MW00564493

U-BOATS

THE ILLUSTRATED HISTORY OF THE RAIDERS OF THE DEEP

U-BOATS

THE ILLUSTRATED HISTORY OF THE RAIDERS OF THE DEEP

DAVID MILLER

Brassey's
Washington, D.C.

First published in the United Kingdom by Pegasus Publishing Ltd.

Copyright © 2000 Pegasus Publishing Ltd.

ISBN 1-57488-246-5 (alk paper)

Printed in Singapore on acid-free paper that meets the American National Standards Institute Z39-48 Standard

Brassey's
22883 Quicksilver Drive
Dulles, Virginia 20166

First Edition

10 9 8 7 6 5 4 3 2 1

CONTENTS

INTRODUCTION

The U-boat war of 1939-1945 exercises a special fascination for a number of reasons:

• U-boats operated against the Allies in almost all of the world's oceans, although the main action took place in a limited arena - the Atlantic and Arctic Oceans.

• It was virtually the only campaign that lasted, without respite, from the first to the last day of the war.

• The *Ubootwaffe* (U-boat arm) was commanded by one man – Karl Dönitz – from its foundation in 1936 to its dissolution in May 1945 and fought according to his concepts of doctrine, training, and organization.

• The campaign was fought very hard, but with a reasonable degree of fairness and honor on both sides; there was little place for political ideology at sea.

• It pitted men against men – life was as tough, unpleasant, and chancy aboard the U-boats as it was in the small enemy warships and merchant ships above them.

• It pitted scientists against scientists, with the technological balance swinging first one way and then another.

• Once Hitler had abandoned the idea of invading the British Isles the U-boats were the only weapon capable of bringing the British to their knees.

• The *Ubootwaffe* was the only element of the German armed forces which took the war to Canada and the United States.

This book looks at the various classes of U-boat and their vari-

ous weapons and sensors, and at the men who manned them and conducted this very protracted and hard fought campaign. It is divided into four parts:

• Part One covers the U-boat in German naval service from the very earliest days, through its first great test in World War I to the clandestine campaign between 1919 and 1935, which was designed to keep U-boat technology and practice alive, despite the terms of the Versailles Treaty.

• Part Two covers the major technological areas in the period 1935-1945, including descriptions of the various types of U-boat, their weapons, communications, sensors, and propulsion systems.

• Part Three describes the campaigns, the men, their training, the sorry saga of *Luftwaffe* co-operation, U-boat losses, and the end of the campaign.

▽ A U-boat is surprised on the surface by aircraft of RAF 105 Squadron on June 5 1942. U-boat crews frequently put up a good fight with their AA guns, shooting down many Allied aircraft, but if the aircraft attack was successful, few if any of the crew would have survived. There was little an aircraft could do other than drop a life-raft, if carried, or radio the boat's position to a friendly ship in the area.

AUTHOR'S ACKNOWLEDGEMENTS

Many people have helped in the preparation of this book and I would particularly like to thank the following.

Museums. Many museums play an invaluable role in preserving our heritage and in helping researchers, almost invariably on very low budgets. For U-boat research, help is always forthcoming from the indefatigable Horst Bredow at the *Traditionsarchiv Unterseeboote*, at Altenbruich bei Cuxhaven, Germany, and his contribution to this book is gratefully acknowledged. There is also, however, a vast amount of U-boat material in British museums, and I have received great help from: Maggie Bidmead and Debbie Corner at the Royal Navy Submarine Museum, Gosport, Hampshire; Derek Gurney at the Museum of Naval Armaments, Priddy's Hard, Gosport; Lieutenant Commander Bill Legg at the Royal Navy Electronics Museum, HMS Collingwood, Gosport; and Dr Peter Thwaites, Royal Signals Museum, Blandford Camp.

Private individuals. Many individuals also made their expertise and resources available. They included Kenneth Wynn. In preparing to write this book, I conducted a great deal of research over a number of years on the U-boats. I was about to go into the details of individual U-boat voyages when Kenneth Wynn's encyclopedic and painstakingly researched, two-volume work *U-boat Operations Of The Second World War* appeared. Kenneth Wynn's work is destined to become the standard work on this particular aspect of the U-boat war and, as a result, where U-boat voyages are concerned I have, with his permission, used his data, but if there are any differences then the responsibility is mine. Ian Hogg, prolific author on gunnery matters, answered many queries on weapons. Bruce Robertson gave unstinted access to his extensive private archive.

Photograph suppliers. Particular thanks must go to the picture researcher Tony Moore; to Bruce Robertson; to Marilyn Gurney, Director and Command Historian of the Maritime Command Museum, Halifax, Nova Scotia, Canada, which was especially generous in the provision of excellent pictures concerning *U-899* and Royal Canadian Navy operations in the Atlantic; and to TRH Pictures.

Maps and diagrams. Michael Haywood has produced many excellent maps and diagrams which add greatly to the value of this book.

Data sources. Finally, much work was carried out at the Public Record Office, Kew, London, whose staff, as always, were not only extremely knowledgable, helpful and efficient, but also charming and very patient.

David Miller
Devon, England, 1999

PART ONE

WORLD WAR 1

THE BEGINNINGS

The first practical German submarine, *Brandtaucher*, was demonstrated by its inventor, Wilhelm Bauer, in Kiel harbor in 1850. Naval officers were not impressed, however, nor did they express any interest in other prototype submersibles produced in 1891 and 1897. Indeed, throughout this period their attention was devoted exclusively to the 'naval race' with Great Britain, which involved only surface warships; new-fangled submarines were an unnecessary complication. As a result, the Imperial German Navy (IGN) was the last of the major navies to build submarines, *U-1* being launched in August 1906.

At first, U-boats were considered solely as defensive weapons, but this changed in 1912, when they proved their value in large-scale exercises. This resulted in a plan for 58 U-boats: 36 to be stationed in the Heligoland Bight, in the mouth of the Elbe River, off Hamburg, defending the High Seas Fleet's main operational bases; 10 in reserve; and, in a significant change of emphasis, 12 for offensive operations.

The planned number of 58 was due to be reached by 1919 and when World War I broke out in August 1914 only 20 boats

▽ *U-96*, one of three boats which formed a sub-group of the larger U-93 class. These boats were launched in 1916-1917, displaced 1,000 tons, and were part of a vast design and building undertaking designated the '*Mobilization*' (Ms) program.

were in service, with a further 15 either under construction or working-up.

THE CAMPAIGNS

The Imperial German Navy's World War I U-boat war can be divided into five phases:
- August 1914 to February 1915: the opening round.
- February to September 1915: the first major offensive.
- March to April 1916: the second major offensive.
- October 1916 to January 1917: the third offensive.
- February 1917 to November 1918: unrestricted warfare and ultimate failure.

The major operational areas for these campaigns were the North Sea and the North Atlantic. U-boats also operated in the Mediterranean with considerable success, but their activities in the Baltic and Black Seas were of only minor significance.

THE OPENING ROUND: AUGUST 1914-FEBRUARY 1915

The first two months of the war were notable for several U-boat 'firsts.' *U-15* achieved the dubious distinction of being the first to be sunk in war when it was surprised and rammed while lying on the surface by the British cruiser *Birmingham* (August 9 1914). Three days later *U-13* failed to return from patrol for rea-

sons which were never established, thus becoming the first of many in the fighting navies of all sides in both wars to be designated an 'operational loss.'

These disasters were offset by several major successes. The first was on September 5 1914, when *U-21* torpedoed the British cruiser *Pathfinder*, but this was completely overshadowed on September 22 when *U-9* sank three elderly British cruisers, *Aboukir*, *Cressy*, and *Hogue* within an hour of each other, thus firmly establishing the U-boat as a major threat to surface warships. Another equally significant event took place on October 20, when *U-17* sank the British merchant ship SS *Glitra* (866grt) in an engagement in which the U-boat's captain obeyed the Prize Rules to the letter. He sent a boarding party to verify the ship's papers and then not only ensured that all crew members were safely in the lifeboats before the sea-cocks were opened, but also towed the lifeboats to within a few miles of the Norwegian coast to ensure the men's safety. This relatively gentlemanly operation was, however, more than offset on October 26 when *U-24*, which had been sent into the English Channel to sink troopships (a legitimate target), saw the French vessel *Amiral Ganteume* (4,590grt) and, mistaking the passengers lining the rails for the troops he was expecting to see, the captain launched a torpedo without warning. In fact, the passengers were Belgian refugees and 40 were killed in the ensuing panic.

The traditional British strategy against a continental adversary was to blockade supplies by sea and this was repeated in 1914, using the might of the Royal Navy to achieve a rapid and very effective cessation of German overseas trade. This forced the Germans to seek ways of either breaking or countering the blockade, neither of which could be achieved by the much-vaunted High Seas Fleet, since this was effectively confined to the North Sea by the British Grand Fleet.

The early merchant ship sinkings were, however, sufficient to encourage a number of German naval officers to propose an

△ The UC-16 class coastal minelayer, *UC-27*, was responsible for sinking 52 enemy merchant ships during World War I. With a displacement of 511 tons and a crew of 26, it carried 18 UC-200 mines. *UC-27* survived the war and was broken up in 1921.

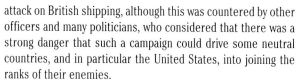

▽ *U-9* photographed by a British merchant captain just before it sank his ship. *U-9* sank three vessels within an hour of each other on September 22 1914.

attack on British shipping, although this was countered by other officers and many politicians, who considered that there was a strong danger that such a campaign could drive some neutral countries, and in particular the United States, into joining the ranks of their enemies.

THE FIRST MAJOR OFFENSIVE: FEBRUARY TO SEPTEMBER 1915

The Germans decided to go ahead with their plans to attack British shipping. They signaled their intentions by publishing an official warning that all waters around the British Isles had been declared a War Zone where British shipping would be attacked without warning, although a channel which would allow neutral ships access to German ports was also designated. The number of U-boats available was woefully inadequate for the task (an average of seven boats at sea through most of 1915) and they actually sank only a very small proportion of the British mercantile fleet, but the threat had a major impact. The British responded by deploying thousands of small auxiliary vessels (for which an encounter with a U-boat was simply a matter of luck) and by placing a series of dense minefields across the Straits of Dover. The most fruitful area for the U-boats was in the South-Western Approaches to the English Channel, which acted as a funnel for the great majority of shipping heading for British ports, but the Dover barrier caused the larger U-boats to take the much longer route northwards around Scotland, greatly reducing their time on station.

Three major incidents resulted in bringing this first offensive to a close. On May 7 1915, *U-20* sank the British liner *Lusitania* (30,396grt); 1,201 passengers, including 128 United States citizens, lost their lives. The resulting outcry led to intense diplomatic discussions, with Germany assuring the United States that attacks on passenger liners would cease. Relations between the two countries were not helped by the sinking of two more liners, *Arabic* (15,801grt) on August 19 and *Hesperian* (10,920grt) on September 6; although casualties were light (76 lives lost, of which only three were US citizens), the Germans were forced to impose such stringent controls on their U-boat commanders that this first campaign petered out in September.

This phase of the U-boat war, in which an average of nine were at sea at any one time, resulted in 365 ships (532,116grt) being sunk.

THE SECOND MAJOR OFFENSIVE: MARCH TO APRIL 1916

By late 1915 the High Seas Fleet was still in its bases, while the German cruisers which had been cruising in the Pacific and Indian Oceans when war broke out had long since been eliminated. The only aggressive action was being undertaken by the U-boats, and, due to the restrictions, even that was at a relatively low level of activity. Nevertheless, the only possible naval solution seemed to lie in an intensification of the U-boat campaign and after further lengthy discussions concerning the danger of dragging the United States into the war the German High Command decided to go ahead. Limitations were imposed, however: the U-boats could attack all enemy vessels inside the War Zone without warning and outside the War Zone if the targets were armed, but passenger ships were not to be attacked, whether inside or outside the zone.

With the U-boat commanders subjected to such strict 'rules-of-engagement' the campaign was never likely to be a success, but then a cross-Channel ferry was sunk off Dieppe with the loss of a number of American citizens.[1] An extremely stern US warning resulted in yet more restrictive rules and the campaign was called off in April, although a few boats at sea failed to receive the recall signal and carried on sinking merchant ships until May 8.

THE THIRD OFFENSIVE: OCTOBER 1916 TO JANUARY 1917

Apart from operations against merchant shipping, the German naval staff tried on numerous occasions to use U-boats as part of an overall plan against the British Grand Fleet. Thus, in May 1916 U-boats were positioned at various points off the British coast and the High Seas Fleet left harbor on the night of May 30/31 with the intention of enticing the British to advance across the lines of U-boats. Although the British did put to sea, the ambush failed and the two battle fleets met each other in the engagement known to the British as the Battle of Jutland and to the Germans as the Battle of the Skaggerak; the surface action was inconclusive and U-boats failed to engage any British ships.

△ Reports of accidents with foreign submarines using petrol engines led to early German submarines being fitted with Kîrting kerosene engines. Unfortunately, as in this picture of *U-1*, this fuel resulted in a dense white cloud, which was visible for miles.

▽ The German Navy's first U-boats, fore-runners of the U-boat fleets which nearly defeated the Western Allies in two world wars. From left to right: *U-1*, *U-2*, *U-3*, *U-4*.

A second attempt took place in August when U-boats were placed in a series of lines covering expected British lines of advance and the High Seas Fleet put to sea with the intention of bombarding the British port of Sunderland, in the north east of England, as 'bait.' This time U-boats sank two British light cruisers but the overall operation was a failure.

By September 1916 the Central Powers were in a most disadvantageous position. There now seemed little prospect of the High Seas Fleet defeating the Grand Fleet, while on land the Battles of Verdun and the Somme had resulted in enormous German casualties for very little gain. In the East, Austria-Hungarian forces were being pushed back by the Russians, while Romania had recently joined the Allies. On top of all this, the domestic situation was becoming very serious. Thus, at the end of August the naval staff recommended to Kaiser Wilhelm II that the only way to bring Great Britain to its knees was to impose a counter-blockade by the unrestricted use of U-boats against the British merchant fleet.

There were long arguments about the dangers posed by such a policy, the Army being concerned that a renewed U-boat campaign might bring Denmark and the Netherlands into the war on the Allied side, giving them yet further fronts on which to fight. The politicians and diplomats, however, were more concerned that it would bring in the United States. But it was decided to restart the campaign according to Prize Regulations at once, with the aim of converting to unrestricted warfare as soon as the time was deemed to be right.

The campaign re-opened in October 1916, increasing in intensity until February 1 1917 when an unrestricted campaign began in earnest. By this stage there were 105 *frontboote* (ie, operational U-boats) available: 46 ocean-going boats operating out of Germany's North Sea naval bases, 23 based in Belgian ports, 10 in the Baltic, and 26 in the Mediterranean. As always, however, the number actually at sea was very considerably less: a maximum of 44 each day in February, rising to 58 in April.

Footnote:
1. SS *Sussex*, a French-registered cross-Channel steamer was sunk on March 24 1916 by *UB-29*. In addition to the crew it carried 325 passengers (24 of them United States citizens), of whom 50 died.

UNRESTRICTED WARFARE AND ULTIMATE FAILURE: FEBRUARY 1917-NOVEMBER 1918

Despite the relatively small number of U-boats at sea, they inflicted immense losses on Allied shipping in the first three months: 1,945,243 tons in all, of which 1,931,102 tons (977 ships) were British. The worst month was April when 873,754grt (413 ships) were sunk. Earlier in the war the majority of engagements had been carried out on the surface using gunfire, but in this later phase submerged attacks using torpedoes — and, thus, an absence of warning — predominated, although guns were occasionally used, principally in order to conserve torpedoes.

However, the German onslaught had two effects which, in combination, spelt the end for Germany. First, and with the greatest impact on the war as a whole, was precisely the outcome German diplomats had forecast: a Declaration of War by the United States on April 6 1917. This resulted in the reinforcement of the Allies by huge numbers of men for the land and air war in France, but, in addition, many US warships joined the Allied fleets, including not only battleships and cruisers, but many smaller vessels, as well. A second consequence was that the British, after much hesitation, introduced convoys.

Convoys had, in fact, started on cross-Channel routes in January 1917 but, following the escalating losses in early 1917, they came into force on the Gibraltar-UK route in April and on the trans-Atlantic route in May. The move was very successful and the impact on the U-boat campaign was immediate, since the oceans were no longer covered with highly vulnerable merchantmen sailing on their own, which had given the U-boats a succession of very soft targets. Instead, the ships were in tight groups, which were not only much more difficult to find, but when found were protected by escorts. Fortunately for the U-boats, however, these escorts were not particularly effective: their only means of detecting a submerged U-boat being hydrophones, which were unreliable and liable to interference from the escort's own motion and propellers.

The convoy scheme at first affected only shipping in-bound to the UK, but outward-bound ships were included from August 1917 and British coastal shipping from July 1918. The increasing

△ *U-35*, most successful submarine of all time, which sank 224 ships (535,900grt) under four captains: Kophamel; von Arnauld de la Perrière; von Voigt; and von Heimburg.

▽ Although operating in the Black Sea and under the Turkish flag, *U-38* was part of the Imperial German Navy. The animal carcasses and sacks of rice indicate that it is setting out on a long patrol.

use of Allied air patrols around the British Isles also had an effect, especially when the aircraft (including seaplanes and airships) gave up conducting area patrols (which had proved singularly unproductive) and began, instead, to serve as part of the convoy escort force. Although they lacked electronic sensors and any effective anti-submarine weapons, these aircraft sighted and attacked large numbers of U-boats with light bombs which, while never accounting for a single sinking, nevertheless contributed to the overall deterrent. Despite all these measures merchant ships were still sunk, but the numbers involved fell dramatically and by mid-1918 the amount of new tonnage built started to exceed that sunk by the U-boats.

THE MEDITERRANEAN THEATER

At the start of the war the Central Powers' situation in the Mediterranean was complicated, since Germany was bound by treaty to assist Austria-Hungary, but when Italy declared war on May 23 1915 it did so only against its neighbor, Austria-Hungary, and not against Germany. However, Germany was determined to help its ally and did so by sending U-boats to the Adriatic: the larger types went by sea through the Atlantic and Mediterranean, but the smaller ones were dismantled and sent by railroad. The German U-boats operated out of Pola and Cattaro (now Pula and Kotor, respectively, in the Adriatic) using an Austrian depot ship, *Gäa*, as their base. A separate group of U-boats operated from Constantinople, Turkey.

In a highly unorthodox arrangement, the German U-boats were commissioned into the Austria-Hungarian Navy, flew the Austria-Hungarian naval ensign, and were allocated numbers in the Austria-Hungarian numbering sequence. The crews, however, remained full members of the German Navy and retained their German uniforms, although a single Austrian liaison officer went to sea with each boat. Thus, for example, the German *UC-12* became the Austria-Hungarian *U-25* in which guise it blew up on its own mines outside the Italian Taranto naval base on March 16 1915 and its true identity was established by Italian divers. This subterfuge, which fooled nobody, continued after Italy declared war on the Central Powers, ending only on October 1 1916.

When U-boat operations started in September 1915 the

Pola/Cattaro-based group was by far the most successful and the Allies tried to confine them to the Adriatic by installing a barrage across the 44 mile (71km) wide Straits of Otranto with nets hauled by drifters, but these, in three years of hard work, accounted for the loss of precisely one U-boat. Allied merchant losses continued throughout 1916, the U-boats' tasks being made easier by the Allies' desperate shortage of anti-submarine vessels, coupled with a steadfast refusal by senior Allied officers to implement convoys. It was in this situation that the most successful cruise by any submarine took place, when *U-35* sank 54 ships (90,350grt) between July 26 and August 20 1916.

In total the German and Austria-Hungarian U-boats sank 325 ships (761,060grt) in the Mediterranean and Adriatic Seas, while the U-boats based in Constantinople sank a further 57 ships (32,830grt) in the Black and Aegean Seas.

THE U-BOATS

When it became obvious that the one way to break the British grip was to impose a counter-blockade by sinking merchant ships, the initial German estimate, made in February 1915, was that some 200-250 U-boats would be required, although at that time the navy possessed just 36 operational boats, with a further 29 under construction. Steps were taken to speed the delivery of U-boats for what was still thought would be a short war. A series of 'Mobilization' (*Ms*) programs were rushed through, consisting of improvements to designs already in production; thus, the *U-57* class was an improvement on the *U-51* class, which had itself been based on the *U-41* class, and so on. The second step was to produce a series of new and simplified designs, which led to the *UB-* series of coastal attack boats and the *UC-* series of coastal minelayers.

A further measure was to impress boats under construction for foreign countries, although this gained only one boat, about to be delivered to Norway, which became, instead, the German *U-A*. However, this was offset by the Italians doing the same thing to Germany when they confiscated the Fiat-Laurenti boat which was about to be delivered to Germany as *U-42*.

One novel way of breaking the blockade was to build sub-

△ *U-1*, Germany's first submarine, was designed by a Spaniard, Raymondo d'Equevillay-Montjustin, built by Germaniawerft at Kiel and launched on August 4 1906. It is now on public display at the *Deutschesmuseum*, Munich, where it is cut-away to show the primitive and dangerous conditions in which its crew lived.

mersible freighters and ten were originally planned. On the only successful voyage in 1916, the first, *Deutschland*, delivered 163 tons of dye to the USA, plus new diplomatic codes for Germany's overseas embassies, and returned with 782 tons of urgently needed nickel, rubber and tin. The next voyage was undertaken by the second to be completed, *Bremen*, but this disappeared on the outward voyage in early 1917, cause unknown. When the United States entered the war in April 1917, the purpose for which these boats had been built disappeared and they were converted to U-cruisers, becoming the *U-151* class.

ANTI-SUBMARINE WARFARE

LOCATING THE U-BOATS

Allied naval leaders were nonplussed by the submarine campaign which was of a nature and on a scale which had been unimaginable before the war. Throughout the war destroyers and a very large number of miscellaneous small vessels, such as armed yachts, sloops, and fishing vessels (mostly trawlers and drifters) were employed on anti-submarine patrols. Unfortunately, they lacked any means of finding a submarine other than by luck, and despite giving the appearance of great energy they actually achieved comparatively little.

It was quickly appreciated that one method of locating a submerged submarine was to use a hydrophone to detect the noise of a submarine's propellers, but the problems of eliminating other noise sources (eg, fish and other marine vessels) and of the hunting vessel's self-noise (from propellers and the motion of the hull through the water) had to be overcome. Some successful attacks using hydrophone did take place, however: on August 21 1917, for example, the noise of the minelayer *UC-41*'s electric motors was detected by minesweepers, which then carried out a successful attack.

A variety of new anti-submarine devices were tried. Indicator nets some 330ft (100m) long and 33ft (10m) deep, fabricated from steelwire, were towed slowly across known U-boat routes. If fouled by a U-boat, a flare was ignited to show where it was on the net, whereupon it was attacked by nearby patrol vessels. They accounted for precisely one U-boat.

WEAPONS

Not only were there no anti-submarine sensors in 1914, but there were no anti-submarine weapons either, leaving surface ships with only two methods of attacking a surfaced submarine: ramming and gunfire. During the war 21 U-boats were despatched by ramming; five were by merchant ships. One measure which appealed to the British navy and public alike were RN-manned merchant ships with hidden armament (popularly known as 'Q-ships' from their 'Q' pennant numbers), which deliberately exposed themselves to attack. When a surfaced U-boat was sufficiently close, the Q-ship's 'merchant seamen' crew dropped the gun covers and engaged the enemy. Some 200 ships were converted for this role; they sank 11 U-boats for the loss of 27 of their own number.

Submerged submarines posed a much more acute problem. The first attempt at a weapon was the 'explosive sweep' which consisted of a loop of cable, whose ends were attached to the ends of a wooden beam towed astern of the hunting ship. Nine 70lb (32kg) explosive charges were secured to the cable, and these were fired electrically from the ship when the beam was seen to swing on engaging an obstacle. This system accounted for just one submarine: *U-8*, sunk by a destroyer in March 1915.

Next came the explosive paravane which contained 80lb (36kg) of TNT. It could be deployed quickly and towed at speeds of up to 25 knots. It accounted for two victims: *UC-19* in 1916 and *UB-69* in 1918.

The first depth-charge entered service in late 1915, early versions being detonated mechanically by a lanyard of the desired length, which was secured to a float. However, this method was quickly replaced by a hydrostatic fuse, which could be preset aboard the ship before being dropped. Depth charges were large; by 1917 the British standard depth charge contained 300lb (137kg) of TNT while the US Navy in 1918 was using one containing 600lb (272kg) of TNT. The problem with depth-charges was that they were essentially being dropped by guess-work and yet they needed to detonate within about 13-16ft (4-5m) of the U-boat's hull. By the war's end depth-charges had accounted for 26 U-boats.

ANTI-SUBMARINE MINEFIELDS

The effort devoted to minefields not only shows how seriously the Allies regarded the menace of the U-boats but also demonstrates how threats compel adversaries to devote considerable resources to countermeasures. The British laid a total of 128,000 mines, while the USA, which did not enter the war until 1917, laid 56,000. Some were aimed at surface ships, but the great majority were aimed at U-boats, first by preventing them from transiting the Straits of Dover and later with the even grander aim of confining them to the North Sea.

The Dover minefields were intended to prevent U-boats from interfering with the extremely busy cross-Channel traffic which was the only method of moving British troops and resources to the European continent. Both ends of the minefields rested on Allied territory and the waters were relatively shallow, but laying was complicated by the very strong tides. In early 1916 a 'zareba' of mines stretching for some 40 miles (64km) along the Belgian coast was laid, followed by a dense barrage stretching from the South Goodwin Shoal to the Snow Bank off Dunquerque, consisting of three lines of deep mines with mined nets 550yd (500m) apart. These defenses were reinforced in 1917/18 by the Channel Barrage with new fields stretching from Cap Gris Nez on the French coast to the Varne Shoal and from the north side of the Varne to the English coast at Folkestone. Searchlights were placed on the coast to illumi-

△ *U-124* was a UE-II type ocean minelayer completed in December 1917. It displaced 1,468 tons, had a crew of 40, and carried 42 mines. Armament comprised four torpedo tubes and one 5.9in (150mm) gun. U-boat design had moved a great distance in ten years compared to the *U-1* (opposite).

nate any surfaced U-boat, with more at sea aboard vessels anchored at intervals across the Channel, and five patrol boats were located at each end for instant response. This involved some 10,000 mines, and claimed 10 U-boats, while the shallower fields sank one more.

The Northern Barrage was on a much larger scale, stretching in a 240 mile (386km) dog-leg from just outside Norwegian territorial waters (Norway was neutral) to the Orkneys, off Scotland, and involving 10 US and 4 British minelayers, which laid 56,033 and 15,093 mines, respectively. This required considerable industrial capacity, extensive transport arrangements, including 24 ships sailing constantly between US and Scottish ports, and a network of special depots in Scotland where the mines were stored and then issued for laying. The actual laying began on June 8 1918 and was completed in October, following which strong British and US diplomatic pressure resulted in the Norwegians mining their own waters, completing the barrage.

During the war Allied mines were known to have sunk 34 U-boats, 19 of them in 1918, but it is also possible that a fairly large proportion of the 37 operational (i.e., unexplained) losses were due to mines as well.

ELECTRONIC WARFARE

World War I was the first major naval conflict in which electronic warfare played a significant role, and the Germans suffered two major setbacks in the first weeks, which were as significant in their way as any battle at sea. In the first, which took place before dawn on August 5 1914 (the day after war was declared), the British cableship *Teconia* lifted the submarine cables off the port of Emden, which carried all Germany's overseas telephone and telegraph circuits, cut them and returned them to the sea. As a result, for the rest of the war all German international communications, particularly to the United States, were routed either by radio or by cables which passed through enemy territory, both of which were constantly monitored by the British from that day on.

The cable-cutting was the result of British pre-war planning, but the second setback to the Germans was the result of pure luck. On August 26 1914, the German cruiser *Magdeburg* ran aground and was scuttled in the Gulf of Finland. A few hours later a vessel of the Imperial Russian Navy recovered the body of an *unteroffizier* whose lifeless hands grasped the fleet signal book and other 'top secret' documents. Two months later the Russians, in an act of notable generosity, handed over copies of all documents to the British, who were in the process of setting up their naval cryptanalysis center in 'Room 40' at the Admiralty. With this priceless start, Room 40 rapidly gained in expertise and provided an increasing amount of information to the planning staffs at the Admiralty.

A tremendous amount of work was still required by the British; a team of cryptanalysts had to be set up from scratch, and they gradually began to break the German naval codes. After the Battle of Jutland the Germans laid ever-increasing emphasis on submarine warfare and Room 40 concentrated on the U-boats, which used a special version of the naval key. The British were so successful that by August 1916 the Germans became suspicious and changed their key, but this, too, was broken.

THE END OF WORLD WAR I

DISPOSAL

At the end of the war the Allies showed a grim determination to rid themselves once and for all of U-boats, of which there were 176 in service and a further 149 in various stages of construction. Most of the latter were scrapped on the ways, but the Allies took over the serviceable boats, all of which were ordered to move to the UK, although 19 were lost while under tow. Of those that arrived:

- France received 45; 10 were put into service, the remainder scrapped.
- Italy received 10, all of which were scrapped.
- Japan received 7, all of which were given IJN numbers, but were then scrapped.
- The UK received 95, all of which were scrapped.
- The USA received 6, all of which were sunk as targets.

In addition, the Netherlands was allowed to keep one U-boat which had sunk in Dutch waters and had been raised by them.

A BALANCE SHEET

Although submarines had been in service with major navies since about 1902, few pre-war pundits had foreseen the impact they would have on naval warfare. The grand total of British, Allied and neutral shipping sunk by U-boats was 5,282 vessels (12,284,757grt). The U-boats also caused repeated crises, particularly in the UK, achieving results out of all proportion to their numbers, although in the end they precipitated the one act which led inexorably to their country's defeat by bringing the USA into the war.

Losses to the U-boat arm were also great, however. The German Navy began the war with 28 U-boats and a further 343 were commissioned between August 1914 and November 1918. In all, 178 U-boats were lost, of which 87 were sunk by Allied ships: 57 of them on the surface and 30 submerged. Of the 91 other losses, mines accounted for 35, and accidents/unexplained for 56. A further eight were interned in Sweden and Portugal. Losses in manpower were also great: 1,400 captured, and 511 officers and 4,576 ratings killed, at least some of them due to the absence of an adequate escape apparatus, which made the chances of escaping from a stricken submarine extremely slim.

Although they were not to know it at the time, the German U-boat command missed a golden opportunity. The use of convoys was, without a doubt, the key to the Allies' success, but the escorts were equipped with only the most basic sensors – hydrophones – which gave them little real chance of locating U-

LOTHAR VON ARNAULD DE LA PERIÈRE AND U-35

The German World War I U-boat *U-35*, remains the single most successful submarine in any navy, having sunk 224 ships (535,900grt) in 25 patrols around the British Isles, in the Mediterranean, and off the West African coast. Nor is that all, since one of its captains, *Kapitänleutnant* Lothar von Arnauld de la Perière, is the most successful of all submarine captains.

Launched on April 18 1914, *U-35* was armed with four 15.75in (500mm) torpedo tubes (two bow, two stern), for which it carried six torpedoes. A gun was mounted on the foredeck: originally an 88mm, but replaced by a 105mm in 1916. On the surface *U-35* was powered by two MAN diesels, giving it a speed of 15.4 knots and an endurance of 7,600 nautical miles. When submerged, it had a speed of 9.5 knots and a maximum endurance of 80 nautical miles.

U-35 had a crew of 35 who served under four captains, the first being *Kapitänleutnant* Waldermar Kophamel who commanded for the boat's first eight patrols. The first two were for training, but these were followed by three operational patrols around the British Isles, on the third of which Kophamel sank 14 ships (23, 539grt). *U-35* then sailed to the Mediterranean, arriving at Pola, the main Austro-Hungarian naval base, on August 23, having sunk three ships en route. Kophamel then carried out a further two patrols, the first in the Aegean, the second in the Mediterranean, before handing over to a new commanding officer at the beginning of October 1915.

The new commanding officer, *Kapitänleutnant* Lothar von Arnauld de la Perière, was descended from a Huguenot soldier who had settled in Prussia. He was born in Posen (Poznan) in 1886 and entered the Imperial German Navy in 1903, being commissioned in 1906. He served in various sea-going appointments before becoming adjutant to Admiral von Pohl, Chief of Naval Staff, in 1913. He spent some months learning the language in England in 1914, but hurried home when war broke out. He volunteered for the newly established naval air arm, although he was reclaimed by Admiral von Pohl after a few months.

De la Perière next volunteered for U-boats and after the mandatory course at the U-Boat School he was posted as commander of *U-35*. He sank three merchant on his first cruise, and three more plus a British sloop, HMS *Pimula*, on the second. The third cruise was marked by sinking a large British merchantman, *Minneapolis* (13,543grt), but he was subsequently forced to return to base with mechanical problems. His next cruise, however, was a triumph, and operating in the western end of the Mediterranean he sank 40 ships (56,818grt). The largest of these was the Italian *Mongibello* (4,059grt) and 19 were under 1,000 tons (four were under 50 tons).

De la Perière's fifth cruise (see map), during which he sent 54 ships (90,350grt) to the bottom, remains the most successful by any submarine commander. On leaving the Adriatic, he disposed of his first 11 victims off the Tunisian coast before sailing north-westwards to operate off the French port of Marseille.

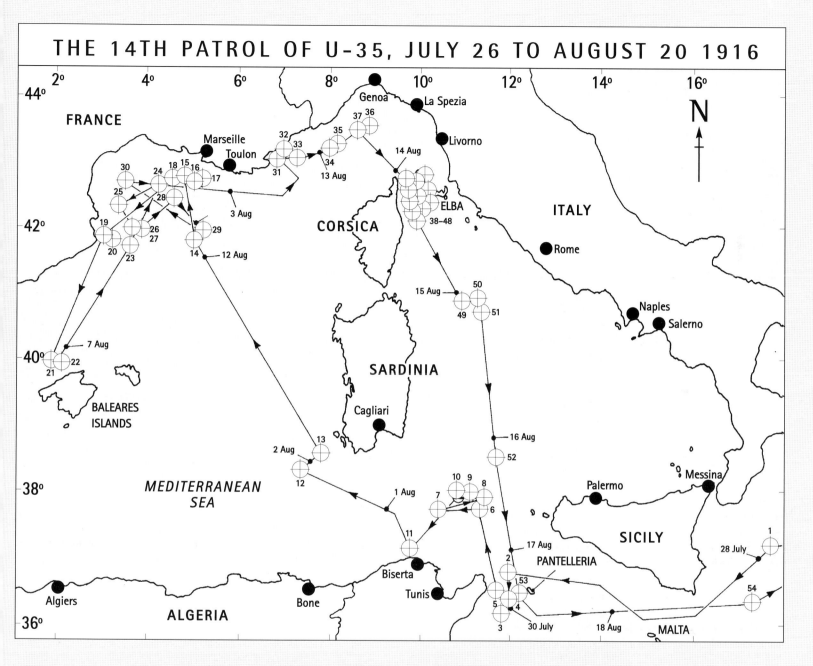

THE 14TH PATROL OF U-35, JULY 26 TO AUGUST 20 1916

After a brief foray down to Majorca, he sailed eastwards along the French coast before turning south and claiming 12 victims in two days in the straits between Corsica and Elba. Returning southwards he sank a few more ships off the Tunisian coast, before going home. Prior to his patrol he had used his high-level contacts to obtain one of the finest gunlayers in the High Seas Fleet and of his 54 successes only four were sunk by torpedoes, the rest being despatched by his master gunner.

The exploits of De la Perière earned him his country's highest honour, *pour le mérite*, on October 11 1916. He relinquished his Mediterranean command in March 1918 to take over an

Atlantic boat, *U-139*. He carried out one patrol (September 11 to November 14 1918) which took him to the United States coast and during which he sank five ships (7,008grt). His total successes in 16 patrols amounted to 194 merchant ships (453,716grt), plus two small warships (2,500t). *U-35* was broken up in Germany in 1920.

Von Arnauld de la Perière commanded the cruiser *Emden* (1928–30), lectured at the Turkish Naval Academy (1932-38), and returned to Germany in 1939. Promoted to Vice-Admiral in 1940, he was en route to take command in the Mediterranean when he was killed in an air crash at Le Bourget, Paris, on February 24 1942.

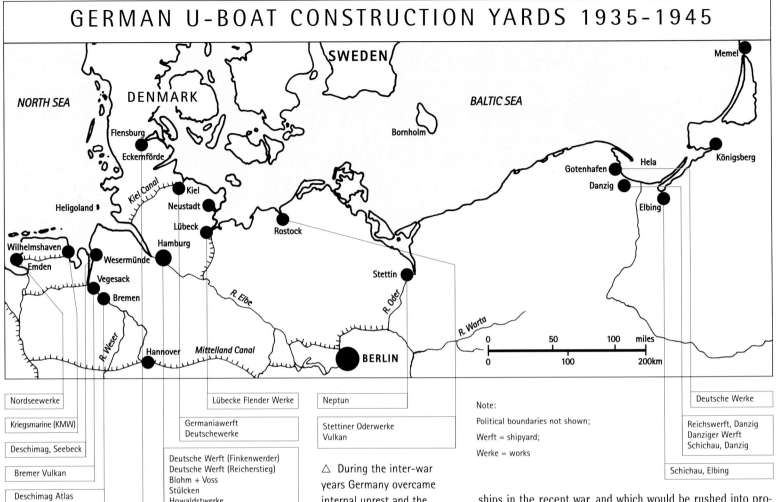

GERMAN U-BOAT CONSTRUCTION YARDS 1935-1945

SWEDEN

DENMARK

NORTH SEA

BALTIC SEA

Memel

Flensburg

Eckernförde

Bornholm

Königsberg

Heligoland

Kiel Canal

Kiel

Hela

Gotenhafen

Neustadt

Danzig

Lübeck

Elbing

Rostock

Wilhelmshaven

Hamburg

Emden

Wesermünde

Vegesack

Stettin

R. Elbe

Bremen

R. Oder

R. Weser

R. Warta

Hannover

Mittelland Canal

BERLIN

| 0 | 50 | 100 | miles |
| 0 | 100 | 200km | |

Nordseewerke

Lübecke Flender Werke

Neptun

Deutsche Werke

Kriegsmarine (KMW)

Germaniawerft
Deutschewerke

Stettiner Oderwerke
Vulkan

Reichswerft, Danzig
Danziger Werft
Schichau, Danzig

Deschimag, Seebeck

Note:

Bremer Vulkan

Deutsche Werft (Finkenwerder)
Deutsche Werft (Reicherstieg)
Blohm + Voss
Stülcken
Howaldstwerke

Political boundaries not shown;

Werft = shipyard;

Schichau, Elbing

Deschimag Atlas

Werke = works

Flensburger Schiffau

boats. Radios were not as sophisticated in 1917 as they were in 1939-42, but they were installed in many U-boats and there seems to be no reason why 'wolf-pack' tactics could not have worked; indeed, they might well have overwhelmed the escorts and wrought havoc among the convoys. That opportunity was to be taken 22 years later, however.

THE INTER-WAR YEARS

The Versailles Peace Treaty, signed by Germany on June 28 1919, laid down the most stringent limitations on German armaments, among the harshest being Article 191, which imposed a total prohibition on the 'construction or acquisition of any submarine of any type.' Once the internal unrest within Germany had been overcome, however, the leaders of the newly created and very weak navy, now renamed the *Reichsmarine*, started making plans for a future war, one element of which was a series of designs for 'mobilization' warships, based on the best of their

△ During the inter-war years Germany overcame internal unrest and the *Reichsmarine* (new name for the navy) set up manufacturing plants for warship production, in clandestine preparation for a new war. In contravention of the Versailles Treaty, Germany began designing and building new warships under the subterfuge of building and testing them for foreign customers. This map shows the U-boat construction yards working from 1935 through to the end of the next war in 1945.

ships in the recent war, and which would be rushed into production as soon as conditions permitted.

The *Reichsmarine* had three commanders-in-chief in the inter-war years, Admiral Behnke (1919-1924), Admiral Zenker (1924-1928), and Admiral Raeder (1928-1942). They worked tirelessly for the navy's recovery and beteeen them produced sound and practicable plans which were inherited by, rather than initiated by, Hitler's National Socialist government. From the start, and in direct contravention of the Versailles Treaty, the *Reichsmarine* made a particular effort to preserve the U-boat design and construction skills that had been acquired during the war. This was achieved by establishing a network of quasi-civilian companies, which carried out work for foreign navies, hut always with the aim of furthering Germany's own naval expertise and ambitions.

One of these quasi-civilian companies was *Mentor Bilanz*, which was based in Berlin and staffed primarily by Naval Ministry design officials. A political storm in 1928 meant that this 'company' had to be disbanded, although, in the event, it was simply renamed *Ingenieurbüro für wirtscnaft und Technik Gmbh* (= engineering office for economics and technical matters), usual-

GERMAN SUBMARINE DESIGNS BUILT FOR FOREIGN NAVIES – 1920–1940					
BUILT FOR	TURKEY	FINLAND	SPAIN[1]	FINLAND	FINLAND
Class Name	Birindci Inönö	Vetehinen	E-1	Saukko	Vesikko
German class	Pu-66 (improved UB-III)	Pu-89 (improved UC-III)	Pu-111 (improved UG)	Pu-110	(improved UB-II)
Launched	1927	1930–31	1932	1930	1932[2]
Building yard	Fijenoord, Netherlands	Crichton-Vulkan Türkü, Finland	Kchevarrieta, Cadiz, Spain	Hietelahden, Helxsingfors, Finland	Crichton-Vulkan, Türkü, Finland
Number built	2	3	1	1	1
Displacement (submerged)	620t	715t	965t	142t	399t
Dimensions Length Beam Draught	193.6ft (59m) 19.0ft (5.8m) 11.5ft (3.5m)	206.7ft (63m) 20.0ft (6.1m) 10.5ft (6.1m)	237.5ft (72.4m) 20.3ft (6.2m) 13.1ft (4.0m)	108.3ft (33.0m) 10.5ft (3.2m) 10.5ft (3.2m)	134.2ft (40.9m) 13.5ft (4.1m) 13.8ft (4.2m)
Range surfaced submerged	7,500nm at 6kt 80nm at 4kt	4,000nm at 10kt 75nm at 3kt	7,000nm at 10kt 160nm at 4kt	500nm at 8kt 50nm at 4kt	1,960nm at 8kt 61nm at 4kt
Maximum speed surface submerged	14.5kt 9.5kt	14kt 8kt	17kt 8.5kt	10kt 6.3kt	13kt 8kt
Guns	1 x 75mm 1 x 20mm	1 x 76mm 1 x 20mm	1 x 105mm 1 x 20mm	1 x 13mm MG	1 x 20mm
Torpedo tubes (torpedoes)	6 x 450mm (17.7in) (10)	4 x 533mm (21in) (6)	6 x 533mm (21in) (10)	2 x 450mm (17.7in) (2)	5 x 533mm (21in)
Mines	–	20 (mine shafts)	–	9	–
Crew	29	30	32	15	16

1 This boat was built for Spain as E-1, but was never delivered and was purchased by Turkey as Gur in 1934.
2 It was not handed over to the Finnish Navy until 1936.

ly abbreviated to *Igewit*, and carried on work as normal. *Mentor Bilanz/Igewit* had two main functions: translating *Reichsmarine* U-boat staff requirements into designs and seeking to obtain foreign customers for whom the designs could be built and tested. In order to achieve the latter, another 'company' headed by a former chief U-boat designer at the Germaniawerft, was established in the Netherlands: *NV Ingenieurskaantor voor Scneepsbouw* (*IvS*). Some of the funding for these activities came from German shipbuilding firms, but most came, via clandestine channels, from the German government itself.

Even though Japan had been an enemy during World War I and had received a number of U-boats in the post-Armistice division of spoils, it was one of the first countries to do business with post-war Germany. This involved purchasing a number of U-boat plans direct from the *Kriegsmarine* in 1920 and subsequently inviting the Germans to supervise their construction and testing in Japan. A similar project for the Argentine Navy fell through, as did the first proposal for Spain, but an order by Turkey resulted in two boats being built by the Dutch yard Fijenoord, in Rotterdam, to German design. These were launched in early 1927, tested by a German crew and then delivered in 1928.

A further success was achieved in Finland. Three minelayers

▽ Smiling crewmen aboard *UC-105*, a coastal minelaying submarine. At the end of the war it was handed over to the Royal Navy and broken up in 1922.

were built to a German design at Türkü, although, since the Finns were inexperienced in submarine construction and also because no work was possible in the winter months, construction took no less than three-and-a-half years from laying down to launch.

One of the 'mobilization' designs prepared by the *Kriegsmarine* in the early 1920s needed to be built and tested, and Spain was targeted for this work. The negotiations proved to be complex and protracted, but it was eventually agreed that bell sections would be constructed by Fijenoord, while the engines and most of the equipment would be produced in Germany, and would be shipped to Spain for assembly in a small, privately owned Spanish yard, Echevarrieta, in Cadiz. This went to plan, but the design, known as the *E-1*, seemed jinxed: the yard went bankrupt (as a result of which the project had to be fully funded by the *Kriegsmarine*), the boat ran aground immediately after launch, and the Spanish Navy lost interest. However, the boat was later porchased by Turkey, which commissioned it as the *Gür*, while the general design formed the basis of the subsequent German Type IA.

In 1924 the Finnish Navy produced a requirement for a small submarine for use in minelaying on Lake Ladoga for which *IvS* produced several designs, but it was not until 1929 that the Finns placed a firm order and the boat was launched in 1930. Finland had signed the Treaty of Dorpat with the USSR in 1920, one of whose provisions was that no warship on Lake Ladoga could exceed 100 t, so the declared displacement of *Saukko* was 99t; the actual figure was 142t, but this subterfuge proved irrelevant since the boat was never used in Lake Ladoga.

At one stage the *Saukko* design was under consideration as the basis for the *Kriegsmarine*'s requirement for a coastal mobilization design, bet it was rejected as being too small. The German Naval Staff considered a displacement of some 250t to be the minimum and a new design, codenamed *Liliput*, was prepared, which was offered for export so that it could be tested. The Estonian Navy rejected it (they later bought two much larger submarines, the *Kalev*-class, from Vickers-Armstrong in the UK) and the *Liliput* was then offered to Finland. The Finns insisted on waiting until they had tested the first of their three *Vetehinen*-class boats, but they did then place an order for a *Liliput*-class boat in October 1930. This boat, *Vetehinen* (*C-707*), was built under *IvS* supervision at the Chrichton-Vulkan yard at Türkü, being launched in May 1933. The trials were conducted by an all-German crew and the Germans managed to extend the trials until 1936 so that a succession of men of the clandestine U-boat arm could be trained in it. This design, with little change, subsequently became the *Kriegsmarine*'s Type II.

It is thus clear that, even in the chaotic years following the end of World War I, the *Reichsmarine* followed a consistent policy of renewal and that, in particular, it was determined to circumvent the terms of the Versailles Treaty in order to create a new U-boat arm. This policy was in place well before Hitler entered the political arena; his role was simply to provide the political will to bring the fruits of that policy out into the open.

PART TWO

THE U-BOATS, WEAPONS, AND EQUIPMENT

TYPE IA

BACKGROUND

When the decision to restart the U-boat arm was taken in Autumn 1932 two classes were proposed, each of eight boats. To mislead the watchful media, however, these were designated 'Motorenversuchsboot' (*MVB* = experimental motor boats). One class, designated *MVB-1*, was to displace 500 tons, with the design based on that of the Vetehinen-class, which had been built to German design for the Finnish Navy. The other class, *MVB-2*, was to be somewhat larger, displacing 800 tons, and based on the German design which had been built in Spain as the *E1* class (later sold to the Turkish Navy as the *Gür*-class).

Although the Type I was the first to be designed (and received the first designation in the Type list), the two boats involved were neither the first to be ordered, nor the first to be launched. Then, despite the fact that they had been developed from the *E1* design, they proved to be less than satisfactory; they had poor stability, which made them bad sea-boats and they were both slow to dive and difficult to maneuver underwater. In addition to all this, they also proved to be mechanically unreliable. As a result, following their initial trials it was decided not to build any more and they were relegated to training, experimental and 'showing the flag' missions.

DESIGN

With a submerged displacement of 983 tons, the Type I was somewhat smaller than contemporary foreign boats intended for ocean-going missions: the British T-class, for example, dis-

placed 1,575 tons and the US Salmon class 2,210 tons. Nevertheless, the *Kriegsmarine* considered it a large boat, especially as it was being built in the context of the tonnage limitations imposed by the Anglo-German Naval Agreements. The Type I design was based on that of the Spanish *E1*, but with some differences, the most important of which was the use of welding as opposed to rivetting for the pressure hull, thus saving considerable weight. The size of the bridge was also reduced. As with German World War I U-boats, the Type Is carried a netcutter on the bows.

The Type IA design was used as the basis for a variety of new designs, only one of which, the Type IX, was built.

The Type I mounted six torpedo tubes - four bow and two stern - and for the first time in a German U-boat these were of the international standard of 21in (533mm) rather than 19.7in (500mm). There was a single 105mm gun on the foredeck and a 20mm AA cannon on the bridge platform.

OPERATIONAL HISTORY

Despite the fact that they had been relegated to training duties, on the outbreak of war *Kapitän-zur-See* Karl Dönitz was so short of *frontboote* (operational boats) that both the Type IA boats were made operational again. *U-25* made two efforts to go to the Atlantic in 1939 but was forced to abort on both occasions. In January 1940, however, it succeeded in doing so and under the command of Viktor Schütze it sank three merchant ships (13,000grt) off the Shetland Islands and a fourth (2,335grt) in the Western Approaches. Schütze then became the first captain to take a U-boat into the neutral Spanish port of Cadiz on January 30 1940 where he refueled and replenished before returning to sea. *U-25* then developed an engine defect but Schütze managed to return to Germany, sinking two more ships (12,000grt) on the way. *U-25*, commanded by Heinz Beduhn, then took part in the invasion of Norway, but was lost with all hands on August 3 1940 off Terschelling when on a minelaying mission. One possible explanation is that it struck one of its own mines.

U-26 (Scheringer) sailed from Germany in June 1940, and despite repeated engine problems sank three freighters and damaged a fourth, south-west of Bishop's Rock. On July 1 1940 it was attacked by destroyers which were working together with a Sunderland flying-boat of 10 Squadron RAAF. *U-26* was forced to surface, where Scheringer decided to scuttle; all 48 crew members survived and were rescued.

◁ *U-25*, one of two type IAs commissioned, sunk six ships before being lost with all 49 crewmen on August 3 1940, possibly after hitting a mine.

TYPE IA

Displacement (surf/sub) 862/983 tons; 237.5ft (72.4m); speed (surf/sub) 17.8/8.3kt; range (surf/sub) 6,700nm at 12kt/ 78nm at 4kt.

TYPE IA
ROLE: Ocean-going attack submarine
DISPLACEMENT Light surfaced: 707 tons Surfaced: 862 tons Submerged: 983 tons
DIMENSIONS Length: 237.5ft (72.39m) Beam: 20.4ft (6.21m) Draught (loaded): 14.1ft (4.3m) Pressure hull diameter: 14.0ft (4.28m)

PROPULSION
Main engines: Two eight-cylinder, four-stroke M.A.N (MAN 8V 40/46) diesels;
    1,400hp at 470rpm (maximum continuous); 1,540hp at 485rpm (maximum
    for 30 minutes)
Electric: Two double BBC motors; 500hp at 310rpm (maximum for 30 minutes)
Battery: Two 62-cell (9,260amp/hour) (AFA 36 MAK 740)
Fuel capacity: 96 tons (heavy diesel oil)

PERFORMANCE
Maximum speed
    Surfaced: 17.75kt
    Submerged: 8.3kt
Maximum operational depth: 328ft (100m)
Range
    Surfaced: 6,700nm at 12kt
    Submerged: 78nm at 4kt
Minimum crash-dive time: 30 seconds

WEAPONS
Bow tubes: Four 21in (533mm)
Stern tubes: Two 21in (533mm)
Weapons carried:
    Normal — 14 torpedoes
    or 4 torpedoes plus 16 TMA mines
    or 4 torpedoes plus 24 TMB mines
    or 4 torpedoes plus 10 TMA plus 9 TMB
    or 28 TMA (maximum)
    or 42 TMB (maximum)
Guns:
    One 105mm SKC/36 (150 rounds)
    One 20mm Flak/30 (2,000 rounds)

OFFICERS AND CREW: 4 + 39 = 43
NUMBER BUILT: 2
LAUNCH OF FIRST OF CLASS: February 14 1936

TYPE II

BACKGROUND

The Type II was the first of the original designs to be built as part of the *Kriegsmarine*'s reconstruction program and was originally given the cover-name *MVB II* (MVB = *Motorenversuchsboot* = experimental motor-boat). The design was based on that of the CV-707 design produced for Finland.

Because Germany was still bound by the Versailles Treaty, the parts for the first Type IIAs were assembled in great secrecy and permission to begin construction was repeatedly delayed due to the political situation, until the signing of the Anglo-German Naval Agreement cleared the way for a public program. Assembly of the first six Type IIAs was then authorized on February 8 1935, followed by authority to start on the first six Type IIBs a month later. The first four Type IICs were ordered on June 17 1937 and the Type IID in October 1938.

Two Type IIBs were originally ordered by the Chinese Navy and were under construction at the Flender Werft when war broke out. They were then requisitioned by and completed for the *Kriegsmarine* as *U-120* and *U-121*.

DESIGN

TYPE IIA

The Type IIA was designed for coastal operations. Its design was based on the Finnish *Vessiko* (*CV-707*), which in its turn had been based on the German Navy's World War I Type UF. It was a single-hull boat, with an internal main rapid-dive tank, but, whereas the *CV-707* had a rivetted hull, the Type II was all-welded, which was both stronger and lighter. The Type IIA had a smaller bridge and, internally, it was designed to use the new *G7a* and *G7e* 21in (533mm) torpedoes as well as *TM*-type torpedo mines. There was a single periscope in the conning tower. Net cutters were originally fitted on the bows, a carry-over from World War I practice, but these were removed early in World War II.

▷ The bridge of a brand-new Type IIC. Note the helmsman's position (forward, left) with wheel and compass, and the captain's position (forward, right) with voice-tube. The main trunk access hatch is open and behind it is the periscope housing.

▽ *U-1*, first of the Type IIA class soon after being commissioned in 1935. The design was based on that of the Finnish *Vetehinen*, which had, in its turn, been based on that of the German World War I Type UB-III coastal submarine.

TYPE IIB

Design of the Type IIB was in progress even before construction of the Type IIA had begun, with the aim of improving the range. The hull was lengthened by inserting three new frames amidships, which enabled a new oil bunker to be installed beneath the control room, increasing the range to 4,000 nautical miles at 8 knots. Diving time was also improved to 30 seconds.

TYPE IIC

The Type IIC was a Type IIB with a further two frames inserted amidships to accommodate improved radio room facilities and

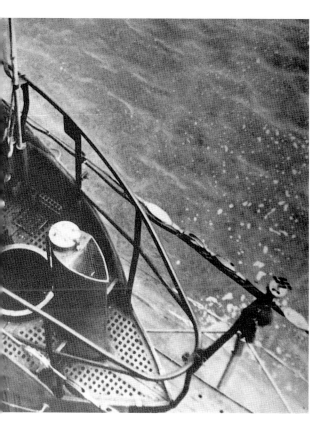

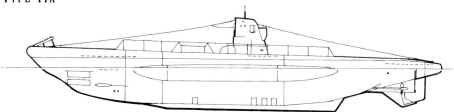

TYPE IIA

Displacement (surf/sub) 254/303 tons; 134.2ft (40.9m); speed (surf/sub) 13.0/6.9kt; range (surf/sub) 1,050nm at 12kt/35nm at 4kt.

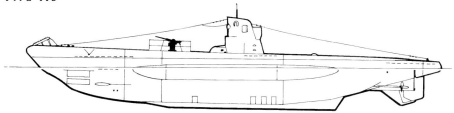

TYPE IIB

Displacement (surf/sub) 279/329 tons; 140.1ft (42.7m); speed (surf/sub) 13.0/7.0kt; range (surf/sub) 1,800nm at 12kt/43nm at 4kt.

a second periscope. This also enabled the fuel bunker beneath the control room to be enlarged yet again (by 35cu ft/1cu m) thus extending the range. In 1943 two Type IICs, *U-57* and *U-58* from the training flotilla, had their after periscope replaced by a *schnorchel*, as part of the development program.

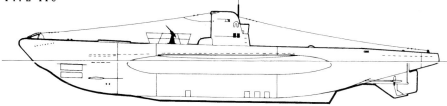

TYPE IIC

TYPE IID

The Type IID was generally similar to the Type IIC, but was fitted with saddle tanks, similar to those on the Type VII. These were used as self-compensating fuel bunkers, with the diesel oil floating on top of seawater, which gradually filled the tank as the oil was consumed. This gave a substantial increase in range to 5,680 nautical miles at 8 knots and enabled the boat to undertake operations around the British Isles. The propellers were fitted with Kort nozzles (a shroud around the propeller), which was intended to improve propulsive efficiency.

Displacement (surf/sub) 291/341 tons; 144.0ft (43.9m); speed (surf/sub) 12.0/7.0kt; range (surf/sub) 1,900nm at 12kt/43nm at 4kt.

DIFFERENCES

The main differences between the sub-types was:
- Each version was slightly longer than its predecessor.
- There were differences in free-flooding slots.
- There were differences in the bridge size and shape.
- From the summer of 1943 the Black Sea boats had enlarged bridges to enable them to mount extra AA guns.
- The Type IID had saddle tanks, Kort nozzles and a greatly extended range.

TYPE IID

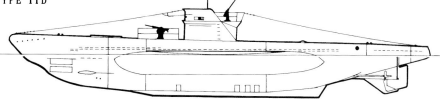

Displacement (surf/sub) 314/364 tons; 144.4ft (44.0m); speed (surf/sub) 12.7/7.4kt; range (surf/sub) 3,450nm at 12kt/56nm at 4kt.

OPERATIONAL HISTORY

The first 12 Type IIs were commissioned in the summer of 1935, with the six Type IIAs going to Kiel for the urgent task of providing basic training for submariners. The second six, all Type IIBs, were employed for advanced training, and were also based in Kiel, where they formed the '*Weddingen*' flotilla,[1] which was established on September 25 1935 under the personal command of Dönitz and which started its training tasks on October 1 1935.

The Type IIs quickly earned the nickname of '*Einbäum*' (plural *Einbäume*), the German word for a dug-out canoe, due to their small size and their very heavy rolling on the surface. Although they were intended principally as training boats and were of limited value in open ocean, the shortage of operational boats on outbreak of war meant that they were used operationally from 1939 to June 1941, when they operated mainly in German coastal waters, in the English Channel, and in the Baltic against the Soviets. As the war continued, however, the operational need for ever-increasing numbers of U-boats and the concomitant requirement for crews forced the *Kriegsmarine* to withdraw the Type IIAs and IIBs from front-line duties and commit them full-time to the training school.

As they were commissioned, the Type IICs *U-56* to *U-62* were assigned to '*U-Flottille Emmsmann*' based at Kiel, which was redesignated '*1 U-Flottille*' on January 1 1940. The Type IICs had an active time between August 1939 and when they were relegated to training, all taking part in the invasion of Norway; all except *U-62* visited the recently opened U-boat bases on the French Atlantic coast at least once in 1940. All were re-allocated to training duties between October 1940 and January 1941 and spent the remainder of the war in the training environment. (*U-63* was lost on February 25 1940.)

One Type IIB, *U-23*, was commanded by *Kapitänleutnant* Otto Kretschmer from October 1937 to March 1940. Kretschmer was one of the most determined officers in the U-boat service and under his command *U-23* carried out nine combat patrols, of which three were minelaying missions. Kretschmer displayed his characteristic aggressiveness, sinking seven merchant ships (26,164grt) and one destroyer, HMS *Daring*.

TYPE II				
	TYPE IIA	**TYPE IIB**	**TYPE IIC**	**TYPE IID**
ROLE	COASTAL U-BOAT	COASTAL U-BOAT	COASTAL U-BOAT	COASTAL U-BOAT
DISPLACEMENT				
Surfaced	253.8 tons	278.9 tons	291 tons	314 tons
Submerged	301.1 tons	328.5 tons	341 tons	364 tons
DIMENSIONS				
Length	134.2ft (40.9m)	140.1ft (42.7m)	144.0ft (43.9m)	144.4ft (44.0m)
Beam	13.4ft (4.1m)	13.4ft (4.1m)	13.5ft (4.1m)	16.4ft (5.0m)
Draught	12.5ft (3.8m)	12.8ft (3.9m)	12.5ft (3.8m)	12.8ft (3.9m)
Pressure hull diameter	13.1ft (4.0m)	13.1ft (4.00m)	13.1ft (4.00m)	13.1ft (4.00m)
PROPULSION				
Diesel (see Note 1)	Two MWM 6-cyl 350hp	Two MWM 6-cyl 350hp	Two MWM 60cyl 350hp)	Two MWM 6-cyl 350hp
Electric (see Note 2)	Two SSW 180hp	Two SSW 180hp	Two SSW 205hp	Two SSW 205hp
Battery (see Note 3)	1 x 62 cells	1 x 62 cells	1 x 62 cells	1 x 62 cells
Fuel	11.61 tons	21.05 tons	22.7 tons	22.7 tons
PERFORMANCE				
Maximum speed (loaded)				
Surfaced	13.0 knots	13.0 knots	12.0 knots	12.7 knots
Submerged (one hour)	6.9 knots	7.0 knots	7.0 knots	7.4 knots
Endurance				
Surfaced at 12kt	1,050nm	1,800nm	1,900nm	3,200nm at 12.7kt
Surfaced at 8kt	2,000nm	3,900nm	4,200nm	
Submerged at 4kt	35nm	35nm	35nm	56nm
Submerged at 2kt	71nm	71nm	71nm	
Diving depth	328ft (100m)	328ft (100m)	328ft (100m)	328ft (100m)
Minimum crash dive time	35secs	30secs	25secs	25secs
WEAPONS				
Bow tubes	Three 21in (533nm)	Three 21in (533nm)	Three 21in (533nm)	Three 21in (533nm)
Stern tubes	None	None	None	None
Torpedoes	Six	Six	Six	Six
Mines	(see Note 4)	(see Note 4)	(see Note 1)	(see Note 1)
Guns	One 20mm Flak Twin	One 20mm Flak Twin	One 20mm Flak Twin	One 20mm Flak Twin
Ammunition	850 rounds	1,000 rounds (see Note 5)	1,000 rounds	1,000 rounds
Officers and Crew	3 + 22 = 25	3 + 22 = 25	3 + 22 = 25	3 + 22 = 25
Number built	6	20	8	16
Launch of first of class	June 15 1935	June 29 1935	September 3 1938	May 18 1940

◁ *U-9* and *U-24* lying in a partially dismantled state on barges during their four-month transportation by road, canal, river, and sea from Germany to the Black Sea. Three Type IIs were sent to Constanza in 1942 and a further three to Feodosia in 1943.

1. Main engines in all versions were twin six-cylinder, four-stroke, Motoren-Werke-Mannheim (MWM) RS 1275 with an output of 350hp at 1,000rpm.

2. Electric motors in all versions were Siemens-Schukert-Werke (SSW) PG VV 322/36 with an output of 180hp at 360rpm. In Type IIC and IID output was raised to 205hp at 360rpm

3. Batteries were manufactured by Accumulatoren-Fabrik-Aktiengesellshcaft, Berlin-Hagen (AFA) and were of two types: (1) AFA 36/MAK/580 with capacity of 7,160 amp/hours, fitted in all Type IIA, all Type IID, and some Type IIB and Type IIC. These batteries gave the performances listed above. (2) AFA 44/MAL/570 with 8,380 amp/hour capacity, fitted in some Type IIB and Type IIC. These batteries improved the endurance to: Type IIB – 83nm at 2kt and 43nm at 4kt; and Type IIC – 42nm at 4kt and 81nm at 2kt.

4. Mines could be carried in one of the following combinations: one torpedo plus 8 *TMA* mines; one torpedo plus 10 *TMB* mines; one torpedo plus 4 *TMA* plus 6 *TMB* mines; 12 *TMA* mines; 18 *TMB* mines.

5. Type IIB boats used in the Black Sea were armed with one 20mm Flak twin plus one 20mm Flak single, with a total of 1,800 rounds.

6. *U-18* was sunk twice. First, it sank after a collision with a surface ship (November 20 1936), but was raised and returned to service. It was subsequently scuttled on August 25 1944.

The Type IIDs were commissioned between June 1940 and January 1942. Some saw brief service, but all had been relegated to training duties by January 1941. Most were made operational again for a short period during the German invasion of the Soviet Union in June-August 1941, but they then returned to training. *U-150*, *U-151* and *U-152* spent their entire service as training boats.

BLACK SEA

Six Type IIBs featured in one of the most unusual deployments ever undertaken by submarines. The first consideration of U-boat operations in the Black Sea was given prior to Operation Barbarossa, but this was not approved by Hitler because he considered that the land attack on the Soviet Union would have succeeded before the boats could be in position. A second proposal in late 1941 was also vetoed, but the third finally achieved success, when Hitler approved the transporting of three U-boats to Romania.

Accordingly, three Type IIBs, *U-9*, *U-19* and *U-24*, were dismantled at Kiel in the summer of 1942, which involved removing the conning tower, diesel engines, electrical motors, batteries, and other smaller items. Three rafts were constructed from five pontoons each and a hull was then placed on its side on each raft. Since each hull weighed some 250 tons and was 134.5ft (41m) long, this was a considerable task. These rafts were moved through the Kiel Canal to Hamburg and then upstream along the River Elbe as far as Dresden. At a landing stage near the city the pontoons were taken out of the water and the hulls cross-loaded onto special transport trailers, each of which was pulled by four tractors, working either one behind the other or four-in-line in two parallel pairs, depending on the road and weather conditions. These transporters then moved with great care and at a maximumn speed of 5mph (8kmh) along the autobahn from Dresden, southwards around Nürnburg to the River Danube at Ingolstadt, where they were cross-loaded back onto their pontoons, which had arrived separately by rail.

From Ingolstadt the pontoons continued their journey until

△ *U-58*, a Type IIC, which was, essentially, a lengthened version of the Type IIB. The very small Type IIs were known to the *Kriegsmarine* as *Einbäume* (dug-out canoes), but they proved quite useful in operations early in the war. Together with *U-57*, *U-58* was used as a test-bed for the newly developed *schnorchel* tubes in 1943/44.

they reached the Austrian city of Linz, where the submarine hulls were floated off, brought upright by flooding their main ballast tanks, and then reinstalled on the pontoons. They then moved on again, with each raft sandwiched between two barges in an effort to disguise what was going on from Allied spies and reconnaissance aircraft. They passed Vienna and continued on through northern Yugoslavia and Romania until they reached Galati, where each hull was put in a floating dock, where it was completely reassembled and then handed over to its crew, who took it on the final leg of the journey to Constanza on the Black Sea coast. They became operational in October 1942.

In August 1942, before the first three boats had even reached their goal, Hitler ordered another three to join them and Admiral Raeder selected three more Type IIBs: *U-18*, *U-20* and *U-23*. Although the transport system had already been tested, winter conditions added to the problems, but the second group of three U-boats also reached the Black Sea successfully and became operational in May 1943.

The six U-boats operated with some success in the Black Sea, sinking a number of Soviet tankers and auxiliaries. *U-9* was sunk and *U-18* and *U-24* were damaged in a Soviet air attack on Constanza on August 20 1944 and were blown up by their own crews on August 20. The other three were offered to Turkey, but when that country refused to accept them they were scuttled off the Turkish coast on September 2 1944.

SUMMARY

Fifty Type IIs were built, of which 11 were lost in combat: 2 to aircraft, 2 to submarines, 2 to mines and 5 to surface ships. As might be expected of a type widely used in training, 4 were sunk in accidents. Another 5, having outlived their usefulness, were stricken in 1944, while 5 were scuttled in the Black Sea. That left 25 still in service at the end of the war: 21 were scuttled in the first week of May 1945 and 4 were taken to the United Kingdom to be disposed of in Operation Deadlight.

Footnote:
1. Otto Weddigen was one of the U-boat heroes of World War I. He was killed when his boat, *U-29*, was rammed and sunk by the British battleship, *Dreadnought* (March 18 1915).

TYPE VII

BACKGROUND

The Type VII was one of the most important designs in the history of the submarine.[1] A grand total of 709 of all sub-types were completed between the first, *U-27* (commissioned August 12 1936) and the last, *U-1308* (commissioned January 17 1945).[2] Despite such large numbers, however, the Type VII was by no means the best submarine of its time, nor was its performance truly outstanding in any one field. But, like many pieces of military hardware, it provided an adequate compromise and suited Dönitz's purposes well. It should be emphasized, however, that at the time the Type VII was selected for production in January 1935 *Fregattenkapitän* Dönitz was still the commanding officer of the cruiser *Emden* and had no influence whatsoever on policy matters such as new types of U-boat.

There were several reasons for the choice of the Type VII. First, and perhaps the most important of all, was that it fitted in well with the requirement for a submarine which could take the trade war well out into the Atlantic. For this the *Kriegsmarine* needed a submarine which would have the range, armament, and seaworthiness necessary for operations in the North Atlantic, to be robust enough to resist enemy attack, to be maneuverable both on the surface and submerged, and to be capable of diving rapidly. Also, because it would be built in large numbers, it had to be relatively easy to build and require a comparatively small crew. Habitability, however, featured very low on

▽ *U-32*, the sixth Type VIIA built, sailing off the coast of Spain between February 2 and May 8 1938, during the Spanish Civil War (note the stripes — red, white, and black — which were indentification marks for neutrals, and the large white figures on the conning tower). *U-32* was sunk on October 30 1940 northwest of Ireland when attacked by two British destroyers.

the list of priorities. A further factor in its selection was that the design was the outcome of steady development starting with the highly successful UB-III of 1917.

Beyond the naval factors, however, was something which was purely political, concerning the 1935 Anglo-German Naval Agreement which allowed the *Kriegsmarine* to build submarines with a total submerged displacement equal to 35 percent of that of the British Royal Navy's, which in 1935 meant that the Germans could build 22,050 tons. This was later amended by mutual agreement in July 1937 to 45 percent of the Royal Navy's tonnage, raising the German figure to 31,500 tons, and in December 1938 to 100 percent (about 70,000 tons). In order to maximize the number of operationally capable, medium-tonnage boats, it was decided to cancel plans for other types such as minelayers and to produce as many Type VIIs as possible. Once in post as *Führer der Uboote*, Dönitz immediately expressed a preference for the Type VII, which he saw as being essential for the one theater that he considered critical in any coming war: the North Atlantic.

Once the two Type IAs and the first Type VIIA had been commissioned they were subjected to a close comparison. This found that the Type VII had much better underwater performance, although the Type IA's twin rudder gave greater maneuverability. The Type IA also had better surface speed and endurance and carried more torpedoes (14 as opposed to 11), all of which were important for boats operating a long way from base. It was decided, therefore, to select the Type VII design for further development and it was reworked to bring it up to the same standard as the Type IA in all respects.

LAYOUT

The overall design of the Type VII was typical of German U-boat practice up to the Type XXI and is given here in some detail.

GENERAL

The Type VII was a single-hull design; that is to say, its pressure hull was also the outer hull, with the strengthening ribs inside the hull. The pressure hull was fabricated from rolled steel, whose thickness varied from 0.73in (1.85cm) amidships to 0.63in (1.6cm) at the ends. The hull was weakest where there were apertures, eg, the main access trunk, torpedo and chef's hatches, diesel exhaust, torpedo tubes, and the numerous small apertures for cables and vents, all of which received a greater or lesser degree of strengthening. There was also a large superstructure, or upper casing, extending from the bow to the stern, which was welded on.

The pressure hull was fabricated from eight modules. Construction began with the erection of the internal ribs at intervals of 23.62in (60cm) and once these were in place sections of the outer skin were welded into position. The internal decking and bulkheads were then added. Once the modules were complete they were placed in the correct order in the assembly shop and then welded together, starting from the central module and working outwards. A large access hole was left on the topside of Module 5 through which were passed all the items required to outfit and equip the submarine. This internal work began at the bow and stern and worked inwards until the

TYPE VIIB

Displacement (surf/sub) 753/857 tons; 218.2ft (66.5m); speed (surf/sub) 17.2/8.0kt; range (surf/sub) 6,500nm at 12kt/90nm at 4kt.

TYPE VIIC

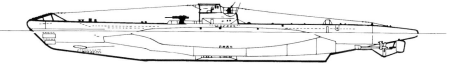

Displacement (surf/sub) 761/865 tons; 220.0ft (67.1m); speed (surf/sub) 17.0/7.6kt; range (surf/sub) 6,500nm at 12kt/80nm at 4kt.

TYPE VIIC/42

Displacement (surf/sub) 999/1,099 tons; 225.4ft (68.7m); speed (surf/sub) 18.6/7.6kt; range (surf/sub) 10,000nm at 12kt/80nm at 4kt.

TYPE VIID

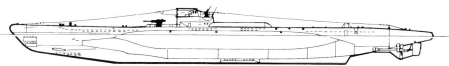

Displacement (surf/sub) 965/1,080 tons; 252.3ft (76.9m); speed (surf/sub) 16.0/7.3kt; range (surf/sub) 8,100nm at 12kt/69nm at 4kt.

◁ The 88mm *Schiffskanone* C/35 was mounted in most Type VIIs. This gun was totaly unrelated to the famous 88mm anti-tank/ anti-aircraft gun used by the Army and *Luftwaffe*; in fact, they could not use the same ammunition.

very last item, the diesel engines. Once this work was complete the hole was closed and the plates welded into place and the superstructure was then added.

FORWARD TORPEDO ROOM

The forward torpedo room accommodated four 21in (533mm) torpedo tubes (mounted 2+2), with the two upper tubes marginally outboard of the lower pair. These tubes were 23ft (7m) long, of which approximately 13ft (4m) projected inboard. The submarine sailed with all four tubes already loaded and with four spare torpedoes in the room: two suspended from the roof and two under the decking. The torpedoes were loaded into the submarine through the forward torpedo hatch and were moved within the compartment using a hoist which ran on rails along

the roof. Torpedoes were loaded into the tubes by five men working together, using a system of pulleys. Most of the crew lived and slept in the forward torpedo room, although there were only six bunks, one of which was occupied by the torpedo petty officer, and the remaining crew found space as best they could.

MAIN ACCOMMODATION

In the forward accommodation section there were, working from forward: a toilet (port), chief petty officers' bunks (port and starboard), wardroom and officers' accommodation (port and starboard), sound room and communications room (starboard), and captain's cabin (port). The toilet was one of two in the submarine, but was the only one that was kept in use throughout the voyage. The four chief petty officers had a bunk each and four officers each had their own bunk and a folding table and bunk seats in each area, which formed the chiefs' mess and the officers' ward-room, respectively. The officers' table could also be used as a makeshift 'operating table' in a surgical emergency. There was no privacy for the chiefs and officers and, as with all accommodation other than the captain's, there was a constant stream of men passing to and fro along the main passageway.

The only person with any semblance of privacy was the captain, whose 'cabin' contained a single bunk and seat, and was screened off by a curtain. This enabled him to work or rest, but he could also hear everything that was going on and he was right next to the control room in the event of an emergency. The sound and radio rooms were also adjacent to the captain and to the control room.

△ Three Type VIIAs on a pre-war inspection, clearly showing the single after torpedo tube, which was externally mounted and thus could not be reloaded at sea. Also clearly visible are the saddle-tanks.

CONNING TOWER

The Type VII had the traditional German arrangement with a conning tower above the main control room and all personnel entering or leaving the pressure hull had to go through the two pressure hatches to get to the bridge. Such a conning position dated back to the earliest submarines, when the tower was fitted with vision ports and was used by the CO when running just below the surface. In the Type VII, however, the CO had no such vision, except by the attack periscope. The Type VII conning tower was very cramped and efforts were made to enlarge it. All personnel entering or leaving the pressure hull had to go through the two pressure hatches to get to the bridge.

CONTROL ROOM

The control room was separated from the rest of the boat by a pressure bulkhead at each end and on all occasions except during an attack the U-boat was controlled from this room, which was immediately below the conning tower access hatch. The second steering position and the two planesmen's controls were on the starboard side. The main controls, such as valves, periscope motors, and main bilge pump were on the port side. At the after end of the control room was the navigator's table. The planesmen were required to keep the U-boat aligned according to the commanding officer's orders and were assisted by bubble attitude gauges and a large depth gauge; a petty officer sat behind them, supervising. The main magazine was located beneath the control room floor and in a surface gun action ammunition had to be passed from there, up the main access trunk to the bridge and thence to the guns.

TYPE VII								
	TYPE UBIII	**TYPE VIIA**	**TYPE VIIB**	**TYPE VIIC**	**TYPE VIIC/41**	**TYPE VIIC/42**	**TYPE VIID**	**TYPE VIIF**
First of class launched	January 6 1917	June 24 1936	April 27 1938	September 19 1940	July 17 1943	None	July 24 1941	March 12 1943
ROLE	Attack boat	Attack boat	Attack boat	Attack boat	Attack boat	Attack boat	Minelayer	Torpedo supply
DISPLACEMENT Surfaced Submerged	516 tons 651 tons	626 tons 745 tons	753 tons 857 tons	761 tons 865 tons	759 tons 860 tons	999 tons 1,099 tons	965 tons 1,099 tons	1,084 tons 1,181 tons
DIMENSIONS Length Beam Draught	181.4ft (55.3m) 19.0ft (5.8m) 12.1ft (3.7m)	211.6ft (64.5m) 19.0ft (5.8m) 14.4ft (4.4m)	218.2ft (66.5m) 20.3ft (6.2m) 15.4ft (4.7m)	220.1ft (67.1m) 20.3ft (6.2m) 15.7t (4.8m)	220.5ft (67.2m) 20.3ft (6.2m) 15.7ft (4.8m)	225.4ft (68.7m) 22.6ft (6.9m) 16.7ft (5.1m)	252.3ft (76.9m) 21.0ft (6.4m) 16.4ft (5.0m)	254.6ft (77.6m) 24.0ft (7.3m) 16.1ft (4.9m)
PROPULSION Diesel Electric Battery Fuel	Two 2,200hp Two 788hp 2 x 62 71 tons	Two 2,320hp Two 750hp 2 x 62 67 tons	Two 2,800hp Two 750hp 2 x 62 108 tons	Two 2,800hp Two 750hp 2 x 62 113 tons	Two 2,800hp Two 750hp 2 x 62 113 tons	Two 2,200hp Two 750hp 2 x 62 159 tons	Two 2,800hp Two 750hp 2 x 62 169 tons	Two 2,800hp Two 750hp 2 x 62 199 tons
PERFORMANCE Speed Surfaced Submerged Range Surfaced Submerged (at 4kt) Diving depth Operational Crush	13.5kt 6.5kt 7,120nm at 6kt 50nm 328ft (100m) 656ft (200m)	16.0kt 8.0kt 4,300nm at 12kt 90nm 328ft (100m) 656ft (200m)	17.2kt 8.0kt 6,500nm at 12kt 90nm 328ft (100m) 656ft (200m)	17.2kt 7.6kt 6,500nm at 12kt 80nm 328ft (100m) 656ft (200m)	17.0kt 7.6kt 6,500nm at 12kt 80nm 394ft (120m) 820ft (250m)	18.6kt 7.6kt 10,00nm at 12kt 80nm 328ft (100m) 656ft (200m)	16.0kt 7.3kt 8,100nm at 12kt 69nm 328ft (100m) 656ft (200m)	16.9kt 7.9kt 9,500nm at 12kt 75nm 328ft (100m) 656ft (200m)
WEAPONS Bow tubes Stern tubes Torpedoes Mines Guns	Four 19.7in (500mm) One 19.7in (500mm) 10 – One 88mm	Four 21in (533mm) One 21in (533mm) 11 22 TMA or 33 TMB One 88mm One 20mm	Four 21in (533mm) One 21in (533mm) 14 26 TMA or 39 TMB One 88mm One 20mm	Four 21in (533mm) One 21in (533mm) 14 26 TMA or 39 TMB One 88mm One 20mm (Note 1)	Four 21in (533mm) One 21in (533mm) 14 26 TMA or 39 TMB One 88mm One 20mm	Four 21in (533mm) One 21in (533mm) 16 26 TMA or 39 TMB One 88mm 20 quad One twin 20mm	Four 21in (533mm) One 21in (533mm) 14 15 SMA One 88mm One 20mm	Four 21in (533mm) One 21in (533mm) 14+27 26 TMA or 39 TMB One 88mm One 20mm
OFFICERS AND CREW	3+31	44	44	44	44	45	44	46
Number ordered Number completed		10 10	24 24	593 577	239 88	165 0	6 6	4 = 1041 4 = 709

[1] From 1944: one 37mm, one twin 20mm

▽ The Type VIIB *U-48* was the most successful U-boat of World War II, carrying out 12 operational patrols under five captains: Schultze, Rösing, Bleichrodt, Atzinger, and Todenhagen. *U-48*'s score was 53 merchant ships (304,981grt) and one Royal Navy sloop sunk, plus four merchantmen damaged. *U-48* was transferred to training duties in October 1943 and was scuttled in May 1945.

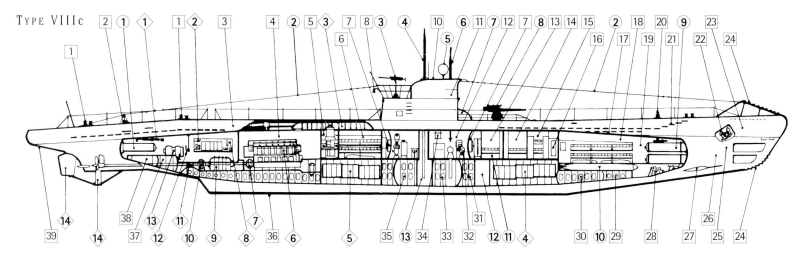

TYPE VIIIc

AFTER ACCOMMODATION

Immediately astern of the control room was the petty officers' (POs') accommodation, with two rows, each of two bunks, on each side of the passageway.

GALLEY

The galley was at the after end of the POs' accommodation and was tiny. It contained two small stoves but the space was restricted even further by a ladder leading up to the chef's hatch and by a panel of circuit breakers on the after bulkhead. It was manned by just one chef, who provided 24-hour coverage 7 days a week. For food storage he had a small refrigerated compartment at the forward end of the POs' accommodation and, by custom, he also had full use of the after toilet for food storage. All of these were, however, nowhere near sufficient. As a result when U-boats sailed there was food in every part of the boat, with joints of meat and fruit hanging from the pipes.

DIESEL ENGINE ROOM

The main engine room housed two diesels, one each side of a narrow walkway, and their mounting rafts. Access to the diesels was reasonably good and the room was permanently manned by machinists, tending their charges. Two types of engine, both with identical dimensions and performance, could be fitted, one made by MAN, the other by Germania.

ELECTRIC MOTOR ROOM/AFT TORPEDO ROOM

The final space housed the two electric motors, the electric controls and indicator panels, and the after torpedo tube. The single 23ft (7m) tube launched its torpedo between the two rudder blades and one torpedo was always in the tube, while the single reload was housed beneath the deck plates. There was a torpedo loading hatch in the roof and the rails of the reloading hoist ran along the ceiling.

ACCUMULATOR ROOMS

There was considerable space beneath the decking, part of

△ Type VIIC hull, weapons and sensors, and propulsion and steering details.

Hull and fittings (figures in squares):
1: Bollards. 2: Navigation light. 3: Aft torpedo hatch. 4: Diesel-engine room. 5: Galley. 6: Chief Petty Officers' accommodation. 7: Pressure bulkhead and hatch. 8: Ship's bell. 9: Conning tower. 10: Bridge. 11: Conning tower (inside). 12: Control room. 13: CO's cabin. 14: Chief Engineer's cabin.

which was allocated to the two accumulator rooms, which were below the forward and after accommodation sections, respectively. Installing and removing the cells was extremely arduous, as each of the very heavy cells had to be loaded through the battery access hatch located just forward of the bridge, maneuvered along the main passageway, lowered into the appropriate accumulator room, maneuvered into a precise position, secured and then wired up; removal was in the opposite sequence. Men had to access the accumulator rooms at sea in order to check the electrolyte levels, top up where necessary, and, in the event of damage, change the wiring.

UPPER CASING

The deck casing covered the whole of the upper part of the pressure hull. It served as a working surface for the seamen, as a cover for piping and ventilation shafts, as an access to the various hatches, and as storage for items such as torpedoes. Most of the casing was covered with wooden planking, which did not

15: Petty Officers' accommodation. 16: Toilet and washroom. 17: Pressure hull. 18: Sailor's accommodation. 19: Forward torpedo room. 20: Capstan. 21: Free-flood holes. 22: Anchor. 23: Forward stabilization tank. 24: Serrated net cutter. 25: Anchor chain locker (inside). 26: Diving tank No. 2. 27: Forward hydroplane. 28: Hydroplane actuators. 29: Trim tank. 30: Torpedo compensating tank. 31: Oil tank. 32: Hydroplane control wheels. 33: Diving tank No. 3. 34: Conning tower access

trunk. 35: Diving tank No. 3. 36: Keel. 37: Aft torpedo compensating tank. 38: Aft trim tank. 39: Diving tank No. 1.

Weapons and sensors (figures in circles):
1: After torpedo tube (1). 2: Wire antenna for HF radio. 3: 20mm *Flak* C/30 cannon. 4: Attack periscope. 5: DF loop. 6: 'Sky' periscope. 7: Magnetic compass housing. 8: 88mm ship's gun C/35 in U-boat mounting C/35. 9: Forward torpedo tubes (4). 10: Reserve torpedo. 11: Radio room (starboard side). 12: Magazine. 13: Attack periscope housing. 14: Air compressor.

Propulsion and steering (figures in diamonds):
1: Steering actuator. 2: Main control board. 3: Engine room air intake trunk. 4: Forward battery room. 5: After battery room. 6: Diesel engines (2). 7: Clutch. 8: Main switch board. 9: Electric motors (2). 10: Clutch. 11: Thrust block. 12: Emergency steering position. 13: Air compressor. 14: Propellers (2). 1 5: Rudders (2).

ice-up and provided more secure footing than a steel deck. The area under the casing was open to the sea through free-flooding holes, whose patterns varied with between dockyards.

HYDROPLANES

There were two sets of hydroplanes, both protected on their forward side by guard rails. The forward planes were set very low on the bow, while the after planes were immediately behind the propellers, which increased their effectiveness.

DIVING

Like any submarine, to run submerged the Type VII had to be properly balanced so that the total weight of the boat and all its contents was equal to the weight of water it displaced. This was not a constant, and varied according to the amount of fuel consumed (which was replaced by an equal amount of seawater, but of a different specific gravity), garbage disposed through the tubes, ammunition expended and so on. It could also be affected by the salinity in the surrounding seawater. The balance was also affected whenever a torpedo was launched and an equivalent amount of water had to be admitted to the torpedo tank exactly as the torpedo left the tube. The boat would not, however, remain stationary at a given depth, but needed the propellers and planes, used in conjunction with each other, to provide a dynamic balance. This balancing and trimming was one of the prime responsibilities of the *Leitende Ingenieur* (*LI* = Leading Engineer).

SURFACING

On the orders of the commander, the electric motors were switched to high speed, the hydroplanes put to 'up' and the reserve fuel pump started so as to prime the engines. Compressed air was then progressively admitted to buoyancy tanks 1, 3 and 5 until the bridge hatch was clear of the surface, at which point the watchkeeping officer led the rush to the bridge to commence all round observation, particularly against air attack. At the same time, the diesels were started, the electric motors stopped, and battery-charging commenced.

DESIGN DEVELOPMENT

TYPE VIIA

All the developments of the Type VII retained the same basic layout and design features set by the Type VIIA, which, in essence, was a single hull design with saddle tanks. There were six watertight compartments, with the main diving tank inside the pressure hull under the control room. This tank did not offer sufficient capacity, however, so further capacity was provided by two saddle tanks, one jutting out from each side of the pressure hull, giving the Type VII its characteristic appearance. There were trim tanks under compartments 1 and 6, and additional diving tanks outside the pressure hull in the bows and stern. Some of the earlier versions were fitted with a serrated-edge netcutter on the bows, a relic of World War I which was soon removed.

There were two special bulkheads at each end of the control room, which could withstand pressure to a depth of 164ft (50m), and there were less substantial bulkheads between the other compartments. A conning tower, from which the commanding officer commanded the U-boat in action, was situated atop the main access hatch, immediately below the bridge. The diesel-oil bunkers were situated inside the pressure hull to avoid leakages when under depth-charge attack.

Ten Type VIIAs were built, six by AG Weser and four by Germania, which were commissioned between July 25 1936 and April 15 1937.

▽ The bridge of a Type VIIB. The captain wears a white cover on his cap, a U-boat tradition, and to his right is the slot for the direction-finding loop, while immediately on his left are the heads of the two periscopes.

TYPE VIIB

As soon as possible after it had been launched, the first Type VIIA was tested and compared with the Type IA. The Type VII was declared the better boat, but it was also decided that various improvements were necessary, of which the most important were increasing the range and speed on the surface, increasing the number of torpedo reloads, and improving the maneuverability. The major changes were in lengthening the hull by 6.56ft (2m) and in increasing the length and breadth of the saddle tanks, which enabled the fuel capacity to be increased by 1,412cu ft (40cu m). The diesel engines were upgraded by fitting superchargers, increasing power output by some 20 percent and speed by about 1 knot. Maneuverability was greatly improved and the turning circle reduced by fitting twin rudders, one behind each propeller. The Type VIIA had also shown a tendency to roll badly on the surface and an attempt to alleviate this was made by fitting *Regelzelle* (compensating tanks) inside the saddle tanks, which acted as roll dampers.

The armament was also revised. The new twin rudder arrangement enabled the single stern torpedo tube to be brought inside the pressure hull, launching its torpedoes between the two blades. The torpedo load was also increased, with two in pressure-tight containers underneath the upper casing and one in the newly created after torpedo room, bringing the total load up to 14. Also, the original Type VIIA mounted

△ A view of *U-402*, a Type VIIC nearing completion, showing the deep hull, saddle-tanks, twin screws and rudders, and the canoe stern.

a single 20mm cannon at deck level abaft the tower, which was principally intended for use against surface ships, but with a secondary anti-aircraft role. However, it was so close to the tower that it had only a limited field of fire and on the Type VIIB it was moved to a platform at the after end of the bridge.

One Type VIIB was ordered for an export customer and was due to be built by Flenderwerft, but the order was canceled and the boat was built as *U-83* for the *Kriegsmarine* instead. A total of 24 Type VIIBs were commissioned.

TYPE VIIC

Dönitz and the U-boat arm in general were very pleased with the Type VIIB, but unfortunately even the longer hull was insufficient to accommodate the new active sonar device, *Sondergerät für aktive Schallortung* (= special apparatus for active sound location), usually known as the 'S-Gerät' (special apparatus). The internal space required for this installation resulted in an additional 23.6in (600mm) frame in the control room (effectively 11.8in/300mm fore and aft of the periscope). This coincidentally also increased the space in the inadequate conning tower by 11.8in (300mm) in length and 2.4in (60mm) in width, and added a further 190cu ft (5.4cu m) to the underdeck fuel tank. Two additional negative buoyancy tanks were also added inside the saddle tanks to reduce diving time, especially in heavy seas. Other minor improvements included a new diesel-oil filtration system to economize in the use of lubricating oil, a new air-compressor, and an updated electrical control system, which used wheel-operated switches in place of knife switches.

Unfortunately, there was no increase in diesel propulsive power to compensate for the greater length, making the Type VIIC slightly slower and with slightly less range on the surface than the Type VIIB. In addition, increasing displacement without any increase in electrical propulsive power meant that submerged speed was marginally slower. The *S-Gerät* also proved not to be ready for operational use and could not be installed in the earlier Type VIICs.

A total of 577 Type VIICs were commissioned.

TYPE VIIC/41

The British anti-U-boat offensive in 1940/41 showed that there were a number of operational areas where the performance of the Type VIIC needed to be improved. These included a higher surface speed and increased weatherliness on the surface, both of which were needed to increase the ability to catch up with targets. It was also considered necessary for the boats to dive deeper to escape depth-charge attacks.

This led to a major weight-saving exercise, in which no less than 11.5 tons were pared off the equipment weight, mainly by substituting newer, lighter items. Ten tons of the weight saved was taken up by increasing the thickness of the pressure hull from 0.73in (18.5mm) to 0.83in (21mm), which enabled the normal operating depth to be increased to 394ft (120m) and the crush depth to 820ft (250m). The requirement to improve seakeeping was met by lengthening the bow by 5in (13cm) and widening the foredeck to produce what was nicknamed the 'Atlantiksteven' (Atlantic bow), the same name as that given to a similar modification to the bows of the battlecruisers *Scharnhorst* and *Gneisenau*.

The modifications were not considered sufficiently great to warrant a new sub-type number, but the changes were indicated by adding the suffix '41' because the executive decision to proceed was given in 1941. Thus, this modified boat became the Type VIIC/41 and a total of 88 were completed. The last, *U-1308*, built by Flensburg, was commissioned as late as January 17 1945.

TYPE VIIC/42

With the Type VIIC/41, the basic design seemed to have been developed to its limits, but there were still urgent demands from the operational crews for yet more surface speed and deeper diving, resulting from the increase in enemy convoy speeds, greater dispersal of convoy routes, and improved ASW methods. This could be achieved only by greater engine power and a plan was prepared to add a second-stage supercharger and to increase the engine speed, resulting in 2,200hp at 530rpm. To accommodate the additional equipment, the engine room needed to be lengthened by 31.5in (80cm), which because of counterbalancing at the forward end, added an extra 5.1ft (1.54m) to

TYPE VIIC BOWS

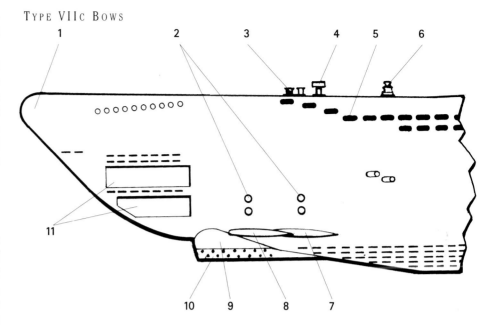

△ The bow of a Type VIIC showing the layout of weapons and equipment of a typical 1944/45 boat.

1: Bows.
2: Underwater telephone transducers.
3: Bollards.
4: *KDB* (*Kristall Busisgerät* = listening device).
5: Free-flood holes.
6: Capstan.
7: Forward hydroplane.
8: Fixed fin/guard.
9: *Balkan Gerät* (Balcony device).
10: 24 hydrophones (*Gruppen Hörsch gerät*).
11: Torpedo tubes.

the overall length of the boat. This increased the top surface speed by 1.6 knots and doubled the endurance at 10 knots.

The pressure hull was also increased by 11.8in (300mm) in diameter and constructed of Krupp 1.1in (28mm) 'CM-351' armored steel, which resulted in a normal test depth of 656ft (200m) and a crush depth of 1,640ft (500m). The saddle tanks were widened by 14in (350mm) to increase bunker capacity to extend range. A hydraulic clutch between the diesel and electric motor drive shafts was substituted for the earlier friction type, and a dehumidifier was added for tropical cruising.

It was planned to build a total of 174 Type VIIC/42s and contracts were placed in July 1942 for a first delivery in August 1944. In the event, however, none was ever laid down, let alone completed.

TYPE VIIC/43

The Type VIIC/43 was planned as a development of the Type VIIC/42, but with a much heavier torpedo armament, comprising six bow and four stern tubes. These extra tubes were to have been accommodated by making changes to the forward and stern torpedo compartments only. This design was canceled in May 1943.

TYPE VIID

In the early war years the *TMA* torpedo-tube-launched mine was not yet ready for service, while the large Type XBs were intended for laying shaft-launched *SMA* mines in distant waters. There was, therefore, a perceived need for a specialized minelayer to lay *SMA* mines at shorter ranges, particularly in British coastal waters, and the Type VIID was developed to meet this requirement. This was, in essence, a Type VIIC with a 32.2ft (9.8m) 'plug' between the control room after bulkhead and the petty officers'

mess. This 'plug' accommodated five vertical mine shafts, each containing three *SMA* mines, together with five compensating tanks, which were flooded as the mines were released. The upper end of the mine shafts penetrated the upper deck and was accommodated in a small superstructure immediately abaft the conning tower, while the bottom end of the mineshafts was open. Further space in the 'plug' was used to accommodate two extra bunks and two refrigerators to store food. The saddle tanks were also lengthened, enabling a further fuel tank, ballast tank, and compensating tank to be added on each side.

Because the mine shafts were accommodated in the 'plug,' the original torpedo and gun armament was not affected and the Type VIIDs were capable of being employed as normal attack boats. The range was somewhat greater than that of the Type VIIC but maximum speed was marginally less. It was also less maneuverable and had increased diving time. Six of this very specialized sub-type were commissioned between August 30 1941 (*U-213*) and January 24 1942 (*U-218*).

TYPE VIIE
The Type VIIE was intended as a test-bed for a new Deutz lightweight V-12, two-stroke diesel engine. Apart from the engines it would have been identical to the Type VIIC except that the weight saved in the engine installation was to have been used in a thicker pressure hull, thus allowing greater diving depths. In the event, the engine program was terminated and the Type VIIE was never laid down.

TYPE VIIF
Experience between 1939 and 1941 showed that, apart from fuel, one of the major limiting factors in U-boats' endurance was run-

△ Three Type VIICs lying at Wilhelmshaven in 1945, with a Type IX in the background. Note that these later Type VIIs do not have a net-cutter or main gun, but the foredecks of the outboard pair have a recess for a *schnorchel* tube and watertight containers for rescue gear.

ning out of torpedoes. On some occasions it was possible for boats which had expended their supply to obtain unused torpedoes from boats returning home, but such availability could not be guaranteed. It was decided, therefore, to develop a specialized torpedo carrier, the Type VIIF. This was produced by adding a 34.5ft (10.5m) 'plug' abaft the control room, of which 25.6ft (7.8m) was used to accommodate 24 torpedoes, in four layers, each of six, with an additional torpdeo hatch on the after deck to enable these torpedoes to be embarked and disembarked. As with the Type VIID, this 'plug' also provided space for additional bunks and refrigerators. The hull had a much increased beam, but in all other respects the Type VIIF was identical to the Type VIIC and had the same armament.

Four boats were ordered and were not completed until mid-1943, by which time the slow and laborious transfer of torpedoes, involving two U-boats sitting on the surface for several hours, was simply not a practicable proposition. They were therefore used in transport missions, with *U-1062* actually delivering a full load of torpedoes to Penang in 1944.

THE END OF THE TYPE VII
The end of the Type VII came with Dönitz's decision to concentrate on mass production of the Type XXI. All contracts for future production of Type VIIs were withdrawn on September 30 1943, although those already under construction were to be completed. As a result, the last of the Type VIICs from the larger yards were commissioned by mid-1944, the only exception being the small Flensburg yard which was not involved in the Type XXI program and continued to construct a few more Type VIIC/41s.

With the value of hindsight it is surprising that instead of undertaking the massive Type XXI program no attempt was made to update the Type VIIC. The post-war programs undertaken by the US and British navies showed that the performance of existing types could be substantially improved by increasing the battery power and streamlining the external hull, and there seems no reason why the same could not have been applied to the Type VIIC. If it had, it might have been rather more effective than the technically risky and resource-hungry Type XXI.

VARIATIONS, MODIFICATIONS AND CONVERSIONS

The Type VIIs were so widely used, for such a long period and for such diverse purposes that numerous modifications (most official, a few unofficial) were inevitable.

ANTI-AIRCRAFT WEAPONS

Once the war started, the very rapid increase in the air threat meant that urgent steps had to be taken to improve the Type VIIs' anti-aircraft capability, giving rise to a series of conversions.

BRIDGE CONVERSION I. The first improvement consisted of the addition of two twin 15mm MG151 machine guns to the existing single 20mm cannon. The MG151s were mounted on the bridge and, since they were not waterproof, they retracted into vertical, cylindrical, watertight mountings, while the 20mm cannon was mounted at a slightly lower level, on what came to be known as the 'wintergarden' (a protective structure). One boat only, *U-533*, received this modification, and following a highly critical report by the captain a slightly modified version was installed in two boats operating with *29 U.Flotille* in the Mediterranean: *U-81* and *U-453*. This involved two twin Breda 13.2mm machine guns in place of the MG151s.

BRIDGE CONVERSION II. The next attempt consisted of two single 20mm C/38 abaft the bridge: one was on a platform at bridge-deck level, the second on a lower platform ('wintergarden'). This was also regarded as an interim measure pending arrival of the twin and quadruple mounts, but a number of boats were fitted.

BRIDGE CONVERSION III. The Type VIID minelayer had six vertical mineshafts immediately aft of the bridge, which meant that the bridge could not be extended aft to accommodate the increased armament. As a result, the *flak* platform was widened to enable two 2mm C/38 singles to be mounted.

BRIDGE CONVERSION IV. This was intended as the ultimate solution for the Type VIIC and involved two twin 20mm C/38 on the bridge platform and either a quadruple 20mm or a single automatic 30mm on the 'wintergarden.' The first twin 20mm mounts were relatively close together, but, in answer to requests

△ Seven Type VIICs were converted to '*flak*' (anti-aircraft) boats between May and November 1943. This is the first, *U-441*, with (from right [forward] to left [aft]): quadruple 20mm (*flak vierling*); bridge; *Hohentwiel* radar antenna; second quad 20mm; single 37mm. *U-441* had some early successes but Allied aircraft soon developed tactics to overcome these defenses and the surviving *flak* boats later reverted to standard Type VIICs. On one occasion *U-441* had all its officers killed or wounded by aircraft, except for the doctor, who took command and brought it back to port.

from the crews, protective shields were fitted which involved mounting the guns slightly further apart. Bridge conversion IV became mandatory for all operational boats from August 1943. In October 1943 the new automatic 37mm cannon became available, although for some time the delivery rate was slower than expected. As they became available these were mounted in place of the quad 20mm which had proved less than fully satisfactory.

BRIDGE CONVERSIONS V AND VI. These two conversions consisted of the bridge conversion IV with an additional platform forward of the bridge, which was intended to strengthen the AA defenses yet further. In the conversion V the sides of the forward platform were plated over, which resulted in even more spray than usual on the bridge. To alleviate this the conversion VI had a slightly lower platform with open sides, but this resulted in increased diving time and difficulties in maintaining a set depth. Only one boat had a conversion V (*U-362*) and two boats had conversion VI (*U-673* and *U-973*).

BRIDGE CONVERSION VII. This was the final *flak* conversion with a structure which completely encircled the bridge and provided two gun platforms, one forward of the bridge and one aft. Each platform accommodated a twin 37mm gun mount.

BRIDGE CONVERSION VIII. This consisted of a platform each side of the bridge, a platform forward of the bridge, and a bridge platform and a 'wintergarden' aft.

UNDESIGNATED AA CONVERSIONS. There were, inevitably, a small number of other conversions. For example, *U-84*, a Type VIIB, had a second 20mm C/38 aft, but instead of being mounted on a 'wintergarden' it was mounted on a small raised platform, which was separated from the bridge structure. Another conversion involved a small platform mounted on the forward side of the bridge which accommodated a single twin MG-151 mounting. As far as is known this was fitted only to *U-338*.

FLAK U-BOAT. The various bridge conversions were intended solely to improve the U-boats' own defensive power, but a '*Flak* U-boat' design was developed which was intended to provide an air defense umbrella for a group of U-boats. This involved longer and wider extensions both fore and aft of the bridge, plus a 'wintergarden,' on which were mounted two quadruple 20mm mounts and a single 37mm. To compensate for the additional armament and ammunition, only five torpedoes (ie, one in each tube) could be carried.

Two boats were actually converted, *U-256* (which had been badly damaged in air attacks in September 1942) and *U-441*, and another five (*U-211*, *U-263*, *U-271*, *U-621* and *U-953*) were set in hand. The first to be ready was *U-441*, which set out on its first cruise with the captain under orders to take aggressive action against Allied aircraft. On the second day at sea (May 24 1943) it shot down an RAF Sunderland, but incurred serious damage in the process. Three more *Flak* boats were completed, but it was soon decided that the operational concept was flawed. The *Flak* boats were of no value in the North Atlantic, while their fuel bunkers and

▽ The business end of a Type VIIC with the torpedo tube covers open and the doors retracted. Note also the very low position of the forward hydroplanes.

reduced torpedo load made them inadequate for operations in more distantwaters. As a result, the idea was scrapped and in November 1943 all were modified to bridge conversion VI standard.

PROBLEMS. While obviously providing an increased air defense capability, these conversions caused as many problems as they solved:
• They added considerably to the top weight, thus reducing stability on the surface.
• The considerable hydrodynamic resistance of the guns and their mounts increased the diving time and reduced underwater speed.
• Ammunition supply created difficulties, since only small numbers of ready-use rounds could be held near the guns. This meant that ammunition had to be passed from the magazine inside the boat, up the tower trunk and thence to the mount, which was further complicated where the ammunition had to be carried around the gun on the bridge platform (which would have been in use) to the gun on the 'wintergarden.' The fact that the guns were automatic increased the ammunition supply requirements.
• The increasing number of men on the upper deck meant that crash-dives took even longer, as they all tried to get down the one hatch.
• Appreciating that the AA defenses had been strengthened, Allied aircraft ceased making solo attacks and circled just out of range until air and sea reinforcements arrived. The aircraft waited until the U-boat started to dive and then swooped into attack.

Fortunately for the U-boat crews the advent of the *schnorchel* meant that their U-boats could cruise at periscope depth to recharge their batteries, which greatly reduced – although by no means eliminated – the danger of air attack.

REPAIR BOATS Two Type VIICs, *U-235* and *U-236*, were completed as 'repair boats.' After working-up both spent most of their careers in the training flotilla at Gotenhafen: *U-235* from October 1943 to March 1945, and *U-236* from September 1943 to April 1944, following which it went to Pillau until March 1945. Both were used to test the new *schnorchel* device in 1943, but both became *frontboote* in 1945 and were ordered to Norway. *U-235* was sunk by a German MTB in Norwegian waters on April 14 1945, while *U-236* was so severely damaged in RAF bombing attacks on May 3 1945 that it was scuttled the next day.

TORPEDO TUBE VARIATIONS Several Type VIIs were completed with fewer than the normal array of torpedo tubes, due to shortages at the time of construction. Some had only two bow tubes and were employed in the training flotillas throughout their career: *U-72*; *U-78*; *U-80*; *U-554*; and *U-555*. Others had no stern tubes, but were employed as normal *frontboote*

(except for *U-351* which served with the training flotilla): *U-83*; *U-203*; *U-331*; *U-352*; *U-401*; *U-431*; *U-651*.

MINE FITTING VARIATIONS A number of Type VIICs did not have the fittings necessary to enable them to handle and lay mines. Such fittings were not fitted in Type VIIC/41 from *U-1271* onwards.

OPERATIONAL HISTORY

The Type VII was at the forefront of the U-boat battles in the North and central Atlantic, in the Mediterranean, and in the Arctic, and sank by far the greatest proportion of Allied ships. They were by far the most important single type of U-boat in service throughout the war. Type VIIs sank an immense tonnage of enemy ships and carried out some of the most notorious sinkings. One such took place on the first day of ther war when *U-30* (Lemp) sank the liner, SS *Athenia*, on September 3 1939; in this tragedy 118 died including several children and 28 US citizens. Two more military successes occurred when *U-47* (Prien) sank the British battleship *Royal Oak* in Scapa Flow (October 8 1939), in which 833 lives were lost, and when *U-29* (Schuhart) sank the aircraft carrier *Courageous* south-west of Ireland (September 19 1939), in which 518 lives were lost.

U-744

U-744 (Blischke) was heading towards convoy HX.280 when it was detected at approximately 1000 hours on March 6 1944 by an ASW escort group consisting of six frigates (five Canadian, one British) which proceeded to hunt the U-boat remorselessly. *U-744* was subjected to 24 separate attacks, in which just under 300 depth-charges, as well as Hedgehog and Squid, were used. Blischke handled his boat with great skill and despite the determination of the surface forces managed to survive for over three-and-a-half hours. Conditions inside the U-boat became critical, as the attacks had resulted in damage to the outer hull, the diesel engines were virtually unusable, and there was much minor damage. On top of this, the boat had been submerged

△ A brand-new Type VIIC leaves the Blohm & Voss yard at Hamburg, one of many built at this famous yard. The pattern of the free-flood holes suggest that it is in the group *U-575* to *U-620*.

since the previous night and, as a result, the carbon dioxide level was high and the crew was rapidly reaching the extremes of exhaustion. In the end Blischke was left with no choice but to surface, where the crew abandoned the sinking submarine, which was given the *coup de grace* by a torpedo from one of the escorts. Blischke was among the 12 lost.

U-371

U-371 (Fenski) was operating in the Mediterranean and early on the morning of May 3 1944 it attacked and damaged USS *Menges*, using an acoustic torpedo. It was then hunted over an extended period by five ships (two US, one British and two French) and at one point Fenski took his boat down to 600ft (200m). Fenski then lay on the bottom for no less than 21 hours, at the end of which the inevitable reasons – low batteries and foul air – forced him to surface. The surface ships were still patiently waiting for him and started to fire as soon as *U-371* surfaced but, even while they were abandoning ship, Fenski still found time to fire an acoustic torpedo, which hit a French frigate. Four of *U-371*'s men were lost, but 49, including Fenski, survived.

U-530, U-977

Two Type VIIs made extraordinary voyages at the war's end, sailing undetected from Norway to Argentina. The first to arrive was *U-530* (*Oberleutnant* Wermuth) which entered Mar Del Plata on July 19 1945, followed by *U-977* (*Oberleutnant* H Schäfer) on August 17 1945. *U-977* managed to spend no less than 66 days submerged, using only the *schnorchel*, an unparalleled feat of endurance which made life inside the boat most unpleasant. Both crews were interned by the Argentine authorities and their boats were handed over to the USA, who sailed them to the United States.

Footnote:
1. In the original scheme for the *Ubootwaffe*, the MVB-VII was the designation for a U-boat intended to carry two motor torpedo boats. When this proposal was dropped in 1934 the number 'VII' was reallocated to the new 500-ton Atlantic boat.
2. It is difficult to reconcile the numbers, since some orders were canceled before construction started, and some were canceled after construction had started.

TYPE IX

BACKGROUND

Although it was overshadowed by the far more numerous and smaller Type VII, the Type IX was the long-range partner to the medium-range Type VII, and from the beginning to the end of World War II these two types combined to form the backbone of the *Kriegsmarine*'s U-boat arm. The origin of the Type IX lay in a 1935 requirement for a long-range U-boat which could travel fast to and from distant operational areas, while carrying an adequate number of torpedoes or mines for essentially solo missions. This led to the design of a boat which was based on the Type IA but which was longer, with more powerful diesel engines, greater speed and range, and increased torpedo-carrying capacity. More than 200 Type IXs were built in seven sub-types, making it the second most widely used of the German World War II boats.

The Type IXs were excellent sea boats and spent much of their time in the South Atlantic, Indian Ocean, and Far East waters, although they also went to the east coast of North America. One pre-war plan was that they would also escort German merchant ships in voyages across the Atlantic or further afield.

▽ *U-37*, the first Type IXA to be completed, heads out to sea in this pre-war photo. The gun on the foredeck is a 105mm weapon, while the anti-aircraft 37mm does not appear to be mounted.

DESIGN

The Type IX, whose design and layout were quite different from those of the Type VII, was an ocean-going submersible, whose design could be traced back via the Type IA to the U-81 series of 1916, which had been the most successful of the World War I *Ms* (*Mobilization*) boats. The design and layout of the Type IX was, however, quite different from that of the Type VII.

The Type IA was taken as the starting-point for the Type IX design in order to save time and resources. One criterion was increased surface speed so that it would reach the distant operating areas more quickly. This was achieved by using 9-cylinder diesels instead of the 8-cylinder diesels in the Type IA and by installing superchargers, which boosted output per unit from 1,540hp to 2,400hp. To balance the much heavier and longer engines, the entire interior was redesigned, with all accommodation forward of the control room and the engines immediately abaft the control room.

The control room was further aft than in the Type I and actually lay in the center of the boat, with the conning tower and bridge immediately above it. As in the Type VII the helmsman's normal position was in the conning-tower and he was joined by the commanding officer and the 1WO when at action stations.

The Type IX had a full double-hull with the pressure hull

TYPE IX								
	U-81 CLASS	TYPE IXA	TYPE IXB	TYPE IXC	TYPE IXC/40	TYPE IXD$_1$	TYPE IXD$_1$ (CARGO)	TYPE IXD$_2$	TYPE IXD/42
ROLE	World War I long-range boat	Long-range attack boat	Long-range attack boat	Long-range attack boat	Long-range attack boat	Long-range attack boat	Tansport	Long-range attack boat	Long-range attack boat
DISPLACEMENT									
Surfaced	1,002 tons	1,032 tons	1,051 tons	1,120 tons	1,144 tons	1,610 tons	1,610 tons	1,616 tons	1,616 tons
Submerged	1,250 tons	1,153 tons	1,178 tons	1,232 tons	1,257 tons	1,799 tons	1,799 tons	1,804 tons	1,804 tons
DIMENSIONS									
Length	234.9ft (71.6m)	251.0ft (76.5m)	251.0ft (76.5m)	252.0ft (76.8m)	252.0ft (76.8m)	287.4ft (87.6m)	287.4ft (87.6m)	287.4ft (87.6m)	287.4ft (87.6m)
Beam	20.7ft (6.3m)	21.3ft (6.5m)	22.3ft (6.8m)	22.3ft (6.8m)	22.6ft (6.9m)	24.6ft (7.5m)	24.6ft (7.5m)	24.6ft (7.5m)	24.6ft (7.5m)
Draught	12.8ft (3.9m)	15.4ft (4.7m)	15.4ft (4.7m)	15.4ft (4.7m)	15.4ft (4.7m)	17.7ft (5.4m)	17.7ft (5.4m)	17.7ft (5.4m)	17.7ft (5.4m)
PROPULSION									
Diesel	Two MAN; 2,400hp	Two MAN; 2,200hp	Two MAN; 2,200hp)	Two MAN; 2,200hp	Two MAN; 2,200hp	Six Daimler-Benzr; 1,500hp	Two GW; 1,400hp	Two MAN;2,200hp	Two MAN; 2,200hp
Electric	Two SSW; 615hp	Two SSW; 500hp	Two SSW; 500hp)	Two SSW; 500hp)	Two SSW; 500hp	Two; 500hp	Two 500hp	Two MWM; 580hp	Two MWM; 580hp
Battery	Two 110-cell	Two 62-cell	Two 62-cell	Two 62-cell	Two 62-cell	Two 62-cell	Four 62-cell	Two 62-cell	Two 62-cell
Fuel	119 tons	154 tons	165 tons	208 tons	214 tons	?	203 tons	442 tons	442 tons
PERFORMANCE									
Speed									
Surfaced	16.8kt	18.2kt	18.2kt	18.3kt	18.3kt	20.8kt	15.8kt	19.2kt	19.2kt
Submerged	9.8kt	7.7kt	7.3kt	7.3kt	7.3kt	6.9kt	6.9kt	6.9kt	6.9kt
Range									
Surfaced	11,220nm at 8kt	8,100nm at 12kt	8,700nm at 12kt	11,000nm at 12kt	11,400nm at 12kt	—	9,900nm at 12kt	23,700nm at 12kt	23,700nm at 12kt
Submerged	56nm at 5kt	65nm at 4kt	64nm at 4kt	63nm at 4kt	63nm at 4kt	57nm at 4kt	115nm at 4kt	57nm at 4kt	57nm at 4kt
WEAPONS									
Bow tubes	Four	Four	Four	Four	Four	Four	—	Four	Four
Stern tubes	Two	Two	Two	Two	Two	Two	—	Two	Two
Torpedoes	16	22	22	22	22	24	—	24	22
Mines	—	—	—	—	—	—	—	—	—
Guns	One 105mm	One 105mm One 37mm One 20mm	One 105mm One 37mm One 20mm	One 105mm One 37mm One 20mm	One 105mm One 37mm One 20mm	One 105mm One 37mm One 20mm	One 37mm Two twin 20mm	One 105mm One 37mm One 20mm	One 105mm One 37mm One 20mm
Rotary-winged kite	—	—	—	—	—	One Focke-Achgelis FA-330	One Focke-Achgelis FA-330	One Focke-Achgelis FA-330	One Focke-Achgelis FA-330
Officers and Crew	4 + 35 = 39	4 + 44 = 48	4 + 44 = 48	4 + 44 = 48	4 + 44 = 48	4 + 51 = 55	57	57	57
Cargo	—	—	—	—	—	252 tons	—	—	—
Commissioned	40	8	14	54	87	2	2	28	1

almost entirely surrounded by an outer hull. It had a wide, flat upper deck, with almost perpendicular sides, which gave sufficient space for 10 torpedoes in pressure-tight containers to be housed. The diameter of the pressure hull was 4.72in (12cm) greater than that of the Type IA.

The original armament was one 105mm gun, one 37mm AA cannon and one C/30 machine gun, but there were many changes as the war progressed. Like the Type IA, the Type IX had a single 105mm gun on the foredeck, but the anti-aircraft armament was increased from one 20mm to one 20mm and one 37mm. In line with the requirement for more torpedo tubes, there were four bow tubes and two stern tubes. A total of 22 torpedoes were carried: forward torpedo room - four in tubes plus four reserve; after torpedo room - two in tubes plus two

spare; under upper casing – 10 in watertight containers.

TYPE IXA

The Type IXA was the original version, of which eight were built, the order for the first four being placed in June 1936 and the second four in December. The first, *U-37*, was launched at Bremen on May 4 1938 and was commissioned on August 4 1938.

TYPE IXB

The Type IXB had greater fuel bunkerage (154 to 165 tons), thus increasing the maximum range to 12,000 nautical miles. Externally, the only visual difference was that the forward 105mm gun was mounted slightly closer to bridge. The first two were ordered in July 1937 and 14 were built.

▷ September 1 1940, and officers and sailors on the bridge of a Type IXA cheer to mark the first anniversary of the start of World War II. There were to be few causes for celebration as the war continued and U-boat losses mounted.

TYPE IXC

The Type IXC was a further evolutionary development of the design, the main difference being yet further increases in the size of the fuel bunkers located between the outer and pressure hulls, increasing capacity to 208 tons. Fifty-four were commissioned between March 1939 and July 1942.

TYPE IXC/40

The designers managed to find space for yet another 6 tons of fuel resulting in the Type IXC-40. This led to orders for a total of 163 but, in the event, only 95 were laid down, of which 87 were actually commissioned. A total of 76 were canceled in 1944 so that production could be concentrated on the Type XXI and Type XXIII.

TYPE IXD

It was appreciated early in the war that there was an operational requirement for a submarine which combined very long range with high speed, but it was also clear that to develop a totaly new type and place it in production would cause excessive complications in the shipyards and at ancilliary manufacturers. It was therefore decided to meet the new requirement with relatively inexpensive and rapid modifications to the Type IX, to be produced in two versions, which were designed and developed in parallel, differing only in the engine installation; one maximized speed (Type IXD₁), the other range (Type IXD₂). Totals commissioned were: Type IXD – 2; Type IXD₂ – 28; Type IXD₁-42 – 1.

All three versions shared the same pressure hull, which was constructed of the same material and had the same diameter as that for earlier Type IXs, but was longer to provide the increased living space and stowage needed for long-range missions. The outer hull was both wider and higher than that in earlier Type IXs and also enclosed the whole of the pressure hull. Both designs had two periscopes, as in the Type IXC. The first contracts (for one Type IXD₁ and three IXD₂) were placed with AG Weser in May 1940.

TYPE IXD₁

The Type IXD₁ was designed as the high speed version and was given a unique engine installation using six unsupercharged Daimler-Benz MB-501 fast diesels, with fresh-water cooling. These engines were standard installation in the contemporary German motor-torpedo boats (known as 'S-boats' in Germany and as 'E-boats' by the Allies) in which they had been very successful. In the Type IXD₁ three of these diesels were installed on each shaft giving total power of about 9,000hp at 1,600rpm, which resulted in the high surface speed of 20.8 knots.

Two were built, *U-180* and *U-195*, being commissioned on May 16 1942 and September 5 1942, respectively. The engine installation proved to give severe problems, however. The cooling system was prone to leaks, the heat in the engine

TYPE IXA

Displacement (surf/sub) 1,032/1,153 tons; 251.0 ft (76.5m); speed (surf/sub) 18.2/7.7kt; range (surf/sub) 8,100nm at 12kt/65nm at 4kt.

TYPE IXB

Displacement (surf/sub) 1,051/1,178 tons; 251.0 ft (76.5m); speed (surf/sub) 18.2/7.3kt; range (surf/sub) 8,700nm at 12kt/64nm at 4kt.

TYPE IXC

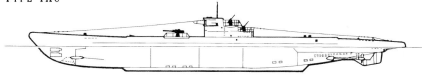

Displacement (surf/sub) 1,120/1,232 tons; 252.0ft (76.8m); speed (surf/sub) 18.3/7.3kt; range (surf/sub) 11,000nm at 12kt/63nm at 4kt.

TYPE IXD₁

Displacement (surf/sub) 1,610/1,799 tons; 287.4ft (87.6m); speed (surf/sub) 20.8/6.9kt; range (surf) not known, (sub) 57nm at 4kt.

TYPE IXD₂

Displacement (surf/sub) 1,616/1,804 tons; 287.4ft (87.6m); speed (surf/sub) 19.2/6.9kt; range (surf/sub) 23,7900nm at 12kt/57nm at 4kt.

room when the engines were running was intolerable, the engines were very fault-prone and, perhaps most dangerous of all, they emitted a huge cloud of dense white smoke, which was visible over long distances. The range was also very disappointing.

TYPE IXD₁ (TRANSPORT)

After their very unsatisfactory first voyages, both were taken out of service, but when the need arose for transport submarines to operate on the Far East route *U-180* and *U-195* were taken in hand and their unsatisfactory engines removed. These were replaced by two standard Germania 6-cylinder, 4-stroke supercharged F-46 diesel engines, as fitted in the Type VIIs. These were much more reliable and did not emit smoke. On the other hand, the maximum speed (on the surface) dropped to 16.5 knots. During this work a much enlarged battery was also fitted, considerably extending the submerged range. All six torpedo tubes were removed. A *schnorchel* was also fitted. In this new

△ *U-106*, a Type IXB, was damaged in an air attack during the morning of August 2 1943 and headed towards a rendezvous with three German E-boats to escort it back to port. Concerned that he would be late for the rendezvous, the U-boat captain surfaced and was promptly spotted and attacked by two Sunderland flying boats. *U-106* sank after 25 minutes: 36 men were rescued by the E-boats; the remainder were lost.

transport guise the Type IXD₁ was able to carry 252 tons of cargo.

TYPE IXD₂

The Type IXD₂ had the same hull as the Type IXD₁ but with a different propulsion system. This comprised two MAN 9-cylinder, 4-stroke M9V 40/46 supercharged diesels, as in the Type IXC, but with the addition of two MWM 6-cylinder, 4-stroke RS 34.5S unsupercharged diesels. The MWM engines were used for cruising, thus enabling the main MAN engines to drive the electric motors as generators to recharge the batteries. Maximum speed on the surface was 19.2 knots. These boats had bunkers carrying 4,412 tons of fuel giving them the exceptional range of 30,500 nautical miles.

TYPE IXD-42

The Type IXD-42 incorporated minor changes from the Type IXD₂, but of 79 ordered only one was completed: *U-883* on March 27 1945. The remainder were canceled in favor of the Type XXI.

VARIATIONS

There were various minor differences in a number of boats. For example:

- Four Type IXCs (*U-183*, *U-184*, *U-185*, *U-187*) were fitted with a 49ft (15m) radio mast to improve long-range communications. The hinged base was mounted on the casing abaft the bridge on the port side, with the mast lying on the upper casing when not in use. It was difficult to raise and lower, and appears to have been of little value, since it was deleted after only two voyages.

- *Schnorchel*s were installed in later boats. This was hinged on the forward, starboard side of the bridge and the well required for the tube in its lowered position displaced three torpedo containers.

- Type IXA and B had three periscopes: one in the control room and two in the conning tower. The control room periscope was deleted in the Type IXCs and Ds, however.

- The diving speed of the Type IX was somewhat slow and the addition of extra anti-aircraft weapons made this even worse. In an effort to overcome this some (but not all) Type IXC/40s had the foredeck narrowed to reduce the crash-dive time. However, this did reduce the number of spare torpedoes that could be carried.

▽ *U-123*, a Type IXB, coming alongside at the end of a patrol. This boat had an unusually long history, carrying out 13 war patrols during which it sank 44 merchant ships (225,132 grt) and the British submarine *P-615*. Decommissioned at Lorient in June 1944, it was found there by the French Navy, who refitted and recommissioned it to serve as *Blaison* (*S-10*) until August 1959.

- A number of Type IXCs and Type IXC/40s were not fitted to carry mines.

- Some boats were fitted with the *FuMo 29* radar, which had a fixed antenna array on the front face of the bridge. This was later replaced by the *FuMo 30*, which had a rotating antenna mounted on the port side of the bridge.

- Some boats were also fitted with *Naxos*.

- Most Type IXDs and some Type IXCs carried a single *Focke-Achgelis Bachstelze* rotary-winged kite. This was a collapsible aircraft, which was housed in a cylindrical container on the upper deck.

WEAPONS

As with the Type VII, the armament underwent a number of changes, leading eventually to a variety of 'wintergardens.' Originally all except the two Type IXDs had a 105mm gun on the foredeck, 37mm automatic on the afterdeck, and a 20mm on a platform at the rear of bridge. However, the foredeck was usually awash so the forward gun was deleted and the platform at the rear of the bridge was extended to form a 'wintergarden,' which mounted a 37mm and two 20mm or, in some cases, a 37mm and a quad 20mm. The base of this extension was also used to accommodate two reserve torpedoes.

U-Boats for Japan

Hitler presented two U-boats to the Imperial Japanese Navy (IJN). The first, *U-511*, a Type IXC, was already in service in the *Kriegsmarine*, having been commissioned in December 1941. It was transferred to the IJN in July 1943 and was sailed to Japan by its German crew, under the cover name Satsuki No 1. It was handed over to the IJN on arrival in Japan on September 16 1943 and was commissioned by them as *RO-500*. It was used for a short while by the IJN, but they did not consider there was much for them to learn from it.

A second boat, *U-1224* (Type IXC/40) was also handed over to the IJN, but in this case it was a brand-new boat, manned by Japanese sailors who had been sent to Germany to collect it. They were fully trained before their boat was commissioned at Kiel on October 20 1943 as *RO-501*. After working-up in the Baltic the boat sailed for Japan, but was sunk with all hands off the Azores on May 31 1944.

Three other Type IXs were in Japanese-controlled ports on May 8 1945 and were immediately taken over by the IJN: *U-181*

△ An unusually clear picture of the control room of *U-889*, looking aft. In the foreground are the ladder and access trunk leading to the conning tower, and the voice-pipe. The plate identifies the boat as having been built at the Bremen yard of Deutsche Schiff- und Maschinen Bau AG (usually known as Deschimag), works number 1097, completed in 1944.

(Type IXD₂); *U-195* (Type IXD₁); and *U-862* (Type IXD₂). They were commissioned into the IJN as *I-501*, *I-506* and *I-502* respectively, but were little used and were surrendered to the Allies in August 1945.

OPERATIONAL HISTORY

TYPE IXC – *U-505*

Most sailors in most navies believe that certain ships are 'unlucky,' and suffer more than their fair share of problems and disasters; *U-505* was just such a one. It was a Type IXC built by Deutsche Werft, Hamburg, and commissioned under *Korvetten-Kapitän* Axel-Olaf Loewe on September 26 1941. Its first operational voyage was from Kiel to Lorient, which it reached on February 3 1942 and after a brief pause for replenishment it sailed again on February 11 to operate off the west coast of Africa. It returned on May 7, having sunk four ships (25,041grt). On its next voyage (June 7 – August 25 1942) *U-505* operated in the Caribbean and had sunk three ships (12,748grt) when the

captain became ill and was relieved by his 1WO. Having obtained authority from *Befelshaber der UBoote* (*BdU* = commander-in-chief, U-Boats) for an early return, *U-505* refueled and replenished the outward bound *U-214*, arriving in Lorient on August 25 1942.[1]

Its next voyage was to the central Atlantic under a new commanding officer, *Kapitänleutnant* Zschech. *U-505* sailed on October 4 1942 and was off Trinidad on November 7 where it sank a merchantman (7,173grt). Alerted to its presence, air patrols were flown by RAF Hudsons and one of these aircraft found the U-boat on the surface on November 11 and attacked. In a very low pass, a bomb hit the after gun, causing a major explosion which not only badly wounded two men and caused much damage aboard the submarine, but also destroyed the Hudson, killing all four crew. *U-505* managed to obtain spares to effect repairs from another boat and passed one of the wounded men to *U-462*, a Type XIV tanker, which had a doctor aboard. During the return voyage, Zschech launched six torpedoes at a lone freighter; all six missed. The boat reached

△ A Type IXC passes down the Kiel Canal, fitted with an unusual, heavily reinforced bow for use in Arctic waters.

Lorient on December 12.

U-505 then underwent some major repairs and did not sail again until July 1 1943, but returned almost immediately for some small repairs, sailing again on July 3. On July 8 the U-boat was attacked by an RAF aircraft and suffered some damage, including some to the *Metox* radar detector and the GSG hydrophone system. A few hours later *U-505* was found and attacked by destroyers, but Zschech managed to escape, although he then decided to return to base, arriving in Lorient on July 13. Next, *U-505* attempted to sail on three separate occasions (August 1, 14 and 21) but in each case returned the following day due to loud noises which came apparent when the boat descended below 164ft (50m). The *Kriegsmarine* believed sabotage had occurred, and a number of French dockyard workers were arrested and shot. After yet further repairs and inspections, *U-505* sailed again on September 18. It had only been away for six days when the boat was spotted by an Allied aircraft and Zschech was forced to crash dive, during which a pump was overloaded and damaged. Judging that this affected

◁ *U-889*, Type IXC/40, bridge, looking aft. On the right (front to rear) are: *UZO* mount, *Hohentwiel* radar antenna (in well), and twin 20mm cannon.
Center (front to rear): attack periscope head, *runddipol* antenna (fixed mast), second periscope head and (partially obscured), the single 37mm AA gun. On the left is another twin 20mm cannon mount. Such hydrodynamic resistance makes it unsurprising that these U-boats were slow underwater

▽ *U-39*, a Type IXA, starts its dive on peacetime maneuvers.

the boat's operational capability, Zschech returned to Lorient, arriving on September 30. The boat sailed yet again on October 9 but on October 23 it was the target of a very intense depth-charge attack, during the course of which Zschech shot and killed himself.

The unfortunate 1WO, *Oberleutnant* Paul Meyer took command, extricated the boat from the attack, buried Zschech at sea, and returned to Lorient, which he reached on November 7. With a new captain, *Oberleutnant* Harald Lange, *U-505*'s next voyage was also brief. It was despatched on Christmas Day to rescue the survivors of a German torpedo-boat, which had been sunk in the Bay of Biscay. It achieved this successfully, but as it entered Brest one of the main electric motors burned out and *U-505* was once again put in the hands of the dockyard.

The worst, however, was yet to come. *U-505* sailed on March 16 1944 for operations in the central Atlantic where, as usual, it suffered from a series of breakdowns and mechanical problems. Lange managed to get all these repaired at sea, rather than use them as an excuse for an early return. *U-505* was found by aircraft operating from USS *Guadalcanal* (CVE-69) on the morning of June 4 and after a very accurate depth-charge attack from a destroyer, USS *Chatelaine* (DE-149), Lange had no option but to surface, abandon ship and scuttle. Lange was first onto the bridge and was immediately badly wounded and knocked out, but the crew got away from the boat, which they thought was sinking and so the demolition charges were not set, nor were the secret documents and equipment destroyed. This

△ The Focke-Achgelis Fa-330 was an unpowered, rotary-winged kite, deployed only in Far East-bound Type IXs. It was stored in a cylinder and assembled in a few minutes, using interconnecting tubes and quick-release shackles. Launching was not difficult, but recovery was time-consuming and if under threat the U-boat captain cut the cable and submerged, leaving the unfortunate pilot (a petty officer) to seek his own salvation.

was unfortunate for *U-505* since the commander of the attacking group, Captain Dan Gallery, USN, had given his crews very thorough training in capturing a surfaced U-boat. Men from USS *Pillsbury* (DE-133) got aboard and secured the boat before it could sink; it was then towed to Bermuda by *Guadalcanal*.

TYPE IXD₁ – *U-180*

U-180 was commissioned on May 16 1942 and sailed on its first voyage from Kiel on February 9 1943. Aboard were two passengers, the more important being the Indian nationalist Subhas Chandra Bhose, who was being sent to the Far East to foment anti-British feeling among Indian prisoners-of-war in Malaya. *U-180* rendezvoused with the Japanese submarine *I-29* on April 25 1943 south-west of Madagascar, transferred its passengers and received two Japanese officers and some cargo in exchange, before returning to France. The captain (Musenberg) sank two ships (13,298grt) during the voyage and achieved the main goal of his mission, but he was most unhappy with the engines, especially the dense smoke which was emitted when on the surface. As a result, once *U-180* returned to Bordeaux on July 2 1943 it was taken out of service.

U-195, carried out one deployment in its original form between March 20 and July 23 1943, when it operated in the Cape Town area of South Africa. It sank two merhchant ships (14,391grt) and damaged a third, but its captain (Buchholz) also submitted a very unfavorable report on the boat's characteristics and on its return to Bordeaux it, too, was taken out of service.

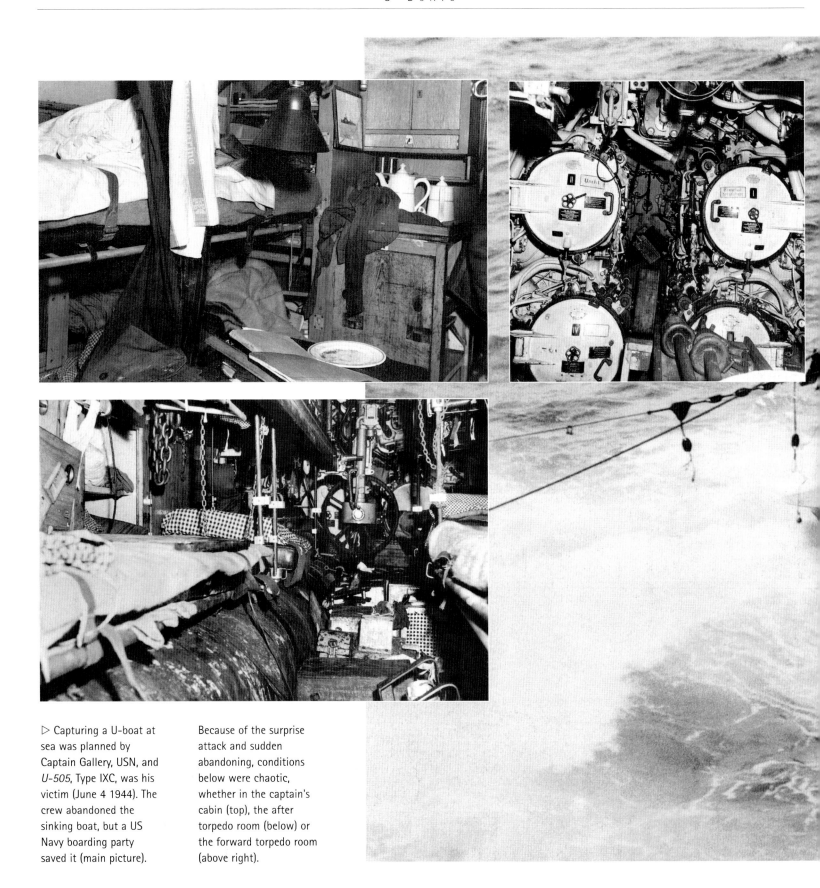

▷ Capturing a U-boat at sea was planned by Captain Gallery, USN, and *U-505*, Type IXC, was his victim (June 4 1944). The crew abandoned the sinking boat, but a US Navy boarding party saved it (main picture).

Because of the surprise attack and sudden abandoning, conditions below were chaotic, whether in the captain's cabin (top), the after torpedo room (below) or the forward torpedo room (above right).

◁ *U-873*, a Type IXD₂, in drydock in the US Navy's Portsmouth Navy Yard on June 30 1945. The after hydroplane and twin rudders are placed immediately aft of the propellers to ensure maximum effectiveness. Above the rudders are the doors for the two stern torpedo tubes.

Having been converted to a transport, *U-180* sailed for the Far East on the first mission in its new role on August 24 1944 but disappeared two days later, presumably having struck a mine. *U-195* left Bordeaux on August 24 and reached Batavia in the Dutch East Indies without major incident on December 28 1944. It set out on the return voyage on January 19 1945 but developed a fault and returned to Batavia on March 4. It then moved to the German repair base at Soerabaya and was still there at the time of the German surrender, when it was taken over by the Japanese as *I-506*.

TYPE IXD₂ – *U-181*

U-181, a Type IXD₂, was commissioned at Deschimag, Bremen, on May 9 1942, its first commanding officer being *Korvetten-Kapitän* Wolfgang Lüth, who had previously commanded *U-13*, *U-9*, *U-138*, and *U-43*. His first operation in *U-181* started from Kiel on September 12 1942 and took him around the British Isles and straight down the central Atlantic, the Type IXD₂'s range making a refueling stop in a French port unnecessary. He sank 12 ships (58,291grt) and returned to Bordeaux on January 18 1943.

The boat's second voyage was one of the longest by any U-boat. It sailed on March 23 1943 and on April 11 was off Monrovia, Liberia, when Lüth attacked the *Empire Whimbrel* (5,983grt) which was hit by several torpedoes but failed to sink. As on several other occasions Lüth decided to use guns to finish off his victim, although the 37mm seems a strange choice. Unfortunately, the first round exploded in the barrel, wounding three men, one of whom, the boat's cook, died shortly afterwards. The merchant ship was finished off with the 105mm gun and the dead man was buried at sea, while the most severely wounded of the survivors was put aboard a returning U-boat. Lüth then proceeded to the southern end of the Mozambique Channel where he sank the *Tinhow* (5,232grt) on May 11 and the Swedish *Sicilia* (even though he knew it to be a Swedish boat and, therefore, neutral) on May 27. He then sank the tiny ammunition ship *Harrier* (193grt) before being ordered by *BdU* to proceed to a replenishment rendezvous with the tanker *Charlotte Schliemann*, since it had been decided to extend the duration of his patrol. The replenishment lasted from June 23 to 26 and included 9,890cu ft (280cu m) of diesel fuel, rations and other supplies.

Lüth next moved northwards between the French island of Reunion and Madagascar, where between July 2 and August 12 he sank a further six ships (32,290grt). Then, since his *Enigma* keys were on the verge of expiring and he needed the latest settings for his voyage back to France, he was ordered by *BdU* to obtain a set from *U-197* (Bartels). The numerous morse messages between the two U-boats required to make the arrangements were duly picked up and decoded by the Allies. The rendezvous took place on August 19 and Lüth then set off for another rendezvous, this time with *U-196* (Kentrat) on August 20.

Unfortunately, a message transmitted by Lüth on August 18 had been monitored and Dfed in South Africa and Allied aircraft were despatched on August 20. They duly found not *U-181* but *U-197* and sank it. Both *U-181* and *U-196* searched for survivors but could find none and Lüth then set out for home. The voyage was uneventful, although there was a further complication when the *Enigma* keys received from Bartels expired on October 1, which meant that Lüth was unable to transmit or receive any *Enigma* messages after that date. So, rather than transmit in plain lan-

△ Type IXC leaves Kiel on a North Atlantic operational patrol.

▽ *U-848*, Type IXD₂, was sunk en route to the Indian Ocean on its first operational voyage.

guage, he kept quiet. *U-181* arrived in Bordeaux on October 14 1943, 206 days after it had left.

TYPE IXD₂ – *U-862*

A Type IXD₂ was the farthest traveled of all U-boats, under an intrepid commanding officer, *Korvetten-Kapitän* Heinrich Timm, who, like a number of other U-boat officers, had been in the merchant marine before joining the *Ubootwaffe*. Timm's first command was *U-251*, a Type VIIC, which he operated in the Arctic, his activities including attacking convoy PQ-17 and reaching Spitzbergen. He left *U-251* in September 1943 to take command of a new Type IXD₂, *U-862*, in which he sailed for the Far East in June 1944.

The voyage out was full of incident. He sank the US ship *Robin Goodfellow* (6,885grt) in the central South Atlantic (July 25 1944) and then, having rounded the Cape of Good Hope, he sank *Radbury* (3,614grt) while south of Madagascar August 13). As he headed across the Indian Ocean he added another three to his score: *Empire Lancer* (7,037grt) on August 16; *Nairung* (5,414grt) on August 18; and *Wayfarer* (5,068grt) on August 19. Not surprisingly, the award of the *Ritterkreuz des Eisernen Kreuzes* was announced on September 17 1944 on his arrival in Batavia, in the Dutch East Indies.

Timm had sailed in Australian waters while in the merchant service and he made this his target when he sailed from Batavia on November 17 1944. He headed down the Australian west coast and then turned east. The first the Australians knew of his

presence was when he carried out a gunfire attack in broad daylight on the Greek tanker *Ilissos* (4,724grt) on December 9 1944, causing some damage, but he submerged when the tanker fired back. He went on to sink the US Liberty ship *Robert J Walker* (7,180grt) on December 24 off the coast of South Australia, followed by another Liberty ship, *Peter Silvester* (7,176grt), on February 6 1945 off the west coast on his way back to Batavia, which he reached on February 15.[2] The Australians spent much effort in trying to find Timm after his first attack on December 9, but never obtained the slightest trace of his boat, apart from when he sank the ships.

Timm holds a remarkable record, having carried out combat patrols in the Arctic, Atlantic, Indian and Pacific Oceans, an achievement not matched by any other *Kriegsmarine* officer. Credit also should go to the design of the Type IXD₂, however, since its long range enabled it to sail from France to the East Indies without refueling and to undertake a solo patrol as far as the east coast of Australia.

SUMMARY
As shown in the table, 194 Type IXs of all sub-types were commissioned, every one of which saw action. Of these, 151 (78 percent) were lost at sea: to surface ships – 58; to submarines – 5 (all in the Far East); to aircraft – 74; to mines – 8; to collision – 1; by unknown – 4; and captured (*U-505*) – 1. In late 1940 the only surviving Type IXAs were transferred to training in the Baltic, and six of all sub-types were stricken since they were

△ A Type IXD₂ under attack from US aircraft. The *flak vierling* is firing forwards, indicating that the boat is under attack from two directions; its chances of survival are virtually nil.

beyond repair. Five went to the Imperial Japanese Navy, two as gifts, while three were requisitioned when Germany capitulated on May 8 1945. Twenty-four survived the war, some of them surrendering while at sea, while others were trapped in port.

Footnotes:
1. Loewe was diagnosed as suffering from appendicitis. His appendix was removed, but he was replaced in command of *U-505* and left the *Ubootwaffe*.
2. *U-862* was still in Batavia on May 8 1945, when it was taken over by the Imperial Japanese Navy as *I-8*.

THE FATE OF THE TYPE IX U-BOATS								
FATE	IXA	IXB	IXC	IXC/40	IXD₁	IXD₂	IXD/42	TOTALS
Sunk at sea by:								
Surface ships	4	5	18	28		3		58
Submarines				3		2		5
Aircraft	1	5	27	29		12		74
Mines	1		1	4	1	1		8
Collision				1				1
Unknown		1		1		2		4
Captured at sea			1					1
Sunk in port by Allied bombing		2		3		1		6
To IJN			1	1	1	2		5
Stricken		1	3	1		1		6
To training	2							2
Survived			3	16		4	1	24
TOTALS	8	14	54	87	2	28	1	194

TYPE XB

BACKGROUND

With a submerged displacement of 2,177 tons and a length of 294.6ft (89.8m) the eight Type XB minelayers were by far the largest submarines built for the *Kriegsmarine*. Their origin lay in the mid-1930s when the navy was developing a series of submarine-laid mines. The first mines, TMB and TMC, were designed to be launched from a standard 21in (533mm) torpedo tube, making every attack submarine, such as the Type VIIs and IXs, a potential minelayer, but such mines had their limitations. First, they could be carried only at the expense of torpedoes and, secondly, they were designed for a maximum depth of 66ft (20m) and used either acoustic or magnetic detonation. It was decided, therefore, that there was a further requirement for a larger, anchored mine, which was designated the *Sonder-Mine A* (*SMA* = Special Mine, Type A), and it followed that there would be a requirement for a purpose-built minelayer to deploy it. A further complication was that the original *SMA* required the detonating mechanism to be set by hand immediately prior to laying.

▽ *U-118*, a Type XB, under attack. These big minelayers were used as replenishment tankers and paid a heavy price, as their mid-ocean rendezvous were frequently known in advance to the Allies through Ultra intercepts of the *Enigma* communications.

TYPE X/TYPE XA

Two boat designs were prepared for the new minelayer, both based on the need to set the mechanism prior to launch. They were based on the World War I Project 45 (*U-117*) class and, as in Project 45, the majority of mines would have been stored in a large chamber aft, in which their mechanisms could be set manually, before the mines were outloaded using a conveyor-belt system. Unlike Project 45, however, it was planned that additional *SMA* mines, with preset mechanisms, would have been wet-stored in eight vertical shafts, two mines to each shaft, mounted in the saddle tanks. Both types were scheduled to be armed with four bow torpedo tubes and the only substantial difference between the two was that Type XA had a greater beam than Type X and thus a greater displacement. Both would have been very large boats, displacing some 2,500 tons.

TYPE XB

Design work on the Types X and XA had proceeded for some time when the problem of remotely setting the *SMA* mechanism was overcome, enabling the mines to be wet-stored. As a result, the design, which Dönitz did not like since he thought it far too big, was altered, becoming the Type XB. In this the after mine

chamber was deleted and a series of vertical shafts enabled it to carry a very useful load of 66 mines, but in a somewhat smaller hull.

The first to be commissioned, *U-116*, reached France in May 1942, but could not be employed as a minelayer because the delivery of *SMA* mines had been delayed, since several had exploded prematurely during tests and more work was needed to identify and cure the fault. However, the large size of these boats made them suitable for use as supply boats until the mines were available, and *U-116*, *U-117* and *U-118* were regularly employed in this role. Even when the *SMAs* did become available, the boats were then used on combined mining and resupply missions. Towards the end of the war two boats, *U-219* and *U-234*, were converted for use as long-range transport boats to deliver men, equipment and weapons to Germany's ally, Japan.

DESIGN

The Type XB was a large, fully double-hulled boat, with a pressure hull divided into seven watertight sections. The foremost section was occupied by six vertical mineshafts, each containing three *SMA* mines in wet storage and, as in the Type VIID, the head of these shafts protruded above upper deck level. There were no forward torpedo tubes and at the after end of this mine space was a toilet on the port side.

The second section housed the main accommodation, with the ratings forward and, most unusually for this era, a second accommodation level below the main deck, with another eight bunks; at least these sailors did not, for once, have to share their living space with torpedoes. Next came the chief petty officers' mess, and the officers' wardroom. Finally, in this section there was a relatively spacious commanding officer's cabin to port, with the communications and sonar rooms directly opposite.

The third section was the control room, which had curved, watertight bulkheads at each end, with a relatively spacious conning tower above, leading to the bridge. As usual, there were two periscopes.

Aft of the control room came the petty officers' accommodation and then the galley, with a toilet and wash-room to port. Next came a large engine room, containing the two main diesels, and then the motor room, with two electric motors. In the after ends were mounted two torpedo tubes, together with another eight bunks for sailors.

Below the main deck were the two accumulator rooms, with 12 lateral two-mine shafts on each side. The outer hull, which was virtually square in cross-section, completely enclosed the pressure hull. The space between the outer and pressure hulls accommodated lateral diving tanks, additional diving tanks in the bow and stern, fuel oil bunkers, three pairs of pressure-tight torpedo containers, and a variety of pipes and control ducts.

▽ After its surrender in mid-Atlantic, *U-234* is unloaded at Portsmouth, NH. Part of its cargo for Japan was a quantity of uranium oxide whose purpose in Japan and disposal in the United States have never been properly explained. (See page 163.)

PROPULSION

Surface propulsion was by means of two Germaniawerft 9-cylinder, 4-stroke, supercharged diesel engines, with a sustained output of 2,100hp at 470rpm, or 2,400hp at 490rpm for 30 minutes. Once submerged the boats were powered by two double AEG electric motors, giving 550hp at 275rpm, which were driven by two batteries, each containing 124 cells, which were housed in two accumulator rooms in the lower deck level. The diesel-oil bunkers had a capacity of 368.2 tons, which gave these boats a range of 21,000 nautical miles, enabling them to travel from Germany to Japan without refueling.

ARMAMENT

The torpedo armament was designed solely for self-defense and consisted of two standard 21in (533mm) tubes mounted low in the stern. A total of 11 torpedoes were carried: two in the tubes, three under the main deck in the torpedo room and the remainder in three pairs of pressure-tight containers beneath the casing on the upper deck.

The original gun armament comprised one 105mm on the foredeck, a 37mm *Flak* aft and a single 20mm on the platform at the after end of the tower. Experience showed that the 105mm

served little purpose and by 1944 all had been removed, but the AA armament was increased, to comprise a single 37mm *Flak* and two twin 20mm aft.

SUPPLY BOAT CONVERSIONS

Some limited work was done to make the boats more suitable for use as supply boats. At least one boat, *U-119*, had additional stowage for eight torpedoes for supply to other U-boats. There were two pallets on each side on top of the saddle tanks, the forward pallet carrying one torpedo and the after pallet carrying three, with a shield welded in front of the forward pallet to cut down the water resistance. Since *U-119* carried out combined mining and supply voyages it must be assumed that these extra torpedoes did not prevent the lateral mine tubes from being used.

TRANSPORT CONVERSIONS

U-219 and *U-234* were both converted for use as transport boats on the Far East run, the former in Brest, the latter in Germania Werft. The major work involved removing the 24 lateral mine shafts to create four large cargo holds. The six forward mine shafts were not altered but were used to stow cargo in containers, each container being the length of three *SMA* mines and held in place by the normal mine mechanism. A *schnorchel* was also fitted on the starboard side. When raised it fitted into a large clamp on the forward edge of the bridge and when lowered it was housed in a trough, displacing one of the torpedo containers. A *Luftwaffe*-pattern *Hohentwiel* radar was also installed. The single 105mm gun was removed, the single 37mm was replaced by a twin 37mm and the after end of the bridge was extended to enable two twin 20mm to be mounted.

OPERATIONAL HISTORY

U-116 was commissioned on July 26 1941 and after working up in the Baltic it sailed from Norway on April 25 1942, arriving in Lorient, France, on May 5 1942. Since the *SMA* mine was not

TYPE XB

Type XB
ROLE: Ocean-going minelayer
DISPLACEMENT
Surfaced: 1,763 tons
Submerged: 2,177 tons
DIMENSIONS
Length: 294.6ft (89.8m)
Beam: 30.2ft (9.20m)
Draught: 15.4ft (4.7m)
Pressure hull diameter: 15.6ft (4.75m)
PROPULSION
Diesel: Two GW nine-cylinder, four-stroke F46a-9pu supercharged diesel engines; 2,100hp at 470rpm (sustained), (2,400hp at 490rpm for 30 minutes)
Electric: Two double AEG GU720/8-287; 550hp at 275rpm
Battery: Two AFA 124-cell 33MAL800W batteries; 9,160amp/hours at 20 hour rate
Fuel capacity: 368.2 tons
PERFORMANCE
Maximum speed
Surfaced: 16.4kt
Submerged: 7.0kt
Range
Surfaced: 14,450nm at 12kt
Submerged: 188nm at 2kt
Operational diving depth: 394ft (120m)
WEAPONS
Bow tubes: None
Stern tubes: Two
Torpedoes carried: 15
Mine shafts: Six vertical shafts in forward hull, three mines each = 18 mines; vertical shafts in side tanks, two mines each = 48 mines
Mines: 66 SMA
Guns:
Original — One Utof 105mm/45 (200 rounds)
One 37mm AA (2,500 rounds)
One 20mm AA (4,000 rounds)
1943 onwards   One 37mm AA (2,500 rounds)
Two twin 20mm AA (8,000 rounds)
OFFICERS AND CREW: 5 + 47 = 52

TYPE XB

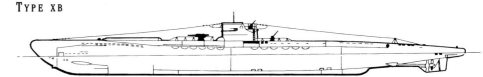

Displacement (surf/sub) 1,763/2,177tons; 294.0ft (89.6m); speed (surf/sub) 16.4/7.0kt; range (surf/sub) 14,450nm at 12kt/93nm at 4kt.

SHIPPING SUNK/DAMAGED BY TYPE XB MINELAYERS					
TYPE XB	**DATE**	**TARGET**	**TONS**	**WEAPON**	**FATE**
U-116	July 12 1942	*Cortona*	7,093	Torpedo	Sunk: shared with *U-201*
	July 12 1942	*Shaftesbury*	4,284	Torpedo	Sunk
U-117	April 11 1943	*Matt W Ransom*	7,200	Mine	Damaged
	April 28 1943	*Empire Morn*	7,092	Mine	Damaged
U-118	Feruary 7 1943	*Baltonia*	2,013	Mine	Sunk
		Mary Slessor	5,027	Mine	Sunk
		Empire Mordred	7,024	Mine	Sunk
	February 8 1943	*Duero*	2,008	Mine	Damaged
		Portland	2,648	Mine	Sunk
	February 22 1943	*Thorsholm*	9,937	Mine	Damaged
		Wivern	1,120	Mine	Damaged
U-119	June 4 1943	*Halma*	2,937	Mine	Sunk
	July 25 1943	*John A Poor*	7,176	Mine	Damaged
U-219	None				
U-220	October 17 1943	*Delisle*	3,478	Mine	Sunk
		Penolver	3,721	Mine	Sunk
U-233	None				
U-234	None				

cleared for operations, *U-116* was pressed into use as a supply boat, carrying fuel, food and torpedoes. It sailed to US waters on May 16 1942 as part of *Gruppe Hecht* and then, having returned to Lorient to replenish, it went south with *Gruppe Hai*, also as a supply boat, from June 27 to August 23. Even though it had only two stern tubes, *U-116* managed to sink one merchantman (4,284grt) and to share in the sinking of another. *U-116* disappeared in the North Atlantic on (about) October 11 1942; cause unknown.

U-117 was commissioned on October 25 1941 and, after what appears to have been a long working-up period, sailed on its first operational patrol on October 12 1942. It laid mines off Reykjavik, Iceland, refueled eight U-boats and then reached France on November 22 1942. Its next patrol was also a refueling mission, in which it replenished 10 boats (one of them twice) between December 23 1942 and February 17 1943. Its next mission (March 31 to May 13 1943) involved laying a minefield off Casablanca (which claimed two merchant ships - 14,292grt), followed by more refueling off the Azores. *U-177*'s final patrol commenced on July 22 1943, but it was sunk on August 7 west of the Canary Islands while rendezvousing with *U-*

△ *U-118*, a Type XB minelayer, under attack on June 12 1943. This view clearly shows the six open-ended mine tubes on the foredeck. Each tube housed three *SMA* mines and more were carried in the side tanks.

66. All 62 aboard were lost.

U-118 was commissioned on December 6 1941 and arrived in France on October 16 1942, having refueled four other U-boats in the North Atlantic en route. In its first patrol from France (November12 – December 13 1942) it laid mines in the Straits of Gibraltar (four ships sunk [16,712grt], three ships damaged [13,065grt]) and then sailed to the Azores where it refueled 11 U-boats before returning to France. The next patrol, which began on May 25, involved refueling operations off the Canaries and *U-118* had replenished three U-boats when it was caught on the surface on June 12 by aircraft from USS *Bogue* and sunk; 44 men were lost and 15 were rescued.

U-119, commissioned on April 2 1942, arrived in France on April 1 1943, having laid mines of Reykjavik and refueled 10 U-boats north of the Azores en route. It sailed for Canadian waters on April 25 1943, refueling three boats on the way, and then laid mines off Halifax, Nova Scotia. These mines sank one merchant ship (2,937grt) and damaged a second, which resulted in considerable disruption of assembling convoys until the area had been swept. On the return voyage *U-119*, in company with two

caught on the surface by aircraft, while replenishing the last of these - usually a recipe for disaster - but managed to escape, reaching France on January 1 1944. It then underwent an eight-month refit for use as a transport to the Far East, which included fitting a *schnorchel*, removing the 105mm gun, and replacing the single 20mm cannon by two twin 20mm weapons. It left France after D-day, on August 23 1944, arriving in Jakarta on December 11. En route it was attacked by two US Navy aircraft, an Avenger and a Wildcat, which usually proved a fatal combination, but again *U-219* was lucky and, with the aid of its heavier AA fit, it shot down the Avenger and escaped. It was still in Jakarta when Germany surrendered in May 1945 and was taken over by the Japanese Navy as *I-505*. It was surrendered to the Allies in August 1945.

U-220 was commissioned on March 27 1943, and its first and only mission was to lay mines off the Canadian coast, sailing from Norway on September 6 1943. Having laid its mines off St John's, Newfoundland, which claimed two merchant ships (7,199grt), it successfully refueled two U-boats north of the Azores and was in the process of refueling a third on October 28 1943 when they were caught by an Avenger/Wildcat team from USS *Block Island*. The other boat escaped but *U-220* was lost with all 56 hands.

U-233 commissioned on September 22 1943 and, like earlier Type XBs, its first mission, which started from Kiel on May 27 1944, was to sail to Canada, mine one of the convoy ports, refuel other U-boats in the central Atlantic and then go to a French port. However, it was caught on the surface when south of Newfoundland by an aircraft which summoned an escort group and these forced *U-233* to the surface where it was rammed and sunk (July 5 1944). Thirty-two crewmen were lost and 30 were saved.

U-234, the last of the Type XBs, had a career quite unlike any of the others. Its completion was delayed by bomb damage and it was not commissioned until March 2 1944. It then returned to the dockyard to undergo a lengthy modification in which it was converted into a specialized transport boat. It eventually sailed from Norway for Japan just before the war's end, on April 17 1945. It surrendered to the US Navy at sea on 16 May and was taken into Portsmouth, New Hampshire. *U-234*'s load on this operation included 12 passengers (10 Germans and two Japanese) and 260 tons of cargo, including plans for advanced German weapons and equipment broken down into small components. Of greatest significance, however, it also carried containers of uranium oxide in the forward mineshafts, whose purpose and destination have never been fully explained. The US Navy made a very determined effort to capture *U-234* and when it was taken into Portsmouth, New Hampshire, the uranium oxide was removed rapidly and in great secrecy, and has never been accounted for since.

other U-boats, was caught on the surface by British aircraft and was damaged but not sunk. One of the aircraft, however, called for support from 2nd Escort Group, one of whose ships rammed and sank *U-119*; all 57 aboard perished.

U-219 was commissioned on December 12 1942, but did not leave Germany until October 5 1943, when it followed a long and circuitous route via Brazil and the Azores to France, in the course of which it replenished five other U-boats. *U-219* was

△ *U-234* enters Portsmouth, NH, naval base, with US Navy sailors topsides. Note that the foredeck has been narrowed in an effort to reduce diving time and a *schnorchel* tube is housed on the starboard side just forward of the bridge.

TYPE XIV

BACKGROUND

It was clear to German U-boat planners in the inter-war years that in a future conflict U-boats operating at any distance from their bases in Germany would need replenishment at sea (RAS) and the first known proposal for such a supply U-boat was made in 1934. Designated the Type IV, this would have displaced some 2,500 tons, but the project was dropped because at that time the navy was bound by the Anglo-German Naval Treaty which limited the tonnage that could be built. As a result, the Naval Staff required the maximum possible tonnage to be available for operational U-boats, such as the Type IA, Type II and, in particular, the Type VII, rather than for tankers.

Dönitz raised the request again in a letter to Naval Headquarters on September 8 1939, in which he proposed the construction of three supply boats with a displacement of approximately 2,000 tons. This request led directly to the Type XIV. Because of their role, these boats were known throughout the *Ubootwaffe* as *milchkuh* (milk-cows).

DESIGN

The Type XIV was required to have good storage capacity together with an upper deck suitable for handling stores, heavy items such as torpedoes, small boats, and fuel lines. Accordingly, the designers took the Type IXD design and made it shorter, wider, and deeper, thus considerably increasing the internal volume, together with a flat and clear upper deck. The first boat was launched in September 1941 and became operational in March 1942.

To ease construction and supply problems various components from the Type VIIC were utilized, including the propulsion unit and many smaller components such as the anchor, winch, watertight hatches, and pumps. The bridge was virtually identical to that of the Type IX.

The pressure hull was constructed from 0.85in (21.5mm) steel plate enabling it to dive deeper than the Types VII and IX, which were constructed of 0.73in (18.5mm) plate.

ARMAMENT

The Type XIV had no torpedo tubes and possessed only a limited self-defense capability. This consisted of two quick-firing 37mm guns in single mounts, one before and one abaft the bridge, and one 20mm cannon, also a single mount, on a platform at the after end of the bridge.

CREW

The Type XIV had a large crew for the size of boat: six officers and 47 enlisted men. The officers consisted of the commanding officer, two watch-keeping officers, an engineer, a supply specialist and a doctor.

TYPE XIVA

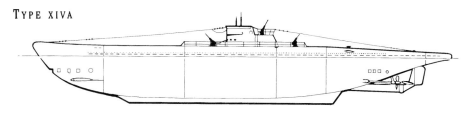

Displacement (surf/sub) 1,688/1,932tons; 220.0ft (67.1m); speed (surf/sub) 14.4/6.2kt; range (surf/sub) 9,300nm at 12k/55nm at 4kt.

BUILDING PROGRAM

Initial orders were placed for 24 boats, but only 10 were actually built: six by Deutsche-Werke, Kiel, and four by Germaniawerft. Of the remainder, three were nearly complete when construction was suspended in mid-1944, while orders for the remaining seven were canceled in May 1944.

OPERATIONAL HISTORY

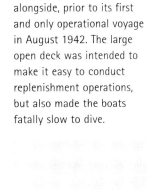

▽ *U-464*, a Type XIV replenishment tanker, lying alongside, prior to its first and only operational voyage in August 1942. The large open deck was intended to make it easy to conduct replenishment operations, but also made the boats fatally slow to dive.

At the mid-ocean rendezvous the Type XIV would take the receiving boat in tow and then float the fuel pipe down with a telephone cable attached. Having made all the connections, the replenishment operation then started, with the two boats proceeding on the surface at a speed of some 3-4 knots on the electric motors. The amounts of fuel supplied varied between 706-194cu ft (20-55cu m) according to the receiving boats' requirements, and the time taken could be up to five hours.

The transfer of stores was a more difficult task. The Type

XIV had a wide upper deck and extra deck hatches, each with an associated davit, which were intended to enable stores to be passed up easily and quickly. However, the freeboard was insufficient to prevent the sea from washing over the deck in anything except the calmest of conditions: as a result the conning-tower hatch was normally used and the crew frequently had to employ lifelines to ensure that they were not swept overboard. Sea-state 4 was the practical upper limit. Once the stores were on deck the next problem was to pass them over to the other boat. The Type XIV was provided with a single 19.7ft (6m) inflatable dinghy for this task, but this generally proved less than adequate.

A different and more reliable method involved the receiving boat traveling to port of the supplying boat, its foredeck abeam the latter's afterdeck and some 82-131ft (25-40m) distant. A manilla line was then passed by pennant-pistol and stores were pulled across in mesh nets suspended from a traveler - an arrangement remarkably similar to that being developed concurrently by the United States Navy in the Pacific. *U-490*, the last

being sunk by aircraft and one by surface ships.

They suffered from two major weaknesses, neither of which was due to the design of the class, but rather to shortcomings in the original operational requirement. First, their replenishment activity had to be carried out on the surface and was very time-consuming. Secondly, the replenishment rendezvous had to be arranged (and not infrequently amended) by radio resulting in considerable radio traffic. Such traffic was monitored by the Allies who used Ultra to extract the content of the messages transmitted by *BdU* and HF/DF to locate individual boats. As a result, the Type XIVs presented excellent targets to the Allied ASW forces.

U-459

Commissioned on November 15 1941, *U-459* carried out five successful resupply missions, but was sunk on July 24 1943, while on its sixth operation in the Bay of Biscay. *U-459* was attacked on the surface by a British Wellington ASW aircraft which dropped two depth-charges, seriously damaging the U-boat. The

U-tanker to be completed, was equipped with an underwater refueling gear, but was sunk before it had a chance to use it.

One of the more imaginative facilities aboard the Type XIVs was a bakery, with a capacity for producing 80 one-kilo ryebread loaves in a 10-hour shift. This fresh bread was greatly appreciated by the crews of the operational boats.

The transfer of torpedoes was also not an easy task. The Type IXs were fitted with special transporting gear to enable them to transfer the torpedoes stored in their upper decking into the bow and stern tubes, and this apparatus was also used for torpedoes received from a resupply ship or U-boat. However, it was a time-consuming activity and not one relished by the crew, because of the physical exertions involved.

In modern parlance these boats would be described as 'force multipliers' since they enabled operational U-boats to remain on patrol for far longer and to patrol in more distant stations than they could have done using only their own resources. This capability was quickly recognized by the Allies who made them a particular target and they were steadily eliminated, nine

Wellington was itself shot down, however, and crashed on the casing, causing further damage. After an attack by a second aircraft, the crew scuttled *U-459*; there were 19 crew dead, the remainder being rescued by a Polish destroyer, operating under British command.

U-460

Commissioned on January 30 1942, *U-460* like *U-459* carried out five successful voyages and was sunk on the sixth (October 5 1943). It was surprised on the surface by aircraft from USS *Card* while in company with three Type VIICs: *U-264*, which had just completed refueling, *U-422*, which was about to refuel, and *U-455*, which was awaiting its turn. The group of four boats was spotted by a US Navy Avenger which attacked at once, dropping a bomb between *U-264* and *U-460*. According to *BdU*'s standing orders, *U-460* should have dived first, but did not do so, possibly because of damage. When more aircraft arrived, *U-264* and *U-422* remained on the surface to defend the tanker, but to no avail, and *U-460* was sunk with the loss of all hands (62).

◁ *U-459*, Type XIV, was commanded by the redoubtable Georg von Wiliamovitz-Möllendorf, who had served in the Imperial German Navy during World War I. The first aircraft to attack *U-459* was shot down but crash-landed on the U-boat's deck and the crew, seeing unexploded depth-charges among the wreckage, rolled them overboard. The depth-charges were fitted with shallow-set fuzes and exploded, making diving impossible. An attack by another aircraft finished the boat. The captain, following naval tradition, saluted his crew and went down with his ship.

U-461

Commissioned on January 30 1942, *U-461* was sunk on its sixth operation. It was crossing the Bay of Biscay on the surface in company with *U-462* (see below) and *U-504* (Type IXC/40), when they were surprised by Allied aircraft. A fierce battle ensued during which *U-461* was sunk by an RAAF Sunderland; 54 died and 15 survivors became prisoners-of-war.

U-462

Commissioned on March 5 1942, *U-462* carried out two successful resupply missions, but had to return early from the third having suffered damage in an attack. It sailed again on June 20 1943 but was again damaged and forced to return to Bordeaux, where it suffered yet more damage in an RAF bombing raid. It sailed on July 27 and was surprised on the surface when sailing in company with *U-461* and *U-550* (see *U-461* above). Having been severely damaged by aircraft, which prevented it from diving, *U-462* then came under gunfire from the Allies' 2nd Escort Group, which had been called to the scene by the aircraft. The captain ordered 'abandon ship' and *U-462* was scuttled; three died, 64 survived.

U-463

Commissioned on April 2 1942, *U-463* conducted four successful resupply operations, but was sunk on the fifth. It sailed on May 10 1943 and was found on the surface on May 16 1943 by an RAF Halifax which attacked immediately. *U-463* was sunk with the loss of all hands (56).

U-464

Commissioned on April 30 1942, *U-464* left Bergen, Norway, on its first mission on August 14 1942 and was nearing its operational area off Newfoundland when it was found and attacked by a US Navy Catalina. *U-464* tried to fight it out on the surface but was very badly damaged and unable to dive. The captain ordered the boat to be scuttled but all 52 survivors were taken off by a nearby Icelandic trawler. Shortly afterwards they were taken aboard a British destroyer and made prisoners-of-war.

U-487

Commissioned on December 21 1942, *U-487* successfully refueled 12 U-boats during its first voyage from Bergen, Norway, to Bordeaux (March 27 to May 12 1943). On its second operation *U-487* successfully refueled nine other boats between July 6 and 12 1943, but then needed to replenish its own fuel stocks. It was arranged that *U-160*, an outward-bound boat, would top-up *U-487*'s bunkers and then return to base. The inevitable radio traffic alerted the Allies and an Avenger/Wildcat team from USS *Core* found *U-487* on the surface on July 13 1943. They used cloud cover to get close to the U-boat without being seen and, astonishingly, as they swept in they caught some of the U-boat's crew sunbathing on the casing. The Avenger dropped bombs on *U-487*, causing serious damage, but the U-boat gun crews then

△ A Type XIV, with its crew standing-by for a replenishment operation. Known as *Milchkuh* (= milk cow), these U-boats were intended to be force multipliers but the Allies made a determined and successful effort to finish them all off very quickly. Astonishingly, Dönitz and his staff failed to realize that their *Enigma* codes had been compromised.

shot down the Wildcat. A second Avenger then arrived, which sank *U-487* with depth-charges: 31 were killed and 33 survived to be taken prisoner.

U-488

Commissioned December 21 1942, *U-488* carried out two very successful operations. During the first (May 18 to July 10 1943) it refueled 14 boats, then replenished from three other tankers which were returning to base, and went on to replenish another eight attack boats. On its second operation (September 7 to December 12 1943) *U-488* supplied fuel and other stores to 11 attack boats. It sailed on its third operation on February 22 1944 but, having refueled five U-boats, it was found and sunk by four US destroyers on April 26 1944. There were no survivors.

U-489

Commissioned on March 8 1943, *U-489* sailed from Kiel on July 22 1943. It survived an attack by an RAF Hudson on August 3, but on the following day it was attacked by an RAF Sunderland, which inflicted severe damage before being shot down itself; the aircraft crashed into the sea, leaving six survivors. *U-489* was critically damaged and sank with the loss of one man, the remaining 58 being rescued to become prisoners-of-war.

U-490

The last of the U-tankers to be completed, *U-490* was equipped with an underwater refueling gear, and, having been commissioned on March 27 1943, it then spent a full year in the Baltic, working up and trialing the submerged refueling gear. It sailed from Kiel on May 4 1944 bound for the Indian Ocean, where it was to take on the task previously performed by the surface tankers, *Charlotte Schliemann* and *Brake*. It was south of the Azores on June 11 when it was found by US Navy aircraft, which directed surface warships to the scene. After a long hunt it was sunk on June 12 (one crewman died, 59 survived), never having had the opportunity to test its submerged gear on operations.

TYPE: XXI

BACKGROUND

The Type XXI was one of that small number of weapons systems which totaly changed the face of warfare. Before the Type XXI, submarines should properly have been termed submersibles, since they spent most of their time on the surface and could submerge for only limited periods, where they were slow and relatively unmaneuverable. The Type XXI, however, was designed from the start as a true submarine whose natural habitat was in the depths. However, as will be seen, the full effect of the Type XXI was not to be felt during the war, since, despite the vast amounts of energy and resources devoted to this brilliant concept, the reality was that only two Type XXIs ever conducted a war patrol.

The Type XXI had its origins in the realization in late 1942 that the Allies were achieving an increasing ascendancy in the anti-submarine battle and that the two major designs available then - Type VII and Type IX - were no longer able to cope. Allied surface ships and aircraft were sinking U-boats in ever-increas-

Type XXI		
Role: Long-range, attack *elektroboot*		
Displacement Surfaced: 1,621 tons Submerged: 1,819 tons		
Dimensions Length: 251.6ft (76.7m) Beam: 21.65ft (6.6m) Draught: 20.67ft (6.3m)		
Propulsion Diesel engines: Two MAN M6V 40/46; 2,200hp Electric motors: Two SSW 2 GU 365/30; 2,500hp Creep motors: Two SSW GW323/28; 323hp Battery: Three 124-cell batteries Fuel capacity: 250 tons		
Performance Maximum speed Surfaced: 15.65kt Submerged: 17.2kt Range Surfaced: 11,150nm at 12kt Submerged: 285nm at 6kt		
Weapons Bow tubes: Six 21in (533mm) Stern tubes: None Torpedoes carried: 23 Alternative: 14 torpedoes plus 12 TMC mines Guns: Two twin 20mm		
Officers and Crew: 57		
Launch of first of class: April 19 1944		
Commissioned: see table		

△ A Type XXI is launched without ceremony in 1944/45. These boats were intended to change the course of the war in Germany's favor, but of hundreds built only a handful ever attained operational status.

ing numbers and German countermeasures were simply not working. For example, main guns had been removed in order to increase the anti-aircraft armament but, except in a few isolated cases, this did not enable a surfaced U-boat to 'fight it out' with aircraft. In addition, the extra weapons substantially increased underwater resistance, thus decreasing range and speed. The *schnorchel* was essentially a palliative and the various electronic devices, such as *Metox* and *Naxos*, had failed to restore the balance.

Meanwhile, Professor Walter had been hard at work designing new, streamlined submarines with excellent underwater performance and incorporating his revolutionary air-independent propulsion system. This led to the proposed hydrogen-peroxide-powered Type XVIII, which displaced 1,652 tons and had an underwater speed of 24 knots. In May 1943, however, it was suggested that this Type XVIII hull design could be adapted to take a conventional diesel-electric propulsion system and this was seized upon with enthusiasm, not least because the designers realized that the large hull would enable many changes to conventional practice to be made. In view of the seriousness of the situation in the U-boat war, progress was rapid and the sketch design was approved by Dönitz on June 19 and the program was approved on August 20. Indeed, so great was the urgency that tooling up, initial production, and detailed design took place in parallel and the first example of Module I left the builders on December 18 1943. The first of these revolutionary boats was launched on April 19 1944 and 120 had been launched by the surrender on May 8 1945. However, only two boats ever started operational patrols and the program was, in reality, a massive failure.

△ A Type XXI at sea. Note the streamlined hull and sail, retractable forward hydroplane, and complete absence of clutter on the deck, all intended to enhance underwater speed and maneuverability. Maximum submerged speed was 16 knots, compared with the Type VII's 7 knots.

DESIGN

The fact that Walter's Type XVIII design had been selected meant that much time was saved, since the tank tests and hydrodynamic calculations had already been completed. Nevertheless, almost everything about the Type XXI was new. There was a streamlined outer hull, in which everything was done to minimize hydrodynamic resistance. There were no deck guns and the two twin 20mm cannon were mounted in streamlined housings at each end of the bridge. On the bridge all extending devices such as the *schnorchel*, radar antenna, and DF loop withdrew into the superstructure when not in use and, instead of the traditional open bridge, there were three small, individual openings, one for the watchkeeping officer, the others for two lookouts. The pressure hull was fabricated from a special steel-aluminum alloy, and was 1in (26mm) thick in the central sections, reducing to 0.71in (18mm) at the ends. In cross-section the pressure hull was a figure-of-eight, but with the upper section of rather greater diameter than the lower, which considerably increased the usable internal volume.

Internally, the battery size was tripled (hence the name *elektroboot*), the new electric motors were much more powerful than previous designs, and two 'creep' motors were added for silent running, driving the main shaft directly using 12 parallel V-belts. There were two batteries (port and starboard), each of which was separated into three partial batteries, with each partial battery accommodated in one of three separate *Akkuräume* (battery compartments). The two forward battery rooms were located under the forward accommodation section, the after battery under the after accommodation section. Individual cells were AFA 44MAL740E model and the total battery weight was 238.8 tons.

In addition, a number of developments which had been designed for the canceled Type VIIC/42 were incorporated into the Type XXI, including the main electrical switchboard and the diesel engines. These engines were the well-proven, six-cylinder MAN M6V 40/46, but with a special BBC Büchi exhaust-gas turbo-supercharger, which increased their power output from 1,050hp to 2,000hp (see below).

The armament consisted of six bow torpedo tubes, which gave two more in a first salvo than in the Type VIIC, but, in addition to this, the Type XXI had a new type of rapid reloading system. This meant that the Type XXI could launch three six-torpedo salvoes in 20 minutes, thus increasing the number of targets it could attack per convoy. Further, because of the greater space, the number of torpedoes carried was 23.

When compared with its predecessor, the Type VIIC, the Type XXI was considerably longer - 251.6ft (76.7m) compared to 220ft (67.1m) - had a much greater displacement - 1,819 compared to 865 tons - and was very much more spacious inside. Of greatest importance, the submerged performance was improved out of all recognition: 16 compared to 7 knots maximum speed and an endurance of 72 hours at 5 knots compared to 45 hours at 5 knots. In addition, it was a much more difficult target for enemy ASW to find and hit, since the streamlined shape offered a much smaller target for sonar and it was much quieter. US post-war tests showed that the Type XXI at 15 knots emitted the same acoustic signature as a US Navy Balao-class boat at 8 knots.

CONSTRUCTION

The revolutionary production system introduced for the Type XXI is an integral part of the story, as it was decided from the very start to construct the submarine on a modular basis, with construction and assembly spread widely across the territory of the Third Reich. The prime reason for this was that it would achieve the most economical use of resources, particularly shipyard facilities, construction equipment and, very importantly, scarce manpower. Thus, the new system would reduce the time each hull occupied the ways at a shipyard, enable more men to work on the program at the same time, and would also enable both individuals and groups of workers to develop great expertise, by specializing in a particular task. Decentralization would also present Allied bombers with many more and smaller targets. Finally, traditional submarine construction methods involved installing large, bulky and heavy equipment, such as engines, motors, and batteries, through hatches or soft patches, whereas the new method enabled such items to be installed direct into the open-ended modules.

As a result of these new practices startling reductions in manpower were at least theoretically possible, the labor per boat being reduced from 460,000 man-hours on a Type XB to some 300,000 for the Type XXI.

STAHLBAU (STEEL ERECTORS)

The construction facilities engaged in the program were divided into three categories, the first in the chain being *Stahlbau*, which assembled individual modules. This work involved fabricating the pressure hull, bulkheads and tanks, fitting the outer hull, and installing the foundations and some hull fittings. These *Stahlbau* were selected from bridge builders, boiler shops, and structural steel plants, few of which had been previously involved in ship-

building. In overall terms there were three clusters of *Stahlbau*: one in the Silesia/Danzig area; the second in central Germany; and the third (and largest) in western Germany.

SEKTIONSWERFTEN (FITTING-OUT YARDS)

The second link in the production chain were the *Sektionswerften* where the modules were outfitted. These were all submarine yards with previous experience of building Type VIIs and Type IXs. Most were responsible for only one module, although a few of the larger and more experienced were responsible for several: Bremer Vulkan, for example, produced Modules 3, 5 and 6, while Danziger-Werft produced Modules 2, 3 and 8. The tasks carried out by the *Sektionswerften* included installing the main electrical motor and gears, steering and diving systems, auxiliary machinery, wiring looms, pipework and furniture, and concluded with the final interior coat of paint. Module VA, the conning tower, was mated to Module V at the *Sektionswerften*. All such yards set up production lines, moving the module along as work was completed, according to a precise timetable, although this was frequently changed.

MONTAGE-WERFTEN (ASSEMBLY YARDS)

The final stage took place at the three *Montage-Werften*: Blohm+Voss, Hamburg; AG Weser, Bremen; and Schichau,

◁ The forward end of *U-2502*, before fitting the bow section. The section has been completely fitted-out internally prior to assembly.

TYPE XXI

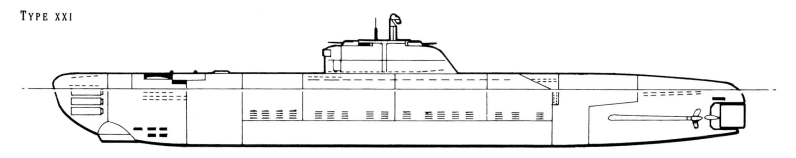

Displacement (surf/sub) 1,621/1,819tons; 251.6ft (76.7m); speed(surf/sub) 15.6/17.2kt; range (surf/sub) 11,150nm at 12kt/285m at 6kt.

Danzig. The modules arrived by pontoon and the first action was to install the diesel engines and gears in Module 3. The modules were then stored until a way became available, when they were set up in their correct order by a large crane. Each module rested on a sledge, which enabled the modules to be aligned using hydraulic jacks for lateral and longitudinal adjustments, and large presses for height adjustment. This alignment process was originally regarded with great suspicion by the more conservative shipbuilders, but turned out to be relatively simple and very precise. It involved drilling three small holes in each bulkhead and when the modules were correctly aligned a light in the control room could be seen through the holes. This align-

▽ A Type XXI is moved from the building bay for final fitting-out. Behind the right-hand tug is a recently arrived barge carrying a hull section for another Type XXI. The dispersed construction system was heavily dependent upon Germany's inland waterways to move the components.

ment and assembly process started with Module V and then proceeded outwards to the bow and stern.

Once the sections were aligned and the pressure-hull joints mated, the two sections of the pressure hull were welded together, the welders obtaining access through a 32in (80cm) gap in the outer hull. The welders worked in a team of four, under the control of a foreman who kept watch at the sighting holes, adjusting the welding to ensure proper alignment. This welding process normally took about eight hours and had to be non-stop to ensure an even and continuous weld, which meant that the men could not halt, even for air raids. Once the weld had been completed and tested for watertightness and any

TYPE XXI

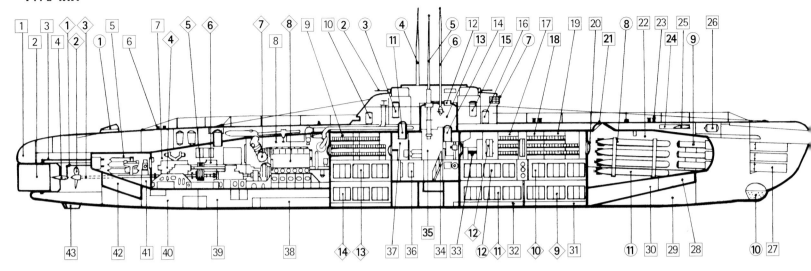

△ Main details of the Type XXI hull, propulsion, weapons, and sensors. Details of sensors on the bridge/sail are shown in the diagram on page 103. Note that it has not been possible to show all facilities on these diagrams.

Hull (figures in squares):
1: Stern. 2: Rudder. 3: Rudder actuator mechanism. 4: After hydroplane. 5: Workshop.
6: Bollards (retractable).
7: Electric motor room.
8: Main diesel engine room.
9: Crew accommodation.
10: Dinghy container (watertight). 11: Galley access hatch. 12: Main access hatch.
13: Conning tower.
14: Control room access hatch. 15: Ready use ammunition container (watertight). 16: Dinghy container (watertight).
17: Officers' accommodation.
18: Chief POs' accommodation.
19: POs' accommodation.
20: Torpedo room access hatch. 21: Torpedo loading hatch. 22: Torpedo room. 23: Bollards (retractable).
24: Forward hydroplane

retraction slot. 25: Forward hydroplane. 26: Dinghy container (watertight). 27: Torpedo doors. 28: Trimming tank. 29: Ballast. 30: Torpedo compensation tank. 31 and 32: Ballast (fixed). 33: Captain's cabin. 34: Lower deck access stairs. 35: Control room. 36: Refrigerated storage rooms. 37: Galley. 38: Ballast. 39 and 40: Diesel oil bunker. 41: After WC. 42: Trimming tank. 43: Fixed fin.

Propulsion (figures in diamonds). 1: After hydroplane actuator mechanism.
2: Propeller, three- bladed (two). 3: Propeller shaft (two). 4: Main electric motor (two). 5: Creep motor driving belts (two). 6: Creep motor (2). 7: Main engine supercharger (2). 8: Main engine

(2). 9 to 14 : Accumulator rooms.

Weapons and sensors (figures in circles).
1: *Torpedowarn–und anzeigegerät* (*TAG* = torpedo warning and indicating device). 2: Twin 20mm cannon. 3: Ready-use ammunition (watertight).
4: Extending radio mast.
5: *Standesrohr* (periscope).
6: *Nachluftzielsehroh* (night/sky observation periscope).
7: *Sonderapparat für Uboote* (special apparatus U-boats), also known as '*Nieberlung*.'
8: Torpedo storage racks (3 + 3 + 2). 9: 21in (533mm) torpedo tubes (six). 10: *Balkon Gerät* (hydrophone array). 11: Torpedo under-floor storage (one). 12: Sound locating room.

external connections made, a belt was welded around the outer hull thus closing the 32in (80cm) gap. Final pre-launch tasks included installing the propeller shafts and propellers.

Once all was complete, the U-boat was launched and the final fitting out took place, including installing radios, radars, periscopes, and final wiring. In addition, the boat was balanced;

the pallet on which the diesel engines rested could be finely adjusted and ballast moved.

One problem that arose was that the *Montage-Werften*, with their rows of almost-complete hulls presented a very valuable target to Allied bombers and to overcome this a start was made on the construction of huge covered assembly halls, similar in concept to the U-boat 'pens' in the Atlantic and Norwegian U-boat bases. U-boat construction would have been on a 'flow-line' principle and at the largest - Valentin, in Bremen - would have delivered one new Type XXI every 56 hours. Work was started on a number of these assembly halls but none was ever completed, and, despite their impressive walls and roofs, they were not impervious to the large bombs (Tall Boy and Grand Slam) introduced by the RAF in 1945.

TRANSPORTATION

With all the movement involved, transport became a major consideration. Smaller components were moved by rail or road, but the size and weight of the completed modules made overland travel impossible. However, Germany did possess a very efficient network of inland waterways and it was these that made the entire concept feasible. Being shipyards, the *Sektionswerften* and *Montage-Werften* all had immediate access to a river or the sea, but some of the *Stahlbau* were deep inland and some were up to 6 miles (10km) from the nearest waterway. In most of these cases special transporters were built to move the completed modules to the nearest canal or river, but in one case the company concerned leased a site on a riverbank where the sections were constructed. On the canals and rivers transportation was by means of Rhine barges or small ocean-going ships. One of the problems encountered was that the huge sections could become distorted during transportation, especially if mounted in a horizontal position, and large 'spiders' (tempo-

TYPE XXI U-BOATS: THE PRODUCTION PROCESS

1: Shafts and propellers.
2: Schnorchel.
3: Direction finder.
4: Vertical antenna.
5: Main engines and reduction gears.
6: Main motors and gears.
7: Auxiliary machinery.
8: Electrical installations.
9: Local wiring.
10: Torpedo tubes.
11: Rudder and diving planes.
12: Bunks and lockers.
13: Plates and shapes.
14: Pressure hull glands.

Steel erectors (*Stahlbau*)	Fitting-out yards (Sektionswerften)	Assembly yards (Montage-Werften)	Post-launch outfitting	Test
40 days	5 days	50 days	4 days	50 days

15: Foundations.
16: Doors and manhole covers.
17: Cast steel parts.
18: Radio and sound.
19: Sanitary installations.
20: Torpedo handling gear.
21: Switchboards.
22: Ballast.
23: Fittings.
24: Conning tower.
25: Power cabling.
26: Batteries.
27: AA guns.
28: Periscopes.
29: Bridge equipment.

TYPE XXI: MODULAR ASSEMBLY

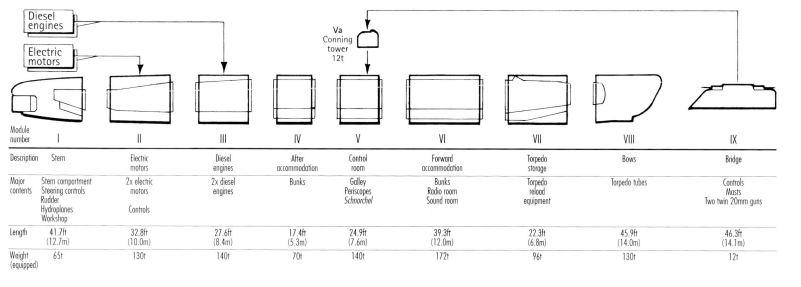

Module number	I	II	III	IV	V	VI	VII	VIII	IX
Description	Stern	Electric motors	Diesel engines	After accommodation	Control room	Forward accommodation	Torpedo storage	Bows	Bridge
Major contents	Stern compartment Steering controls Rudder Hydroplanes Workshop	2x electric motors Controls	2x diesel engines	Bunks	Galley Periscopes *Schnorchel*	Bunks Radio room Sound room	Torpedo reload equipment	Torpedo tubes	Controls Masts Two twin 20mm guns
Length	41.7ft (12.7m)	32.8ft (10.0m)	27.6ft (8.4m)	17.4ft (5.3m)	24.9ft (7.6m)	39.3ft (12.0m)	22.3ft (6.8m)	45.9ft (14.0m)	46.3ft (14.1m)
Weight (equipped)	65t	130t	140t	70t	140t	172t	96t	130t	12t

◁ One of the many peripheral devices developed for the Type XXI construction process was this large sled, which prevented the forefoot from striking the slip during launch.

Type XXI Forecast/Actual Deliveries						
	Forecast Deliveries		**Actual Deliveries**			
	Jan 11 1943	Jan 6 1944				
Yard			Blohm+Voss	Deschinag	Schichau	TOTALS
Place			Hamburg	Bremen	Danzig	
Hulls			2501-2531; 2533-2546; 2548; 2551; 2552	3001-3041; 3044	3501-3530	
April 1944	3					0
May 1944	9	2				0
June 1944	18	5	1	0	0	1
July 1944	27	9	1	1	1	3
August 1944	33	19	3	3	1	7
September 1944	33	26	5	1	2	8
October 1944	35	29	7	3	3	13
November 1944	37	33	5	3	4	12
December 1944	38	33	6	6	8	20
January 1945	38	33	5	11	6	22
February 1945	38	33	6	6	0	12
March 1945	38	33	6	8	5	19
April 1945	38	33	2	0	0	2
May 1945			1	0	0	1
TOTALS	385	288	48	42	30	120

rary internal frames) had to be fitted to overcome this.

Transport between the yards was not the only problem and considerable effort had to be devoted to movements within the yards themselves. Thus, movement systems had to be designed and then the necessary tracks, cross-tracks, turntables, power capstans, special transporters, and cradles provided. The complexity and cost of these intra-yard facilities had not been anticipated by the original planners and the requirement for a total of some 50,000 tons of scarce steel came as a distinct surprise.

THE REALITY

The theory was fine but in real life this program was affected by shortages of material and of labor, disruption of the transportation systems, air attacks on submarine construction facilities by Allied bombers, and numerous design problems disrupting the production process. In addition, there were major difficulties with the completed boats, and in working up the crews. As a result, this very ambitious and complicated program was soon well behind schedule.

Politics also entered the program on numerous occasions, one of the more extreme being the pressure brought on Schichau, Danzig, to launch *U-3501* in time for Hitler's birthday (April 20). This was achieved on April 19 1944, but the boat had to be kept afloat by buoyancy bags and was immediately towed to a drydock to be completed. In the event, the first Type XXI to enter

service was *U-2501*, built by Blohm+Voss. It was taken over by the *Kriegsmarine* on June 15 1944 and entered service on June 28. This was followed by *U-3501*, which entered service on July 29.

PROBLEMS

Tremendous pressure was brought to bear on all those involved in the system to achieve high results, one consequence of which was that numbers of older officials collapsed under the strain. The production forecasts were deliberately over-optimistic, which was supposed to spur the yards to greater endeavors, but the result was that the forecasts were continuously having to be adjusted downwards, leading to the discrediting of the system and discouragement throughout. Also, in an attempt to meet the schedule, modules were sent onwards with parts missing, which then had to be installed by the next link in the chain, adding to the confusion. As the table shows, 120 Type XXIs were commissioned from June 1944 onwards, but the *Ubootwaffe* paid a heavy price for the desperate rush into a totaly new system of production and for the lack of prototypes, and it was inevitable that such an ambitious program would encounter numerous problems.

DESIGN

The design process included the construction of a full-size, completely outfitted wooden mock-up, but, despite this, numer-

△ Three Type XXIs in final assembly at the Blohm & Voss yard in Hamburg. Note at the forefoot of the right-hand hull the large cylindrical housing, which accommodated the *Balkan Gerät* sonar transducer assembly.

ous parts of the design were found to be unsatisfactory. The hydraulic system, for example, was taken straight from that intended for the Type XVIII and, because of the pressure of work in the design office, it was not until late November 1943 that it was realized that not only were the plans incomplete, but they were also unnecessarily complicated and required an excessive amount of precision machine work. By the time this discovery was made, however, materials had already been ordered and the first modules were already under construction, so it was decided to go ahead and complete the Type XVIII design. But this proved highly unsatisfactory and over-complicated and the early boats with this system had to be modified. A simpler and much more satisfactory system was designed for the later boats.

ALLIED BOMBING

In the early days of the Type XXI program, the direct effect of Allied bombing was limited, although raids on the MAN and Siemens-Schuckert factories in January 1944 caused serious delays in the supply of diesel engines and electric motors, even though these were not the only production centers for engines and motors.[1] The indirect effects were also serious. The disruption of power supplies, for example, regularly brought work to a standstill, while workers were frequently absent looking after their families, dealing with the after-effects of a raid, or because there was no transport to bring them to work.

POST-LAUNCH MODIFICATIONS AND REPAIRS

Some post-trials repair work is to be expected on any new submarine, but the modifications required for the Type XXI were far beyond the normal. Some of these affected just individual boats: for example, *U-2501* had to return to the yard for urgent repairs in July 1944, the problems lying almost exclusively in a badly constructed Module II. Other problems were more fundamental, being the outcome of an over-hasty rush through the design stage. Thus problems were found in engine installations, motor installations, pipework design and routing, ventilators, *schnorchel*, and pumps. As a result of these discoveries, not only did many modifications have to be incorporated into new production, but in many cases boats already completed had to be modified.

The hydraulic system has already been mentioned, but the decision to install a *schnorchel* was not taken until much of the design work had been completed and production had started, which meant that the early boats were completed without it and had to be returned to the yards for it to be installed. Such work not only delayed the boats' entry into service, but also took yard workers away from their basic tasks in the Type XXI production process, delaying the production schedule yet again.

There were also a number of problems with the batteries, some of which led to minor explosions. A particular problem

▽ Eight Type XXIs in various stages of progress at the Blohm & Voss yard in Hamburg in May 1945. The Type XXI program was a massive industrial undertaking which was ultimately a total failure, since only one boat entered service before the capitulation.

arose when it was discovered that the main electrical lead supplying DC current from the battery to the electric motors ran down one side of the boat and returned along the other. This was a neat solution from the production point of view, but was potentially disastrous at sea, since it set up a magnetic field which could easily trigger a magnetic mine. Again, boats had to be returned to the yards for the cabling to be rerouted.

The six-cylinder diesel engines were selected because they had already been developed for the Type VIIC/42, but, as mentioned earlier, a special supercharger had been developed to raise power from 1,000hp to 2,000hp. When the early boats were tested, however, it transpired that the supercharger had little effect in its intended task of raising speed when *schnorcheling*. Then, since surface performance was less important than submerged performance, the supercharger was deleted, and the resources devoted to its development were wasted.

There were also flaws in the design. For example, in order to achieve a good diving time there were numerous free-flood holes in the upper deck, but it was found that once submerged these created considerable hydrodynamic turbulence, which significantly reduced the underwater speed. There were also problems with the *schnorchel* operation, due to changes which had been made to the diesel-engine.

One unsatisfactory feature of the design, which could not be rectified in the time available, concerned the single rudder which was centrally mounted and normally lay outside the wash of the twin propellers, which were angled slightly outwards. This resulted in a large turning circle: some 3,280ft (1,000m) on the surface and 1,500ft (450m) at 6 knots submerged. Varying the speed of the propellers or stopping the inboard propeller altogether effected a small improvement.

OPERATIONAL HISTORY

The normal system for accepting a new U-boat into the *Kriegsmarine* involved the crew in 'standing-by' their new boat as it neared completion and then taking it over on the commissioning day. The crew was then involved in testing the individual submarine in conjunction with the construction yard and, when all was satisfactory, they then took the boat to one of the training flotillas in the Baltic for shaking-down and training in the latest operational techniques. The same system should have applied to the Type XXI, but, since virtually all the equipment was new and because the Type XXI represented such a radical increase in underwater performance, everything took much longer, despite the previous experience of some members of the crew on earlier Type VIIs and Type IXs.

Desperate efforts were made by the Type XXI crews to make their boats ready for operations before the war came to an end. But, as described above, many of those boats completed needed modifications or repairs which simply could not be done in the conditions then holding good in the remaining German

before returning to port.

The performance of the Type XXI had a number of significant features for operations. Once a convoy had been located, either visually or by radar or sonar, the Type XXI had sufficient underwater speed and endurance to close the convoy, evade the ASW screen, whether surface ships or aircraft, and attack the merchant ships. The Type XXI was also capable of launching three full salvoes of six torpedoes each in 20 minutes, enabling it to engage multiple targets over a short space of time. Then, once the attack was completed, the great strength of the pressure-hull, deep-diving capability, and long endurance at 'creep' speed (60 hours at 5 knots) enabled the boat to escape. In addition, the much greater fuel and torpedo capacity meant that it would be able to range the North and South Atlantic without needing replenishment, as had been the case with the Types VII and IX.

The Type XXI would have posed many problems for the enemy, not least being that the Allies were mentally attuned to a battle in which the enemy could move at only about 3 knots and had a strictly limited underwater endurance. It would have taken several months to overcome such a mindset.

As described above, until late 1944 Allied bombing had a disruptive rather than a disastrous impact on the Type XXI program. The situation changed radically in 1945 when massive raids resulted in the destruction not only of U-boats still on the ways but also of completed U-boats fitting out, or, in some cases, after commissioning and while undergoing training. Thus, quite apart from the damage to the construction facilities, 17 completed Type XXIs were sunk in harbor between December 31 1944 and May 8 1945: Hamburg – seven; Kiel – six; and Bremen – four.

REASONS FOR FAILURE

In essence the Type XXI simply introduced too much that was new simultaneously and demanded too much of those involved in the program. The reasons for this were diverse. In part it was due to the impending defeat on the high seas and the desire to do something - anything - to prevent it. There was also a fascination in Germany for anything that was new and militarily impressive. With hindsight, there also appears to have been an air of unreality about many of the activities and decisions, some of which may have been due to the pressure of work and others to plain 'woolly-thinking.' Unfortunately for the *Kriegsmarine*, the outcome of all the pressure and the cutting of corners was that the boats that were actually completed were constantly having to return to the yards for repair or modification, resulting in delays in attaining full service status.

dockyards. Nevertheless, a number of boats left German ports heading for the U-boat bases in Norway. *U-2511*, the first to become operational, sailed for Norway on March 18 1945, where its most immediate task was to carry out deep-diving trials in Oslo-fjord, such tests having been impossible in the shallow waters of the Baltic. This showed that some modifications were necessary, which were carried out in the local yard at Horten, but, astonishingly in view of the desperate state of the war, only after the work-force had taken its Easter vacation. In a second test in early April *U-2511* reached 560ft (170m), but Dönitz was not satisfied and *U-2506*, which left Germany on April 14, carried out further tests on April 26, when it reached 720ft (220m). Some of the other boats which reached Norway were undergoing *schnorchel* trials and getting ready for sea when the war ended.

The first of the two war patrols started on April 30 1945 when *U-2511* put to sea from Bergen, Norway, with orders to go to the Caribbean. The boat was detected by a British anti-submarine patrol group off the Scottish coast but escaped with ease. On May 3, just after receiving the surrender order by radio, *U-2511* had the British cruiser HMS *Suffolk* in its sights at a range of 656yd (600m) and the commanding officer (Schnee) went through the motions of an attack but broke off at the last minute, dived under the target and made off for Norway without being detected. The other war patrol was conducted by *U-3008* which sailed from Wilhelmshaven just before the surrender and carried out an undetected dummy attack on a British convoy

△ The four forward sections of a Type XXI at the Deschimag yard in Bremen. The sections had to be aligned very precisely using light beams and then arc-welded. Each weld took eight hours to complete and had to be continuous to ensure that it would be effective; the welders were not allowed to halt, even for bad weather or air raids.

Footnote:
1. The diesel engines were of MAN design and were built by MAN itself, but also by Klöckner-Humboldt-Deutz, Ulm; and Wumag, Görlitz. The electric motors were built by SSW, Berlin; AEG, Berlin; and Brown-Boverie et Cie (BBC).

TYPE XXIII

BACKGROUND

The Type XXIII coastal U-boat was one of the most brilliant submarine designs of World War II, although its success has been overshadowed by that of its larger and more glamorous contemporary, the Type XXI.

By 1941 the only Type II coastal U-boats left on strictly operational duties were the six in the Black Sea, the remainder having been relegated to training duties in the Baltic. This meant that operations around the British Isles were being undertaken by the much larger Type VIIC. When design work on modifying Walter's Type XVIII to form the Type XXI was starting, however (see Type XXI above), a proposal was put forward for a new type of coastal boat, which would incorporate the same ideas of sectional construction, streamlining, and high underwater performance. Dönitz gave his approval to the idea in early 1943,

although he added two provisos: that the boat should also be deployed in the Mediterranean and Black Sea theaters, which meant that it needed to be transportable by rail; and it had to have 23ft (7m) long torpedo tubes, rather than the 16.4ft (5m) tubes favored by Walter.

Walter's Type XXII was the start point for the design work, although the Type XXIII which was eventually produced bore little similarity to Walter's design. In the design work, a deliberate effort was made to keep everything about the new boat simple and to use well-tried components wherever possible. The preliminary sketch design was ready by July 30 1943, while ambitious construction plans for mass-production were prepared in parallel. Deutsche Werft was designated the lead yard, but assembly of the modules, and the fitting out and testing of individual boats, was to be conducted in the proposed theater of operations by local firms acting as sub-contractors: Atlantic and North Sea – Hamburg; Mediterranean – Toulon Arsenal in German-occupied France, and Genoa and Monfalcone in German-occupied Italy; Black Sea - Nikolayev, German-occupied USSR.

▽ This picture gives a good idea of the small size of the Type XXIII. This particular boat entered service as *U-2365* in 1945 but was scuttled in the Kattegat en route to Norway on May 5 1945. It was raised and refitted for service with the *Bundesmarine* and is seen here being placed in the water in 1956. It sank on September 14 1966; 19 men died.

TYPE XXIII	
ROLE: Coastal submarine	
DISPLACEMENT Surfaced: 234 tons Submerged: 275 tons	
DIMENSIONS Length: 113.8ft (34.7m) Beam: 9.8ft (3.0m) Draught: 25.3ft (7.7m)	
PROPULSION Diesel: One MWN 6-cylinder, 4-stroke RS-34-S unsupercharged diesel; 630hp Electric motor/generator: One AEG GU 4463-8 double-armature; 35ehp Electric creep motor: One BBC GCR-188 single-cummutator electric motor Battery: One 62-cell AFA 2 x 21 MAL-740E battery; 5,400amp/hour Fuel capacity: 18 tons	
PERFORMANCE Maximum speed Surfaced: 9.7kt Schnorchel: 10.75kt Submerged: 12.5kt Creep: 4.5kt Range Surfaced: 4,450nm at 12kt Submerged: 285nm at 6kt Crash dive: 9 seconds	
WEAPONS Bow tubes: Two 21in (533mm) Stern tubes: None Torpedoes carried: Two Guns: None	
OFFICERS AND CREW: 2 officers, 12 enlisted men = 14	
SUBMARINES ORDERED: 280	
LAUNCH OF FIRST OF CLASS: April 17 1944	

TYPE XXIII

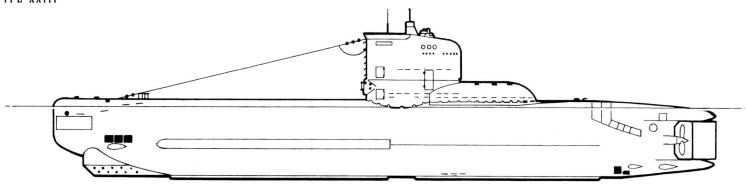

Displacement (surf/sub) 234/275 tons; 113ft (34.7m); speed (surf/sub) 9.7/12.5kt; range (surf/sub) 4,450nm at 6kt/194nm at 4kt.

However, the program was seriously affected by three factors: the distances to these remote construction sites; Axis reverses in the face of the advance by the Allied land forces; and Allied bombing.

Assembly of the first-of-class *U-2321* was started at the Deutsche Werft on March 10 1944; the boat was launched on April 17 1944 and commissioned on June 12 1944. By July 1944, however, it was clear from Allied advances in both east and west that the foreign yards would no longer be available, and as a result all assembly was concentrated at Germaniawerft, Kiel, and Deutsche-Werft, Hamburg. The program was given very high priority, and a director of another ship-building company, Stülcken, was placed at its head.

DESIGN

The Type XXIII had an all-welded single hull; indeed, it was probably the first ever truly single-hulled submarine in any navy. The cross-section of the forward pressure hull was, like that of the Type XXI, in the form of a figure–of–eight. Aft, the pressure-hull was cylindrical in section and underneath were housed non-pressurized fuel oil bunkers and diving tanks. There was no superstructure apart from the relatively small bridge and a small 'hump' immediately abaft the bridge, which covered the diesel exhaust silencer. The stern tapered to a knife-edge, as in the Type XXI, but with a single, three-bladed propeller and a single rudder. The original design had no forward hydroplanes, in line with Walter's ideas, but these were added later.

The requirement for transportation by rail had a significant effect on the design and the boat was designed to be broken down into four elements, although the bridge also had to be removed. Also, in order to meet the rail transportation requirement, the forward section containing the torpedo tubes was kept as short as possible, with the result that no space was left to enable torpedoes to be loaded in the usual way from inside the boat. This meant that the two torpedoes had to be loaded by

△ The performance of the Type XXIII was optimized for the submerged regime. There were two bow torpedo tubes, each containing an externally loaded torpedo; there were no reloads. Note the *Balkon Gerät* beneath the bow and the single propeller in a 'knife-edge' stern.

ballasting the boat down by the stern to bring the tube bow caps clear of the water so that the torpedoes could be loaded externally from a barge. A further consequence was that no reloads could be carried.

Fairly late in the design stage it was discovered that the boat was overweight, but this proved relatively easy to solve, since all that was necessary was to add a 7.2ft x (2.2m) long section amidships. Due to the modular construction methods employed this did not prove difficult.

The propulsion plant involved a single MWM RS-348 diesel engine, which was already in use as a diesel-generator in the Type IXD₂, and the AEG GU 4463/8 electric motor, which was a simplified version of the model in wide-scale use in the Type VIIC. There was also a creep motor which, like that in the Type XXI, was connected to the main shaft by a conical belt reduction system. This creep motor could be used either for low-noise, low-speed submerged cruising, or when *schnorcheling*, since this enabled the diesel engine to drive the electrical motor as a generator to charge the battery. In line with the *elektroboot* concept, there was a large, 62-cell battery.

The Type XXIII proved to be an excellent boat. The design was optimized for submerged performance; underwater speed was 11.2 knots in early versions but, after the forward walkway had been removed and the free-flood holes were reduced in number, this rose to 12.5 knots. Surface speed was just over 9 knots and the Type XXIII had an extending *schnorchel* which could be used at a maximum speed of 10.75 knots. The boat submerged quickly, although this meant that the crew had to take quick action to ensure that it did not exceed the permitted maximum diving depth. It was also very maneuverable, both when submerged and when on the surface. One drawback was that the bridge was large in proportion to the size of the hull in order to house devices such as the periscope and *schnorchel*, and to accommodate watchkeepers. As a result the bridge contributed some 39 percent of the boat's underwater resistance.

It was planned to coat all Type XXIIIs with *Alberich* but, in

ALLIED SHIPS SUNK BY TYPE XXIII U-BOATS			
DATE	**BOAT**	**TARGET**	**TONNAGE (GRT)**
February 25 1945	U-2322	Egholme	1,317
April 16 1945	U-2324	Monarch	1,150
April 23, 1945	U-2329	Sverre Helmerson	7,209
May 7 1945	U-2336	Sneland	1,791
	U-2336	Avondale Park	2,878
TOTALS		5	14,345

the event, this was achieved only from *U-4709* (launched on February 8 1945) onwards. The Type XXIII also had the first practical 'swim out' torpedo tubes, in which the dynamically stable torpedoes left the tube at about 8-10 knots.

OPERATIONAL HISTORY

By the time the war ended on May 8 1945 a total of 62 Type XXIIIs had entered service, of which 18 were stationed in Norway and the remainder at various ports in northern Germany. Ten boats are known to have carried out operational missions, which resulted in five Allied merchant ships being sunk for no loss to the attacking submarines.

The unfortunate *Avondale Park*, which was sunk at 2300 on the night of May 7 1945, achieved the dubious distinction of being the last enemy merchant ship to be sunk by a German U-boat in World War II.

Seven Type XXIIIs were lost either under training or while in transit from German ports to Norway:

- *U-2331*: October 10 1944. Disappeared while on training in the Baltic; cause unknown.
- *U-2342*: December 26 1944. Hit mine in the Baltic.
- *U-2344*: February 18 1945. Sunk, having collided with *U-2366*, while on training in the Baltic.
- *U-2359*: May 2 1945. Sunk by British aircraft in the Kattegat.
- *U-2338*: May 4 1945. Sunk by British aircraft in the Baltic.
- *U-2367*: May 5 1945. Sank following collision with another U-boat in the Great Belt area.
- *U-2365*: May 5 1945. Sunk by British aircraft in the Kattegat.

▽ The two submarine designs which were supposed to restore the initiative to the *Kriegsmarine*: inboard are three Type XXIs; outboard is a single Type XXIII.

THE WALTER BOATS

Helmuth Walter, a gifted engineer and inventor, played a very important role in German U-boat development between 1935 and 1945, although only a few of his many designs were built and none actually became operational. He was working on turbine development for the Germania company in the early 1930s when his mind turned to submarines and he foresaw the need for U-boats capable of traveling underwater at speeds of up to 30 knots and which would remain submerged for many days, both of which ideals were far beyond the capabilities of any submarine then either in service or under development. Although his name has become associated with propulsion systems, Walter's submarine interests were comprehensive and he was equally concerned with shape and control.

His initial idea was for a closed-cycle propulsion system in which a diesel engine would be supplied with oxygen obtained from the disintegration of high-test hydrogen peroxide[1] thus enabling it to operate underwater without the need for an air supply. By 1934, however, he was advocating a somewhat differ-

▽ Professor Walter's revolutionary 4-man submarine, *V-80*, seen here in 1940, had a sustained underwater speed of 26.5 knots, far greater than any submarine at the time or before.

ent process in which the steam produced by the disintegration of the hydrogen peroxide was used to drive a turbine. He proposed two rather different systems, the 'direct' and 'indirect,' but as the latter was never proceeded with it is only the 'direct' Walter process that need concern us here.

In the 'direct' system (see diagram) the hydrogen peroxide was fed into a catalyzer where it broke down into steam and oxygen[2], both of which then passed into a combustion chamber, where they were mixed with water and diesel fuel, and ignited. This produced steam (88 percent) and carbon dioxide (12 percent) at a much higher temperature and pressure, which were used to drive a turbine; they then passed into a condenser, where the gas/water mixture was separated, the excess water and carbon dioxide expelled into the surrounding sea-water, and the remaining water cooled before it re-entered the cycle at the condenser or combustion chamber. The result was a powerplant that was light in weight, very compact, and totaly independent of an external air supply. Unfortunately, it also used great amounts of hydrogen peroxide, consuming approximately 25 times as much fuel per mile by volume as a diesel engine.

A demonstration model of the system was running by mid-1936, by which time Walter felt sufficiently encouraged to break away from Germania to set up his own research and development company - *Walterwerke* (Walter works) - which became involved in many projects (several totaly unrelated to submarines) for both the *Kriegsmarine* and the *Luftwaffe*.

V-80

Walter's work led to a revolutionary demonstration submarine, the four-man *V-80*, which was built by Germania in great secrecy and launched on January 19 1940. *V-80* had a design displacement of 80 tons (hence the name), although, in reality, it displaced over 100 tons. The pressure hull had a figure-of-eight hull cross-section and was shaped like a fish; there were no forward hydroplanes, it had a single propeller, and it carried no weapons. It was powered by an early version of the Walter process, in which the turbine was driven by steam direct from the catalyzer (ie, there was no combustion chamber), with the high revolutions of the turbine being reduced by a gear train to 1,000rpm. Power output was some 2,000hp at the turbine, which, after transmission losses and operating auxiliaries, was reduced to 1,875hp at the shaft. The hydrogen peroxide was stored in plastic bags outside the pressure hull, using the normal pressure of the seawater to force the fuel into the boat.

The tests were successful, with *V-80* demonstrating a sustained submerged speed of 26.5 knots, far faster than that of submarines in any other navy. Walter's system of dynamic control was also a success, with one control stick being used for both lateral and vertical control, making the boat very maneuverable, although the Flettner flaps were over-complicated. Surface performance and handling were poor, however, although this was not a major significance in a boat designed to spend the great proportion of its time submerged.

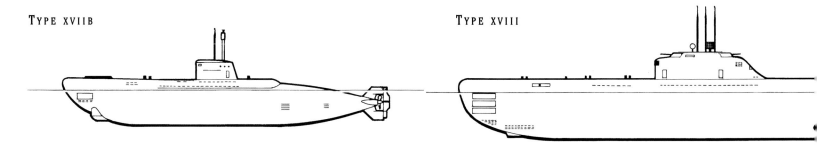

TYPE XVIIB

TYPE XVIII

V-300

Walter was keen to press on to test the 'hot' system (ie, with a combustor) and his initial designs for a new 300 ton displacement boat, *V-300*, were ready in September 1942. This was much larger than *V-80*, but of a similar 'fish'-type shape and it lacked forward hydroplanes. In view of the high consumption of hydrogen peroxide, two diesels were installed for economical surface travel, with two Walter turbines for fast submerged use and two 'creep' electric motors for slow use. Armament consisted of two 23ft (7m) long tubes and four torpedoes. To Walter's annoyance, he was unable to prevent interference by both Germania, the intended builders, and *OKM* design staff, which led inexorably to growth and eventually to a traditional long, thin hull design with forward hydroplanes and a 600 tons displacement. The maximum submerged speed also dropped to 19 knots which, while still fast, was much less than Walter hoped for. A contract was placed with Germania for one example, *U-791*, in February 1942, but was canceled in July 1942 after relatively little work had been done, since Walter had persuaded Grand Admiral Raeder that the design should be dropped.

△ Professor Walter's Type XVII was ordered in two virtually identical versions: 12 -Bs from Blohm+Voss and 12 -Gs from Germania. In the event only three -Bs were completed, none of which entered service.

△▷ The Type XVIII was designed by Walter to meet a requirement from Dönitz for a new, faster ocean-going boat powered by the Walter propulsion system. It was never built but was the basis of the Type XXI design.

◁ A wooden model of the Type XVII built at the Walter works for hydro-dynamic testing. Note the exceptionally smooth hull lines and absence of forward hydroplanes (left) and the cruciform after empennage (below).

WA-202; WK-201/-202

One of the prime causes of problems with the *V-300* design had been with Germania and Walter obtained agreement that his new design should be developed in conjunction with B+V (Blohm & Voss). This caused a major row, since Germania considered itself the parent design yard for all submarines. The result was a typically unsatisfactory compromise, with two separate versions being produced, both of which were originally designated '*201*'; the B+V design being *Wa-201* (Wa = Walter) and the Germania design, *WK-201* (WK = Walter-Krupp), although the latter was soon changed to *WK-202* to differentiate it more clearly from the B+V boat. Both designs were prototypes for the Type XVII and were built to operational standards, although none of them carried torpedo tubes, the torpedo room being used instead to instruct the crew in the Walter process.

The two yards were given considerable latitude in their work on Walter's basic design; analysis and testing of their proposals began in March 1942, with both designs being amended in light of the tests. Orders for two examples of each design were placed in mid-1942; construction commenced at B+V in December 1942 and Germania in February 1943, with *U-792 (Wa-201)* being launched on September 28 1943 and *U-794 (WK-202)* on October 7 1943. In the subsequent tests both encountered numerous problems, although this was to be expected in such revolutionary designs. Surface handling left much to be desired, while submerged handling below 5 knots was difficult due to the lack of forward hydroplanes. Despite this, the two boats were transferred to the trials unit at Hela in the Baltic in December 1943, where a number of problems were encountered with the propulsion system, particularly with the proportioning device. Dönitz visited Hela in March 1944 and went to sea in *U-794*; the run was extremely successful and Dönitz returned to Berlin full of enthusiasm. It was generally agreed that the B+V boat, which was slightly longer and with less beam than its competitor, was better designed; it was also agreed that B+V's internal layout was much better and that the standard of workmanship was much higher.

Both *U-793* (Wa-201) and *U-795* (WK-202), the second boat from each yard, were commissioned in April 1944. These had minor differences from the first two, including only one Walter turbine each, resulting in reduced performance. After builders' trials, both joined the test program at Hela.

TYPE XXII

TYPE XXVI

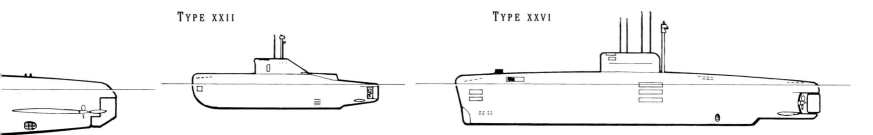

The trials showed the potential of Walter's 'hot' system, the highest underwater speed achieved being 24.78 knots and the longest submerged run 4 hours 25 minutes. Many faults were found, although as far as the propulsion plant was concerned these were almost all concerned with the proportioner and little difficulty was found with handling, storing or controlling the hydrogen peroxide. Some problems were encountered with the overall design, mainly concerning the size of the rudders and the lack of forward hydroplanes. All four boats were taken out of service by late 1944 and laid up. They were scuttled in May 1945, but were subsequently raised by the Allies: the two B+V boats (*U-792* and *U-793*) were then taken to the UK as war prizes for use in trials; but the two Germania boats were scrapped.

TYPE XVIIB/G

While these experimental boats were building, Dönitz continued to press for a production order for Walter-propelled boats in sufficient numbers for realistic operational trials to be undertaken. This resulted in orders for 24 boats, 12 Type XVIIB (*U-1405* to *U-1416*) from B+V, and 12 Type XVIIG (*U-1081* to *U-*

△ The Type XXII was a 12-man Walter boat intended for operations around the British Isles. Two were laid down, but neither was completed.

△▷ Type XXVI was designed as a Walter-powered Atlantic boat but of similar size to the Type VIIC. Four were being assembled when the war ended in May 1945.

▽ *U-1407*, one of the three Type XVIIBs to be completed, in drydock in May 1945.

1092) from Germania. These were slightly enlarged versions of the earlier *Wa-201* and *WK-202* boats, with two torpedo tubes and carrying four torpedoes. Both were fitted with *schnorchel*s.

The entire Germania contract was canceled in September 1943 as was the contract for the last six boats from B+V, to enable both yards to concentrate on the Type XXI program. B+V did complete three boats, however, although due to labor shortages and the pressure of other commitments (particularly to the Type XXI) these were much delayed, being commissioned in December 1944 (*U-1405*), February 1945 (*U-1406*) and March 1945 (*U-1407*). They saw no operational service and all were scuttled on May 5 1945, but all were subsequently raised. *U-1405* was scrapped, but *U-1406* went to the USA for trials, while *U-1407* went to the UK where it was commissioned as HMS *Meteorite* and used in trials for several years. The remaining three boats laid down by B+V were never completed.

TYPE XVIII

At a meeting with Dönitz on January 2 1942, the admiral told Walter of the need to concentrate on boats for the war in the Atlantic. So, as soon as he returned to Kiel, Walter immediately started work on a project to meet the admiral's requirements, which was initially given the designation *V-301*. For his part, Dönitz did all he could to promote the new project, culminating in a crucial meeting at the Reichs Chancellery in September 1942 where Hitler, always excited by technological innovation, gave his full backing to the program. As a result, the previously reluctant naval procurement staff were suddenly seized with enthusiasm, the new project being designated the Type XVIII by the *Kriegsmarine* and *Pr276* by the *Walterwerke*. This started as a scaled-up version of the *Wa-201*, but with twin-screw propulsion, which Dönitz preferred. The boat had a submerged displacement of 1,182 tons and was powered by two Walter turbines, giving it a maximum underwater speed of 27 knots and a submerged range of 243 nautical miles at 25 knots. It was armed with six 16.4ft (5m) tubes and carried 20 torpedoes. Dönitz approved, except for his usual demands for 23ft (7m) torpedo tubes and anti-aircraft armament. That said, he urged Walter to pester the naval procurement chiefs to order at least two Type XVIIIs.

Having reworked the design to meet Dönitz's demands, two boats were duly ordered, numbered *U-796* and *U-797*. By May 1943

THE WALTER DRIVE

▷ In the Walter drive system, diesel oil tanks were outside the pressure hull; fuel floated on top of seawater. Aurol (high-test hydrogen peroxide) was contained in flexible plastic bags outside the pressure hull. A = catalyzer; B = combustion chamber; P = pump.

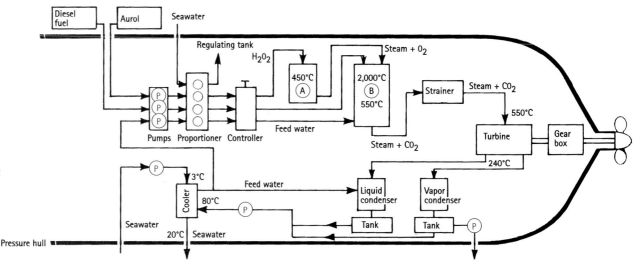

◁ Walter proportioning devices and combustion system under test in a shore-based rig.

◁ The neat, compact Walter double-flow turbine, built for the Type XVIII U-boat.

the design had grown yet again, this time displacing 1,652 tons, and powered by two 7,500hp Walter turbines, giving it a submerged speed of 24 knots. But it was suggested at this point that, instead of Walter turbines, the design could be converted to take a conventional diesel-electric power train, but with triple the normal battery size, which would occupy the space intended for the hydrogen-peroxide bunkers. Thus was born the Type XXI, an idea which was greeted with great enthusiasm and Dönitz sent Walter a letter of apology, telling him that his Type XVIII would no longer be required. Undeterred by the 'hijacking' of his Type XVIII design, Walter's fertile brain switched to other new projects.

TYPE XXII

The Type XXII was a Walter design intended for use in the Mediterranean and in coastal waters around the British Isles. It displaced 200 tons, had a crew of 12, and was powered by a single Walter turbine. Armament comprised two bow tubes and a third on the upper casing facing aft. It was the first Walter design to feature the knife-edge stern. At one time it was planned to build 72, but only two (*U-1153* and *U-1154*) were laid down and neither was completed, although the design became the basis for the Type XXIII.

TYPE XXIV

In 1943/44 considerable thought was given to increasing the number of ready-to-use torpedoes. The Type XXI had six bow tubes, but this was considered insufficient. This gave rise to a proposal to rework Walter's original Type XVIII design yet again, this time to include an additional six or eight side tubes, located towards the bows but facing aft. This proposal was not pursued.

TYPE XXVI

It was considered by some in the *Ubootwaffe* that the Type XXI was too large for Atlantic anti-convoy operations and the *Walterwerke* attempted to produce a successor — even though

the *elektroboot* was not yet in service! – which combined high speed with a size nearer that of the Type VIIC. This was done by enlarging the Type XVII and the resulting Type XXVIA displaced approximately 500 tons, had a single Walter turbine, and was armed with 10 torpedo tubes (four bow, six lateral).

There were a number of 'official' designs to meet this requirement, Type XXVIB and two variants of the Type XXVIE, to which Walter responded with an improved version of the Type XXVIA, the Type XXVIW. This had a longer hull and a different type of bridge. In a significant development, it was also the first large U-boat design not to have a conning tower, placing the CO in the control room in action, as in British submarines. There were 10 21in (533mm) torpedo tubes: four in the bow and three each side facing aft in an arrangement known as a 'Schnee-organ'. In other respects, however, the Type XXVIW made the maximum use of existing components. It had a maximum speed of about 25 knots submerged and an unusually high surfaced speed of 18 knots.

△ *U-1407*, one of three Type XVIIBs completed. Scuttled on May 5 1945, it was raised, inspected by Royal Navy officers (as seen here) and taken to England, to be commissioned as HMS *Meteorite*. British interest in Walter's propulsion system was so strong that they built two new boats using it. *Meteorite* was scrapped in 1950 after many tests.

When Dönitz considered the four competing designs to meet this requirement he decided that the Walter design was superior. It was intended to build the Type XXVIW in modules, as for the Type XXI, with the *Montage-Werft* being Schichau at Danzig, which would phase out Type XXI assembly. Schichau duly received an order for 100 Type XXVIW in March 1944, but it then transpired that only B+V had the expertise to construct Module 2, which included the Walter turbine installation. Since it would be very hazardous to transport the modules from Hamburg to Danzig by sea and impossible by land, it was decided in September 1944 that B+V would become the *Montage-Werft* and Schichau withdrew from the project.

Many of the lessons learnt at such cost in the Type XXI project were incorporated into the design of the Type XXVIW, especially in making it much easier to construct, and eliminating known problems, by fitting a hinged rather than a telescopic *schnorchel*, for example. Also, a full-scale wooden mock-up was constructed and completely outfitted to ensure that everything

would fit in, that junctions between modules (eg, in pipework) would match, and that all equipment would be accessible. It was also proposed to complete the first-of-class as a prototype, which would be fully analyzed before series production commenced. The original plan was to order 250 Type XXVIW, to enter service from mid-1945 onwards, replacing the Type XXI. U-boat construction plans were repeatedly amended as the situation in Germany deteriorated, and the final plan for the Type XXVIW authorized the construction of 100. This figure remained, even though it was plainly impossible to realize; ultimately only four boats (*U-4501* to *U-4504*) were being assembled as the war ended.

HYDROGEN PEROXIDE SUPPLY

One potential problem associated with the Walter process was the growing requirement for hydrogen peroxide, which was variously known as *Ingolin*, *Aurol*, *T-Stoff* and *Oxylene*. This substance was required by the *Luftwaffe* for various aircraft applications, by the Army as fuel for the V-2 missile, and elsewhere in the *Kriegsmarine*: eg, for torpedoes. The original production plant was at Bad Lauterburg, most of whose output went to the *Luftwaffe*, and three more plants were under construction by the war's end. It would seem likely that, had a significant number of U-boats using Walter propulsion systems entered service, the hydrogen peroxide supply situation would have become critical.

WALTER IN RETROSPECT

Walter had a profound influence on German U-boat design and his fertile mind produced many very sound ideas. His analysis of the need for air-independent propulsion was brilliant and his hydrogen peroxide system was technically sound. In addition, he had many practical ideas on submarine design in general.

△ *U-793*, a Type Wa-201 boat, was designed and built by Blohm + Voss and was powered by a single Walter turbine. It was commissioned in April 1944 and scuttled in May 1945, but was later raised and taken to the UK for use in Royal Navy trials.

Like many inventors, however, Walter tried to introduce too many new ideas in each design, resulting in lengthy development at a stage in the war when time was no longer on Germany's side. Thus, among the many concepts included in most designs were: a revolutionary shape; a completely new and untested propulsion system; a novel control system, without forward hydroplanes, with one- instead of two-man operation; and an automatic depth-keeping device. Many of his ideas were simply too complicated. For example, the *Wa-201/WK-202* had Flettner rudders and hydroplanes, adopted from aircraft practice. This system, which was intended to enable the U-boats to be controlled manually at high speeds, involved small fins at the trailing edge of the planar surfaces, which operated first until they were hard over, when an actuator automatically moved the main plane, with the fins reverting to their normal position. This proved to be over-complicated to produce and impracticable in operation, and later designs reverted to simple planes with hydraulic operation.

Walter was so keen to avoid traditional, stereotyped thinking that he deliberately recruited staff from other disciplines. The scientist (Poschen) who studied hull resistance and submerged control, for example, had originally designed printing machines.

Many of Walter's ideas came to fruition with other navies in the 1950s, but, although several boats powered by his system and designed according to his precepts were completed for the *Kriegsmarine*, none ever undertook an operational cruise.

Footnotes:
1. High-test peroxide was given a number of cover-names by the Germans. For use in aircraft and missiles it was designated *T-Stoff*, for ship and submarine use it was *Aurol*, and for torpedoes it was *Ingolin*. It was also known as *Oxylene*.
2. Chemically: $2H_2O_2 = 2H_2O + O_2$
   (water) (oxygen)

PROJECTS THAT WERE NEVER COMPLETED

Type III. The Type III was a 1934 project for a specialized minelayer. It was based on the Type IA but with the hull lengthened by 24.6ft (7.5m) giving it a planned full load displacement of 970 tons. It would have carried 54 *TMA* or 75 *TMB* mines and would have mounted two 105mm guns and one 20mm cannon. It would also have carried one small boat intended to assist in minelaying.

Type IIIA. This was initially designated the Type VII but was later redesignated either Type IIIA or Type III (modified). This would have had the same pressure hull as the Type IA, but with a somewhat larger outer hull. A large, watertight, cylindrical hangar on the after deck was intended to carry two small motor-torpedo boats. Forty-eight *TMA* mines were also to have been carried. This proposal was dropped when it was realized that there would be little practical use for such a composite vessel, and that, in any case, there would be great difficulty in launching and recovering the MTBs.

Type IV. The Type IV was a proposed supply and workshop submarine, which was intended to meet operational U-boats in mid-ocean and to supply them with fuel, torpedoes, mines, provisions, potable water, and spares, as well as carrying out limited repair work. The Type IV was required to be capable of spending a minimum of 90 days at sea and would have displaced approximately 2,500 tons (surfaced).

Type V. Project. Walter boat.

Type VI. The Type VI was a proposal to convert a Type IA to be driven by a Schmidt/Hartmann steam plant for both surfaced and submerged propulsion. This was surprising in view of the generally bad experiences of all navies which had tried steam propulsion plants over the previous 30 years. The project was quickly terminated.

Type VIIE. The Type VIIE was intended as a test-bed for a new Deutz lightweight V-12, two-stroke diesel engine. Apart from the engines it would have been identical to the Type VIIC except that the weight saved in the engine installation was to have been used in a thicker pressure hull, thus allowing greater diving depths. In the event, the engine program was terminated and the Type VIIE was never laid down.

Type VIII. This designation may have been allocated to a proposed 600 ton design, which was intended for production in the event of mobilization. This type was mentioned briefly in 1935 and, so far as can be traced, was never mentioned again.

Type X, XA. See Type XB entry.

Type XI. The German Type XI was to have been an 'artillery boat,' with a completely new hull design; it would have had a submerged displacement of 4,650 tons and its main armament was to have consisted of four 127mm guns, mounted in two twin turrets. It was also to have carried an Arado Ar231 floatplane, which could be broken up into small elements and housed in a vertical, watertight cylinder just forward of the bridge. It would have been hoisted out and replaced by a crane mounted alongside the tower. Four boats (*U-112* to *U-115*) were laid down in 1939 but all were canceled on the outbreak of war. Had they been completed these would have been the largest U-boats in the *Kriegsmarine*, by a very considerable margin.

Type XII. The Type XII was a projected 'fleet' design, with a submerged displacement of 2,041 tons, developed from the basic Type IX. It was planned to build nine, but no orders were ever placed.

Type XIII. This was a 1939 project for a small submarine developed from Type II.

Type XV. This was a preliminary design for a transport and repair submarine, displacing 5,000 tons.

Type XVI. This was also a preliminary design for a resupply and workshop submarine, but somewhat smaller, with a displacement of 3,000 tons.

Type XVIIK. The 'one-off' Type XVIIK was intended to test a closed-cycle propulsion system developed by Deschimag, based on the widely used Daimler-Benz DB-501 diesel engine. A prototype of the closed-cycle engine was quickly running ashore and it was decided in March 1943 to have a boat built to test the concept; development was given high priority, only for it all to be canceled in August 1943. But, following representations from the companies, the project was resurrected in December 1943 and it was suggested that the Type XVIIG might be modified, under the designation Type XVIIK. The contract was placed in February 1944 for a single boat, *U-798*, to be constructed at Germania, and work on both the boat and the propulsion unit continued at a fairly slow rate. By June 1944, however, Germania was deeply involved in other, much more urgent programs, and all further work on the Type XVIIK program was suspended.

Type XVIII. The Type XVIII was a Walter design for an attack boat using the Walter propulsion system, with a 1,887 ton submerged displacement. Its overall design and appearance were used for the Type XXI and the Type XVIII was canceled (see Type XXI entry). Two hulls (*U-796, U-797*) were laid down in 1943 but construction was canceled in March 1944.

Type XIX. The Type XIX was a transport submarine project. The design was based on that of the Type XB minelayer and would have been unarmed.

Type XX. The Type XX was also a transport submarine design, developed from Type XB. It would have been shorter than the Type XB, with greater beam and draught, and a large keel. Displacement was to be 3,425 tons. Thirty were laid down in 1943, but construction was suspended in 1944. Work on three (*U-1701* to *U-1703*) restarted in August 1944 for employment as hydrogen peroxide carriers, but ceased again in early 1945.

Type XXI. The basic Type XXI was used as the start-point for a host of projects, none of which ever came to fruition, due to the Allied victory. These included:

Type XXIB. A 1943 idea for the development of Type XXI with additional six 'side' torpedo tubes (three on each side), sited amidships and angled outwards, facing aft, designed to increase the number of immediately available tubes.

• Type XXIC. A further development of Type XXI, but with an additional 12 'side' torpedo tubes (six per side).

• Type XXID. A late 1943 project for a U-tanker carrying 430 tons diesel fuel.

• Type XXIE. Transport submarine with no torpedo tubes and capable of carrying 665 tons of cargo.

• Type XXIT. Another transport submarine project, which would have been similar to the Type XXIE but with reduced (275t) cargo load.

• Type XXIV. Another resupply submarine project, similar to Type XXID, but carrying reduced payload.

Type XXII. A Walter design intended for use in Mediterranean and coastal waters. It was to have had a displacement of 200 tons and a crew of 12. It was designed to be powered by a Walter engine and armed with three 21in (533mm) torpedo tubes. At one time it was planned to build 72, but only two (*U-1153, U-1154*) were laid down and neither was completed. The design was used as the start-point for the Type XXIII *elektroboot* design.

Type XXIV. Another Walter project which was essentially an ocean-going development of the Type XVIII. It was to have carried 14 21in (533mm) torpedo tubes, six of which were in a conventional arrangement in the bow. The other eight were to have been located four on each side, facing aft, in a 'Schnee-organ'.

Type XXV. A projected coastal submarine, with a 160 tons dis-

placement, which would have been powered by batteries only; ie, it would have had to return to harbor to recharge its batteries.

Type XXVI. The Type XXVI was slightly more complicated, as there were two different projects, one by Professor Walter under the designation Type XXVIW, the other an 'official' design, the Type XXVI.

• Type XXVIW. The Type XXVIW was a Walter design for an ocean-going submarine with a displacement of 1,160 tons. It was based on the Type XVIIA, but with a longer hull and a different type of bridge. It would have been the first U-boat design not to have a conning tower, placing the commanding officer in the control room. There would have been 10 21in (533mm) torpedo tubes: four in the bow and three each side facing aft in a *Schnee-organ*. The Type XXVIW was intended to be built in sections, as for the Type XXI and the sections for the first four (*U-4501* to *U-4504*) were under construction as the war ended.

• Type XXVIA. The basic official design was the Type XXVIA, which was to have was to have displaced 1,124 tons and be armed with 12 21in (533mm) torpedo tubes, loaded externally. Six tubes would have been in the bow and there were to be three aft-facing tubes on each side in a *Schnee-organ*.

• Type XXVIB. The Type XXVIB was similar but would have displaced 1,124 tons and the torpedoes were to be loaded internally, in the usual way.

• Type XXVIE. There were also two variants of the Type XXVIE planned, both of which were to have had more powerful battery and electric motors. Type XXVIIE1 was to have had a MAN diesel and eight torpedo tubes, while the Type XXVIE2 was to have had a Deutz diesel and 12 torpedo tubes.

Type XXVIII. The Type XXVIII was a 1943 design for a 200 ton displacement boat intended for use in the Mediterranean and coastal waters. It was generally similar to the Type XXIII, and would have used the Walter indirect propulsion system, but this was not ready and the project was abandoned in March 1944.

Type XXIX. The Type XXIX was a series of design studies carried out in 1944 for an attack boat displacing between 681 and 1,100 tons, which was intended to replace the ubiquitous Type VIIC. The design was kept simple and it was intended to use Type XXI propulsion with single propeller. The major differences between the various designs lay in the length and cross-sectional shape of the pressure hull, the propulsion system and the number of torpedo tubes.

• Type XXIXA. This was the basic design with a displacement of 681 tons and an armament of eight bow-mounted torpedo tubes.

TYPE XI

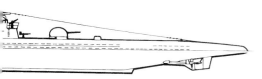

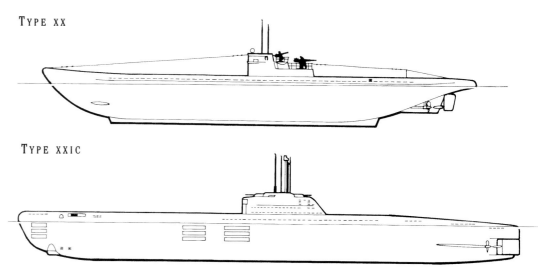

TYPE XX

TYPE XXIC

• Type XXIXB, -B2; -C; -D. These were improved designs, prepared in response to increasing staff requirements. Type XXIXB, -B2 and C were to have been armed with eight bow-mounted torpedo tubes, while Type XXIXD had eight in the bow plus four side-mounted, aft-facing tubes. The Type XXIXB2 was declared the most promising design but no production order was ever placed.

• Type XXIXF; -GK; -H.[1] These, again, were minor variations on the same theme. The torpedo tube fits varied: Type XXIXF was to have had four bow and four side; Type XXIXGK six bow, six side; and Type XXIXH six in the bow only.

• Type XXIXK. The Type XXIXK was to have been powered by a 'Kreislauf' closed-cycle diesel system. There were to have been four versions, Type XXIXK1 to –K4, with different diesels, while -K1 and -K2 would have stored the oxygen in pressurized flasks, and -K3 and -K4 in liquid form. -K3 was intended to maximize underwater speed and, on paper, was capable of 21.5 knots.

• Pressure hull. The cross-sectional shape was:
Types XXIXA-D. Circular tapering to figure of 8 at the bow.
Type XXIXH. Circular.
Type XXIXF and -GK. Figure of 8 cross section throughout.
Type XXIXH. Elliptical.

Type XXX. The Type XXX was similar to the Type XXI but with only one diesel, a 62 cell battery instead of 124, and a single propeller. The pressure hull was circular in shape, except for the fore-ends which were figure-of-eight. There were two variants:

Type XXXA: twelve torpedo tubes: eight in bows, four in *Schnee-organ*; Type XXXB: eight torpedo tubes, all in bow.

Type XXXI. The Type XXXI was very similar to the Type XXX, but with figure-of-eight pressure hull, shorter overall length, and armament as for Type XXXA. The Type XXXI was considered to be better than either of the two Type XXX versions.

Type XXXII. A projected two-man, mini U-boat, similar to the Type XXVIIB '*Seehund*' but without a diesel engine. The batteries would have given an estimated four day endurance. Two torpedoes were to be carried.

Type XXXIII. The Type XXXIII was a 1944 design for a small

submarine to operate around the British Isles. It was to have been powered by a closed-cycle diesel system, using liquid oxygen. It would have carried four torpedo tubes. None was ordered.

Type XXXIV. A three-man coastal U-boat project, the Type XXXIV would have had a closed-cycle diesel propulsion system, and two torpedoes were mounted on the hull. None was ordered.

Type XXXV. The Type XXXV was an ocean-going submarine designed to replace the Type XXVI if the *Aurol* fuel could not be produced in sufficient quantities. The Type XXXV was essentially similar in design to the Type XXIXB2, but was 16.4ft (5m) longer to accommodate the oxygen tank. No orders were placed.

Type XXXVI. A projected alternative to the Type XXXV but based on the Type XXVI, and 16.4ft (5m) longer to accommodate the oxygen tank. No orders were placed.

Towed containers. As explained elsewhere, U-boats made rather poor transports as they had little spare capacity. Thought was therefore given to submersible containers, which would be towed by a U-boat and which would be kept submerged by the forward motion. This arose in response to the need to transport fuel to the Axis land and air forces fighting in North Africa. In early 1943 two containers, one capable of carrying 150 tons, the other 450 tons, were designed, but the loss of Tunisia removed the requirement. A prototype was built and the feasibility of submerged towing was demonstrated. A proposed production order was canceled in late 1944.

△ Three of the many U-boat designs that were never built. The Type XI was a 1930s design for an 'artillery boat', armed with four 127mm guns. Type XX was a development of the Type XB, optimized for the resupply role. Type XXIC was a modified version of the basic Type XXI, with 12 additional torpedo tubes, six on each beam.

Footnote:
1. No trace of Type XXIXE can be found. Type XXIXGK is correct, but no reason for this unusual designation can be found.

FOREIGN U-BOATS

The *Kriegsmarine* obtained a number of submarines from foreign sources in the course of the war. Some were under construction for foreign buyers and were requisitioned; others were captured when German land forces overran foreign countries in 1940-41; some were requisitioned when Italy signed an armistice with the Allies in 1943; and one was captured at sea.

TURKEY

Turkey ordered four submarines from Germany in the late 1930s, of which three were the Ay class (1,210 tons), which was based on the Type IXA, but with certain Turkish requirements. Two were built in Germany and delivered in 1938, while the third was built in Turkey under German supervision. The fourth, *Batiray* (1,375 tons) was a minelayer, capable of carrying 40 mines which were launched through the torpedo tubes. It was slightly larger than the other three. It was also built in Germany and, unfortunately for the Turks, was just reaching completion as war broke out and was requisitioned by the *Kriegsmarine*. It was given the first of the 'foreign boat' designations as '*UA*' on September 21 1939. Because it had been built in accordance with German design practices, *UA* was easily absorbed into the *Kriegsmarine*, the only significant difference being the mounting of the 105mm gun at bridge level, a feature of many British designs of the time.

UA was very active in the early years of the war. It took part in the invasion of Norway in April 1940, where it carried supplies, and it also carried out several operational sorties in 1940/41, during which it sank seven ships (40,716grt) and damaged one (5,728t). It was later used as a supply boat, carrying out one operation in March/April 1942. It was eventually stricken at Neustadt, Holstein, in May 1944 and returned to Kiel where it was scuttled on May 2 1945.

▽ The *Kriegsmarine* impressed into service a number of foreign submarines, one of them the former British minelayer, HMS *Seal*. This boat was captured at sea in May 1940 and served under the German flag as *U-B*, being used in the training role until July 1941.

UNITED KINGDOM

The British modern, Porpoise-class minelayer, HMS *Seal*, had been launched in September 1938 and was laying an offensive mine barrier in the southern end of the Kattegat on May 2 1940 when it was damaged by a mine and was unable to dive. It was captured by the Germans, repaired and then commissioned as *UB*. Because it was specifically designed to lay British Mk XVI mines, it could not be used for German mines and was employed on training duties until 1943, when it was stricken. It was scuttled at Heikendorf on May 2 1945.

NORWAY

In 1940 the Norwegian Navy operated nine submarines and when the Germans overran the country they found that one (*B-1*) had escaped to the UK and the remainder had been scuttled in port. The Germans raised a number of these, of which three were commissioned into the *Kriegsmarine*: *UC-1* (ex-*B-5*); *UC-2* (ex-*B-6*); and *UC-3* (ex-*A-3*). *UC-3* was never employed, however, while *UC-1* and *UC-2* were used for training for a short period and then stricken.

NETHERLANDS

When the Germans invaded the Netherlands, there were 27 submarines in commission in the RNethN, of which 15 were in the Dutch East Indies and 12 were in home waters. Seven of the latter managed to reach the United Kingdom and five were captured either in port or still under construction. Apart from *O.8*, which had been built in 1915, the other Dutch submarines were up-to-date, well-designed and well-armed, and were enthusiastically taken into service by the *Kriegsmarine*. On taking them over the Germans noted that *O.25*, *O.26* and *O.27* were all fitted with the Dutch-designed *schnorchel* tube. That on *UD-4* (ex-

O.26) was tested in 1941, but the tests were terminated at the end of the year and the tubes removed from all three boats. *UD-1* was used on training tasks, but the others were all employed operationally in the North Atlantic.

UD-1. The Dutch *O.8* was originally built for Britain's Royal Navy as HMS *H-6* and commissioned in 1915. It was wrecked on the Dutch coast in 1916, but it was salved and interned by the Dutch, who purchased it from the British and commissioned it as *O.8*. It served throughout the inter-war years and was still in service when the Germans invaded in 1940. Despite its age, the Germans commissioned it as *UD-1* and it was used for training for most of the war, being scuttled at Kiel on May 4 1945.

UD-2. The Dutch *O.12* was launched in 1930 and was scuttled at Den Helder when the Germans attacked on May 14 1940. It was raised and repaired, and was commissioned into the *Kriegsmarine* as *UD-2* on January 28 1941. It was stricken at Kiel on July 6 1944 and scuttled there on May 4 1945.

UD-3. *O.25* was one of three boats of the very modern O.21 class which were captured incomplete by the Germans, and then completed and commissioned into the *Kriegsmarine*. *O.25* was launched on May 1 1940 and scuttled almost immediately in the dockyard, but was raised in June 1940. It entered service on March 1 1942 and served in the North Atlantic, where it sank one ship, *Indra* (5,041grt), on November 26 1942. It was lying at Kiel on October 13 1944 when it was severely damaged in an Allied air raid and was subsequently broken up.

UD-4. *O-26* was still under construction in May 1940 and was completed by the Germans, launched on May 23 1940, and commissioned into the *Kriegsmarine* as *UD-4* on January 28 1941. It

△ The Turkish submarine *Batiray* was built in Germany, its design being based on the Type IXA but with certain modifications, such as mounting the main gun on a raised platform before the bridge. On the outbreak of war it was taken over by the *Kriegsmarine* and commissioned as *U-A*. It served from September 1939 to May 1944.

was completed with a German-type bridge and twin 20mm cannon in place of the Dutch 40mm. It served operationally in the North Atlantic and was also used as the tanker in the trials of an underwater refueling system, such trials being held in the Baltic in September-October 1943. *UD-4* was scuttled at Kiel on May 4 1945.

UD-5. *O-27* was also completed by the Germans, launched on September 26 1941 and commissioned on January 30 1942. Like *UD-4* it had a German-type bridge. It sank one merchantman, *Primrose Hill* (7,628grt), on October 29 1942 in the North Atlantic. It was captured intact at Bergen in May 1945 and was returned to the Dutch Navy, with which it served until 1959.

FRANCE

The *Kriegsmarine* obtained three French submarines in June 1940, all of which were of the latest L'Aurore class.

UF-1. *L'Africaine* was under construction at Chantier Worms at le Trait. It was taken over as a German prize and commissioned as *UF-1* in May 1941, but was not completed during the German occupation.

UF-2. *La Favorite* was launched in September 1938 and was still in the dockyard hands when the Germans took it over in June 1940. It was commissioned as *UF-2* in May 1941 and entered service in November 1941. It was stricken at Gotenhafen on July 5 1944 and scuttled there in May 1945.

UF-3. Like *L'Africaine*, *L'Astree* was still under construction when the Germans arrived in 1940. It was commissioned as *UF-3* in May 1941 but never became operational.

ITALIAN TRITONE CLASS BOATS					
BOAT	**ITALIAN NAME**	**LAUNCHED**	**FATE**		
			MEANS	**PLACE**	**DATE**
UIT-7	Bario	January 23 1944	1. Sunk by British bombs 2. Scuttled	Monfalcone Monfalcone	March 16 1945 May 1 1945
UIT-8	Litio	February 19 1944	1. Sunk by British bombs 2. Scuttled	Monfalcone Monfalcone	March 16 1945 May 1 1945
UIT-9	Sodio	March 16 1944	1. Sunk by British bombs 2. Scuttled	Monfalcone Monfalcone	March 16 1945 May 1 1945
UIT-10	Potassio	November 22 1943	Scuttled incomplete	Monfalcone	May 1 1945
UIT-11	Bame	November 4 1943	Scuttled incomplete	Monfalcone	May 1 1945
UIT-12	Ferro	November 22 1943	Scuttled incomplete	Monfalcone	May 1 1945
UIT-13	Piombo	November 4 1943	Scuttled incomplete	Monfalcone	May 1 1945
UIT-14	Zinco	November 4 1943	Scuttled incomplete	Monfalcone	May 1 1945
UIT-15	Sparide	February 21 1943	1. Scuttled 2. Sunk by British bombs	La Spezia Genoa	September 9 1943 September 4 1944
UIT-16	Nurena	April 11 1943	1. Scuttled 2. Sunk by British bombs	La Spezia Genoa	September 9 1943 September 4 1944
UIT-19	Nautilo	March 20 1943	Sunk by British bombs	Pola	January 9 1944
UIT-20	Grongo	May 6 1943	1. Scuttled 2. Sunk by British bombs	Monfalcone Genoa	September 9 1943 September 4 1944

ITALY

ROMOLO CLASS

Although various attack submarines in many navies have been misemployed as transports, only four classes of specialized transports have ever been built. The first of these was the two-boat Deutschland-class, built for the Imperial German Navy in World War I, the second and third the Yu100 and Yu1001 classes for the Japanese Army in the World War II, and the fourth the Italian Romolo class. The latter were designed in 1941-42 to meet the requirement for a specialist transport submarine to carry vital war goods between Italy and North Africa, although with a potential alternative role of carrying goods between Axis Europe and Japan. With a submerged displacement of 2,560 tons, they could carry 600 tons of cargo in four holds. They were lightly armed, with two 450mm torpedo tubes in the bow and three 20mm AA cannon.

Twelve were laid down, of which two were completed before the Italian armistice on September 8 1943. The German Navy made a determined effort to obtain these two boats from their ally, but the Italian naval chief refused and then both boats were sunk within weeks of entering service, both, by chance, on the same day, July 18 1943: Romolo by an RAF Wellington off Augusta, and Remo by the British submarine, United, in the Gulf of Taranto.

The remaining boats in the class were numbered from R-3 to R-12. R-3, R-4, R-5 and R-6, which were under construction at Taranto in the south, were not completed during the war. R-7 to R-12 were under construction in northern yards and were

immediately taken over by the Germans and given numbers prefixed by 'UIT'.

• UIT-1. Originally R-10, this was launched on July 12 1943 and scuttled at La Spezia on September 9 1943. It was raised by the Germans, who transferred it to Genoa where fitting out started on September 13 1944. It was sunk in that port on October 4 1944 in a British bombing raid.

• UIT-2. This was launched as R-11 on August 6 1943 and taken over by the Germans on September 9 1943. It was transferred to Genoa and fitting out started on September 13 1944, but it was sunk on April 24 1945 in a British air raid.

• UIT-3. R-12 was launched on September 9 1943 and completion work started under German supervision on September 29 1943. It had not been completed when it was scuttled at La Spezia on April 24 1945.

• UIT-4. Formerly R-7, this boat was launched on October 21 1943 and was sunk by British bombs at Monfalcone on May 25 1944.

• UIT-5. Formerly R-8, this boat was launched on 28 December 1943 and was sunk by British bombs while still at Monfalcone on 20 April 1944.

• UIT-6. Formerly R-9, this boat was launched on February 27 1944. Fitting out work started on September 13 1944, but the boat was sunk by British bombs at Monfalcone on March 16 1945.

TRITONE CLASS

Twelve of these boats were under construction for the Italian Navy at the timeof the armistice and the Germans tried very hard to get them completed and into service (see table).

CM1 CLASS

The Italian Navy operated a number of small submersibles and 'human torpedoes'. A class developed in 1942/43 was the 'Costieri Monfalcone' (= coastal, Monfalcone). These were in the Monfalcone yard when it was taken over by the Germans on September 8 1943.

UIT-17. This was launched as CM-1 three days before the German takeover, but was not commissioned in the Kriegsmarine until January 4 1945. It was captured by partisans in April 1945 and taken to an Italian-controlled port.

UIT 18. CM-2 never left the dockyard at Monfalcone. It was bombed there in May 1944 and later scuttled.

THE ITALO-GERMAN TRADE DEAL

In 1942/43 the Germans became increasingly concerned with the question of trade with Japan, but were reluctant to divert too many of the *Kriegsmarine*'s attack boats to the transport role. Long-term plans were considered for new boats such as the Type XX and shorter-term plans for a transport version of the Type VIIC. However, there were a number of Italian submarines operating out of French ports and, since Dönitz had a low opinion of their performance as attack boats, it was suggested that they should be used as transports. When this was first proposed (February 23 1943) Hitler rejected it, but within a month a deal had been negotiated with the Italians in which nine Italian submarines would be used for transport to the Far East (with Italian crews), in return for which the Germans would supply the Italian Navy with 10 new Type VIICs.

Two of the nine boats covered by this deal were sunk before they could be converted: *Archimede* off the Brazilian coast (April 16 1943) and *Leonardo da Vinci* in the Bay of Biscay (May 24 1943). The tenth Italian boat operating out of Bordeaux, *Ammiraglio Cagni*, was excluded from the deal by the Italians, partly because it was the most modern, but also because it had already carried out a very successful 137-day patrol in the south Atlantic (October 6 1942–February 20 1943) and was scheduled to carry out another starting in June.

The seven Italian submarines were converted to their new role very quickly. Sixty tons of cargo could be accommodated internally without any further work, but six weeks in Bordeaux dockyard enabled them to carry a further 150 tons by converting part of their bunkers, although this meant that they would have to be refueled during the voyage. The work was given high priority and the boats were given the nickname *Aquila* followed by a number.[1] *Aquila I-III* left for the Far East in May 1943, followed by *Aquila V* and *Aquila VI* in June. Of those five, two were sunk within days of departure from Bordeaux, but three successfully completed the voyage, arriving in Singapore in July/August. *Aquila IV* and *Aquila IX* were due to leave in mid-July, but the fall of Mussolini on July 25 1943 delayed their departure.

ITALIAN SUBMARINES SEIZED BY GERMANY

A period of confusion in Italy culminated in the armistice which came into effect on September 8 1943 and the *Kriegsmarine* immediately seized all the Italian submarines it could get its hands on. These comprised three boats in Bordeaux (*Finzi* and *Bagnolini*), two in Singapore (*Giullani* and *Torelli*), and one in Sabang, in Dutch East Indies (*Cappellini*). Like the other submarines, they were given numbers in the '*UIT*' series and were:

UIT-21. Giuseppe Finzi (Pietro Calvi class) was at Bordeaux on September 8 1943 and was taken over by the Germans on the following day. It was designated *UIT-21*, but it was never made operational, being scuttled in Bordeaux harbor on August 25 1944, just before the arrival of the Allies.

UIT-22. Alpini Bagnolini (Liuzzi class) was taken over at Bordeaux on September 10 1943 and commissioned as *UIT-22*. It

△ The Italian *Archimede*, seen here at Bordeaux, was to have been re-roled for use as a supply boat on the Far East route under a deal between the German and Italian governments, but was sunk near Brazil before it could be converted.

was manned by a German crew and sailed for the Far East on February 8 1944, only to be sunk by a South African bomber on March 11 1944 while rounding the Cape of Good Hope.

UIT-23. Reginaldo Giuliani (Luizzi class) left Bordeaux on May 16 1943, arriving in Singapore on July 17 1943. It was still there when the Italian armistice came into force and was seized by the Japanese on September 10 1943, but was later handed over to the Germans, who commissioned it as *UIT-23*. It took some time to assemble a German crew but this was eventually achieved and it sailed from Singapore on February 13 1944 but was sunk by the British submarine *Tally Ho!* in the Straits of Malacca on the following day.

UIT-24. Commandante Capellini (Marcello class) left Bordeaux on May 11 and arrived at Sabang in the Dutch East Indies on July 9 1943. It was lying there at the time of the armistice and was seized by the Japanese. It was handed over to the Germans who commissioned it as *UIT-24*. They sailed it to Kobe, Japan, and it was still there when the Germans surrendered on May 8 1945 and was taken over by the Japanese as *I-501*.

UIT-25. Luiggi Torelli (Marconi class) sailed from Bordeaux on June 18 1943 and arrived in Singapore on August 26. It was turned around remarkably quickly and was about to sail homewards carrying a valuable cargo when it was seized by the Japanese on September 8 1943. After the usual prolonged negotiations it was handed over to the Germans who commissioned it as *UIT-25*. It was given a German crew and sailed to Kobe. It was still there in May 1945 when it was taken over by the Japanese as *I-504*.

Footnote:
1. The allocation of *Aquila* nicknames was: *Enrico Tazzoli - Aquila I; Reginaldo Giulani - Aquila II; Commandante Cappellini -Aquila III; Giuseppe Finzi - Aquila IV; Barbarigo - Aquila V; Luigi Torelli - Aquila VI; Leonardo da Vinci - Aquila VII; Ammiraglio Cagni - Aquila VIII; Capitano Bagnolini - Aquila IX.*

WEAPONS

TORPEDOES

The weapon that really mattered to U-boats was the torpedo, known to the crews as an *Aal* (= eel), for which there was no alternative for submerged attacks and which, when surface attacks were still possible, was also often used in preference to the gun. The torpedo was, however, one of the most expensive and complicated weapons of its time, and suffered from many problems, particularly in the *Kriegsmarine*. In essence, the torpedo was a weapons system, consisting of six elements: the torpedo itself, the propulsion and guidance systems, the warhead, the pistol, and the depth-keeping device. These will be considered in turn.

◁ U-boats' primary weapon system was the torpedo, of which only a limited number could be carried. This Type VIIC, for example, could carry 14 such as that shown here.

▷ *Federapparat Torpedo* (*FaT* = area-search torpedo) made an immediate course change (max 135° in 1° steps) followed by a straight line, minimum 547yd (500m) extendable in 110yd (100m) steps. On completing this leg the torpedo entered the 'ladder' phase, starting with a left or right turn which was set before launch. Each leg was either 875yd (800m) or 1,750yd (1,600m) long but each course reversal had a set radius of 164yd (150m). The speed of the torpedo was a constant 30 knots, but its speed of advance during the course reversal stage was either 5 knots (1,75yd legs) or 7 knots (875yd legs). The diagrams show (top) left turn/long leg, and (lower) right turn/short leg.

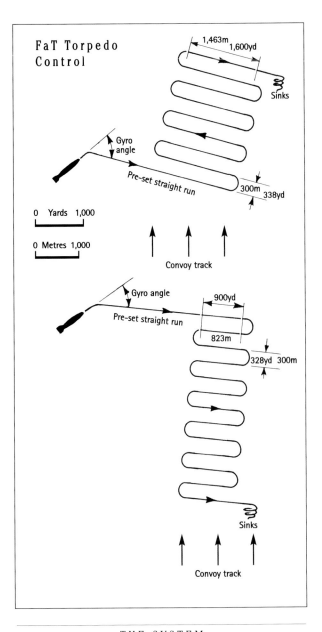

FaT Torpedo Control

1,463m / 1,600yd

Sinks

Gyro angle

Pre-set straight run

300m / 338yd

0 Yards 1,000

0 Metres 1,000

Convoy track

Gyro angle

900yd

Pre-set straight run

823m

328yd 300m

Sinks

Convoy track

THE SYSTEM

One of the major lessons of U-boat warfare in World War I was the need for a torpedo which did not leave a tell-tale trail of air bubbles, and an early electric torpedo was running by 1918. Although forbidden by the Versailles Treaty, development of this weapon was continued by a German cover company in Sweden from 1923 onwards, with trials being carried out at Karlskrona in 1929. The electric torpedo had slower speed and shorter range than the air-propelled torpedo, but the benefits of trackless-ness were considered to more than offset such disadvantages.

Throughout World War II the *Kriegsmarine* used 21in (533mm) torpedo tubes and all were 23.5ft (7.16m) long, except for a small number designed by Professor Walter, which were

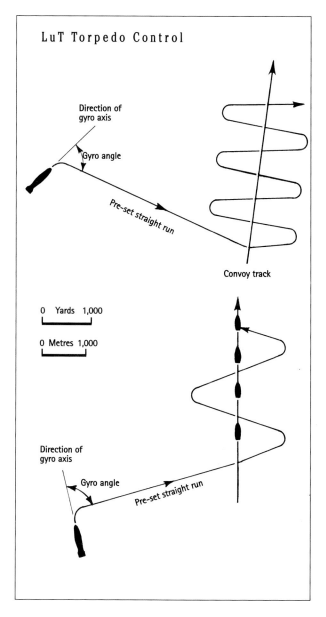

LuT Torpedo Control

Direction of gyro axis

Gyro angle

Pre-set straight run

Convoy track

0   Yards   1,000

0   Metres   1,000

Direction of gyro axis

Gyro angle

Pre-set straight run

◁ *Lagenunabhängiger Torpedo* (*LuT* = position-independent torpedo) — the subject of the top diagram — had two significant differences to *FaT*. First, a further course-change could be made at the end of the straight run. Second, the length of the straight legs in the 'ladder' phase was fully variable between zero and 1,750yd (1,600m), enabling the speed of advance to be adjusted between 5 and 21 knots. In the final development, *LuT II* — lower diagram — the angle of the course reversal could also be adjusted.

16.4ft (5.0m) in length. These torpedoes had a design number, consisting of a capital 'T' followed by an individual number (Roman numeral: eg, *T IV*) and which was sometimes given a letter suffix (eg, *T IIIb*). They also had a three-digit type deignation, the initial letter denoting the model (dating back to the first models, pre-1910); all World War II torpedoes were 'G' followed by a number that denoted its length in meters (either '7' or '5'), and the final letter denoted the drive system (a = steam; e = electric; ut = Walter turbine, etc). In addition, towards the end of the war torpedoes were also given codenames, either of fish or birds.

Two basic operational torpedoes were used by the U-boats throughout the war: the *G7a* and *G7e*. Both were 21in (533mm) in diameter and 23.5ft (7.16m) long, both contained the same warhead, were controlled by a conventional depth-keeping sys-

tem involving a bellows and pendulum, and were steered directionally using a gyroscopic control. Indeed, the only significant difference lay in their propulsion systems.

T I (G7A)

The *G7a* was propelled by a gas-steam system, which at the outbreak of war provided three possible settings: 44 knots to 5,500yd (5,000m); 40 knots to 8,200yd (7,500m); 30 knots to 13,700yd (12,500m). However, early operational experience showed that the 44 knot setting overloaded the engine and this setting was banned until a modified engine was introduced in the middle of the war. The propulsion system meant that the *G7a* left a trail of bubbles, and thus, ideally, it should have been only used at night.

Another of the problems with the *G7a* was that, as originally designed, it was a very sophisticated weapon. It was difficult and expensive to manufacture, requiring a considerable amount of strategic materials (for example, 816lb/370kg of copper), took 3,730 man-hours to build and was very expensive (24,000 *Reichsmarks*). In a major program, which took place early in the war and which attracted little attention, the weapon was completely redesigned so that, with only minimal effect on performance or effectiveness, the labor input dropped to 1,707 hours, the copper content to 373lb (169kg) and the cost to 13,500*Reichsmarks*.

The *G7a* was designed to hit a ship's side, and was fitted with an impact pistol (*Aufschlagzündung*). More than one torpedo hit was usually required to sink a target and if the opportunity for such a second shot did not occur the target frequently managed to limp home.

T III (G7E)

The *G7e* had an all-electric propulsion system, being powered by a lead-acid battery which was some 8ft (2.44m) long and weighed 0.7tons (711kg).[1] There were 52 cells, arranged two abreast, which delivered 92amp/hr, housed in a battery container which could be slid in and out on two rails.[2] An important feature was that the battery container included a series of heating elements which were used to preheat the battery, using eternal power, to 86degF (30degC), thus extending the range by some 60 percent. The battery drove an eight-pole, series-wound DC motor operating at 1,755rpm and producing 96hp for 5.66 minutes. The *G7e* had a maximum range of 5,470yd (5,000m) at 30 knots, which was reduced by up to 1,400yd (1,280m) if the battery had not been heated prior to launch. Although it shared many components with the *G7a*, including the warhead, pistol, depth-gear, and gyroscope, the *G7e* was much simpler and cheaper.

Surprisingly, the British had no knowledge of the successful development of an electric-powered torpedo until some parts of one were recovered from the sea-bed in Scapa Flow following the sinking of the battleship *Royal Oak* by *Korvetten-Kapitän* Gunther Prien in *U-47*.[3]

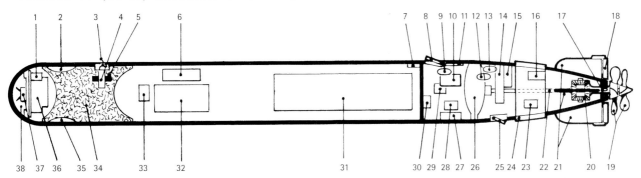

TORPEDO TV (*G7 es*) ACOUSTICALLY-GUIDED, ELECTRICALLY-PROPELLED TORPDO

A *T V* acoustic torpedo and *TZ 5* Pistol. Length, 23.54ft (7.175m); diameter, 21in (533mm); weight, 3,318lb (1,505kg) +/- 68lb (31kg); negative buoyancy, -353lb (160kg) +/- 75lb (34kg); speed, 24 knots; range (with heated battery), 6,015yd (5,500m).

Key: 1: Thermal relay for safety range. **2:** Upper receiver coil. **3:** Propeller for setting safety range. **4:** *Pi 4c* contact (inertia) pistol. **5:** *TZ 5* magnetic pistol coil. **6:** 4-valve amplifier for pistol circuits. **7:** Battery heating plug access cover. **8:** Starting lever. **9:** G-switch access cover (for battery charging and adjusting homing control). **10:** Electric generator (homing gear supply). **11:** G-switch. **12:** Depth-control gear access cpver. **13:** Gyroscope angular setting access cover. **14:** *TA 1* depth-control gear. **15:** Gysroscope. **16:** Discriminator box. **17:** Movable hydroplanes. **18:** Movable rudders. **19:** Contra-rotating, twin-bladed propellers. **20:** Gearbox (single: contra-rotating conversion). **21:** Fixed fins (4). **22:** Propeller shaft. **23:** Smoothing box. **24:** Transmitting coil (surrounds torpedo). **25:** Touching lever switch. **26:** Main electric motor; 40hp, 1,210rpm. **27:** Pistol distribution box. **28:** Resistance converter (converts DC to AC). **29:** Charging plug. **30:** Main switch for motor circuit. **31:** Battery; 36 cells. **32:** Compressed air reservoir (five vessels). **33:** Fuzing relay. **34:** *KE 1* warhead (604lb/274kg). **35:** Lower receiver coil. **36:** Acoustic amplifier. **37:** Acoustic receiver. **38:** Glycerine/ethyl-eneglycol filling (to ensure good noise transmission to the hydrophones).

TORPEDO CONTROL

The control systems fitted to the various types of torpedo became increasingly sophisticated as the war progressed. Originally, torpedoes could be programmed to make one turn immediately after leaving the launch tube (the 'offset'); initially, this was 95 degrees, but was later increased to 135 degrees. Having made that turn, however, the torpedo then continued in a straight line until it reached its maximum range, where it automatically sank.

F A T

A new torpedo control system bacame operational at the end of 1942: *FaT* (*Federapparat Torpedo* = spring apparatus torpedo).[4] This enabled the guidance system to be set before launch so that, in addition to the standard initial 'offset,' the torpedo was programmed to run in a straight line for a pre-set distance, at which point it began a 'ladder' search pattern (see diagram on previous pages). Such weapons were intended to be launched from abeam a convoy and the prime intention was that the hit should take place during the straight run; however, if this failed then the 'ladder-search' would then, sooner or later, ensure a hit. *FaT* was originally fitted to the steam-powered torpedo (*G7a FaT I*) and because this left a slight bubble wake it was initially allowed to be used only in darkness.

This proved successful, not least because the commanding officer did not need to be so precise in launching the torpedo. One potential problem with *FaT* lay in the risk of a 'blue-on-blue' accident, since if several U-boats got in among a convoy and launched *FaTs* the torpedo had no means of differentiating between an enemy ship and a U-boat. As far as is known, however, no such sinkings took place.

A slightly different version, *FaT II*, was fitted to the electrically powered torpedo, which came into use as the *T III FaT II* (*G7e*) in March 1943. This was intended to be launched from the

stern tube to attack pursuing escort warships and, following the initial 'offset' course change, its only patterns were either a long loop or a circle (always to the left). *FaT II* was introduced in May 1943, but it was not a success, mainly because of its short range of 5,470yd (5,000m). As a result a new version, *T IIIa FaT II* (*G7e*), was rapidly developed, which had a larger battery, giving it a range of 8,000yd (7,315m).

L u T

Next to appear, in March 1944, was *LuT I* (= *Lagenunabhängiger Torpedo* [position-independent torpedo]), which was developed from *FaT*, but incorporated two significant differences in the search pattern. First, an additional course-change at the end of the straight run was possible, which enabled the commander to program the torpedo onto the same course as the convoy. Secondly, the length of the straight legs in the 'ladder' phase was fully variable between zero and the maximum of 1,750yd (1,600m), instead of having only two possible settings as in *FaT*. Thus, the speed of advance could be varied between 5 and 21 knots. *LuT I* was installed in the steam-propelled torpedo as the *T I LuT I* (*G7a*) and in the longer range version of the electrically powered torpedo as *T IIIa Lut I* (*G7e*). A second version, *LuT II*, enabled changes in course of over 180 degrees to be made. *LuT* was not used operationally until late 1944 and about 70 torpedoes fitted with the device were launched.

T IV (*G7es*) '*FALKE*'

By early 1943 the Allied ASW forces were becoming very effective, forcing U-boats to launch their torpedoes from greater distances and under more disadvantageous circumstances. In addition, the *Kriegsmarine* had an increasingly urgent requirement for a fast torpedo which could be launched quickly and effectively against an approaching surface warship.

Research into an acoustic torpedo which would home on a target's noise signature was pursued in Germany from 1934 onwards and it was quickly apparent that the major limitation lay in the torpedo's 'self-noise,' which was mainly due to the propeller. Some improvement resulted from better blade design but, essentially, the technology of the time limited the designers to a maximum speed of 25 knots. This meant that the targets to be attacked had to be moving between a lower limit of 12 knots, because below that speed the target did not generate sufficient noise to attract the seeker, and an upper limit of 19 knots, because of the need to enable the torpedo to close with the target.

The first weapon – *T IV (G7es) Falke* (= falcon) – entered testing in 1940 and was originally meant to enter service in 1942, but development problems caused long delays and the early models were not tested at sea until early 1943. Then, however, two out of three successes resulted in the weapon being declared satisfactory and it was cleared for service from July 1 1943. *Falke* had a contact pistol, a 604lb (274kg) warhead[5], the relatively low speed of 20 knots and a range of 8,200yd (7,500m). It was in service for a brief period only and a few U-boats were adapted to take it, before it was replaced by the much better *Zaunkönig*. Approximately 100 *Falke* were manufactured, of which some 30 were launched in anger.

T V (G7ES) ZAUNKÖNIG

The need for an effective weapon against hunting warships became increasingly urgent and Dönitz pressed ever harder for a new weapon. He had originally agreed to an in-service date of early 1944 for the definitive anti-escort weapon, but in May 1943 he brought this forward to October 1 1943, and then, on July 13, to August 1. Astonishingly, no fewer than 80 of the new torpedoes were ready on that date, as demanded, and they were at sea in September.

The new torpedo – *T Vb (G7es) Zaunkönig* (= wren)[6] – was developed from the existing *T III* and had a maximum range of 6,290yd (5,750m).[7] The *T III*'s speed of 30 knots had to be reduced to 24.5 knots due to the problem of 'self-noise,' while the sensitivity of the acoustic receiver meant that targets had to be moving faster than 10 knots and less than 18 knots.

Of necessity the arming range was short – 274yd (250m) – and it was not unknown for one of these torpedoes to try to sink the U-boat that had launched it. This meant that the U-boat had to dive deep immediately after launch, depriving it of the opportunity to observe the success (or otherwise) of the torpedo, and leading to somewhat exaggerated claims of its effectiveness. Thus, it was not until Spring 1944 that Dönitz began to suspect that *Zaunkönig* was not as good as was being claimed.

The Allies knew a great deal about *Zaunkönig* from intelligence reports and were thus able to design, produce, and issue counter-measures before it ever entered service. Thus, as soon as they had confirmation that an acoustic torpedo was being used they introduced noise-makers (known as 'foxers') which were towed behind warships to decoy the acoustic hunting head in the torpedo. Realizing what was happening, the Germans developed *T XI (G7es) Zaunkönig II*, in which the seeker was

△ External tubes, such as this after tube aboard a Type VIIA, were located outside the pressure hull, thus releasing internal space for other uses, but could not be reloaded at sea.

more accurately tuned to ships' propeller noises, thus making it less vulnerable to noise-making decoys. *Zaunkönig II* also had a more powerful battery (17T) to give greater range, improved propeller design (thus reducing self-noise and enabling targets moving at 9 knots to be tracked), and was capable of being launched at depths of up to 164ft (50m), compared to 49.5ft (15m) for *Zaunkönig I*.

WARHEADS

During World War I the standard German torpedo explosive was *Hexanite*, a mixture of *hexanitrophenylamine* (HND) and the standard explosive *trinitrotoluene* (TNT) which proved to be very stable. A major increase in explosive power was introduced in 1933 when the *Kriegsmarine* started adding powdered aluminum to *Hexanite* in the torpedo warheads. It had been discovered in the early 1900s that adding powdered metals to explosives added considerably to their power and the new German mixture (known as *TNT/HND/Al*) contained 25 percent aluminum by weight.

At the start of World War II both *G7a* and *G7e* torpedoes were fitted with an identical warhead (*Kopf* = head) containing 617lb (280kg) of *TNT/HND/Al*. The only major variation in service torpedoes was with those with an acoustic head (eg, *TIV Falke* and *TV Zaunkönig*) where the warhead was displaced from the very front of the torpedo and was slightly reduced in size to 604lb (274kg).

PISTOLS

The torpedo warhead included a self-contained *Pistole* (*Pi* = pistol), which could be of two types: an impact fuze (*Aufschlagzündung*) or a magnetic influence fuze (*Magnetzündung-pistol*). The former was intended to fire the detonators on hitting the target, the latter as the torpedo passed through the ship's magnetic field.

Pi. 1

In September 1939 the standard pistol for *G7a* and *G7e* torpedoes was the *Pi.1*, which had both impact and magnetic functions. The latter consisted of a longitudinally mounted armature which was spun by a propeller in the nose. When it entered a magnetic field an electric current was induced, closing a relay and firing the detonators. There was also a safety device which armed the warhead once the torpedo had traveled 270 yards (250m) from the tube.

The impact element was simple and dated back to World War I. It comprised a direct-action firing pin and four 'whiskers' which were intended to react to a glancing blow. Once combat operations began, however, there were large numbers of torpedo failures, and U-boat commanders reported that they had seen torpedoes blow up as soon as they had passed the safety distance. The designers of the pistol had known that there were a number of problem areas and that the spinning armature device was liable to incorrect operation for several reasons. First, the effect of the torpedo moving through the Earth's magnetic field, a problem exacerbated by changes in the Earth's magnetic field due to changes in latitude. Secondly, there was the problem of mechanical vibration, which could either change the torpedo's own magnetic field or shake the relays so much that they closed. The designers and the *Torpedoversuchanstalt* (*TVA* = torpedo test establishment) had sought to balance these known problems against the rapid fall-off in the magnetic influence of the target with depth, but they made the fatal error of deciding to base everything on detailed theoretical calculations and failed to conduct proper trials in the open ocean and also at high latitudes.

Dönitz's first response to the magnetic problem was to issue an order on October 2 1939 that only the impact element of the pistol was to be used until further orders.[8] Then it was also discovered that the contact fuze did not always function correctly either, due to poor design of the whiskers (which resulted in a minimum impact angle of approximately 20 degrees) and the striker. Perhaps the most devastating example occurred on October 30 1939 when *U-56* (Zahn) launched a salvo of *T 1(G7a)* torpedoes against the British battleship, HMS *Nelson*, and the captain observed three hits but not one explosion.

Permission to start using the magnetic element again was given on November 10 1939 but further malfunctions led to more

△ Torpedoes normally sank themselves at the end of their run, but this German *G7* ran ashore on the Dutch island of Aruba. The warhead is the black section containing 617lb (280kg) of explosive, which was activated by one of the four 'whiskers' in the nose hitting a solid object. This particular torpedo subsequently exploded, killing four men.

trials, after which the torpedo specialists finally admitted that the pistol was faulty. Matters came to a head during the Norwegian campaign when furious U-boat commanders returned from patrol to report numerous failed attacks due solely to malfunctioning torpedoes. As a result, every attack was carefully analyzed and *Gross-Admiral* Raeder set up a formal enquiry which resulted in several members of the *TVA* being court-martialed for dereliction of duty during the period 1936-39. Dönitz was told by one official that one of the torpedoes had been accepted for service after just two test runs, neither of which had been completely satisfactory. As a result, the *TVA*, which until then had been a totaly civilian establishment, was completely reorganized, with a naval officer at the head of every section.

An improvement program was set in train, but Dönitz had no alternative but to issue an order that only the impact fuze was to be used and that even then the torpedo was to be set to run shallow (which reduced its effect). Despite this, the success rate began to increase. There was another spate of failures in February 1941 with one commander reporting that he had launched no fewer than seven malfunctioning torpedoes. Yet another enquiry suggested that this might have been due to embarking the torpedoes under severe winter conditions, although nothing was proved.

Not surprisingly, these problems had an adverse effect on the U-boat service as a whole. First, it infuriated the captains and crews, who repeatedly got their boat into the correct position for an attack, only for all the effort to be wasted by an unreliable torpedo. Secondly, it caused a great deal of friction between the U-boat service and the *TVA*, especially when the latter tried to argue that the problems were due to faulty aiming by the U-boat captains.[9]

Pi 2

The *Pi 2* was a nose-mounted combined impact and magnetic

pistol used in the *G7e* only, the impact element being similar to that of the *Pi 1*. The magnetic function, however, was quite different and was based on a horizontally mounted coiled rod (420,000 turns), coupled by a valve amplifier to a relay system. The circuit was arranged to fire when the voltage dropped after a specified value had been reached, which was intended to ensure that it fired as the torpedo passed under the target's keel.

Unlike the *Pi 1* there was a cut-out switch for the magnetic function, enabling the pistol to be used for impact-only, if required. Current to operate the electric circuits of the *Pi 2* was obtained from the torpedoes' main battery.

PI 3/MZ 3

So severe was the pistol problem that the Germans even turned to their despised Italian allies for help and the Italians supplied a number of their S.I.C magnetic pistols, which entered *Kriegsmarine* service as the *MZ 3* in August 1943. This pistol used coiled rods connected to a valve amplifier and thence, via relays, to the detonators. The impact element, *Pi 3*, was similar to *Pi 1*. The original versions were supplied direct from the Italian Navy, but the pistol was later manufactured in Germany as the *MZ 3a*.

TZ 5/PI 4s

When the *T V* torpedo was being designed it was clear that the acoustic sensors would prevent the warhead and pistol from being located in their customary position at the front of the torpedo. This meant that the contact pistol could not depend upon the traditional firing-pin and 'whiskers' which were activated by physical contact with the target. Similarly, since the torpedo was likely to approach the target from astern, where the speed differential between target and torpedo would be low, the magnetic pistol could not depend upon rapid changes of magnetic flux. In addition, the guidance system would make sudden changes of course, which meant that both pistols had to be proof against rapid angular forces. These factors led to two new pistols, the *TZ 5* active magnetic pistol and the *Pi 4c* contact pistol, both of which operated on totaly new principles.

With the *TZ* the torpedo was surrounded by a symmetrical magnetic field which was distorted by the presence of a target, causing the pistol to fire the detonators. The new *Pi 4c* was inserted into a well in the top of the torpedo. It functioned on the inertia principle, using two pendulums with their axes at right-angles, which resulted in a variable sensitivity, maximized forward and upward.

The *TZ 5/Pi 4c* combination was potentially the best pistol combination produced by any navy during World War II. According to German records, some 600 *T V* torpedoes were launched in combat, of which 58 caused explosions, a success rate of just 9.7 percent, but it proved impossible to attribute the cause of the failures.

△ At the start of the war, all German torpedoes were 'straight runners' as shown by this torpedo hitting a British merchant ship amidships.

DEPTH-KEEPING

One of the most important aspects of torpedo performance was that it should maintain the correct depth: when fitted with an impact fuze the torpedo had to run shallow enough to hit the target, while if fitted with a magnetic fuze it needed to run underneath the target. It was also important that the torpedo should not break the surface at any time during its run, since that would alert a watchful enemy, possibly enabling him to take evasive action.

TIEFEN APPARAT I (TA I) (= DEPTH APPARATUS NO.1)
Both *G7a* and *G7e* torpedoes were fitted with *TA I*, a conventional device incorporating a directly coupled pendulum and hydrostatic valve. Unfortunately, this was not tested properly in the pre-war years, which was due, at least in part, to a pre-war assumption that only the magnetic setting would be used, which meant that precise depth-keeping was not too important. As a result the depth-keeping was poor and the immediate remedial action ordered by *BdU* was to set the torpedo to run shallow, which reduced the effect. The instruction aboard *U-570* (which was captured by the British) showed that even as late as Spring 1941 these depth-keeping problems were still a matter of major concern.

TIEFEN APPARAT II (TA II) (= DEPTH APPARATUS NO.2)
Four separate influences led to the development in 1943 of a new depth-keeping device, *TA II*. First, there was the general unreliability of *TA I*. Second, there was a new problem in that the *FaT* and *LuT* guidance systems caused torpedoes to alter course rapidly under full helm, resulting in a violent roll which sometimes caused them to break surface. Third, the *T IIIa FAT II* torpedo was fitted with a larger and heavier battery to give it extra range, but this increased its negative buoyancy, making depth-keeping difficult. Fourth, U-boats were being forced to launch

their torpedoes from ever greater depths and with the direct coupling of the hydrostatic valve and pendulum in the *TA I* this led to the torpedo broaching before correcting action became effective.

The *TA II* was intended to overcome these problems and contained improvements. The maximum running depth was increased from 40ft (12m) to 50ft (15m) and an extending connection was fitted between the hydrostatic valve and the pendulum, to enable torpedoes to be launched from depths of up to 130ft (40m) without broaching.

TA II only partially solved the turning problems with *LuT*s and, as a result, these torpedoes were fitted with extensions to the horizontal fins, which were activated by an air cylinder after the torpedo had left the tube. The fins reduced the rolling but increased the turning circle, so similar devices had to be fitted to the vertical rudders as well.

END-OF-RUN

All torpedoes were designed to sink automatically if they had not been detonated after a set distance. However, they frequently detonated, on some occasions (as far as could be ascertained) due to hitting the sea-bed and on others due to the collapse of the pistol due to the pressure of the water. Towards the end of the war a device designated the *Enddetonierersicherung* (= end-of-run detonation preventer) was produced to prevent this. It consisted of a hydrostatically operated valve which flooded the pistol when a depth of 492ft (150m) was reached.

TORPEDO PROPULSION

At the start of the war there were two standard methods of powering U-boat torpedoes. The first of these was the internal combustion engine in the *G7a*, which used *Dekalin* (decahydronaphthalene) as a fuel and compressed air as an oxidant.

△ Inside a 'U-boat bunker' the crew of a Type VIIC exercise great care as they load a *G7* torpedo into their boat. For reasons which are now difficult to understand the German censor has obliterated the torpedo's tail fins and propellers.

This had a power output of 350bhp at 1,470rpm, and range and speed could be traded off against each other. (The three-setting system, and the problems with propulsion, have been described under the section on *TI (G7a)* torpedo.)

The second method was the electric-powered *G7e*, whose prime advantage was that it left no discernible wake. The battery was some 8ft (2.44m) long and weighed 0.7tons (711kg). There were 52 cells, arranged two abreast, which delivered 92amp/hr, and these were housed in a battery container which could be slid in and out on two rails. An important feature was that the battery container included a series of heating elements which were used to preheat the battery, using external power, to 86degF (30degC), thus extending the range by some 60 percent. The standard battery was designated the *13T* but later torpedoes used a larger battery, designated *17T*, to give greater range.

In both *G7a* and *G7e* the power unit drove a propeller shaft, which in turn drove a gearbox powering two contra-rotating propellers, which were necessary to overcome the effects of torque.

PRODUCTION

Between 1934 and 1939 German torpedo production was about 70 per month, which increased rapidly once war broke out, reaching 1,000 per month in early 1941, and peaking at 1,700 per month in 1943. Production fell to 1,400 per month in 1944 and then tailed off, due a combination of Allied bombing and transportation difficulties, coupled with shortage of labor and materials. According to a British estimate, the Germans produced some 70,000 21in (533mm) torpedoes during the war, of which approximately 10,400 were launched in anger. Of these 9,300 were unguided (7,000 electrical *G7e* plus 2,300 steam-powered *G7a*); 500 were pattern-runners (*FaT* and *LuT*); and 600 were acoustic.

NAVAL TORPEDO SCHOOL

The main torpedo training school for U-boat officers was at Mürwick and the course had to be attended by all 1WOs and by commanding officers who had not perviously attended a course. Subjects covered included the care and maintenance of torpedoes, tubes and control devices; plotting; and control and launching drills. The facilities at the school were excellent and included 15 rooms for practising U-boat control drills. Practical lessons were given aboard a number of minesweepers, which had been specially converted for the task, with two torpedo tubes removed from S-boats mounted on the fo'c'sle and a simulated U-boat control room below decks.

TORPEDO PROJECTS

WALTER DESIGNS
Dr Walter's wide interests in submarine matters extended to

torpedoes, where he set about designing a hydrogen-peroxide drive. His design bureau produced some 16 different designs of which three were actually in production as the war ended, although none actually entered service. The differences between these models lay in the length and negative buoyancy of the torpedoes, rather than in the propulsion system, which was essentially the same.

The propulsion system in the *T VII (G7ut) Steinbarsch* (= perch) provides a typical example. This used five substances: *Dekalin* (fuel); *Ingolin* (oxidant); fresh water (coolant); *Helman* (catalyst); and compressed air (pressurizer).

As soon as the torpedo began to move down the tube a valve was opened, releasing the high-pressure air to act on the *Dekalin, Helman, Ingolin*, and fresh water, although matters were so arranged that the four did not arrive in the combustion chamber simultaneously. First to arrive were the *Helman* and *Dekalin*, followed very shortly afterwards by the water and, after about one second's delay, the *Ingolin*. The *Helman* was self-igniting, starting the reaction, whereupon the supply of *Helman* ceased. The *Ingolin* and *Dekalin* were sprayed in through concentric nozzles at one end of the chamber while the water was sprayed in from the other end.

The water kept the heat of the reaction within manageable limits (2,300degC). It also turned into high-pressure steam, which then passed into a single-stage, axial-flow turbine, generating 435bhp at 23,000rpm, which was geared down to drive twin, contra-rotating propellers at a speed of 1,550rpm. This reduction gearing was also used to compensate for the torque effect of the turbine, with the first (and heavier) gear turning in the opposite direction to the turbine. This gave a speed of 45 knots and a range of 8,750yd (8,000m).

As the torpedo contained such volatile ingredients it was essential that there were adequate safety precautions. The fresh water tank was cylindrical in shape and some 6ft (1.83m) long, and occupied the middle part of the main body of the torpedo. The *Dekalin* tank was placed at the front of the water tank and the *Ingolin* tank at the rear, thus not only keeping them physically separate but also ensuring that if there was a rupture (for example, in a depth-charge attack) the two substances would be so diluted by the water that they would not react with each other. A further precaution was that there was a lever-operated valve in the *Ingolin* supply line which was released only as the torpedo left the tube, thus ensuring that the torpedo was well clear of the U-boat before the reaction began.

By far the heaviest (and bulkiest) ingredient was the fresh water; a variant designated *Schildbutt* was under development which used seawater instead, thus enabling considerably more *Dekalin* and *Ingolin* to be carried and extending the range to 19,700yd (18,015m). A yet further development was *Steinwal* which not only used seawater injection, but also replaced the compressed air (and its heavy container) by pumps, giving an even greater range of 23,000yd (21,030m).

△ The torpedoes took up a great amount of space inside the submarine, but, when required, they had to work first time, every time. This meant that they had to be maintained regularly and here torpedo men carry out routine maintenance on their charges.

OTHER PROJECTS

Numerous other U-boat torpedo projects were considered both before and during the war. One was for a closed-cycle propulsion system, using the *Kreislauf* principle, in which a mixture of oxygen and exhaust gas was fed into an otherwise conventional engine. Experiments began in the early 1930s and in 1937 the aircraft-engine manufacturer, Junkers, was given a development contract. The proposed *M5* torpedo had a diameter of 29.6in (750mm) and would have been powered by a 425hp closed-cycle engine, but this was dropped and the engine was redesigned to fit in a 21in (533mm) torpedo. Forty engines had been built and some torpedo runs undertaken when in 1943 it was decided to concentrate all development efforts on the Walter torpedoes.

Another torpedo designer, Dr Kauffmann, developed a closed-cycle torpedo drive, using an Otto engine. Work proceeded very promisingly until just before the war, when Kauffmann, a Jew, was forced to leave Germany and development ceased. A rocket-propelled torpedo, designated *Hecht* (= pike) was also considered, although whether this would have proved feasible in the light of contemporary hydrodynamic knowledge is not known.

Other development efforts were aimed at the guidance systems and one very ambitious 1944-45 project sought to use wake-homing, although this proved to be a very complex area and was not perfected. The *G7es Geier* (= vulture) was a torpedo which attempted to overcome the shortcomings of the passive acoustic torpedoes, by using active acoustic homing.[10] This transmitted three pulses per second at a frequency of 80kc/s, giving an acquisition range of 280yd (250m), and a returning echo above a set value was used to operate the rudder to turn the torpedo towards the target. The *Geier* was nearly at the production stage in May 1945, but it is doubtful whether problems such as surface echoes had been solved, although it appeared that it would overcome the problems caused by noise-making

decoys (eg, 'Foxer').

One of the most significant torpedo projects was *G7es Lerche* (= lark)[11] which was connected to the U-boat throughout its passage by an insulated copper wire which was paid out simultaneously from the torpedo (through the hollow propeller shaft) and from the U-boat's torpedo tube. *Lerche* had a passive, acoustic detection system, which transmitted signals down the wire to the operator aboard the U-boat, who was better able to discriminate between different targets, and to identify spurious echoes, than any electronic device of that era. Five different orders could be passed down the wire: torpedo turn left, torpedo turn right, gyroscope, acoustic receiver train left, acoustic receiver train right. *Lerche* is believed to have been fitted in one U-boat for trials purposes in 1945, but did not enter production, although the wire-guidance technique was to be widely copied in many weapons systems in the post-war era.

△ Loading a torpedo was a dangerous and time-consuming business, which involved a complex array of frames, pulleys and winches. It was even more complicated below where most of the accommodation had to be totaly rearranged to enable the 'fish' to reach their stowage spaces.

TORPEDO LOADING AND MAINTENANCE

Torpedoes were long, heavy, unwieldy and coated in heavy grease, which combined to make them exceptionally difficult to handle in the cramped interior of a U-boat. They were loaded through either the forward or after torpedo access hatch, using a special deck-mounted derrick and a trough. Once below, the torpedo had to be maneuvered to its desired place, either in a tube, in a rack or under the floorboards.

At sea, there was a regular maintenance program to ensure that the torpedoes would be fully ready for use when required. This involved all torpedoes in the tubes being removed once every 4-5 days when they were inspected. At such times, in the case of steam-propelled torpedoes (*G7a*), their compressed air supply was checked and if necessary topped-up, or, in the case of electrical torpedoes (*G7e*), their batteries were checked and, if necessary, the electrolyte was topped up. This

activity caused great upheaval in the torpedo compartments, where bunks, hammocks, and bedding had to be moved while that day's torpedo was removed, serviced and replaced.

The torpedo mate was so closely involved with his charges that he did not live in the petty officers' mess, but in the forward torpedo room.

TORPEDO TUBES

The forward torpedo tubes were mounted with about one third of their length inboard and about two-thirds outside the pressure hull, supported by frames. Throughout World War II, U-boats used a bubble-free ejection system, in which compressed-air was admitted into the inboard end of the tube, where it acted against a free-floating piston. This pushed the torpedo down the tube at a velocity of some 33ft/sec (10m/sec). The piston was, however, prevented from leaving the tube by a set of grooves and was then forced back by the pressure of the sea-water while the torpedo proceeded under the power of its motors. As the piston was pushed back the compressed air behind it was vented into the submarine, until the piston came to a halt against the tube doors.

This system ensured that the torpedo left the submarine without releasing any air into the sea-water, which would reach the surface as bubbles, thus revealing the U-boat's presence. It did, however, have a number of disadvantages. First the tubes were both heavy and expensive; secondly, it was depth-limited; thirdly, the piston, a large, cylindrical device weighing 77lb (35kg), had to be removed and replaced every time a torpedo was removed for maintenance, or the tube was reloaded.

CONDUCTING TORPEDO ENGAGEMENTS

Submerged engagements were conducted by the captain from the control center in the conning tower. He used the attack periscope to observe the target and to estimate its size, speed, heading, and draught, passing this information verbally to the 1WO who was with him. Surface engagements, however, were normally conducted by the 1WO, using a special sight mounted on the bridge.

For a submerged attack, the U-boat commander had to locate the target through the attack periscope and then estimate its speed and course relative to his boat, passing the information to the officer (usually the 1WO), operating the torpedo computer as he did so. The required inputs included: torpedo speed; estimated range; estimated target angle on bow; estimated target speed; and a correction factor for the rate of swing of the target. The computer then calculated the director angle, convergence, shot angle, and extreme range, and transmitted the shot angle to the 'shot angle receiver' in the torpedo compartment.

During such an attack the captain had to balance a number

of contradictory factors:

• The more observations he made and the longer they lasted, the better would be the fire control resolution; but the greater the exposure, the more likely it was that the periscope would be detected by the enemy.

• Torpedoes were slow: steam-driven – 40 knots; most electrical – 30 knots; acoustic torpedoes – 24 knots. As a result, the fire control resolution had to predict where the target would be, provided it continued on its present course at a constant speed, by the time the torpedo could reach it.

• Almost all surface vessels, except perhaps extremely slow convoys or already-damaged ships, were faster than a submerged U-boat, which meant that the U-boat needed to be ahead of the target before the engagement started.

• The more torpedoes launched the greater the probability of a hit, but the number of torpedoes carried was strictly limited and resupply at sea, while possible, could not always be arranged, and in any case was very dangerous.

• At the start of the war the torpedoes ran in a straight line from the tube, but then new equipment enabled them to make one alteration of course after leaving the tubes. From 1943, however, new guidance systems came into service which enabled the torpedoes to perform search patterns which considerably enhanced their possibilities of a hit.

• A further factor was to select the right torpedo for the job, which became increasingly complicated as the war progressed. Thus, in the early days of the war each U-boat's load of torpedoes was a simple matter, consisting of either *G7a* or *G7b*, but in May 1943 *BdU* laid down that the load for a Type VIIC would be:

* Forward: four *T I FaT I* (*G7a*) plus six *T III* (*G7e*).
* Aft: two *T III FaT II* (*G7e*).

By April the following year this had changed to:

* Forward: three *T V* (*G7es*) (*Zaunkönig*) plus either five *LuT* or two *FaT I* plus three *FaT II*.
* Aft: two *T V* (*G7es*) (*Zaunkönig*).

The figures given for torpedoes' maximum ranges were misleading because, in practice, engagements against individual ships rarely took place at such ranges. In the early part of the war launching range was usually under 1,000yd (914m), but from 1943 onwards this increased to 2-3,000yd (1,830-2,740m) or more, partly due to the introduction of torpedoes with more sophisticated search patterns, but mainly due to the ever-greater effectiveness of Allied ASW tactics. When faced by a mass of ships in a convoy, however, a U-boat could launch one or more random shots at the densest mass of shipping in a convoy in the hope that it would find a target.

SUBMERGED ENGAGEMENTS

When Type IA and Type II U-boats entered service in the mid-1930s, they used methods virtually identical to those used in 1918, with the 1WO employing tables and a special disc calcula-

▽ The careful preparation of a torpedo, supervised by a chief petty officer (right rear, peaked cap). Grease is applied to ensure that it will leave the tube cleanly and smoothly.

tor to work out angles from the data passed to him by the captain. He then transmitted the relevant information orally to the bow and stern torpedo rooms. As the torpedoes could not be angled, the whole boat had to be aimed-off at an angle calculated by the director, while a spread was achieved by swinging the boat. The order to launch was passed orally to the chief torpedomen in the bow and stern torpedo compartments, who then pulled the launch lever on each tube in turn.

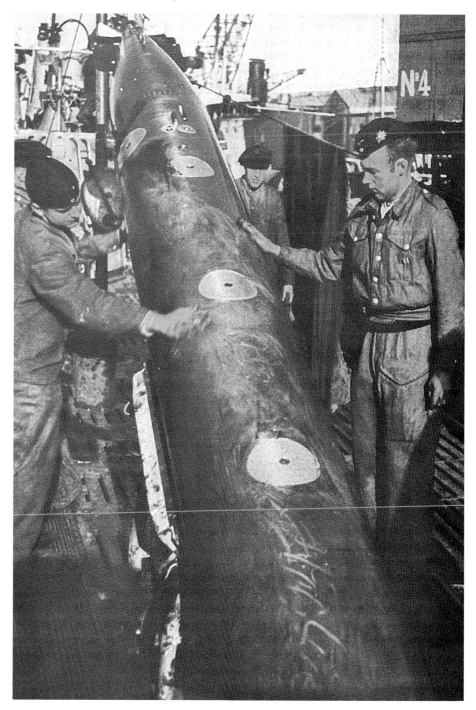

The entry into service of the first Type VIIs and IXs in 1938 coincided with the advent of gyroscope angling for the torpedoes (+/-90 degrees either side of dead-ahead in 1 degree steps) and a new director angle computer (*T.Vh.Re.S.1*) was installed to manage this.[12] Inputs to the computer were: the captain's estimates of target range, speed and its angle to the U-boat's bow; the selected torpedo speed; and any corrections for the U-boat's swing. From these the computer calculated director angle, convergence, shot angle, and maximum range, and transmitted the shot angle to a visual indicator in the bow and stern torpedo rooms. The chief torpedomen watched these indicators and then set the gyro angle manually on each tube.

At first the convergence calculator and director angle calculating clock were separate, but in 1939 some minor changes were made to the director angle computer to incorporate both of these in the main computer. The new device was designated the *T.Vh.Re.S.2*.

Early combat experience showed a number of deficiencies in the systems, which were considered to be over-complicated, and with too many minor differences between the equipments fitted into different types of U-boat. It was also felt necessary to incorporate a greater degree of automation, by enabling the gyro angle to be set remotely from the control room, for example, rather than by hand in the torpedo room. Finally, it was known that *FaT* and *LuT* guidance systems would soon come into service and there was a need to ensure that there was space in the computers to install the new gears.

This new equipment, the *T.Vh.Re.S.3.*, was rather complicated and, since equipment in the conning tower was usually affected by damp, it was relocated to the main control room (*Zentral*) below the conning tower. This required a transmitting

△ In the forward torpedo room the *Torpedomaat* (petty officer with headphones, left) receives orders from the 1WO in the conning tower: 'Tube 2 — prepare! Open tube cap!' When all preparations are complete the *Torpedomaat* reports, 'Tube 2, ready.' The final order is '*Rohr 2 — los*' ('Tube 2 — fire!') and then the crew counts the seconds until the expected detonation against the target.

panel in the conning tower to enable the captain to input the necessary data, and he was also provided with a control panel to enable him to monitor the settings in the system. Firing was also controlled from the conning tower, with an automatic delay of 2.3 seconds between launches in a spread.

A simplified mechanical director angle computer was designed for installation in the Type XVII Walter boat, but this did not enter service. However, the design was adapted and improved for use aboard the Type XXIII coastal boat, in which it was designated the *T.Vh.RGM 3D*.

SURFACE ENGAGEMENTS

On the surface the engagement was normally conducted by the 1WO and in the Types IA and II he used the *Torpedo U-boot Ziel Apparat No.1* (*TUZA 1*) (= U-boat torpedo aiming device), which was slow and complicated to use and, as an additional complication, had to be removed and carried below every time the U-boat submerged. A slightly improved version was produced by Carl Zeiss of Jena in 1936, of which the first variant, *TUZA 2*, was not watertight (and also had to be removed when the U-boat dived) but this was overcome in the *TUZA 3*, which was watertight to 300ft (90m).

In 1939 a new bridge sight was brought into service, again designed by Carl Zeiss of Jena, which was designated the *Uboot-Zieloptik* (U-boat target optical sight). There were two versions: *UZO 1* for Type VIIs and *UZO II* for Type IXs, the latter sight being identical to the *UZO 1* except that it was mounted on a plinth because the Type IX bridge screens were higher. A *TUZA 3*, which could be fitted on the *UZO* mounting, was still carried as a reserve in case the *UZO* was damaged in a depth-charge attack.

The *UZO*, however, suffered from a number of disadvantages. It was complicated and too many minor variations were allowed, making it difficult to use and requiring a lot of specialized instruction at the training schools. In addition, the bridge screens limited it to +/-110 degrees. The *UZO* also leaked if the U-boat dived below 300ft (90m), which was happening more often as the Allied ASW capability increased. Therefore, a new system was developed and, four competing designs from different companies having been assessed, the Siemens *UZS 4* was selected. This was fitted with a pair of Zeiss 10 x 80 binoculars.

INSTALLATIONS

To summarize, in September 1939 all Type VIIs and Type IXs in service had the following torpedo control gear:
- attack periscope;
- *UZO* surface sight (*UZO 2a, 2b, 2c*, or *2d*);
- *TUZA 3* surface sight (as reserve for *UZO*);
- director angle computer (*T.Vh.Re.S.2*);
- shot and spread angle indicators in bow and stern torpedo rooms;
- gyro angling gear (one on each tube, manually set).

The new range of equipment was first fitted into a Type VIIC,

U-69, in 1940 and from December 1941 it was installed in all new-build boats and retrofitted into existing boats (except Types IA and II) during routine refits. It was also installed in Type IIDs (*U-137* to *U-152*). All these boats had:

- attack periscope;
- *UZS 4* surface sight;
- director angle computer (*T.Vh.Re.S.3*);
- shot and spread angles *were* transmitted direct to the torpedo gyroscope (ie, there was no manual involvement in the torpedo rooms);
- a captain's control box fitted in the conning tower.

The torpedo control system then remained virtually unchanged for the remainder of the war, except for the director angle computer *S.3* (*T.Vh.Re.S.3*), a modified version of the *T.Vh.Re.S.2*, which included the new computer gears required when using the new torpedoes equipped with *FaT* and *LuT* guidance systems.

IN RETROSPECT

The German torpedo program offered greater promise than achievement. The greatest single shortcoming was the failure to carry out realistic trials in the pre-war period, which resulted in defective guidance systems, pistols, and depth-keeping. As a result, U-boat commanders lost many opportunities in the years 1939–43. The second major criticism is that in the last 2–3 years of the war there was an uncoordinated (almost uncontrolled) plethora of torpedo projects both within the *Kriegsmarine* and between the *Kriegsmarine* and the *Luftwaffe*. The latter, astonishingly, was allowed to take aerial torpedo design and development away from the Navy in 1943. A further potential problem was that, despite the terrible lesson of the lack of pre-war trials, many of the late-war projects were rushed into production without proper trials (sometimes without any trials at all), although, fortunately for the U-boat captains, the war came to an end before the consequences of this became obvious.

Footnotes:
1. The battery was designated 13T210.
2. The battery installation in the *G7e* was designated 13T210.
3. The British later captured a number of *G7e*s, one of which was passed to the United States. Both countries 'reverse engineered' the *G7e*, which later entered service as the British Mark XI and the US Mark 18, although only the American torpedo saw operational service in the war.
4 Known to the Allied navies as 'Curly.'
5 The reduction compared wih other warheads was due to the increased space taken up by the acoustic head.
6 It was known to the Allies as GNAT (German Navy Acoustic Torpedo).
7 The range was slightly less if the batteries had not been pre-heated prior to launch.
8 This was done by setting the latitude correction to the maximum since there was no cut-out switch.
9 This whole affair had an uncanny parallel in the US Navy. This, too, suffered many torpedo malfunctions in the period 1942–43, which the torpedo specialists blamed on faulty operational procedures but which turned out, in the end, to have been due to lax testing, gross over-optimism, and excessive security during peacetime.
10 It was originally designated *Boje* (= buoy).
11 It did not have a 'T' number.
12 These 'computers' used gears and mechanical linkages to carry out calculations; they were not electronic computers in the modern sense.

MINES

The *Kaiserlichemarine* made extensive use of submarine-laid mines during World War I; its successor, the *Kriegsmarine*, sought to repeat that in World War II. Two approaches were taken, the first being to design mines which could fit inside a standard 21in (533mm) torpedo tube. Designated *Torpedomine* (*TM*), these, in effect, made every U-boat a potential minelayer. The second was to produce mines of maximum effectiveness, but not limited to the 21in (533mm) diameter, which meant that specialized minelayers would be required, fitted with some form of dispensing system, which, in the event, was vertical shafts, hence the name, *Schachtmine* (*SM*) (*schacht* = shaft).

Choosing between the two systems was a matter of balancing advantages. *TMA*s could be launched by any attack submarine. On the other hand, they displaced torpedoes, thus reducing the submarine's primary attack weapon. It also meant that any minefield that was laid was very small. The specialized minelayer carried many more mines of a more powerful type, but carried only a very limited number of torpedoes and was not very suitable for employment as an attack boat. For both types, one of the major problems was that mines needed to be laid in relatively shallow water and in places where enemy vessels were likely to pass, which meant that the minelaying boats were particularly vulnerable.

TORPEDOMINE A (TMA)

The *TMA*, developed in the 1930s, was a moored mine, which meant that it included an anchor and cable which were fairly heavy, and a buoyancy chamber, which took up a lot of volume. As a result, the *TMA* contained a relatively small charge: 474lb (215kg). *TMA* was 11.1ft (3.38m) long, 21in (533mm) in diame-

▽ On Cherbourg beach, in France, July 1944, two members of a US mine disposal team prepare a German mine for destruction by burning. This *SMA* mine was laid by a U-boat to disrupt the D-Day invasion traffic, but had broken loose and washed ashore.

ter, and two could be carried in each torpedo tube. It could be laid in depths of up to 886ft (270m).

TORPEDOMINE B (TMB)

The *TMB* was a ground mine which could be laid in waters up to 66ft (20m) deep and, it being only 7.6ft (2.3m) long, three could be carried in each 21in (533mm) torpedo tube. The complete *TMB* weighed 1,631lb (740kg), of which 1,280lb (580kg) was the explosive charge. The mine could be detonated by either magnetic or acoustic sensors.

TORPEDOMINE C (TMC)

In the early weeks of the war it was discovered that the *TMB* was not sinking as many targets as it should. This led to the *TMC*, which was developed very quickly in November 1939 and which contained virtually twice the amount of explosive: 2,204lb (1,000kg). This was achieved by lengthening the mine to 11.12ft (3.39m), reducing the numbers to two per torpedo tube, as with the *TMA*. Detonation was either magnetic or acoustic.

SCHACHTMINE-A (SMA)

Like the *TMA*, the *SMA* was a moored mine, but considerably larger, with a length of 7.1ft (2.15m) and a diameter of 4.4ft (1.33m). It weighed 3,527lb (1,600kg), of which the explosive charge was 771lb (350kg). Maximum laying depth was 886ft (250m).

These mines required the detonating mechanism to be set just before they were laid and one of the original problems facing the designers in the early 1930s was that this had to be done directly by hand. This necessitated 'dry storage' in which the mines were held in an accessible store and then laid by means of a moving belt. However, the problem of setting the mines in a 'wet store' was resolved, enabling them to be launched from vertical tubes.

EINHEITSMINE SEHROHR-TREIBMINE (EMS)

The *Einheitsmine Sehrohr-Treibmine* (= standard mine/drifting) was a tube-launched mine which entered service in late 1943. It was designed to float on the surface, moving with the current, and to explode on contact with a target. It became active 10 minutes after launching and sank automatically 72 hours later. It carried 31lb (14kg) of explosive.

MINETORPEDO-A (MTA)

The *Minetorpedo-A* was developed to replace the *TMA* and was, in essence, a torpedo with a mine warhead, which was intended to overcome the problem of the vulnerability of U-boats when laying ground mines in shallow waters. A stand-off weapon, the *MTA* could be programmed to run to any distance up to a maximum of 7,655yd (7,000m) in 220yd (200m) increments. On arriving at the set distance, the motor switched off and the torpedo sank to the bottom where it acted as a ground mine. It had to be used in water less than 66ft (20m) deep for maximum effect.

▷ Overhead view of a 105mm gun aboard an unidentified Type IX U-boat. Full designation of the gun was '10.5cm *Schiffs Kanone C/32 in 8.8cm Marine Pivot Lafette C/30D*" (105mm Ship's Cannon, Model C/32, in 88mm Naval Mounting, Model C/30D). The wooden strips were intended to provide grips for the guncrewmen's feet on a wet deck.

SURFACE GUNS

Early submarines in all navies were armed only with torpedo tubes but the Imperial German Navy started to install guns from the *U-19* class onwards. These were principally intended for use as defensive weapons against small surface vessels, for which a torpedo was not a suitable weapon. In World War I, however, it was discovered that guns could also be used in surface actions against merchant ships, to save torpedoes in a surface action, first to force the targets to stop and subsequently to sink them. Thus, calibers grew from 88mm to 105mm, while the 'U-cruisers' were fitted with two 150mm guns. Whatever the caliber, however, there was no escaping the fact that a submarine was a poor gun platform, since it rolled a lot and the seas frequently washed over the weather deck which became slippery and hazardous. Indeed, the gun crew were normally secured by life lines to prevent them being washed overboard. Also, there was no range-finder; as a result, most gun engagements took place at very short range.

The idea of a 'U-cruiser' was resurrected in the 1930s with the Type XI. This would have had a submerged displacement of 3,930 tons and been armed with two twin 127mm guns, plus two 37mm and one 20mm anti-aircraft weapons (plus an Arado 231 aircraft). This ambitious design was canceled, however.

The crew on the foredeck gun itself comprised three men – aimer, layer and loader – but ammunition supply was a major problem. There were a few rounds in a water-tight, ready-use locker under the deck-plates next to the gun, but if more rounds were required a chain of men had to be set up, passing rounds from the magazine, which was below the control room floor, and then up

U-BOAT SURFACE GUNS		
Full title	8.8cm *Schiffskanone* C/35 *in Unterseebootslafette* C/35	10.5cm *Schiffskanone* C/32 in 8.8cm Marine Pivot Lafette C/30D
Short title	8.8cm SK C/35 in Ubts LC/35	10.5cm SK C/32 in 8.8cm MPL C/30D
Mounted in	Types VIIA, -B, -C, -C/41, -D, -F	Types IA, IX (except IXD), XB
Caliber	88mm (3.46in)	105mm (4.13in)
Breech	Semi-automatic	Semi-automatic
Traverse	360°	360°
Elevation	−4° to 30°	−3° to 30°
AMMUNITION High explosive	Weight (complete round)	30.11lb (13.7kg)	51.4lb (23.3kg)
	Muzzle velocity	2,297f/s (700m/s)	2,576f/s (785m/s)
	Range	13,500yd (12,350m)	16,787yd (15,350m)
Armor piercing	Weight	30.7lb (13.9kg)	51.8lb (23.3kg)
Star shell	Weight	24.7lb (11.2kg)	32.4lb (14.7kg)

△ A scene known to every serviceman in every nation: crews in their best uniforms stand around awaiting the arrival of a senior officer. In the foreground is *U-38*, a Type IXA, armed with a 105mm gun. These guns had identical controls on each side for ease of handling in action. Note also the tampion in the muzzle, which had to be removed before going into action.

the main trunk to the bridge, and over the coaming to the deck.

U-boats were very vulnerable when carrying out a gun action, not least because, if taken by surprise, the requirement to secure the gun and ammunition and to get the men below meant that it took much longer than usual to submerge. Thus, guns could be

used only where the captain felt that the situation permitted it and, as the range and capability of Allied air power increased, those opportunities became fewer. A further factor was that the gun exerted a significant hydrodynamic drag, contributing greatly to the slow underwater speed, while its weight and high position contributed to the rolling of the boats on the surface.

It was decided in April 1943 not to install any further 88mm guns in new-build U-boats and to remove the guns from Type VIIs in service, except those operating in special areas such as the Gulf of Finland. The majority of Type IXs, however, most of which operated in the South Atlantic and Indian Oceans, retained their 105mm guns. No large caliber gun installations were planned for any new-build U-boats after the Type XII.

Two types of surface gun were used:

8.8CM SCHIFFSKANONE C/35 IN UNTERSEEBOOTSLAFETTE C/35 (8.8CM SK C/35 IN UBTS LC/35).
The naval 88mm gun installed in Type VIIs was totaly unrelated to the famous 88mm gun used by the German Army and *Luftwaffe*, differing to such an extent that they could not use each other's ammunition. The naval gun was mounted on a low pedestal without a shield and could be laid from either side by the crew of two, who were provided with chestpads.

10.5CM SCHIFFSKANONE C/32 IN 8.8CM MARINE PIVOT LAFETTE C/30D (10.5CM SK C/32 IN 8.8CM MPL C/30D.
The 105mm gun was mounted in Type IA U-boats, all Type IXs except for the Type IXD₁ transport conversion, and the Type XB. It was a simplified version of the 10.5cm naval dual-purpose (anti-ship, anti-aircraft) weapon, mounted on an 8.8cm pedestal, to economize on deck area. There was no gun shield.

ANTI-AIRCRAFT ARMAMENT

The U-boat was at its most vulnerable to air attack if it was caught in the act of diving, and standing orders from *BdU* were not to dive under these circumstances unless the commander was sure he could reach a depth of more than 197ft (60m) by the time the aircraft arrived overhead. If not, he was to stay on the surface and fight it out. As the war progressed, however, Allied aircraft became much faster and appeared so suddenly that it became necessary to have a more effective weapon, and the number and caliber of such weapons increased steadily.

At the start of the war virtually all U-boats had an anti-aircraft armament of a single 2cm *Flak* cannon (*Flak* = *Flugzeugabwehrkanone*), which was usually sited on the casing, either before the bridge (Type IIA and IID), or immediately abaft the bridge (Type VIIA). This had several disadvantages: the bridge created a large dead zone; it took some time to get the gun into action; and, of even greater significance, it took some time for the crew to get inside the submarine in an emergency crash-dive. Therefore, it was decided to move the AA gun to a special platform at the after end of the bridge.

In 1942, however, Dönitz decided that a heavier air defense armament was required, although this coincided with increased demands for AA weapons from all the other German armed forces as well. In the *Ubootwaffe*, trials with both quadruple and

◁△ A 20mm anti-aircraft mounting aboard *U-506*, a Type IXC.

△ Twin *C/38 II* 20mm cannon in the very simple LM43U mounting aboard *U-889*, a Type IXC-40, at the end of the war. Surface anti-aircraft defense was a problem that was never properly solved and heavier armament, while good for crew morale, was not the best answer.

U-BOAT FLAK GUNS			
Full title		2cm *Flugabwehrkanone* C/35 in Lafette C30/37	3.7cm *Flugabwehrkanone* M/42
Short title		2cm Flak 38	3.7cm Flak M 42
Mounted in		Types VIIC, VIIC/41, IX	Types VIIC, VIIC/41, IX
Caliber		20mm (0.79in)	37mm (1.46in)
Breech		Automatic	Automatic
Traverse		360°	360°
Elevation		−2° to +90°	−10° to 80°
AMMUNITION High explosive	Weight (complete (round)	0.711lb (0.32kg)	1.61lb (0.73kg)
	Rate of fire cyclic practical	420–480rpm 220–240rpm	n.k. 50rpm
	Range	13,500yd (12,350m)	16,787yd (15,350m)

twin 20mm mountings had been very successful but, as a result of delays, the first two quadruple 20mm mountings were not fitted until May 1943 and the first twins were not mounted until mid-July. Also, in June a new 20mm shell became available, named *Minengeschoss* (mine shell) which not only was filled with three times the explosive of previous shells but, in addition, the explosive itself, *Hexogen*, was new and much more powerful.

Problems were also encountered with the new 37mm automatic gun which was installed from December 1943 onwards. This proved to be very susceptible to stoppages, many of them attributable to poor workmanship. In addition, the material proved very sensitive to sea-water, which made it necessary to conduct frequent maintenance and test firings. By that stage of the war, however, captains would surface to charge their batteries only at night, and even then they were extra cautious and would not allow artificers to use lights to work on the guns, while there was little value in trying to range the guns in the dark. A great variety of weapons and installations appeared from 1942 onwards but by 1944 it was appreciated that U-boats were unlikely to win a surface engagement with an aircraft, although *Flak* weapons continued to be fitted, even in the Type XXI.

2CM FLUGABWEHRKANONE C/30 IN LAFETTE C 30/37. (2CM FLAK 30)

The Rheinmetall 2cm *Flak 30* entered *Kriegsmarine* service in the early 1930s. It was a recoil-operated weapon and was, in effect, a large machine gun. It had two triggers, side-by-side; the left for automatic, the right for single shots. It fired a variety of fixed rounds, most with tracer. The effective rate of fire was 120 rounds per minute.

2CM FLUGABWEHRKANONE C/30 IN LAFETTE C 30/37. 2CM FLAK 38

The 2cm *Flak 38* was developed by Mauser and was, in essence, a 2cm *Flak 30* with an improved bolt, accelerator, and return spring, which doubled the rate-of-fire. Otherwise it was identical to the *Flak 30* and used the same range of ammunition. This weapon was also produced in a twin version (*Flakzwilling*) with a practical rate of fire of approximately 400rpm, and a quadruple (*Flakvierling*) version, which fired approximately 800rpm.

3.7CM FLUGABWEHRKANONE M/42 (3.7CM FLAK M 42)

The final gun to be developed for U-boats was the 3.7cm *Flak M 42*, which was a navalized version of an army weapon. It was considerably more effective than the 2cm *Flak 38*, since it fired a much heavier shell to a much greater range, although the cyclic rate-of-fire was considerably lower.

ROCKETS AND MISSILES

The idea of launching rockets from U-boats originated in 1941 with a chance conversation between *Korvetten-Kapitän* Fritz Steinhoff, commanding officer of *U-551*, and his brother *Doktor* Ernst Steinhoff, a civilian employed at the rocket research establishment at Peenemünde. Their idea led to some 'unofficial' tests in the summer of 1942 using a wooden frame (actually a *Schweres Wurfgerät 41* [= heavy launcher

model 41]) which carried six 30cm *Wurfkörper 42 Spreng* (= rockets model 42), a type then under development at Peenemünde. The launches were successful, both on the surface and when submerged at a depth of 40ft (12m). Dönitz knew about these tests and expressed interest in the use of such rockets against convoy escorts, but the idea was dropped.

PROJECT URSEL

Project Ursel, which may have been a further development of the tests just described, was a missile intended to be launched from a U-boat against a pursuing surface vessel. The detection element, the *SP-Anlage*, was ready first and demonstrated its ability to detect and locate propeller noise with great accuracy and then, using the U-boat's known depth, to work out the target's precise position. This detection system was capable of working at ranges up to five times the U-boat's depth and was installed in late production Type XXIs. The missiles, however, were still under development when the war ended.

◁ Tests were carried out in May/June 1942 firing 30cm rockets from wooden frames mounted on the upper deck of *U-511* (Type IXC). Both surface and submerged launches (left) were successful, but the frame degraded the boat's underwater performance and the idea was dropped. A different idea (above) was to mount a *V-2* missile in a floating transporter/launcher barge, which would be towed submerged across the Atlantic by a Type XXI. On arrival, the barge would be flooded until it was vertical, the bow doors opened and the missile fueled, the guidance system set and then launched. (The figures of men in the launcher are intended to indicate scale.) It is doubtful that the system could have been made to work with the technology of the time, but the concept was sound and led to the US and Soviet ballistic missile submarines of the 1950s.

THE WURFKÖRPER ROCKET

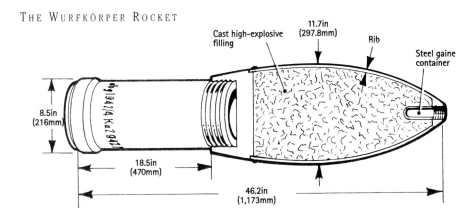

△ The *30cm Wurfkörper 42 Spreng* (Rocket, Model 42) that was used in the 1942 experiments.

V-1

The first of the Third Reich's *Vergeltungswaffen* (= vengeance weapons) was the Fieseler *V-1* (Fi-103), flying bomb, an unmanned, straight-wing aircraft, powered by a pulse-jet, which cruised at 360mph (580kmh) over a range of 148 miles (238km). It was designed to be launched from a ramp at a land site, but the possibility of U-boat launches against remote targets such as New York was considered in July 1943. However, the *V1* was a *Luftwaffe* weapon and the proposition was rejected by the *Reichsluftministerium* (= air ministry) and never resurrected.[1]

V-2

An entirely different project concerned the *V-2* (A-4) ballistic missile and originated with a suggestion from a civilian director of the *Deutsche Arbeitsfront* (German Labor Front) who attended a demonstration of the *V-2* at Peenemünde in 1943. Immediately afterwards he proposed that the missile be placed in a watertight container, towed across the Atlantic by U-boat and launched against New York.

The staff at Peenemünde took this extraordinary proposal seriously but were unable to devote any time to it until late 1944, when it was given the code-name '*Prüfstand XII*' (= test stand 12). The containers were to be approximately 105ft (32m) long, to displace 500 tons and contain one *V-2* rocket each, plus a control room and fuel tanks. The plan was for three such containers to be towed by a single Type XXI U-boat, with the containers being kept submerged by the forward speed of the U-boat. At least one container in each trio would have carried, in addition to the missile and its fuel, a quantity of diesel fuel to resupply the U-boat in the course of its voyage across the Atlantic.

On arrival at the launch position the U-boat would surface and stop, whereupon the containers would automatically float to the surface. Two men would then board each container and open valves to fill the ballast tanks, thus bringing the container to the vertical. Having connected an electrical supply from the U-boat, the men would then enter the control room where they would fuel the missile, set the gyroscopic guidance system, and open the electrically operated doors. When all was ready for launch the two men would return to the submarine, and launch was to be initiated from a remote control aboard the U-boat, with ducts turning the rocket efflux through 180 degrees up the sides of the container and then out into the atmosphere.

German records for late 1944/early 1945 are inevitably incomplete, but it appears that a contract for three prototype containers was placed with Vulkanwerft in December 1944 and that least one was produced. Plans were also made for Blohm+Voss to convert a U-boat, but no actual tests of the system took place.

The system would have been inaccurate, but the effect of a sudden attack by even one or two missiles on New York would have been devastating. The Allies already had intelligence through Ultra about a possible *V-2* attack on New York and had prepared a contingency plan to deal with it. In early March 1945, therefore, when they detected six U-boats in a group, plus at least four others sailing individually, heading westwards across the Atlantic, they assumed that an attack was under way and started 'Operation Teardrop' to counter it. Four U-boats were sunk but the remainder got though, although it transpired that this was not the anticipated missile attack. Nevertheless, the strength of the US response indicates that the possibility of such an attack was taken very seriously.

THE MYSTERY OF U-1053

In an incident which has never been fully explained, *U-1053* (Type VIIC), was lost off the Norwegian coast on February 15 1945, which is attributed by some authorities to 'deep diving trials' and by others to 'rocket trials.' Why a Type VIIC should have been involved in diving tests at such a late point in the war is not apparent. On the other hand, if rocket trials were being carried out it is not known which rockets were being tested.

ANTI-AIRCRAFT ROCKETS

Experiments were conducted in 1942 with a 3.4in (8.6cm) anti-aircraft rocket, which deployed a length of cable when launched. The idea was that a U-boat would launch a number of rockets when under attack and that the cables would snag on the aircraft's wings and tailplane, causing the aircraft either to crash or to abort the attack. At the very least, it would spoil the pilot's aim. This was trialled aboard *U-441*, but was judged a failure and not pursued further. A further proposal was to install high-explosive warheads in the rockets, which would be aimed straight at the attacking aircraft; but, despite intensive development and trials in late 1943, this, too, was dropped.[2]

Footnotes:
1. After the war the US Navy combined a Japanese-designed shelter on the after deck of a submarine with a German-designed F-103 missile (known in the US as Loon) to produce a fully feasible system.
2. Britain's Royal Navy developed two similar anti-aircraft weapons at around the same time: one was the FAM (Fast Aerial Mine), the other the PAC (parachute and cable) rocket. Both were widely deployed in 1943-45, particularly aboard landing-craft, but, so far as is known, did not achieve any successes.

SAIL SENSORS AND WEAPONS

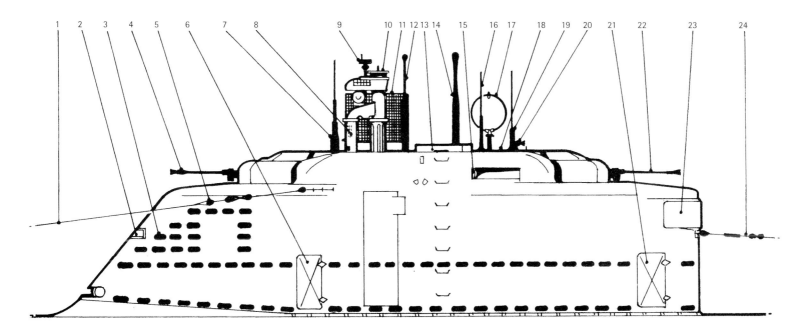

SENSORS

RADAR

Radar was one of the newest and most exciting areas of technological development in the late 1930s, with both the Germans and the Western Allies carrying out a great deal of work. The British appreciated the potential value of airborne radar in the anti-submarine battle as this would enable an aircraft to operate unaffected by conditions of visibility and to cover large areas of sea. Then, once a contact had been made, the radar could be used to direct the aircraft towards its target. The first such Anti-Surface Vessel (ASV) radar was introduced in Allied aircraft in early 1941. U-boat commanders quickly became aware that aircraft were appearing too often for their presence to be due to visual sightings and they concluded, correctly, that radar was to blame; after all, the *Luftwaffe* used *FuG-200 (Hohentwiel)* to good effect in their FW-200 Condor aircraft. As a result, the Germans produced a first-generation detector which enabled U-boats to know when they were being illuminated by radar.

In early 1942 an RAF Stirling bomber carrying a British Mark II ASV set, which operated at centimetric wavelengths, was brought down near Rotterdam, where the wreck was found and analyzed by the *Luftwaffe*. However, due to the single-service rivalry which existed, even in the third year of the war, the resulting report was at first issued only to *Luftwaffe* units and it was some weeks before the *Kriegsmarine* became aware of the discovery.

△ The sail of a Type XXI showing the many sensors being installed at the end of the war.
Key: **1:** HF wire antenna. **2:** Stern light. **3:** Free-flood holes. **4:** Twin 20mm cannon. **5:** Insulating links. **6:** Access door. **7:** Extending rod antenna. **8:** Diesel exhaust **9:** *Bali* antenna. **10:** *Schnorchel.* **11:** *Hohentwiel* radar array. **12:** *Standsehrorh* **13:** Watchkeeper. **14:** *Nacht-Luftziel-Seerohr* (periscope). **15:** Navigation light (starboard). **16:** Rod antenna. **17:** DF loop. **18:** Watchkeeping officer. **19:** Rod antenna. **20:** *UZO.* **21:** Twin 20mm cannon. **22:** Access door. **23:** Sonar. **24.** HF radio antenna.

Nor was the *Kriegsmarine* itself without fault and at this time it, too, suffered from bureaucratic shortcomings. When Vice-Admiral Stummel took over as head of the *Kreigsmarine*'s communications service in 1943[1] he quickly established that research and development efforts up to that point had been uncoordinated and inefficient. After discussing this with Dönitz, Professor Küpfmüller was appointed in December 1943 to take charge of all technical aspects of the electronic war. Dönitz pulled no punches in his directive which was sent to all naval commanders-in-chief, telling them that:

'…for some months past the enemy has rendered the U-boat war ineffective… I have therefore ordered the creation of a Naval Scientific Directional Staff (with) Professor Küpfmüller as head of this staff and directly subordinate to myself. Professor Küpfmüller is invested by me with all necessary authority for the execution of his duties….'[2]

Professor Küpfmüller quickly brought not only a new dynamism to the electronics world, but also introduced a far tighter and more coordinated organizational structure. Among other measures, he established 12 working parties, each covering a specified area, such as radar, intercepting enemy radar, secure communications, acoustics, infrared, ultraviolet, and extremely low frequency. Thus, from early 1944 onwards there was a much more disciplined approach to electronic matters and, while not all the working parties achieved success, many did.

One of the steps taken to get to grips with the problem was to outfit two Type VIICs – *U-406* and *U-473* – with a considerable amount of additional electronic equipment to enable them to monitor all forms of Allied radar and radio at sea. Experienced technicians were also aboard to supervize the operation, the team aboard *U-406* being headed by Dr Greven, but both voyages turned out to be total failures. *U-406* (Dieterichs) sailed on January 5 1944 and operated as part of various groups until February 18 when it was sunk by HMS *Spey*. Forty-one of the crew of 53 survived, including Dr Greven and his team; their different badges of rank meant that they were singled out for interrogation and their role was soon understood by the Allies.

A second attempt to obtain the 'on-the-spot' radar and radio information was undertaken by *U-473* (Sternberg), which sailed from Lorient on March 24 1944, also outfitted with extra equipment and carrying additional specialists. This was *U-473*'s second war cruise, but it was sunk on May 6 1944 after a long and heavy engagement, and 30 men survived, again including some members of the communications team.

Active radar, known as *Funkmessortungsgerät* (radar detection equipment) and abbreviated to *FuMO*, was installed in German surface warships from 1937 onwards, but the first proposal for a U-boat installation was not made until 1939. This involved a radar with the cover name of *DeTe-Gerät* (*Deutsches Technisches Gerät* = German technical equipment), which was tested aboard the research ship *Störtebecker* in the winter of 1939. At one point there was a suggestion that the equipment would be installed in two U-boats, presumably Type VIICs, but this never took place. Indeed, it was not until the increase in air attacks on U-boats in 1942 that radar was given any degree of urgency, and even then the sets were limited by poor power output and low frequencies until a British magnetron was captured and copied in 1943.

FuMO-29 'GEMA'

The first U-boat radar was a converted set originally fitted in surface ships. The U-boat set was designated *FuMO-29*; it used a fixed array around the front of the bridge, consisting of two horizontal rows of six dipoles each, the upper row for transmitting, the lower for receiving. The transmit antennas were divided into port and starboard groups of three each and were energized in turn, in a very early form of phase-shifting. This gave a coverage of about 10 degrees each side of the bows, which could be increased by altering course or even by turning the U-boat in a complete circle. The set operated at 382MHz and range was approximately 8,200yd (7,500m) against surface targets and 16,400yd (15,000m) against an aircraft flying at a height of 1,640ft (500m). *FuMO-29* was installed beginning in 1942 in a few Type VIIs (eg, *U-230*) and a number of Type IXs (eg, *U-156*). *FuMO-29* was often referred to by the crews as the '*GEMA*,' the name of the company that produced it.

FuMO-30

The next radar installation involved the same set, but with a new rotatable antenna, which was mounted on the port side of the

bridge and retracted into an oblong housing. This was designated *FuMO-30*. The antenna array consisted of a tubular steel rectangle covered with a wire mesh and with four pairs of dipoles on the front face and two 'figure-of-eight' antennas on the rear face. This antenna was rotated by a mechanical linkage from a handwheel in the *Funkraum* (= radio room) below.

FuMO-61 Hohentwiel/FuMO-64 Hohentwiel-Drauf

The *Kriegsmarine* looked urgently for a more effective replacement for the *GEMA* set and selected the *Luftwaffe*'s *FuMG-200 Hohentwiel*, which was used in the Focke-Wulf FW-200 Condor maritime patrol aircraft as a ship detection set. This was adapted for U-boat use as the *FuMO-61* '*Hohentwiel-U*' with a mattress-type antenna 4.9ft (1.5m) wide and 3.3ft (1m) high. There were four rows, each of six dipoles. Operating frequency was 556MHz and maximum range was approximately 12.4 miles (20km) against low-flying aircraft and about 4.3 miles (7km) against ships. The first set was installed in a U-boat in March 1944 and by September 64 Type VIIs and IXs had been fitted. A slightly modified set – *FuMO-64* '*Hohentwiel Drauf*' – was installed in Type XXI boats.

△ The sound cabinet aboard *U-889*, showing the operator's display and control wheel. *U-889* was a Type IXC/40. Its first patrol began on April 5 1945 and its mission was to harass shipping off New York Harbor, but en route the surrender was broadcast, and it was spotted by an RCAF Liberator on May 10 flying the black flag. The Canadian Navy inspected (and photographed) it closely, and commissioned it into their service in 1945, but it was transferred to the US Navy in 1946 and it was scuttled in 1947.

FuMO-391 Lessing

The air-warning set, *FuMO-391 Lessing*, was developed for use in the Type XXI, where it used the '*runddipol*' antenna atop the *schnorchel*. *Lessing* indicated the presence of an aircraft but not its height or bearing. Range on a surfaced U-boat was given as approximately 10,900yd (10,000m) against low-flying aircraft and approximately 18 miles (30km) against aircraft flying at 6,560ft (2,000m). It could also be used when the U-boat was *schnorchelling*, but the range was much less: approximately 13,200yd (12,070m) for an aircraft at 3,300ft (1,000m).

HYDROPHONES

It had long been known that sound travels great distances underwater and sound detection devices, 'hydrophones,' had been installed in submarines since World War I. These enabled submarines to detect sources of noise, particularly propellers, and to establish the approximate direction (but not the range), and had the significant bonus of being passive.

Gruppenhorchgerät (GHG)

The *GHG* (= group listening device), which was installed in U-boats from 1935 onwards, consisted of a group of hydrophones, which were mounted in two arcs, one on each side of the bows. Each hydrophone was connected to an electronic timing circuit in the *Funkraum* where the operator made adjustments to obtain the maximum reading, enabling him to establish the direction of the source. The *GHG* originally had 11 hydrophones each side, but this was later increased to 24 to give greater sensitivity and accuracy. However, the hydrophone arrays were fixed, which meant that the system was most effective when dealing with sound sources on the beam and its accuracy decreased rapidly with sources ahead or astern. The range depended on the ambient acoustic properties of the water but, given favorable conditions, single ships could be detected at about 11nm (20km) and convoys at about 54nm (100km).

Kristalldrehbasisgerät (KDB)

The *KDB* (= crystal rotating base device), which was installed in Type VIICs and Type IXCs, was introduced in an effort to improve on the performance of the *GHG* and could give a reading with an accuracy, under favorable conditions, of ±1 degrees. The sensor itself was T-shaped; the cross-piece, some 19.7in (500mm) long, contained six crystal receivers. The *KDB* was located on the upper casing just forward of the capstan and could be rotated from within the U-boat. It suffered from two disadvantages; it could not be used when the U-boat was traveling at high speeds and it was vulnerable to damage from depth-charges.

Balkon Gerät

The *Balkon Gerät* (= balcony apparatus), usually known simply as '*Balkon*' was an improved version of *GHG*, and was first tested in

△ *Balkon Gerät* (balcony apparatus, seen here on *U-889*) consisted of 48 hydrophones in a circular dome at the forefoot. Range varied with sea conditions, but was claimed to be 10,940yd (10,000m) against a destroyer-sized target, with an accuracy of plus/minus 2 degrees.

a Type IXC in 1943. This was a cylindrical device installed at the foot of the stem, in which 48 hydrophones were installed. Coupled with greatly improved electronics, this gave a major improvement in performance compared to the *GHG*, and covered an arc ±170 degrees. *Balkon* was a standard fit in the Type XXI and was also installed in a small number of Type VIICs in 1944-45. Range varied with speed, weather, and sea-state but, as a guide, was stated to be 10,940yd (10,000m) against destroyers and 6,500yd (6,000m) against merchant vessels, with an accuracy of ±2 degrees.

Torpedowarn – und Anzeigegerät (TAG)

The *TAG* (= torpedo-warning and indicating device) was developed later in the war for installation in the Type XXI and later U-boats. It used two receivers in the *Balkon* device, which were connected through special circuits to two loudspeakers, one in the conning tower, the other in the sound room. This device detected unusual noises, such as incoming torpedoes, and gave audible warnings. U-boats were issued with specially prepared gramophone discs in order to train its crews to recognize the various noises which might be detected by the *TAG*.

Sondergerät für aktive Schallortung (S-Gerät)

The *S-Gerät* (= special device for active sound location) was, as its name implies, an active system, transmitting pulses and using the received echoes to locate underwater objects such as enemy submarines. However, it transmitted 20 millisecond pulses at a frequency of 15kHz with an output power of 5 kilowatts, which were easy for an enemy to detect. It was therefore seldom used. It covered an arc of ±120 degrees and, subject to sea-state and weather, had an estimated range of 4,380yd (4,000m) against surface vessels, with an accuracy of ±2 degrees.

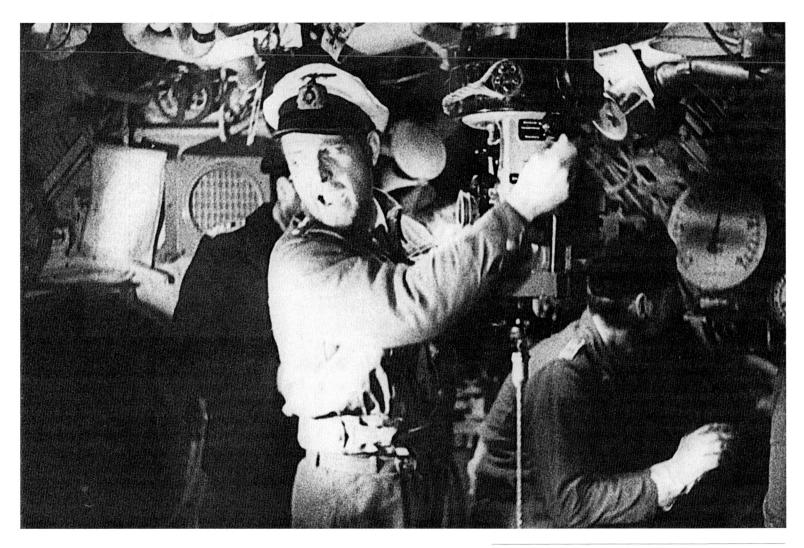

SONDERAPPARAT FÜR UBOOTE (SU-APPARAT)

The *SU-Apparat* (= special apparatus for U-boats), also known as '*Nibelung*,' was an improved type of active/passive device, which required only a few pulses to locate the position and approximate speed of a target. It was originally intended for the Type VIIC/42, but was eventually installed in the Type XXI in a special installation on the forward edge of the bridge, which (due to screening) prevented its use aft. In this installation the passive mode was used to detect the enemy and to establish a bearing, whereupon the operator transmitted a maximum of three pulses, which were sufficient to determine the range, course and approximate speed of the target, without the target being able to gain a 'fix' on the transmitter.

The equipment had not been operationally tested by the war's end, but was estimated to have a range, depending upon a variety of factors such as sea-state, of 4,380yd (4,000m) against a 12,000grt target moving at a speed of 12 knots. Bearing accuracy was assessed as ±4 degrees and range accuracy as ±2 percent of the range taken.

△ 'Down periscope!'
A U-boat captain at an early-wartime periscope.

PERISCOPES

The periscope was the commanding officer's vital eye to the outside world. This consisted of a stainless steel tube through which ran the optical tube, with an eyepiece and prism at the foot and another prism and a lens under a protective glass plate at the head. There were two main types of periscope:

• General use: *Standsehrohr C/2*, with a fixed eye-piece, or the *Angriff-Seerohr* (ASR) *C/12* or *C/13*.

• Attack and night use: *Binokuläre Nacht-Luftziel-Seerohr* (*NLSR*); a special periscope for use at night.

*N*avigation was a problem for a U-boat using its *schnorchel* and a new type of periscope to enable the navigator to take 'fixes' was undergoing trials at the war's end. The *Standsehrohr* was very expensive and took many man-hours to produce; the *Fahrstuhl* was an effort to produce a cheaper substitute. A significant feature was that the CO sat on a bicycle-type saddle which moved up and down with the periscope.

The great majority of boats (eg, Type VII, Type IX, Type XB,

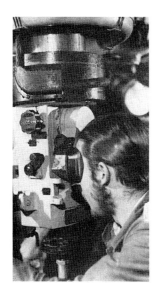

◁ *Kapitänleutnant* Adalbert Schnee using the *Binokuläre-Nach-Luftziel-Seerohr* (*NLSR*) aboard *U-201*, a Type VIIC.

▷ These helical rods were intended to change the natural frequency of the conical element of the tube to avoid resonance with the natural frequency of the eddies. The rods broke the water-flow into general turbulence. The antenna in the foreground is a *runddipol* (circular dipole).

and early Type XXIs) were fitted with one *Standsehrohr* and one *NLSR*, while the smaller boats (Type XVII, Type XXIII) had just one periscope, a shortened version of the *ASR*. Periscopes were produced by Zeiss, Jena; Askania, Berlin; and Nedinsco, in the Netherlands.

PROBLEMS WITH U-BOAT PERISCOPES

In general, there were three main problems. The most important was vibration, which arose because of the long unsupported length of the periscope when extended, when the circular tubes created eddies in the water due to the forward motion of the U-boat. For example, in the Type IXD$_2$ when a new type of 29.5ft (9.0m) periscope was fitted which had an unsupported length of 16.7ft (5.1m), the head suffered from excessive vibration at a speed of 6 knots, making it almost impossible to use. It was then discovered that the frequency of the eddies was the same as the natural resonant frequency of the tube (about 3.2 cycles per second). This was overcome by adding an extending bracket to reduce the unsupported length of the tube which increased its natural frequency to 5.8 cycles per second, thus eliminating the vibration. Similar problems were encountered with the natural resonant frequencies of the conical part of the periscope and these were eliminated by adding a number of helical wires, which broke the water flow into general turbulence without any resonating eddies.

It was obviously important that the exposed end of the tube was watertight, but it was equally important that the internal end was air tight, since any leakage of the U-boat's internal atmosphere into the tube caused fogging. This became of particular importance when *schnorchel* tubes were fitted.

Footnote:
1. His predecessor, Vice-Admiral Maertens, had been dismissed.
2. Dönitz's letter, 'Creation of a Naval Scientific Directional Staff,' dated Berlin, December 14 1943.

COUNTERMEASURES

RADAR WARNING RECEIVERS[1]

FuMB-1 'METOX'

The *Kriegsmarine* became aware in mid-1942 that British ASW aircraft were surprising U-boats crossing the Bay of Biscay and conducting very precise attacks, even at night. They concluded, correctly, that such aircraft must be equipped with VHF radar; it was, in fact, the British ASV Mk 1 (ASV = anti-surface vessel), operating in the 1.4m band. It was obviously essential that a warning device should be produced quickly and, by chance, a French electronics company, Metox-Grandin, had their R.600 VHF receiver available, large numbers of which were hastily ordered. The set was mounted in the *Funkraum* (radio room) where the operator had constantly to tune across the frequency band (1.3 to 2.6 meters). The incoming signal then generated an audible warning, which was broadcast on the boat's loudspeaker system, and the higher the frequency of the radar signal, the higher the audio frequency. This equipment came into use in August 1942 and was considered so important that an additional petty officer (later a chief petty officer) was added to the radio crew to supervize its operation.

In view of the urgency of the requirement it was not possible to fit a properly installed antenna, which would have required holes to be drilled through the pressure hull – not an easy task. So, an improvized device was supplied, consisting of a wooden cross around which were wrapped wires to provide a horizontal and vertical antenna. This had to be carried up to the bridge every time the U-boat surfaced, and mounted in a bracket installed for that purpose, with two leads trailing down the ladder to the *Funkraum*. On the order to 'crash dive' the antenna had to be dismounted and carried below and, not surprisingly, the leads could get in the way, sometimes even preventing the closure of the tower hatch and forcing the captain to order a return to the surface to allow the cables to be sorted out, usually just as the Allied aircraft came in on its attack run.

The equipment gave good warning of the approach of an ASV Mark I-equipped aircraft but, since the antenna was directional, one of the watchkeepers on the bridge had to turn it through 90 degrees at frequent intervals. The unit, officially designated *FuMB-1* (*Funkmess-Beobachtungs-Gerät* = radar observation equipment) was popularly known as '*Metox*,' while the antenna was known to the U-boat crews as the *Biskayakreuz* (= Biscay cross).

In addition to the sets deployed at sea, a land-based network of *Metox* sets was also established, with 14 sites along the French side of the English Channel coast manned by men of the navy's 2nd Radar Division. The sets were later supplemented by the more up-to-date *Samos* equipment. This network was supposed to warn of the approach of radar-equipped Allied aircraft, but the results were very disappointing.

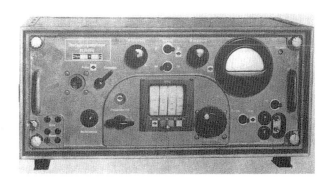

▷ *FuMB-1* (*Metox*) radar warning receiver was fitted from August 1942 onwards. It had some success, but the main problem was with the antenna.

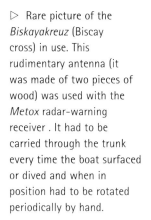

▷ Rare picture of the *Biskayakreuz* (Biscay cross) in use. This rudimentary antenna (it was made of two pieces of wood) was used with the *Metox* radar-warning receiver . It had to be carried through the trunk every time the boat surfaced or dived and when in position had to be rotated periodically by hand.

△ The central mast had a back-to-back radar-warning installation. The horn-shaped '*Mücke*' detected 3cm signals, while the parabolic '*Fliege*' covered the 8- 12cm band (see page 11). The antenna still had to be rotated by hand, and taken below every time the boat submerged.

In early 1943 it became apparent that, despite the wide-scale use of *Metox*, U-boats were again being surprised by Allied aircraft and *Kriegsmarine* technical intelligence staffs sought the reason. At first they thought that the Allies were using some form of supersonic modulation device in the operator's headset. Thus, from March 1943 onwards a device known as a 'Magic Eye' was removed from another set in the U-boat (the Telefunken Ela-10.12 'all-wave' receiver) and added to the *Metox R.600*, to give a visual indication of an incoming signal.

It quickly became clear that this was not the answer and the next suggestion (which came from the U-boat men themselves)

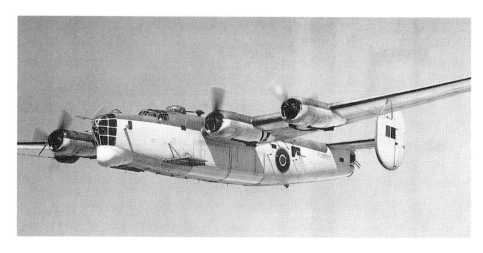

height, known simply as the *runddipol* (= round dipole).

The first few boats fitted with this equipment crossed the Bay of Biscay without incident in August 1943, but the high hopes were quickly dashed when, on September 20, *U-386* (Albrecht), was taken by surprise by an RAF Liberator without having received any warning from its *Wanze*.[3] This was followed by similar attacks on other *Wanze*-equipped boats in October, and on November 5 1943 Dönitz banned the use of *W.Anz G1* as well. It had been known from the start that *W.Anz G1* frequently overheated and radiated, so, as a result of the German fixation with the 'radiation' problem, it was superseded by the improved *W.Anz G2*, which featured improved screening to reduce spurious emissions. In the event, this was not widely used.

FuMB-10 BORKUM

By coincidence, in the week that *W. Anz G1* was banned a new and somewhat primitive stop-gap system became available. Designated *FuMB-10 'Borkum,'* this consisted of a very simple crystal amplifier, which was connected (via the gramophone socket) to the standard Radione all-band receiver in the *Funkraum*. This new equipment covered the frequency band between 3.0 to 0.75 meters, but lacked any form of tuning control and simply gave an audio warning of an incoming signal over the boat's loudspeaker system. *Borkum* had a relatively poor range. Although it covered a wider band of frequencies than the earlier sets, it still did not cover the frequency of the new British ASV Mark III. Despite its limitations, *Borkum* continued to be installed up to the end of the war.

FuMB-7 NAXOS

When the RAF Stirling bomber was shot down over Rotterdam in early 1942 (previously referred to under 'radar') *Luftwaffe* personnel searching the wreckage found a totaly unknown radar working at 9.7cm, a frequency which German scientists had previously considered impracticable.[4] Unfortunately for the U-boat

was that the Allies were using some form of infra-red detection technique. As a result, an infra-red detector was developed and fitted in some U-boats, while others had their upper works painted with an infra-red absorbing paint. Neither had the slightest effect and Allied air attacks continued.

The next suggestion was that the *Metox* set itself was producing a detectable signal from its intermediate-frequency stage (ie, it was radiating) and that this was being used as a homing signal by the Allied aircraft. Soon after the *Metox* entered service the Allies had appreciated that it produced powerful radiations and considered using this phenomenon to home in on U-boats, but their experiments suggested that this was too difficult and the matter was closed. Unaware of this, the *Kriegsmarine* carried out experiments using a *Metox* receiver ashore and an aircraft with a suitable detector, which established that the aircraft could detect *Metox* radiations at 25 nautical miles (46.5km) when flying at a height of 6,560ft (2,000m). This convinced *BdU* that *Metox* radiations were to blame and a signal was sent on July 31 1943 stating that *Metox* was only to be used with great caution, but then, on August 13, a British prisoner-of-war stated under interrogation that the British were, indeed, homing on *Metox* radiations and Dönitz issued a second signal which banned the use of the *Metox* set altogether on August 14.[2]

FuMB-9 ZYPERN (WANZE)

Meanwhile, the German electronics company Hagenuk had developed a more sophisticated set which automatically scanned the radar frequencies (120-180cm) thought to be used by the Allies, although an operator was still needed for the fine tuning. This was officially designated *FuMB-9* with the codename 'Zypern' (= Cyprus), but the alternative designation of *W.Anz G1* (*Wellenanzeiger* = radar warning indicator) led to the more commonly used name '*Wanze*.' (It was also sometimes simply referred to as the '*Hagenuk*' after its manufacturer.) The antenna associated with this set consisted of two small dipoles mounted on a cylinder, which was enclosed in a wire mesh frame measuring 8in (200mm) in diameter and 4in (100mm) in

△ U-boats on the surface were vulnerable to detection by airborne radar, making U-boat radar-warning receivers ever more important. To add to the U-boat problems, the Allies were constantly adopting new weapons in their war against the U-boats. This Liberator GR V (FL927/G) has anti-surface vessel (ASV) Mk III centimetric radar in the nose radome and also has nose outriggers carrying rocket rails, for use in the final run in to the target.

▷ A Lockheed Hudson VI (FK689) fitted with ASV (anti-surface vessel) Mk I radar. The use of such airborne radar gave the Allies a tremendous advantage, enabling them repeatedly to take U-boats by surprise.

crews, this news was initially confined to *Luftwaffe* circles and it was some weeks before the *Kriegsmarine* became aware of it. As a result, the first response to this new threat did not appear until December 1943 when a new detector-receiver warning device, *FuMB-7* 'Naxos,' began to be installed in U-boats. *Naxos* covered the 8-12cm band, although it was principally designed to detect the British ASV Mark III radar. It had a range of only some 5,700yd (5,000m), which meant that an incoming aircraft was already on its attack run by the time it was detected; thus, at best, *Naxos* provided only about one minute's warning.

The antenna was officially designated *Cuba Ia*, but was more commonly known by its nickname, *Fliege*, from its resemblance to a bow tie.[5] It was a parabolic reflector, which was initially mounted inside the DF loop, but this made it dependent upon the radio operator below who rotated the loop using a mechanical linkage, and the *Fliege* was subsequently mounted on its own bracket on the bridge. The parabolic shape of the antenna enabled it to cover a wide horizontal area but it was restricted to a vertical coverage of approximately ±10 degrees of the horizon. However, its major disadvantage was that, like the *Metox* antenna, *Fliege* was not pressure tight, which meant that it, too, had to be rushed below whenever the U-boat dived.

KORFU

One of the first products of the rush to produce a radar detector to cover the 10cm frequencies was a set designated *Korfu*. This employed the first German-produced tunable magnetrons and was tested in four U-boats, starting in December 1943. Not only did it require highly skilled operators, however, but it was also found to radiate strongly, and its use was discontinued.

FuMB-23/FuMB-28 NAXOS ZM

This set was a combination of the original *Naxos* receiver with a totaly new antenna, which rotated at some 1,300rpm, with the output being displayed on a cathode-ray tube. This was deployed on S-boats in late 1944 but a version intended for U-boats was still under development when the war ended in May 1945.

FuMB-26 TUNIS

Naxos was always regarded as a stop-gap and was quickly followed by *Mücke* (= gnat), which was intended to counter the new US 3cm radar, known to the Germans as 'Meddo.' *Mücke*'s antenna was horn-shaped, but gave a similar performance to *Fliege*.

Despite these new equipments, the *Ubootwaffe* decided that it was necessary to retain *Wanze* and *Borkum*, so that by now a U-boat bridge was somewhat crowded. Fortunately it proved possible to combine *Fliege* and *Mücke* by mounting the two antennas back-to-back on a single pole, which fitted into a bracket on the bridge and which was rotated manually by one of the watchkeepers. However, it still had to be taken below every time the U-boat dived. This combined system was designated *FuMB-26* 'Tunis' and was installed in operational boats from May 1944 onwards.

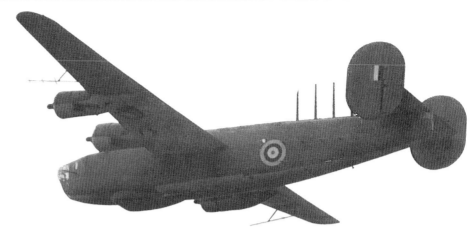

△ A Consolidated Liberator I (AM910). Note the ASV antennas under the wings, on the nose and atop the rear fuselage.

△ *Athos* radar-warning receiver array consisted of two circles of loop antennas: upper – X-band; lower – S-band. The loops were connected internally into four sectors, which, in conjunction with an amplifier and display unit, gave continuous bearing display and 360deg coverage. It was entering production in April 1945.

FuMB-29 BALI

The shortcomings of the various antennas which had to be taken below were apparent from the start and a German firm designed and produced a new antenna designated *FuMB-29* with the code-name 'Bali.' This was a pressure-tight, omni-directional dipole, mounted on a cylindrical wire cage.

FuMB-35 ATHOS/FuMB-37 LEROS

Athos (*FuMB-35*) was the final refinement and had two circular antenna arrays mounted inside a pressurized head atop a telescopic mast. The upper array covered the X-band and consisted of 32 small loop antennas, while the lower array covered the S-band and consisted of 16 larger loops. The electronics were also much more sophisticated than earlier sets, with four separate amplifiers and a display on a cathode-ray tube. The first experimental set had just been installed in one U-boat when the war in Europe ended in May 1945. In a further project, the electronics of *Athos* were combined with the *Bali* antenna (see above) to produce the *Leros FuMB-37* which was installed in some Type XXIs. The antenna was mounted on the *schnorchel* head.

ANTI-SONAR COATING

ALBERICH

One of the responses to Allied sonar was to reduce the U-boats' acoustic signature by the use of a sound-absorbing material to coat the hull. It was hoped this would both contain the U-boats' own noise and also reduce the reflected component of the hostile sonar. This resulted in a system code-named *Alberich* which consisted of a coating of synthetic rubber (Oppanol) which reduced sounds in 10-18kHz range by an estimated 15 percent.[6] It was also believed that the effectiveness varied with changes in temperature and pressure, but these could only be guesses, since the Germans found it very difficult to make comparative tests at sea.

There were two practical difficulties with *Alberich*. The first was that the Oppanol coating came in sheets 0.2in (4mm) thick, which had to be firmly secured to the hull, but contemporary technology could not produce an effective and durable adhesive. The second problem was that applying the sheets had to be done under cover, and was both time-consuming and labor-intensive.

The first boat to be treated was *U-11*, a Type IIB, which was employed by the *Nachrichtenmittelversuchskommando* (*NVK* = Communications Test Command) for tests in 1940. These were sufficiently promising for an operational Type IXC, *U-67*, to be treated immediately after launch, but by the time it arrived at Lorient in August 1941 on its first voyage no less than 60 percent of the coating was missing. Indeed, the worst problems arose when the tiles had come loose but had not yet fallen off, since they flapped in the wake and generated eddies, causing more noise than they were concealing and thus totaly defeating their object. Further trials were made with one of the captured Dutch boats, *UD-4*, but again difficulties were encountered with the adhesive.

Attention then switched to other means of defeating enemy sonar, mainly by diving deeper. Further work was also done on *Alberich* and in 1944 several newly completed Type VIICs were given an *Alberich* coating, using a new adhesive. The first of these, *U-480* (Förster), was commissioned in October 1943 and, following the application of *Alberich*, went to Norway in May 1944 for comparative trials against two other recently completed boats, which lacked the *Alberich* coating: *U-247*, a Type VIIC; and *U-999*, a Type VIIC/41. Following the trials *U-480* sailed for Brest, arriving on July 7, having shot down an RCAF Canso (Catalina) en route. *U-480* operated in the English Channel in August/September 1944, where it sank a Canadian corvette (HMCS *Alberni*), a British minesweeper (HMS *Loyalty*), and a merchantman, (*Orminster* [5,712t]), and seriously damaged another merchantman (*Fort Yale* [7,134t]). Following the sinking of the *Orminster*, *U-480* was hunted for seven hours, but managed to escape, a feat for which the captain gave *Alberich* much of the credit.

U-480 reached Norway on October 4 and left for another patrol in the English Channel on January 6 1945, where it sank another merchantman (*Oriskany* [1,644t]) and was then subjected to a lengthy hunt. This time *Alberich* failed to protect it and it was sunk by British ASW ships on February 24 1945.[7]

Meanwhile, it had been decided that Type XXIIIs and Type XXVIs, then under construction, would receive *Alberich* coatings, although as far as is known only one Type XXIII, *U-4709*, was actually completed with the coating, becoming operational in February 1945.

TARNMATTE

Tarnmatte (= camouflage coating)[8] was a compound of synthetic rubber and iron oxide powder which was used to coat *schnorchel* heads to shield them from Allied radar. It was designed to have its maximum effect at a wavelength of 9.7cm, which corresponded to that used by the ASV Mk III airborne radar carried by British ASW aircraft, and was claimed to absorb 90 percent of such waves.

△ Close-up of a U-boat coated in synthetic rubber, codenamed 'Alberich.' The system provided a substantial reduction in the sonar signature, but the problem lay in finding a reliable adhesive.

SONAR DECOYS

BOLD

Bold was a chemical device intended to confuse hunters equipped with sonar. It consisted of a metal can, 3.9in (100mm) in diameter, containing calcium hydride, which was released from a special launcher. On release, seawater seeped in through a valve and reacted with the calcium hydride to produce a dense screen of hydrogen bubbles. The valve opened and closed, causing the can to hover at around the 98ft (30m) mark where it presented a false target to the attacker's sonar for a period of 20-25 minutes, enabling the U-boat to move slowly away. It was widely used in the *Kriegsmarine* from 1942 onwards, and was also being supplied to the Japanese Navy. New and improved versions of *Bold* were given numbers, the last being *Bold 5*, which was under development in 1945 and was intended for use at depths up to 656ft (200m).

SIEGLINDE

An associated device was *Sieglinde*, which was also expelled from the special launcher, and was intended to give the same acoustic signature as a U-boat moving at 6 knots. It was normally used in conjunction with *Bold 4* and *5*.

SIEGMUND

Siegmund emitted a series of explosions, which were intended to 'black-out' the enemy's listening devices, providing short-term protection while the U-boat moved at high speed to evade an attack.

RADAR DECOYS

APHRODITE

Aphrodite was a 36in (900mm) diameter, hydrogen-filled balloon, tethered by a 164ft (50m) line to a sheet anchor. Just below the balloon there was a cross-bar from which were suspended three aluminum foils to act as radar reflectors; these would, it was hoped, confuse the enemy into thinking a U-boat was present.[9] The device had to be assembled on the upper casing, where the balloon was inflated from a gas bottle; once launched it had a 'life' of about 3-6 hours. *Aphrodite* proved popular with U-boat crews, who tended to release the balloons in large numbers, and it remained in use well into 1944. But by then it was folly for a U-boat to surface in the Bay of Biscay and this, coupled with the advent of the *schnorchel*, led to the demise of *Aphrodite*.

The Allies knew all about *Aphrodite* before it was deployed in September 1943, but even so it undoubtedly caused some confusion among their ASW forces at first.[10] One occasion when *Aphrodite* was used with apparent success was on the night of February 10/11 1944, when *U-413* (Poel), *U-437* (Lamby), and *U-731* (Graf von Keller) broke off an attack on convoy OS.67 and deployed several *Aphrodites* which appeared to confuse the pursuing escorts; all three U-boats certainly escaped.

THETIS

Thetis was the name given to a variety of floating decoys (known to the Allies as the 'Radar Decoy Spar Buoy' [RDS]) which were intended to confuse Allied warship surface search radars. The first, which was intended to give the same response as a surface U-boat, was an entirely passive device consisting of a wooden beam carrying 10 metal dipoles and a thin steel tube, both 16.4ft (5m) long, which were secured to the opposite sides of two cork floats. These devices took up a lot of much-needed space below decks and were awkward to take up through the conning tower and to assemble on the sea-swept deck, but despite this some U-boats carried as many as 30. The dipoles were cut to the frequency of the British ASV (ie, meter-wave) radar. The concept was for all U-boats to deploy a number as they passed through the Bay of Biscay where they would remain afloat for many months and thus, it was hoped, cause confusion to Allied ASW ships and aircraft. The original *Thetis* was first deployed in February 1944, by which time the *Kriegsmarine* had realized that the new Allied airborne radar, ASV Mark III, operated at centimeter wavelengths, making *Thetis*, which was designed to counter meter-length wavelengths, a complete waste of time.

However, there were several later versions of *Thetis* which were intended to simulate the radar response of a *schnorchel* head. Both were small, lightweight S-band corner reflectors: *Thetis S* was assembled by hand and deployed on the surface, while *Thetis US* was launched underwater through the tube normally used for *Bold*. As far as is known, development was given a low priority and, although tested, neither was used operationally.

△ The *Aphrodite* system consisted of a tethered, gas-filled balloon from which was suspended a cross-bar carrying three strips of aluminum foil. This was intended to give the same radar signature as a surfaced U-boat and had some success when first used. but the Allies quickly developed counter-measures.

Footnotes:
1. All *Kriegsmarine* radar warning receivers were known to the Allies under the generic term 'German Search Receiver' (GSR).
2. There is no doubt that a British PoW did make such a statement, even though it was totaly without foundation, but his reason for doing so has never been established.
3. *U-386* was damaged but survived to report the incident to *BdU*.
4. The captured set was in fact a prototype of the H2S system.
5. The direct translation of *Fliege* is a fly (ie, the insect) but it was also the contemporary slang name for a bow-tie, which was part of the formal uniform for all *Kriegsmarine* officers. It was this usage that gave rise to the nickname.
6. *Alberich* was the name of a dwarf in one of Wagner's operas; he made himself invisible by donning a magic coat.
7. Other boats known to have been given an *Alberich* coating were *U-485* and *U-486*.
8. It was also known by the codename *Sumpf* (= swamp, morass).
9. This was very similar in concept to the Allies' 'Window' which, by chance, was first used at the same time as *Aphrodite*.
10. The Allies contributed their foreknowledge of *Aphrodite* to the opportune capture of a document, but it was almost certainly due to Ultra.

THE ELECTRONIC BATTLEFIELD

RADIO COMMUNICATIONS

Radio communications were absolutely essential to Dönitz's concept of command and control, but there were four major problems:

• Technical limitations meant that the U-boats had to be very near or actually on the surface in order to receive and transmit messages.

• Most of the traffic generated by both the U-boats and the shore-based transmitters was encoded using *Enigma*, which the British were able to read for most of the war, giving them a vast amount of information.

• U-boats transmitted numerous messages, enabling the Allies to locate their positions using direction-finding equipment.

• The Allies used a technique known as 'traffic analysis' to examine the patterns of transmissions and moves of transmitters to deduce current and future intentions.[1]

The uses of the radio system were defined by Dönitz in the '*U-Boat Commander's Handbook*.'[2] These were to send important messages, such as:

'1. Enemy reports which make it possible to send other submarines into action.

2. Warnings referring to the positions of enemy submarines or minefields.

3. Reports on the situation in the theater of operation, traffic, possible use of armed forces, description and strength of patrols.

4. Weather reports.

5. Position and reports on movements of ships, insofar as the transmission of these reports is required by headquarters, or seems necessary to enable them to assess the position.

6. Reports called for by headquarters. What reports are required is stated in the operation order.'

These requirements generated a great deal of traffic, but Dönitz's requirements were not all, and traffic was generated for other reasons, particularly when making arrangements for unscheduled meetings of U-boats at sea, which included agreeing a mutually acceptable rendezvous, refueling requirements, passing over *Enigma* keys, exchanging equipment, enabling a sick man to consult a doctor[3] or placing a wounded/sick man on a boat returning to base.

Radio users in all armed forces were well aware that their transmissions could be intercepted and the *Kriegsmarine* certainly learned a great deal from its own monitoring of Allied communications, but senior officers in the *Kriegsmarine* were convinced that their codes and, in particular, their *Enigma-M* machines, were absolutely invulnerable. They were also well

▷ An unusually relaxed scene with three officers enjoying the sun, which they would rarely have been able to do later in the war. The two sloping-wire antennas for high frequency radio communications stretch from the bridge to the stern. HF radio provided an essential link between the boats and base, but also gave the Allied intercept services a vast amount of traffic for analysis.

aware that the Allies had a land-based direction-finding (DF) capability and tried to avoid falling victim to it. But right up to the end of the war they had no idea that DF equipment was also carried aboard Allied escort vessels at sea, nor did they guess that Allied equipment could take an accurate bearing on transmissions lasting 20 seconds or less.

Periodic instructions were issued to U-boat commanders to refrain from using the radio unless absolutely necessary, but this led to new problems. First, *BdU* and his staff frequently felt desperate for information, which led to repeated requests for situation and location reports. Second, the fact that nothing was heard from a U-boat was often (and over-optimistically) taken to mean that the captain was obeying the instruction rather than that his boat had been sunk.

By late 1944 the U-boat service was experiencing very severe communications problems. The Allied advance over France and into Germany overran many transmitter and receiver stations. The operators aboard the U-boats were less well trained and experienced than in earlier years and, on top of this, the U-boat commanders were increasingly reluctant to use their radio, because of hidden fears that the Allies were somehow using such transmissions to locate their boats. As a result, some 50 percent of U-boats did not transmit any messages at all

SELECTED U-BOAT RADIO SETS					
ROLE	**SET**	**FREQUENCY**	**POWER**	**MAIN USE**	**ALTERNATIVE USES**
Transmitters	Telefunken S-400-S	3–30MHz	200W	U-boat to shore	Main set
	Lorenz 40-K-39a	3–30MHz	40W	U-boat to shore	Stand-by to main set
	Telefunken T-200 FKW 39	3–24MHz	200W	U-boat to shore	
	Lorenz Lo 40 K 39a	5–16.7MHz	40W		
	Telefunken	600–800m	150W		
	Telefunken Spez-2113-S	100kz–1.5MHz	150W	Beacon	U-boat to U-boat
Receivers	Telefunken E-437-S	3–30MHz	N/A	Shore – U-boat	Main receiver
	Telefunken E-381-S	15kHz–20MHz	N/A		a. Stand-by to main receiver b. Used as VLF receiver
	Telefunken Ela-10.12	100kHz–1.5MHz	N/A	Beacon	a. Enemy ship-ship signals b. Enemy commercial signals c. Used DF loop antenna
	Radione R.1 or R.2			Stand-by to Ela-10.12	a. Had jack for internal gramophone system b. Listening to enemy propaganda broadcasts c. Used DF loop antenna

GERMAN AND ALLIED DIVISIONS OF RADIO BANDS DURING WORLD WAR II				
GERMAN SYSTEM		**ALLIED SYSTEM**		
GERMAN NAME	**FREQUENCY BAND**	**ALLIED WORLD WAR TWO EQUIVALENT**		
Längstwelle (longest wave)	Less than 100kHz	Very low frequency (VLF)		3–30kHz
Langwellem (long wave)	100kHz–1.5MHz	Low frequency (LF)		30–300kHz
Grenzwelle (intermediate wave)	1.5–3MHz	Meidum frequency (MF)		300kHz–3MHz
Kurzwelle (short wave) Ultrakürzwelle (ultrashort wave)	3–3MHz Above 30MHz	High frequency (HF) Very High frequency (VHF)		3–30MHz Above 30MHz

during an entire operation, except perhaps on arriving off a Norwegian base to request a surface escort – some did not even do that. This had two main results. First, earlier in the war if no message was received from a U-boat for about two weeks it was considered lost, but by late 1944 it took up to the scheduled end of the patrol and a time beyond that before a loss could be assumed. Second, *BdU* received little or no information on the current position at sea and by the time U-boat commanders had returned and were giving oral reports their information was several weeks out of date.

All this traffic was sent in hand-speed Morse at a rate of about 22-25 words per minute. One way of shortening transmission times was to use signals taken from two 'short signal books' (*Kurzsignalheft*), one for convoy sightings and the other for weather reports. Both books enabled the operator to substitute single words or groups of letters for commonly used phrases, which were then encoded using the *Enigma* machine, and identified by prefixing the text with the Greek letter 'beta' with an added bar.

Later in the war, a new device – *KZG 44/2* '*Kurier*' (= courier)[4] – was developed for use in conjunction with a normal trans-

◁ After end of *U-889*'s radio room with (top right) direction-finding receiver *Type T3PLLä38* and (bottom left) the hand-wheel for rotating the bridge-mounted direction-finding loop.

▷ Telefunken Receiver *Type E 436 S* with the front cover down to reveal the large tubes (valves). This was the main receiving set for U-boats covering frequencies from 3-30 MHz.

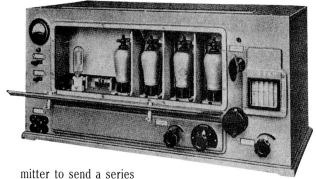

mitter to send a series of letters in Morse-code in an extremely short 'burst' – typically seven letters in 0.4 seconds – over a continuously varying sequence of frequencies. This made direction-finding and interception very difficult, but not impossible, as the British proved. *Kurier* was tested in *U-878* (Rodig) in the Baltic in mid-1944 followed by further trials involving six boats in Norwegian waters on August 9 1944, but both were unsuccessful. However, the problems were overcome and *Kurier* went into production, being installed in about 20 boats by the war's end.[5]

The receiver equipment was far more elaborate, consisting of three Philips CR-101 receivers and a device which displayed the received message on film, from which it was read by an operator. Such bulky receiver equipment could not be accommodated in a U-boat, which meant that *Kurier* could be used only for communications from U-boats to the shore, but not from the shore to U-boats nor between U-boats.

RADIO EQUIPMENT

RADIOS

The type of sets carried varied between U-boat types but all had equipment covering three bands: very low frequency (VLF), medium frequency (MF), and high frequency (HF)(see table). Most of this equipment was manufactured by German companies such as Telefunken, Lorenz, Radione, and Rohde & Schwarz, but some also came from French and Dutch manufacturers. The basic long-range communications between *BdU* and U-boats at sea were radio telegraphy broadcasts using hand-keyed Morse in the HF band, which was known to the Germans as *kurzwelle* (short-wave) (see table).

Inside a U-boat, the sets were located in the *Funkraum* (= radio room) and normally consisted of a main transmitter, one or more less powerful stand-by transmitters, and a variety of receivers. Messages to the U-boats were broadcast from high-powered transmitters in France and Germany, with the address in clear language and the text usually encoded. Submerged U-boats could be out of communications for long periods, so messages to them had to be repeated frequently, until they were acknowedged.

Medium frequency (100kHz-1.5MHz) was used between U-boats at sea and for homing other U-boats to a surface rendezvous. The radio room included a long-wave transmitter and a multi-band receiver, which also served as the stand-by to the main HF receiver. Apart from listening out on U-boat frequencies, U-boat radio operators also monitored the international frequencies 600m and 36m, which were used for distress calls by Allied merchant ships under attack.[6]

ANTENNAS

In the early part of the war the long-wire stretching from the bridge forward to the bows was used as the transmit antenna and one of the two aft wires for receive. For best communications – and to reduce the chance of enemy DF – when using these wires the boat had to be pointing directly at the distant radio station, although captains were not always amenable to the *funkers*' requests for a temporary change of course. Later, a telescopic rod mounted on the bridge was found to be sufficient, although such an antenna transmitted a signal of equal strength throughout 360 degrees. Occasionally, when all attempts to get a message through had failed, an *Aphrodite* balloon was used to raise a long-wire for use as an antenna.

△ The *Lorenz 40 K 39a* was the stand-by transmitter, with power-supply unit (top) and transmitter stage (below). Power output was 40 Watts and it covered the high frequency band: 3–30 MHz.

▽ *Radione R.3* general-purpose receiver, which, among other uses, could receive enemy propaganda broadcasts (if the captain allowed it). It also had a gramophone socket, enabling records to be broadcast around the boat. It normally used the DF loop as its antenna.

SECURITY

The *Funkraum* contained many classified documents, including the *Enigma* code settings (keys), manuals and instructions, and message logs, so access was restricted to the operators and a very few other members of the crew. There were very strict standing orders that in an emergency (eg, on abandon ship) all classified documents and the *Enigma* machine were to be put in a weighted sack and either fired out of a torpedo tube or dropped overboard. In addition, some of the documents, such as the *Enigma* keys, were printed on water-soluble paper and would dissolve if dropped into the bilges.

THE *GOLIATH* TRANSMITTER

Most land-based transmitters used medium and high frequencies to communicate with U-boats, but a new and highly unusual system came into service in the Spring of 1943. U-boats could receive low frequency signals down to about 50ft (15m) but had to come up to the surface to receive medium and high frequency signals. It was discovered, however, that VLF signals (known to the Germans as *längstwelle*) could penetrate to depths of up to 85ft (26m) in the North Atlantic, although this was reduced somewhat in the South Atlantic and Indian Oceans. The *Kriegsmarine* already operated a VLF transmitter at Nauen, near Berlin, but this could not operate at the powers now required, so a new transmitter, named *Goliath*, was designed and built by the electronics company, Lorenz. The *Goliath* site occupied a 642 acre (260 hectare) area located in a loop of the River Milde, some 9 miles (15km) north of Gardelegen (37miles/60km north of Magdeburg).

COMMUNICATIONS BETWEEN U-BOATS

Communications between U-boats at sea was kept to a minimum, but where necessary was achieved by radio unless they were within visual contact, when traditional flags were used. All U-boats were also fitted with *Unterwasser-Telegraphie* (UT), which was intended for use between two submerged U-boats. This involved two pairs of hydrophones (one for transmit, one for receive) on each side of the bows and operated at a transmit frequency of 3.5kHz, but the range was relatively short and depended upon ambient conditions. It was rarely used on operations because its transmissions could be picked up by enemy sonar/asdic.

COMMUNICATIONS BUOYS

BEACON BUOY

The *Schwammboje* (= swimming buoy) was intended to act as a beacon and transmitted a fixed frequency signal to home U-boats onto a convoy. It was generally similar to the weather reporting buoy. It was first used in late 1942, but had fallen out of use by U-boats by mid-1944, although it continued to be used by the *Luftwaffe*.

CONTACT-KEEPING BUOY

The *Fühlungshalterboje* (*Fübo* = contact maintaining buoy) was similar in purpose to the *Schwammboje* but was smaller and used a totaly different technique. It consisted of a cylinder approximately 24in (610mm) high and 12in (304mm) in diameter, beneath which was a 24in rod to which was attached a thin circular weight about 12in in diameter, which kept the buoy upright. The three parts were screwed together on the upper deck and just before it was thrown overboard a lanyard was pulled, igniting a fuze which had a burning time of about 30 minutes, at the end of which the buoy threw up either a colored flare or multi-colored Verey lights. Some U-boats were reported to carry as many as 15 of these devices.

TRANSMITTING BUOY

Another device under test at the end of the war was an expendable communications buoy, which contained a recording device, a transmitter, and a delay switch. Prior to release from the submerged U-boat, the message was loaded, and the transmit frequency and delay set. Once on the surface the buoy waited for the preset delay, which allowed the U-boat to get well clear, transmitted its message, and then sank itself automatically.

U-BOAT D/F

All U-boats were fitted with a *Funkpeilrahmen* (= direction-finding loop) which was usually mounted on the bridge and turned by a mechanical linkage from the *Funkraum* below. This was used to receive incoming signals from the shore or from other U-boats, and, where necessary, to establish an approximate bearing to the transmitter; it was not intended for DF-ing enemy signals. Professor Küpfmüller identified a need to enable U-boats to achieve this and produced two new equipments. The first, codenamed *Presskohle*,[7] was a 'quick-fix' attachment to a standard U-boat receiver enabling it to take bearings on signals between 1.5 and 3.0 MHz in the HF band; 20 percent of operational U-boats had been fitted by the war's end. The longer term solution was intended for Type XXIs and consisted of two crossed DF loops inside the *schnorchel* head, whose anti-radar coating was electronically transparent to incoming HF signals. Like so much German equipment, this had just entered production as the war ended.

B-DIENST

The German Navy's radio interception and decrypting agency was the *Beobachtungs-Dienst* (= monitoring service), known as the '*B-Dienst*,' which had been established in the 1920s and was modeled on the British Admiralty's 'Room 40,' which had been very successful in World War I. It was of considerable value in the U-boat war[8] and penetrated many British codes, including

THE THREE-ROTOR ENIGMA

These pictures and diagrams show the appearance and operation of the three-rotor *Enigma* machine. The four-rotor machine was essentially similar in operation, but added an extra level of complexity. The *Enigma* machine measured 13.4 x 11 x 6in (340 x 280 x 150mm), weighed about 26.5lb (12kg) and consisted of five main elements: a typewriter keyboard (1); a scrambler unit (2); a plugboard (3); a set of lights on a lampboard (4); and a battery (5). The keyboard, plugboard and lampboard had identical 26-key layouts, using the conventional German keyboard which was different from the English/American keyboard:

QWERTZUIO
ASDFGHJK
PYXCVBNML

There were no keys for numerals or punctuation, both of which had to be spelled out in full in the text, nor for the German umlaut (eg, ö, ä, ü) which had to be spelled 'oe', 'ae' and 'ue', respectively.

The scrambler unit consisted of three moving rotors between two fixed plates. Each rotor had 26 spring-loaded terminals in a circle on its right side and 26 flat studs on its left side. Wiring inside the rotor connected each terminal to a stud on the opposite face, but in a random manner. There was a 26-toothed ratchet on the right of the rotor and a 26-letter setting key on the left. Each station held eight rotors, numbered I to VIII, all those with the same number having the same internal wiring.

There were two fixed wheels, one at each end of the well, which also had 26 contacts each. Each contact on the entry wheel was permanently connected to one of the sockets on the plugboard (3), while in the reversing wheel each stud was permanently connected to another stud. At the start of a new code setting

◁ Three rotors assembled on axle.

the operator selected the three rotors designated in that day's key setting, assembled them in the designated order on the axle and placed them in the well. The lever on the left was then closed, pushing the three rotors and two fixed wheels close to each other and ensuring that their studs all made contact. The lid was then shut, leaving the ratchets on the periphery of the three rotors exposed, with one letter on the side of each rotor visible through a small aperture.

The plugfield had 52 sockets, two for each letter, which were connected by double-ended cables, usually with six pairs left unconnected. Finally, the lampfield also included 26 bulbs, and each time a key was pressed a lamp would glow, giving, according to the rotor settings, another letter in the alphabet, but never the original letter itself.

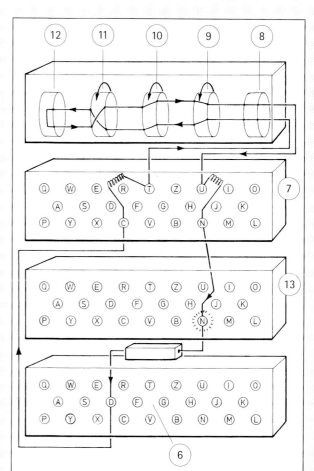

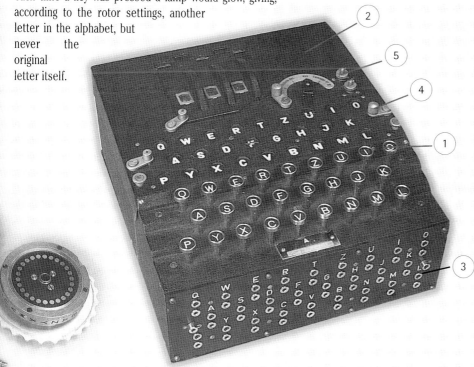

△ Three *Enigma* rotors and axle.

▷ Close-up of rotors, lampfield, and keyboard.

When the operator pressed a key (6) he activated a mechanical linkage, advancing the right-hand rotor and completing an electrical circuit. Current flowed through the plugfield (7) to the entry wheel (8), thence through the three moving rotors (9, 10, 11) to the reflector (12), which returned the current back through the rotors (along a different route), the entry wheel and the plugfield to the lampfield (13), where a lamp glowed. The rotors operated like the wheels on a car odometer. The right-hand rotor moved 1/26th of a revolution for every keyboard hit, the 27th hit moving the central rotor forward 1/26th of a revolution. When the central rotor completed one revolution it moved the left-hand rotor forward 1/26th of a revolution: the system started to repeat itself only after 26 x 25 x 26 = 16,900 key hits. A vital feature of the system (and also in breaking it) was that a key could designate any other letter in the alphabet *except itself*.

the Broadcasting for Allied Merchant Ships (BAMS) code (known to the Germans as *München*), which enabled them to track British convoys for several years.[9] Indeed, by 1942 the *B-Dienst* was even reading the Admiralty's 'U-boat situation reports' which enabled Dönitz to see just how accurate and up-to-date was the British knowledge of U-boat locations (but not how they had obtained them), causing him considerable alarm. By 1943 *B-Dienst* was giving Dönitz very timely and precise information, one example being on March 14 1943 when it told him the whereabouts and course of convoy HX.229, a fast convoy proceeding from Halifax, Canada, to the UK. This information enabled Dönitz to assemble a wolf pack (codenamed *Raubgraf*) which duly intercepted the convoy on the morning of March 16 and sank 13 ships (141,000grt) over a period of 48 hours.

Once the British realized that the Germans had broken BAMS they took immediate steps to change it, although the distribution of new books to many users around the world was neither an easy nor a quick task, delaying the actual changeover to the new code until June 1943. *B-Dienst* broke this new code in September and it was changed again on December 1 1943. But then, during December, the British broke into the German Navy's *Triton* code and learned among other things that the *B-Dienst* was reading BAMS yet again, and changed to a completely new system on January 1 1944. *B-Dienst* had, in fact, been reading the original code (which they named *München*) since 1942 and had been providing *BdU* with decrypted messages within hours, but there was a total break between June and September 1943 before the new code was broken. The code introduced in January 1944 was never broken, however, although this had little relevance since the U-boats were no longer in a position to attack convoys in any strength.

ENIGMA

The *Kriegsmarine* used several different methods of encrypting message traffic, but the most important involved the *Enigma* machine. This device was marketed commercially by a Dr Scherbius of Berlin from 1923 onwards and in 1926 the *Reichsmarine* became the first military service to procure it. The Navy was followed by other services and by the mid-1930s there were several different models in use with all the German armed services as well as with a number of civil organizations. The *Kriegsmarine* model was designated *Enigma M* (M = *Marine* [navy]) of which the essentially similar models M1, M2 and M3 were in service in 1939.

Enigma was an 'off-line' encryption system; that is to say, it did not itself transmit. Indeed, it did not even act as a typewriter to produce 'hard copy' in the form of either a typewritten page or tape. Instead, it had a keyboard and when a key was pressed a complicated electrical circuit was completed which lit a lamp giving an alternative letter, which could be any other letter of the alphabet, but never the original letter itself. Although the

△ The *Telefunken FKW* high-power transmitter, consisted of three modules: transmitter (top); keying and modulating unit (center); and power supply unit (bottom). It covered frequencies from 3.7–15 MHz in 10 bands. Power output was 200 Watts.

entire operation could be performed by one man, there were normally two: one sat behind the machine and typed the message, while the second observed the lamps, wrote down the letters as they lit up and then transmitted the encrypted message using the Morse-key. At the distant end the situation was reversed, with the Morse operator passing the incoming (encrypted) message to the *Enigma* team, one of whom typed the encoded message one letter at a time, while the second wrote down the clear message as the lamps lit up.

All stations needing to talk to each other had to use the same settings, which was achieved by a document known as the *Schlüssel M* (= naval key).[10] Each key covered a calendar month and changes were made daily at 1200 German Standard Time, although more frequent changes could be implemented on receipt of a codeword. When a U-boat sailed it was given sufficient of these keys to cover its anticipated voyage (plus a reserve). These keys were classified *Geheim* (= secret) and were issued on a very carefully controlled basis. Complications arose if U-boats stayed on patrol longer than expected (for example, having been refueled or when sailing to and from the Indian Ocean) and they ran out of *Enigma* keys. In such cases they had to rendezvous with another boat to obtain the keys necessary for use during their return voyage.

Messages containing particularly sensitive information were double-encrypted and the first words revealed to the operator starting the normal decoding process were 'officer only.' This meant that aboard the U-boat the radio operator had to hand the message to the communications officer who, in privacy, decrypted the second crypt.[11] There was also a system for 'officer-to-officer' conversations known as *Funkschlüsselgespräch* (= coded radio conversation), which involved three participants at each end: the officer and two operators. The officer dictated his remarks which were typed out by the *Enigma* operator and then transmitted by the Morse operator, letter by letter, as the lights lit up. At the receiving end the *Enigma* operator typed the message onto the *Enigma* as it was received, with the other operator writing out the clear-text message as the lamps lit up, and passing the text to his officer. The method was slow and cumbersome and gave several clear 'signatures' to Allied listeners, and it was seldom used.

The Germans were aware of a possibility that *Enigma* might be broken, although they considered this to be very remote, and they took several steps to improve the system. From 1939-42 the *Kriegsmarine* divided its *Enigma* users into three communities, each of which used the same settings for its *Enigma*s. The first was for all warships (including U-boats) on the high seas, designated *Ausserheimische Gewässer* (= foreign waters), and also known as *Hydra*. The second was used by all warships in home waters, *Heimische Gewässer* (= home waters), known as 'Heimisch.' The third was used by shipyards, and was known as 'Werft.' However, there were a large number of non-U-boat users on both *Hydra* and *Heimisch*, and Dönitz obtained authority for an exclusive U-boat setting, designated *Triton*, whose introduction on February 1 1942, coincided with introduction of the new *Enigma M4* machine. This was a new version with a fourth rotor, which greatly complicated the decoders' problems; for example, the number of possible starting positions were increased from 17,576 (26^3) to 456,976 (26^4).

GERMAN SUSPICIONS

One of the earliest incidents arousing German suspicions about the Allies accessing *Enigma* naval codes took place on the night of September 27/28 1941. *BdU* was informed by radio of a number of interlocking problems: *U-67*, heading for the South Atlantic, had a crewman with venereal disease, but no doctor; *U-68*, also heading south, was short of torpedoes and had a doctor; and *U-111* was homeward bound with spare torpedoes. *BdU* ordered all three boats to rendezvous at Tarafal Bay, San Antao Island, in the Portuguese Cape Verde Islands, a particularly remote spot which had never been used before. Once there, *U-68*'s doctor would examine *U-67*'s sick sailor and either cure him or send him home aboard *U-111*, which would pass its spare torpedoes to the other boats.

Several messages were required to set up such an unplanned rendezvous, which were duly intercepted and decrypted by the British Ultra organization and, as a result, the British decided to attack. Thus, at about midnight on September 27/28, the British River-class submarine, *Clyde*, met the three U-boats in Talafera Bay and in a confused melee *U-67* was damaged while attempting to ram the British submarine. In the end, all four boats survived and escaped from each other.

Dönitz found it hard to believe that *Clyde*'s arrival had been by chance and convinced himself that the British were reading *Enigma*. As a result, he ordered an immediate change of *Enigma* keys to be followed by an investigation by Vice-Admiral Maertens, Chief of Naval Communications. Maertens' report concluded that such a thing was impossible.

In another incident on January 12 1943 *U-459*, a Type XIV tanker, was instructed by radio to rendezvous with an Italian submarine at a spot 300 miles (480km) east of St Paul's Rock. When *U-459* arrived, however, it found a number of Allied destroyers carrying out ASW searches and the captain concluded that they must have been fully aware of the time and place of the rendezvous. He reported this conclusion to Dönitz, who initiated a further review of cryptographic security. Once again the conclusion was that the Allies could not possibly have broken the codes, not least because the four-wheeled *Enigma* had recently been introduced. These conclusions were reinforced by information obtained by the *B-Dienst* which seemed to suggest that the Allies' use of airborne radar was somehow to blame. A further complication was that in 1942 the Germans had captured a French resistance worker who was accused of transmitting the time and rough destination of all U-boat sailings, which suggested that espionage – always a popular scapegoat in

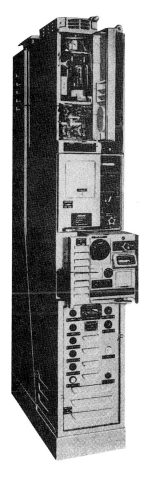

△ *Telefunken T 200 FK 39* was another HF transmitter used in U-boats and was particularly suitable for sending automatic Morse code.

these circumstances – might be to blame.

Yet another incident, this time in the Far East, re-awakened suspicions in 1944. Two German tankers, *Charlotte Schliemann* and *Brake*, were operating in the southern Indian Ocean, refueling U-boats going to and returning from the bases in Malaya. *Charlotte Schliemann* disappeared without explanation on February 11 1944 while *UIT-22* was sunk on March 11 en route to a rendezvous with *Brake*. That tanker was then sunk on the following day by a British destroyer, an event which was observed and reported to *BdU* by *U-168*. The Germans were alarmed to lose two tankers and a U-boat in the same remote and deserted area, all within 50 miles (80km) of their respective rendezvous, and in such a short space of time. So, the Chief of Naval Communications carried out yet another investigation, in the course of which he discovered that *UIT-24*, which had been scheduled to replenish from *Brake* a few days after the first three, had sent some signals from a position South of Mauritius. The usual suspects – compromise of the U-boat codes and treason – were once again examined, as was the possibility of interception of radio traffic to Japan, but nothing could be established and, as had happened after the previous investigations, the matter was left there.

Great efforts were made to eliminate possible sources of leaks, such fears even extending to the naval communications staff in the Admiralty in Berlin. Thus, on September 9 1941 a new system was introduced in which map squares were encoded using a simple code (which was changed at irregular intervals) before the message was passed to the cypher office, so as to conceal the positions even from the otherwise highly trusted communications staff.

In fact, apart from a break of several months in 1943, the Allies were indeed reading *Enigma*. In combination with other technological advances such as DF and airborne radar, this enabled them either to find many U-boats and destroy them, or to re-route convoys in order to avoid them.

Footnotes:
1. It should be noted that it was radio traffic that was vulnerable to interception. Thus, German messages passed between land-based HQs by voice or telegraph over landlines were totaly immune.
2. *The U-Boat Commander's Handbook, New Edition, 1943*, Thomas Publications, Gettysburg, Pa, USA, ISBN: 0-939631-21-0. (Text as translated by US Navy in 1943.)
3. In general, only Type IXs heading for the Indian Ocean, Type XBs, and Type XIVs carried a qualified medical officer.
4. *KZG 44/2 (KZG = Kurz-Zeichen-Geber* [= short signal device]; 44 = year of manufacture; 2 = 2nd model). A *KZG 44/1* was designed but not proceeded with.
5. *U-234*, a Type XB, which surrendered en route to Japan in May 1945 carried *Kurier* equipment as part of its radio outfit.
6. Such ships used the Morse code to signal 'RRR' for an attack by a surface ship and 'SSS' for a submarine attack, followed by the ship's name and location, and a closing repeat of 'SSS' or 'RRR.'
7. *Presskohle* was the name for a briquette made of compressed coal dust.
8. It was known to the Allies as the German 'Y' service.
9. The main source for breaking BAMS was the German raider *Schiff 16* (*Atlantis*) which found parts of the code on three British merchant ships it captured in late 1940.
10. Different 'communities' using the same machine could be set up by issuing each community with its own 'key.' Aboard U-boats, for example, a separate community was created by the use of an 'officer-only' key, which was held by the communications officer.
11. This task was not relished by the officers concerned, who frequently simply asked the radio operator (who was already privy to a great deal of secret information anyway) to carry on with the second decoding.

PROPULSION

The majority of World War II U-boats used diesel-electric propulsion, being powered underwater by electric batteries, while on the surface diesel engines provided power for both propulsion and battery charging. Maximum power on the surface was obtained by using both diesels, with all clutches engaged and electric motors spinning freely. For maximum economy, however, one diesel was used with its clutch to the electric motor disengaged, while on the other side all clutches were engaged with the diesel driving the electric motor in generator mode driving the opposite motor. Thus, both screws were turning and the batteries were being charged, giving a cruising speed of about 6 knots.

DIESEL ENGINES

High speed diesels were used to conserve weight and space, and were mounted on resilient blocks to reduce damage and to cut down noise transference to the hull. All service diesels were four-stroke.

MAIN TYPES

The types of diesel engine fitted in *Kriegsmarine* operational U-boats are shown in the specifications tables accompanying descriptions of the U-boat types. The most important of these were those produced by Germaniawerft (GW) of Kiel and

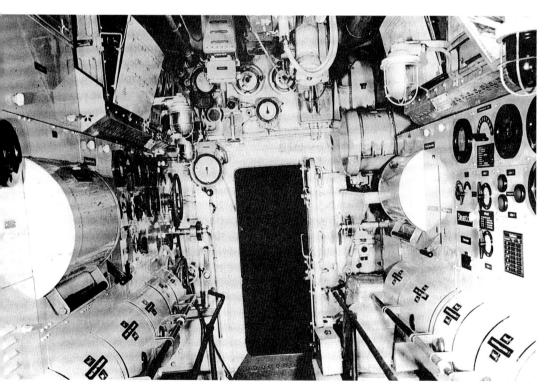

▽ The pristine cleanliness of the electrical motor room of *U-889*, a Type IXC/40. Submerged power was supplied by two *Siemens-Schuckert 2GU 345/34* electric motors.

Maschinenfabrik-Augsburg-Nürnberg (MAN), particularly the virtually identical types they produced for the Type VII. These were the MAN M6V 40/46 and the GS F-46, which in the Type VIIA were unsupercharged, but from the Type VIIB onwards were fitted with *Gebläse* (super-chargers), raising maximum power from 1,050bhp to 1,400bhp per engine. The two manufacturers employed different methods of supercharging: GW used a geared supercharger driven from the engine's main drive shaft (*Kapselgebläse*), while MAN used an exhaust-driven device (*Büchigebläse*). To meet the even greater power requirement of the proposed Type VIIC/42 it was proposed to use the MAN engine with yet further supercharging to bring the power output up to 2,200bhp, but when this new U-boat was canceled the engine was selected for the Type XXI. Once the first few Type XXIs were undergoing trials, however, it was discovered that the superchargers were unnecessary and they were deleted.

With some exceptions, Type IXs were powered by two MAN 9-cylinder, 4-stroke M9V 40/46 supercharged diesels, which proved both reliable and economical. As built, however, the Type IXD₁, was powered by six Daimler-Benz unsupercharged diesel engines, which were in two parallel sets of three. This installation proved to be a dramatic failure and when the two boats were re-roled as transports their engines were replaced by two GW F-46 supercharged diesels. The Type IXD₂ and IXD/42 had a quite different arrangement with two supercharged 9-cylinder MAN diesels for maximum power and two MWM 6-cylinder, RS 34.5S unsupercharged diesels for cruising. This gave them the exceptional surface cruising ranges of 31,500nm at 10 knots or 8,500nm at 19 knots.

STANDARDIZATION

Some efforts were made to achieve standardization. Similar models were installed in different types of U-boat, as described above, but there was also an effort to use engines already in use elsewhere in the *Kriegsmarine*. Thus, the Type IIs' MWM RS-127S 6-cylinder, 4-stroke unsupercharged engines were identical to those installed in R-1 class minesweepers. Similarly, the original Type IXD₁ was powered by six Daimler-Benz MB-501 unsupercharged diesels, as used in the *Schnellboote*. Despite their success in the *S-boote*, these engines proved to be a failure in the Type IXD₁. Similarly, the Type XXIII's MWM RS-348 was originally used as an electrical generator in battleships and as a diesel generator in the Type IXD₂. Other standardization measures included the Type XB using the same engine installation as the Type IX, while the Type XIV had two GW 1,400hp diesels, as in the Type VIIC.

EXPERIMENTAL PROJECTS

As in other areas, there was constant experimentation in an effort to obtain more powerful or more efficient propulsion systems. The most radical propulsion process considered was the Walter process, which is described separately. The idea of a steam plant which could be used for both surface and submerged propulsion was considered at one time or another by most major navies and during the 1930s the *Kriegsmarine* examined the Schmidt-Hartmann process, going so far as to start designing a submarine to test it – the Type VI – but this was quickly dropped. Consideration was also given to Deutz V-12 2-stroke diesels, which would have been much lighter than contemporary diesels and it was planned to use the weight saved to produce a much thicker pressure hull, thus considerably increasing diving depths. A trials boat was designed – the Type VIIE – but the engines suffered lengthy delays and were eventually canceled.

BATTERIES

The lead-acid battery was an unglamorous and often overlooked item of equipment, but its care, maintenance, and good health was absolutely vital to the U-boats' survival and was a major and continuing preoccupation for the captain, the LI and most members of the crew. The battery was used to store the electrical energy which powered the U-boat when submerged, a requirement which included not only the propulsion machinery, but also all electrical devices needed to operate the boat and to sustain life aboard: what is known in modern terms as the 'hotel load.' The design of the individual cells had changed little in the previous 30 years. Each consisted of an outer wooden case housing a hardened rubber box, which contained gridded electrodes and a liquid electrolyte, topped by a sealing plate through which protruded the two terminal posts: the anode (positive) and the cathode (negative). From about 1940 onwards the hardened rubber box was lined with a soft rubber bag.

It should be noted that in the early part of the war and before Allied aircraft became so effective U-boats spent a remarkably small proportion of their time submerged, especially in the central and southern Atlantic, as the figures from *U-505*'s *Kriegtagesbuch* (war diary) show.

BATTERY HANDLING
The cells were located in battery rooms in the bottom of the boat. Each cell was extremely heavy and on installation had to be manhandled down the main access trunk and through the sub-

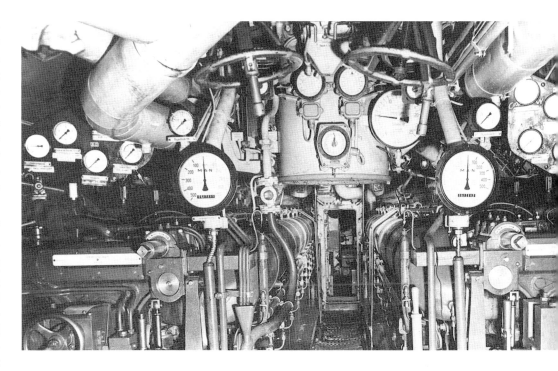

△ The main engine room of a Type IXC/40 showing the two MAN 9-cylinder M9V 40/46 supercharged diesel. Note the after escape trunk above the central passageway.

marine to the battery hatch, where it was lowered into the battery room. Once there it had to be maneuvered into position, wedged tightly in place and then, when this was completed, the cells were connected in series, using copper wire.

On surfacing, and having ensured that there was no sign of the enemy, the first priority for both the captain and LI was to recharge the batteries. This was normally achieved by running one diesel for propulsion, while the other drove its associated electric motor as a generator. Ideally the battery was charged at constant current and increasing voltage until a reading of 2.4 volts was obtained, when the charge was altered to one of constant voltage and decreasing current. Time was of the essence, but too high a charging rate damaged the cells by poisoning the electrolyte, and also generated excessive amounts of hydrogen gas, which could lead to a potentially explosive concentration inside the hull.

The captain, assisted by the LI, had to exercise very careful control over the use of the battery when submerged, since the capacity of the individual cells depended not only upon receiving a full charge when on the surface but also on the rate at which they were discharged when in use. Naturally, the captain preferred to keep his battery as fully charged as possible, but this depended upon the tactical situation. The captain knew that, once submerged and regardless of the enemy, the survival of his crew was limited by two factors: the ability of the battery to continue to power the boat and the ability of the atmosphere inside the hull to enable life to continue. At a low level of electrical consumption and human activity endurance could be as much as three days, but high levels of consumption shortened this dramatically, a fact as well known to the ASW forces on the surface

U-505 TIME SPENT SURFACED/SUBMERGED				
Dates	Operational Area	Distance traveled (nm)		Percentage
		Surfaced	Submerged	
February 11 – May 7 1942	Off West Africa	12,937	316	2.4
June 7 – August 25 1942	Caribbean	12,842	498	3.8
October 4 – December 12 1942	Caribbean	10,876	626	5.7

as it was to the U-boat crews below. In the early years of the campaign the Allies were so short of anti-submarine ships that they could not afford to leave ships in the area of a known contact waiting for it to surface, but from about 1943 onwards this was no longer the case and on numerous occasions they were content to wait until the U-boat captain was forced to surface.

Damage to the cells was a double concern to the captain, the first of which was that he would lose his underwater power. In addition, there was the danger that spilt electrolyte would mix and react with seawater in the bilges, releasing poisonous chlorine gas, for which a rudimentary and not particularly effective breathing apparatus was issued.

The large number of cells were one of the most important features of the Type XXI and Type XXIII *elektroboote*, but they also became a crucial factor in the construction program. The principal battery-supplier, AFA, already had factories in Berlin and Hannover in Germany but, with the encouragement of the *Kriegsmarine*, started in 1943 to develop further factories in Vienna, Austria, and Posen (Poznan) in Poland. This project was given a low priority by Speer's newly created armaments ministry and serious delays occurred. The factories at Berlin and Hannover were badly affected by Allied bombing, both of the cities in general and of the battery factories in particular. They also suffered from the secondary effects such as lack of electrical power and transport, and worker absenteeism. The two new factories took more time than expected to begin production and, in any case, their distance from the shipyards on the coast added to the difficulties.

THE TROPICS

No German U-boats were designed for service in the Tropics and when they began to serve in the southern Atlantic and later in the Indian Ocean numerous problems caused by heat and humidity were discovered. Cells were particularly badly affected, as they failed to hold their charge as well as they did in temperate climates, and overheating became a problem. Indeed, most U-boats returning from the Far East found their batteries only just lasted the voyage. So serious was the problem that the German U-boat repair base at Kobe, Japan, had a special facility for constructing cells.

SCHNORCHELS

Tubes to enable submarines to run their air-breathing diesel engines for propulsion and to recharge their batteries while running underwater were not a German invention. The American submarine pioneer Simon Lake installed such a device in his *Argonaut*, launched in 1894, as did the Japanese in *Submarine No 6*, the first submarine designed and built in Japan, which was commissioned in 1906. This boat was testing its air tube in April 1910 when it appears that the mouth of the tube dipped below the surface; as a result, the submarine was flood-

△ A *schnorchel* head covered in *Tarnmatte*, a radar- absorbing coating. Note also the *runddipol* antenna array.

ed and lost with all 16 men aboard.

The next person to return to the concept was Lieutenant-Commander J.J. Wichers of the Royal Netherlands Navy (RNethN), whose interest lay in enabling crews of Dutch submarines operating in the East Indies to avoid the tropical heat by running their diesels while remaining submerged. His first patent, taken out in the early 1930s, was for a simple extending tube, similar in concept to those employed by Lake and the Japanese, but the problem with all three devices was that they lacked any means of preventing water from entering the tube if the boat dipped. Wichers, however, was the first to come up with the solution, which was to fit a head-valve, using a spherical float which automatically closed the tube. The RNethN was sufficiently impressed by this device for it to be fitted in two submarines (*O-19, O-20*) for trials and when these proved successful improved tubes were incorporated into the 0-21-class during construction. The Dutch devices were quite sophisticated and included an automatic head-valve as well as an electric motor to raise and lower the mast. There was a separate exhaust-gas mast, which was fixed in the case of *O-19* and *O-20*, and manually extended in the case of the others.

When the Netherlands were overrun in 1940 three of these tube-fitted submarines (*O-25, O-26, O-27*) were captured by the Germans, who carried out some trials in *O-25*, but then lost interest, removing the device from all three boats in 1941. The British showed even less interest and removed the masts from their ex-Dutch boats in 1940.

By 1943 it was clear that the time spent by U-boats traveling on the surface recharging their batteries was becoming increasingly dangerous and in May 1943 Dönitz and Professor Walter discussed methods of achieving this while the U-boat remained underwater. This led to a re-examination of the Dutch system, following which a new German design was produced. In this, instead of the air-tube leading directly to the engines, as in the Dutch design, it simply led into the inside of the submarine, from which the diesels drew their air supply in the normal way. It should be noted that the amount of air required was significant: the two diesels on the Type XXI, for example, needed 166,000cu ft (4,700m³) air per hour.

The concept of the 'air buffer' was important, since it meant that the entire internal volume of the submarine acted as a reservoir in the event that the valve was suddenly closed. This meant that the diesels could run on for a short time if the air supply was lost, although this could not go on for very long, since if they were allowed to extract the air from the inside of the submarine for more than two or three minutes it led to giddiness, shortage of breath, burst ear-drums, dental fillings falling out, loss of consciousness and, at least potentially, asphyxiation. Thus, in the early installations it was necessary for an engineer to monitor the tube constantly while it was in use in order to stop the diesels whenever the valve closed, but this was later automated. The diesels had to be modified to run with the *schnorchel*: the MAN M9V in the Type IXC-40, for example, was fitted with special camshafts with a 'normal' position giving an exhaust pressure of 0.1atü and a '*schnorchel*' position, with a pressure of 0.4-0.45atm (atmospheres).

Once the design had been agreed, progress was rapid and prototype tubes were installed in two Type IIs (*U-57, U-58*) in July 1943. These telescopic tubes replaced the after periscope, being raised and lowered vertically by the periscope mechanism. Initial tests in August were successful. As a result, a modified tube was installed in two Type VIIs, *U-235* and *U-236*, in September 1943. The tests in all four boats were successful and showed that, used with care, the *schnorchel*, as it was now named, could be of considerable tactical value.

DESIGN

The retrofitted *schnorchel* tubes in the Types VII, IX, X and XIV were, inevitably, something of a compromise. Each type required its own individual design, which had to be compatible with the height of the periscope, the shape of the superstructure, the arrangement and type of engines, and the available space. In all, eight different types of German U-boats had *schnorchels* and some of those had more than one design.

In the Type VII the *schnorchel* tube was located at the port, forward end of the bridge; it was locked in the upright position by a large clamp and pivoted forwards to lie in a large well inset into the deck. The disadvantage of this arrangement was that the *schnorchel* head-valve and exhaust fumes interfered with

the forward view through the periscope. In the Type IX and Type XB, however, the tube was located on the starboard side of the after end of the bridge and pivoted backwards to lie in a deck-well. The Type XXI and XXIII used a telescopic *schnorchel* which was housed inside the bridge structure.

Two designs of mast entered service, the most widely used being hinged at its foot (*klappmast*) which was raised and lowered by a cylinder and piston, driven by oil pressure from the periscope hydraulic system. In the lowered position it rested in a slot in the upper casing. In the original installations for Type VIIC and IX the *schnorchel* was ahead of the periscope, but even though the head-valve was below the lens of the fully extended periscope the wake of the *schnorchel* and the exhaust gases adversely affected vision ahead.

The second type of mast was telescopic, similar in its action to that used for the periscope. It was operated by an air motor located in the control room, which used mechanical links to drive a pinion wheel engaged in a rack on the side of the mast. The mast extended through the bridge structure and when retracted was housed in a vertical well extending through to the bottom of the boat. A manual stand-by system could be used to raise the telescopic mast but not the hinged mast.

It was originally thought that it would be necessary to

▽ A vertically extending *schnorchel* mast, installed on the Type XXI. It was raised by a special air-compressor which drove a pinion wheel engaged in the rack on the rear side of the mast. Note the *Tarnmatte* and the ball operating the head-valve.

▷ The earlier type of hinged *schnorchel* mast which was retrofitted on existing boats, such as this Type IXC/40.

△ A hinged *schnorchel* lying in its well on the upper deck.

open after the submarine had submerged in order to flood the mast. The ball float did this mechanically as the mast reached the housed position, while the ring float type used a small vent which operated at a depth of about 100ft (30m). Experience showed that each ball and ring valve needed very extensive testing to ensure that it operated properly, both prior to installation and during the U-boat's working-up period. The head was stream-lined so that it left the minimum wake and was covered with an anti-radar coating to prevent location by enemy ASW forces.

The *schnorchel* was not without its problems. Despite early German hopes to the contrary, Allied radar proved capable of detecting an object as small as the *schnorchel* head, although this was obviously much more difficult to detect than a surfaced U-boat.

British experience was that whereas a surfaced U-boat could be spotted at 6 miles (9.6km) a *schnorchel* could be spotted at only about 3 miles (4.8km). Also, the tube, and, in partic-ular, its wake, was visible to the naked eye during daylight.

Inside the U-boat, the noise from the diesels meant that the hydrophones could not be used, making the captain totally dependent on the periscope. Further, protracted submerged operations resulted in new problems; for example, antenna cables and ducts were flooded, rust proliferated, and insulators were broken or disintegrated. Also, the boat was compelled to travel at no more than about 6 knots, since above that speed the periscope, which was essential while using the *schnorchel*, suf-fered from vibrations.

Once Dönitz decided to go ahead progress was rapid. Priority was given to operational boats followed by other in-service boats and then to boats under construction. The first 20 tubes for Type VIICs were ordered in August 1943 and another 100 in September, together with 40 for in-service Types IXC and IXD. These were fit-ted at the operational bases, including Lorient, St Nazaire, La Pallice, Brest, Bordeaux, Toulon, as well as in dockyards in Germany. It was also planned to fit *schnorchels* in Type XIV U-tankers, but all but one had been sunk by the time the final design was agreed. The records show, however, that the last surviving Type XIV boat, *U-488* (Studt), was fitted with a *schnorchel* prior to departing on its final patrol on February 22 1944.

The *schnorchel* was regarded with great scepticism by the operational U-boat crews, an attitude that was not helped when the first operational boat, *U-264* (Looks), was lost in the North Atlantic on February 19 1944 during its first operational voyage. The reason for its loss was unknown to the *Kriegsmarine* at the time but was assumed by the cynics to be due to the *schnorchel*. What had actually happened was that *U-264* had been hunted by British warships until it was forced to surface, where demoli-tion charges were set and the crew abandoned ship, all being rescued. Despite this apparent setback, the *schnorchel* gradual-ly became accepted and by mid-1944 it was in regular use.

deflect the exhaust gases downwards and spread them out in order to avoid detection by enemy ASW forces. German experi-ence seemed to show that this was unnecessary and on the Types XXI and XXIII the exhaust was simply discharged through a series of holes in the side of the mast. The British, however, reported that the diesel exhaust smoke was frequently a help in detecting a *schnorchel*.

Two devices for rapidly closing the air intake were produced. One was an electro-pneumatic device, circular in shape; the other used a floating sphere. The Germans designed two types of head-valve for operational use: the first used a ball float (*Kugelschwimmer*), but this was being replaced by the ring-float (*Ringschwimmer*) in 1945.[1] Both were opened by gravity and closed by the buoyant action of the float, when the upper end of the *schnorchel* became submerged. Both were also required to

Footnote:
1. An electro-pneumatic valve was still under development at the end of the war.

PART THREE

OPERATIONS
THE U-BOAT WAR

Phase 1. September 1939 to May 1940

Dönitz had already deployed his 39 operational U-boats (out of 57 actually in commission) to their war stations when war broke out on September 3 1939, with some in British coastal waters and a few in the Western Approaches. One of the latter, *U-30* (Lemp) became the first to sink a British ship, when it torpedoed the liner *Athenia* (13,581tons) without warning on the night of September 3, in contravention of *Kriegsmarine* standing orders; 112 died, but some 1,300 were rescued. The British saw this as the start of an unrestricted campaign, although responsibility was vehemently denied by the German authorities, who even went to the extreme of altering a number of entries in the boat's *Kriegtagesbuch* (war diary), the only known instance where this happened.

At this stage, the *Ubootwaffe* was equipped with a mix of Type I, II, VII and IX boats. Smallest were the Type IIs, whose range confined them to the North Sea and the coastal waters around the British Isles, and most of which had been reclaimed temporarily from the training flotillas. The largest were two Type Is and an increasing number of Type IXs, which had sufficient range to reach the Azores. In between these in size was the Type VII, upon which Dönitz pinned his greatest hopes as the general-purpose attack boat; Type VIIAs and -Bs could operate in the Atlantic as far as 15°W and down to the Bay of Biscay, while the Type VIIC could operate further westwards and as far south as the Portuguese coast.

In the event, the U-boats were deployed in three waves, although the numbers were unimpressive, peaking at 21 on September 10 and then reducing to 13 (November 23) and, finally, to 9 (February 7). There were also a number of problems: the torpedo arming devices functioned incorrectly, and the pre-war concept of a senior officer exercising tactical command of a 'wolf-pack' from one of the U-boats in the group simply did not work.

▽ October 17 1939, a day when everything seemed possible. Cheering sailors greet *U-47*, Type VIIB, on its return from sinking the British battleship, HMS *Royal Oak*, in Scapa Flow. This exploit made Günther Prien, the commanding officer, a national hero and his fame persists to this day.

Dönitz directed the main effort against unescorted shipping in the South-Western Approaches, although he also deployed U-boats as far south as Gibraltar, as well as conducting mine-laying operations in the coastal waters around the British Isles. The British had closed the English Channel with minefields (as in World War I) and all U-boats had to undertake the long haul northwards from German North Sea ports and around the British Isles before they reached their operational areas.

One of the most widely publicized incidents of the U-boat war took place less than two months after war had been declared. *Korvettenkapitän* Günther Prien took *U-47* (Type VIIB) into Scapa Flow, the Royal Navy's heavily protected base off the northern coast of Scotland, on the night of September 13/14, where he sank the battleship *Royal Oak* with the loss of 833 lives. British naval pride was deeply humiliated and the Germans scored a major propaganda victory, turning Prien into a national hero.

In March 1940 Dönitz was ordered to concentrate all available U-boats to support the invasion of Norway, which even extended to using several boats as ammunition transports. The mass of Allied shipping resulted in the U-boats being presented

with many targets, but they were foiled by a series of torpedo malfunctions, which caused a major scandal. On the credit side, however, Norwegian ports immediately became available for use by U-boats, providing direct access to the Arctic and a staging/refueling point on the way to the North Atlantic.

PHASE 2. MAY 1940 – MARCH 1941

The German assault on the west was launched on May 10 1940, with Belgium capitulating on May 28 and the French armistice being signed on June 22. The U-boats were unable to play a major role in this, partly because the large numbers requiring repairs following the invasion of Norway caused considerable congestion in the shipyards, although boats were back in the Atlantic by June, sinking 63 ships (356,937grt), by far the largest monthly total so far. The land victory in France also resulted in the *Ubootwaffe* obtaining control of the French Atlantic ports, a totaly unexpected bonus, which eliminated the lengthy voyage around the British Isles. Convoys of lorries containing weapons, munitions and general supplies were despatched before the armistice had been signed and the first port, Lorient, was available for use on July 6 1940, with the first boat, *U-30* (Lemp), entering the following morning.

By now it was clear that the concept of command afloat would not work and Dönitz, who had set up his HQ in Paris, assumed personal command of operations in the Atlantic. Thus, in July 1940, wolf-pack operations against Allied convoys began in earnest, with frequent help from the *B-Dienst*, and U-boat successes mounted rapidly. U-boat 'aces' such as Prien, Lemp, and Kretschmer carried out one attack after another on convoys in the North-Western Approaches; successes were frequent and U-boat losses relatively small in what the U-boat crews involved came to look back on as the 'happy time.' The concept of using large numbers of U-boats in night attacks frustrated Allied ASW forces, since their sonar was unusable and they had only visual observation to depend on to find the low-lying, fast-moving U-boats as they slipped through the lanes of ships in the convoy.

The U-boats continued to inflict heavy losses through the winter months, but Allied ASW forces gradually improved their techniques and in early March 1941 no fewer than three U-boat 'aces' were lost. Prien (*U-47*) disappeared without trace on March 7; Schepke (*U-100*) was crushed in the bridge when his boat was rammed by HMS *Vanoc*; but the third, Kretschmer (*U-99*), was so heavily depth-charged that he was forced to surface and abandon, with 40 of his 43 crew surviving.[1]

A significant development in this period was that, at their own suggestion, the Italian Navy established an Atlantic base, known as *Betasom*, at Bordeaux, with the first six submarines starting operations there in November 1940. From then until the Italian armistice in 1943 Italian submarines served in the Atlantic, under German operational control but Italian command.

U-BOATS IN SERVICE: 1939–1945					
MONTH	COMMISSION	TRAINING	PERCENT TRAINING	OPERATIONAL	AT SEA
September 1939	57	18	32%	39	23
October 1939	51	12	24%	39	10
November 1939	52	19	37%	33	16
December 1939	54	20	37%	34	8
January 1940	54	21	39%	33	11
February 1940	50	15	30%	35	15
March 1940	50	16	32%	34	13
April 1940	47	13	28%	34	24
May 1940	49	18	37%	31	8
June 1940	51	24	47%	27	18
July 1940	53	23	43%	30	11
August 1940	55	28	51%	27	13
September 1940	61	34	56%	27	13
October 1940	68	38	56%	30	12
November 1940	74	50	68%	24	11
December 1940	83	56	67%	27	10
January 1941	94	72	77%	22	8
February 1941	103	82	80%	21	12
March 1941	109	82	75%	27	13
April 1941	121	93	77%	28	19
May 1941	139	106	76%	33	24
June 1941	150	112	75%	38	32
July 1941	169	116	69%	53	27
August 1941	184	120	65%	64	36
September 1941	197	124	63%	73	36
October 1941	219	144	66%	75	36
November 1941	238	157	66%	81	38
December 1941	250	162	65%	88	25
January 1942	262	171	65%	91	42
February 1942	276	175	63%	101	50
March 1942	288	177	61%	111	48
April 1942	302	183	61%	119	49
May 1942	318	194	61%	124	61
June 1942	336	210	63%	138	70
July 1942	346	208	60%	138	70
August 1942	358	209	58%	149	86
September 1942	366	194	53%	172	100
October 1942	374	179	48%	195	105
November 1942	385	178	46%	207	95
December 1942	403	199	49%	204	97
January 1943	419	206	49%	213	92
February 1943	421	200	48%	221	116
March 1943	432	203	47%	229	116
April 1943	435	199	46%	236	111
May 1943	420	180	43%	240	118
June 1943	428	214	50%	214	86

Month	Commission	Training	Percent Training	Operational	At Sea
July 1943	417	210	50%	207	84
August 1943	413	239	58%	174	59
September 1943	424	239	56%	165	60
October 1943	425	250	59%	175	86
November 1943	429	267	62%	162	78
December 1943	452	293	63%	169	66
January 1944	456	287	65%	91	42
February 1944	455	287	63%	168	68
March 1944	453	285	63%	168	68
April 1944	453	290	64%	163	57
May 1944	449	287	64%	162	43
June 1944	435	257	59%	178	47
July 1944	423	246	58%	177	34
August 1944	406	248	61%	158	51
September 1944	401	255	64%	146	68
October 1944	403	272	67%	131	45
November 1944	418	288	69%	130	41
December 1944	428	293	68%	135	51
January 1945	453	314	69%	139	39
February 1945	453	297	66%	156	47
March 1945	445	280	63%	165	56
April 1945	389	223	57%	166	54

However, the relationship was not a happy one, with Dönitz developing a very poor opinion of their capabilities and performance, and they were quickly relegated to a secondary role.

PHASE 3. MARCH 1941 TO JANUARY 1942

The loss of three high-grade commanders forced Dönitz to move his U-boats in the North Atlantic further westward, while the Type IXs moved southward, exploiting an Allied 'soft spot' which had been detected off the West African coast. By the summer of 1941 the British had sufficient escorts to provide end-to-end protection for convoys on both the North Atlantic and UK-Gibraltar-West Africa routes. But the numbers of U-boats at sea were increasing rapidly also and a succession of bloody battles were fought as both sides sought to gain the upper hand. Dönitz started to deploy his boats ever further west and by the summer of 1941 they were regularly operating off the Canadian coast.

Many U-boats sought to assist the battleship *Bismarck* during its foray into the Atlantic in May 1941, especially after it had lost the initiative, but heavy weather prevented the boats from getting close, while several boats which got into good firing positions against British warships had already run out of torpedoes. In the event, U-boats were able to pick up just three survivors from the doomed battleship. A number of tankers had been deployed across the Atlantic to replenish *Bismarck* and

▽ Otto Kretschmer (*U-99*) comes ashore at Liverpool on March 17 1941. Later he became a rear-admiral in the post-war navy.

other ships in its group and these were now re-tasked to support U-boats. However, as described elsewhere, they were sunk, one after another, by the British, using Ultra information. Operations in the Atlantic continued at a steady level, but there was a marked increase in the attacks on convoys on the Gibraltar route. Also, U-boats were sent into the Mediterranean to assist Rommel's operations in Libya, with the first six boats arriving in late September (which gave a 30 percent reduction in boats operational in the Atlantic), followed by another four in November. Dönitz's ire at sending U-boats into what he regarded as a secondary theater was somewhat reduced when *U-81* (Benker) sank the British carrier HMS *Ark Royal*, on November 13 1941.

PHASE 4. JANUARY 1942 TO JULY 1942

The Japanese attack on Pearl Harbor (December 7/8 1941) came as a complete surprise to the Germans and, as a result, U-boats were not in a position to take immediate advantage of the United States' entry into the war. Indeed, it was not until January 13 1942 that U-boats arrived off the USA's Atlantic seaboard, in an operation designated *Paukenschlag* (= drumbeat). They started operations off the Atlantic seaboard of the USA and in the coastal waters of Nova Scotia and Newfoundland, but quickly extended southwards to include the Gulf of Mexico and the Caribbean. They inflicted very heavy losses, particularly of tankers – it was known to the U-boat crews as the 'second happy time' – and it was May before the US Navy was able to institute convoys. Once started, however, US ASW arrangements rapidly improved and the U-boats were gradually forced out further away from the coast and out into the Atlantic.

On other fronts, U-boats continued to inflict losses in the Mediterranean and in the Arctic, while Japanese submarines began operations in the Indian Ocean. The latter sank merchantmen as far west as the Mozambique Channel, adding considerably to the British problems.

In general, the *Ubootwaffe* believed that it had done well in the first half of 1942. The successes off the US coast in February-March had been outstanding – 873,000grt of shipping had been sunk – and more U-boats were at sea than ever before.

PHASE 5. AUGUST 1942 TO MAY 1943

Buoyed by their successes, the *Ubootwaffe* decided to make a determined effort to sever the convoy routes linking the UK and North America. It was a battle fought against the background of the worst fall and winter weather of the war, with heavy seas, high winds, and regular banks of fog. The *B-Dienst* had penetrated the latest British naval code, enabling it to provide Dönitz with a regular stream of accurate convoy positions, which *BdU* used to move U-boats into position. Further, not only were more boats at sea, but they were also being refueled on a regular basis, enabling them to spend much longer on patrol. By this stage, also, *BdU* was exercising a sophisticated form of control, with U-boats being formed and reformed into patrol lines and attack groups, although problems were experienced – for example, when the U-boat sighting the convoy was the end boat in a patrol line.

Caribbean operations were ended in September, when rising U-boat losses coupled with the lengthy transit (3-4 weeks) made them unprofitable. Some operations were conducted in the Gulf of St Lawrence, with moderate success.

Also, at this stage the U-boat crews were beginning to think that the Allies were establishing a distinct technological edge. Allied radar was clearly superior and a succession of German radar warning receivers were failing to provide adequate notice of Allied air attack. This, coupled with the greater speed and endurance of Allied aircraft, meant that air attack was causing increasing losses.

At this stage also, Dönitz and his staff realized that sheer numbers of the current types of U-boat would not provide the answer and Dr Walter began to come to prominence, since his proposals for great increases in underwater speed and endurance offered an attractive solution to many of the problems.

One of the more controversial incidents in the U-boat war took place on September 12 1942 when *U-156* (Hartenstein) sank the British liner *Laconia* (19,695grt), which was sailing independently, with 2,732 people aboard: 932 crew, passengers and guards, and 1,800 Italian prisoners-of-war. As soon as he

realized that Italians were among those in the sea Hartenstein started a rescue operation, which soon consisted of one Italian and three German submarines sailing on the surface, with many survivors on the upper deck and in lifeboats, which were being towed. This concentration of U-boats was attacked with bombs and by US Liberator aircraft; some survivors were killed and *U-156*, which was slightly damaged, left the scene, although the other three boats remained until the survivors were taken off by Vichy French warships from Dakar. The incident resulted in 1,621 deaths and caused much bitterness; it also led to an order from *BdU* that no such rescues were to be attempted in future, except that masters and chief engineers would be taken aboard for interrogation.

In October 1942 German intelligence noted an increase in naval activity in and around Gibraltar but having already considered and rejected the possibility of an Allied landing in North Africa they made a wrong deduction. Thus, no U-boat attacks were made on any of the many Allied convoys heading for the North African landings (Operation Torch).

Meanwhile, the U-boat attacks on North Atlantic convoys continued unabated and the predominance of the *Ubootwaffe* in German naval affairs was confirmed on January 30 1943 when Dönitz was promoted to *grossadmiral* and appointed commander-in-chief of the *Kriegsmarine*. Despite this promotion, he retained direct command of the U-boats. His headquarters staff moved from Paris to Berlin on March 30 1943.

△ An Allied tanker burns. This time the crew escaped, but Merchant Navy losses were high.

◁ US Navy sailors watch the convoy they are protecting in the unceasing battle against the U-boats.

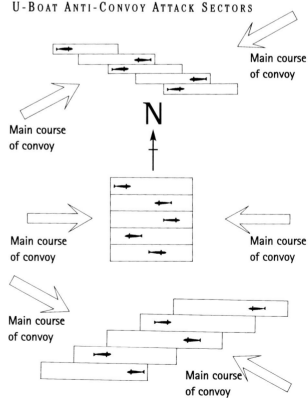

U - B O A T   A N T I - C O N V O Y   A T T A C K   S E C T O R S

Main course of convoy

Main course of convoy

N

Main course of convoy

Main course of convoy

Main course of convoy

Main course of convoy

Main course of convoy

The U-boat campaign in the Atlantic reached its peak in March 1943, helped in part by the fact that many Allied escorts were in port for repairs after the appalling weather of the previous two months. However, U-boat successes were diminishing rapidly, while U-boat losses suddenly increased to a totally unacceptable level: January – 6; February – 19; March – 16 ; April – 15; May – 41. On May 21 Dönitz accepted that matters could not continue as they were and ordered a temporary cessation in the campaign.

PHASE 6. MAY 1943 TO SEPTEMBER 1943

Those in Berlin regarded this reduction in the U-boat campaign as a temporary expedient, attributing the Allied success to a combination of sheer weight of numbers and technological developments, both of which would soon be reversed in Germany's favor. Allied air power was, however, becoming increasingly effective, not least in the Bay of Biscay, the one area which all U-boats had to transit when leaving on or returning

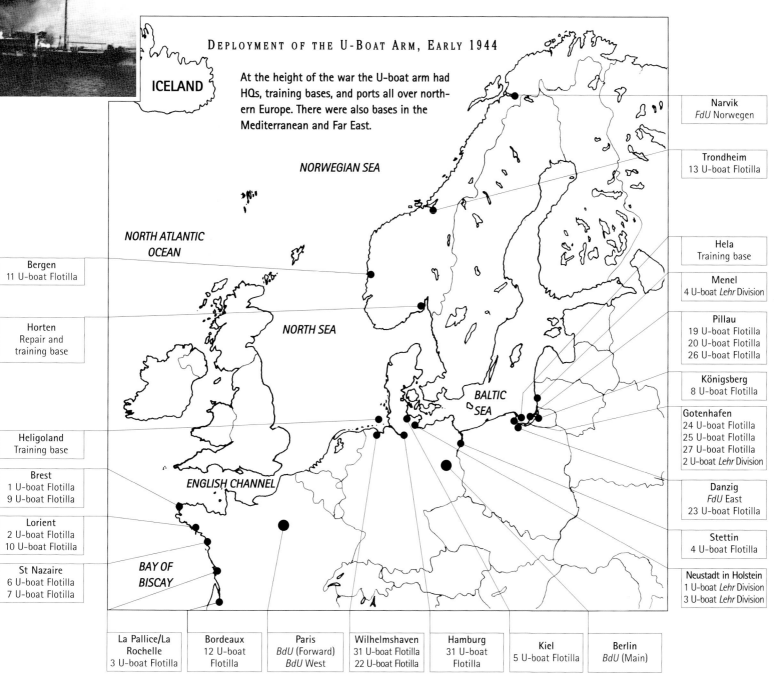

DEPLOYMENT OF THE U-BOAT ARM, EARLY 1944

At the height of the war the U-boat arm had HQs, training bases, and ports all over northern Europe. There were also bases in the Mediterranean and Far East.

ICELAND

NORWEGIAN SEA

NORTH ATLANTIC OCEAN

NORTH SEA

BALTIC SEA

ENGLISH CHANNEL

BAY OF BISCAY

Narvik
FdU Norwegen

Trondheim
13 U-boat Flotilla

Hela
Training base

Menel
4 U-boat Lehr Division

Pillau
19 U-boat Flotilla
20 U-boat Flotilla
26 U-boat Flotilla

Königsberg
8 U-boat Flotilla

Gotenhafen
24 U-boat Flotilla
25 U-boat Flotilla
27 U-boat Flotilla
2 U-boat Lehr Division

Danzig
FdU East
23 U-boat Flotilla

Stettin
4 U-boat Flotilla

Neustadt in Holstein
1 U-boat Lehr Division
3 U-boat Lehr Division

Bergen
11 U-boat Flotilla

Horten
Repair and training base

Heligoland
Training base

Brest
1 U-boat Flotilla
9 U-boat Flotilla

Lorient
2 U-boat Flotilla
10 U-boat Flotilla

St Nazaire
6 U-boat Flotilla
7 U-boat Flotilla

La Pallice/La Rochelle
3 U-boat Flotilla

Bordeaux
12 U-boat Flotilla

Paris
BdU (Forward)
BdU West

Wilhelmshaven
31 U-boat Flotilla
22 U-boat Flotilla

Hamburg
31 U-boat Flotilla

Kiel
5 U-boat Flotilla

Berlin
BdU (Main)

A GLOBAL SYSTEM: U-BOAT OPERATIONS 1939-1945

The main thrust of the German U-boat campaign was in the North Atlantic, but U-boats actually operated against the Allies in all oceans of the world except the Pacific and the Antarctic, as this map portrays.

A. British Isles. The waters around the British Isles were a major U-boat operational area from September 1939 to May 1945.

B. Norway. From June 1940 to May 1945 Norwegian ports were used as refueling bases for U-boats proceeding to and from the Atlantic, as well as operational bases for boats operating in the Arctic Ocean.

C. Bay of Biscay. U-boats operated in the Bay of Biscay from 1939, but used the French Atlantic ports from July 1940 to June 1944.

D. North Atlantic. The decisive operational zone in the U-boat war was the North Atlantic which, from December 1941 also included the United States seaboard.

E. Central Atlantic. Operations in the Central Atlantic became possible from July 1940 once the French Atlantic ports were in use by German naval forces.

F. Mediterranean. Despite the size of the Italian submarine fleet, Hitler ordered that U-boats should go to the German ally's aid in the Mediterranean, the first arriving in September 1941.

G. Gulf of Finland. Operations against Soviet shipping took place from the invasion of the USSR on June 22 1941 to May 8 1945.

H. Black Sea. Type IIs were transported overland and by river to the Black Sea, where they operated from May 1943 to August 1944.

I. Greenland. U-boats transported several meteorological parties to and from bases on the Greenland coast.

J. Caribbean. Once the USA entered the war in December 1941 U-boat operations extended as far as the entrance to the Panama Canal.

K. The Cape. With the deployment of the *Monsun* group, operations extended right down to the Cape of Good Hope, which was first reached by U-boats in May 1943.

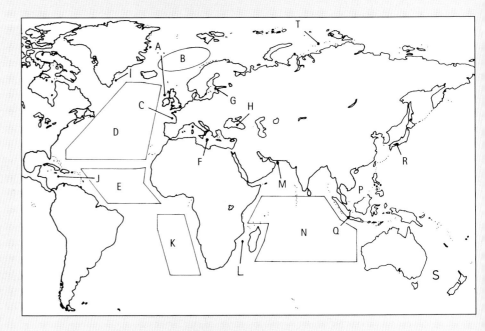

▽ The losses in this global war were high and U-boats were sunk in every ocean of the world.

L. Mozambique Channel. In mid-1943 U-boat operations extended around the Cape and northwards into the Mozambique Channel.

M. Arabian Gulf. Several U-boats penetrated into the Gulf in 1944.

N. Indian Ocean. Numerous U-boats carried out offensive operations in the Indian Ocean in 1943-44, replenishing from German tankers, and proceeding to the base at Penang for rest and repairs.

O. Penang. The main German Far East base was at Penang on the west coast of the Malayan peninsula. The first U-boat entered the port in July 1943.

P. Singapore. A small repair base was established in Singapore from mid-1944 and was operational until May 1945.

Q. Batavia. A second repair base was located in Batavia in Japanese-occupied Indonesia.

R. Japan. A small U-boat base was established at Kobe, including a battery repair and construction facility.

S. Australia. *U-862* (Timm) sailed around Australia in December 1944/January 1945.

T. Kara Sea. Six U-boats operated in the Kara Sea in August 1944.

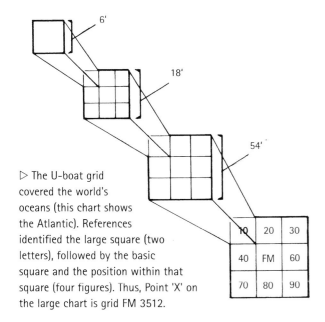

▷ The U-boat grid covered the world's oceans (this chart shows the Atlantic). References identified the large square (two letters), followed by the basic square and the position within that square (four figures). Thus, Point 'X' on the large chart is grid FM 3512.

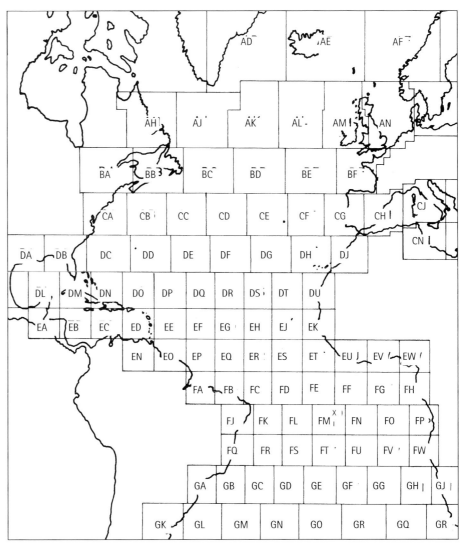

from patrols. One answer was to give individual U-boats a much increased anti-aircraft armament and to convert some special *'Flak'* U-boats, to enable them to fight it out on the surface. These measures achieved some early successes, but Allied aircrew quickly realized what they were up against and devised tactics to overcome them. In the Azores area the carrier-borne aircraft of the United States Navy destroyed the supply U-boats, whose existence had so greatly increased the range of the operational boats.

The Japanese had made several requests for German U-boats to operate in the Indian Ocean, but while the Atlantic campaign was going well Dönitz had not felt the need to comply. With the collapse of the campaign, however, and the need for the *Kriegsmarine* to be on the offensive somewhere, things looked different and, encouraged by reports that the Allied ASW capability in the Indian Ocean was poor, he decided to send a group of Type IXCs to the Far East. Group *Monsun* sailed in June, but the limited range of the Type IXC meant that the boats had to be refueled twice, which turned out to be something of a disaster.

PHASE 7. SEPTEMBER 1943 TO JUNE 1944

In mid-1943 it appeared that new weapons coming into service with the *Ubootwaffe* would begin to erode the Allied technological lead: the failed *Metox* warning device was being replaced by the more effective *Wanze* and heavier AA weapons were being fitted in many more U-boats. The new torpedo, *T5 Zaunkönig* also came into service. The hopes raised by such advances were quickly dashed, however. *Wanze* proved no more effective than *Metox*. Losses from Allied air action remained at a high level and the concept of a *Flak* U-boat was abandoned. To add to the problems it became apparent that early claims about the effective-

ness of *Zaunkönig* were exaggerated.

The U-boats tried to resume the offensive in the North Atlantic, but all attempts were quickly smothered and throughout the fall and winter of 1943/1944 little was achieved in this area. In November a conscious decision was taken to withdraw to the eastern Atlantic and the figures for merchant ship sinkings speak for themselves: November – 6 (23,245grt); December – 7 (47,785); January – 5 (36,065) and February – 2 (7,048grt).

By December 1943 some 20 percent of boats at sea were being lost each month and U-boat crews were becoming increasingly bewildered by the number and variety of Allied ASW sensors and weapons. This feeling was exacerbated by the fact that the great majority of U-boats that were lost were unable to signal that they were under attack; thus, unless the Allies announced the sinking or until any men taken prisoner managed to get the news home, *BdU* had no idea what had happened to the boat or why.

By the beginning of 1944 the voyage across the Bay of Biscay, whic h earlier had taken 3-5 days, was taking up to 12 days, with boats forced to stay underwater for up to 22 hours in every 24. Further, every moment spent on the surface recharging the batteries and compressed air reservoirs was fraught with peril, with reliance placed on alert watchkeepers and the effectiveness of the radar warning receiver. Even that device told them only that a radar was active in their area – it gave no indication of radar type, bearing or range – and it was not even effective against all enemy radar frequencies. To add to these problems, the losses were such that U-boat commanding officers were becoming ever younger and less experienced, many crew members were totaly inexperienced straight out of training, and the vital leavening of experienced and mature petty officers and chief petty officers was becoming spread increasingly thinly.

On top of everything else, it was becoming alarmingly obvious that the long-expected Allied invasion was now imminent and from March onwards the Atlantic U-boats were deliberately held back as a counter-attack force.

The only areas of aggressive activity were in the Arctic, where U-boats continued to contest the passage of convoys to and from North Russia, and in the Indian Ocean, where operations, albeit on a small scale, were reasonably successful.

PHASE 8. JUNE 1944 TO MAY 1945

In late May/early June 1944 the Germans were well aware that an Allied landing on the French coast was imminent, but what they did not know was the time and place, so Dönitz withdrew the great majority of U-boats to ports where they were held at six hours notice to sail. Thus, at the time of the Allies' landing on June 6 1944, there were 79 U-boats available to take immediate action against the Allied fleet, 59 of them in ports (22 in Norway; 37 in France), with another 20 at sea (17 en route from Norway into the Atlantic – 5 of which, unknown to *BdU*, had already been lost – and 3 on weather-reporting duty in mid-Atlantic). Although the invasion was expected, the Allies managed to achieve both strategic and tactical surprise. Dönitz responded by throwing as many U-boats as possible into the fray, although the results achieved, despite the vast numbers of ships concentrated in the Channel, were negligible.

The surviving U-boats were withdrawn from their attacks in the Channel area at the end of August, by which time they had sunk 5 surface escorts, 4 landing ships and another 12 ships (56,845grt), and damaged a few others. Dönitz claimed that the 'old fighting spirit of the U-boat arm has again magnificently stood the test,' although the loss of 20 U-boats and some 1,000 crew (of which 240 were rescued by the Allies) was a high price to pay. Most of the U-boats escaped to Norway.

The period November 1944 to April 1945 showed a surprising increase in merchant ship sinkings and a reduction in U-boat losses. This was partly due to the introduction of a new type of

▽ U-boats inflicted great losses, particularly on merchant vessels: here, seamen are rescued from American steamer *Carlton*, 1942.

schnorchel but also to operations along the enemy's coasts, especially around the British Isles. The noose around the German homeland was clearly tightening, however, and with the failure of the short-lived German attack in the Ardennes the Allied advance from both east and west continued. Despite this, the *Ubootwaffe* continued operations at a high rate in the last four months of the war, even in the face of an increasingly severe shortage of fuel. A few Type XXIII coastal boats became operational, but the most surprising feature was the failure to get the Type XXI into service. There were many in the training organisation and more in emerging from the yards, but they never attained operational status. Meanwhile, the number of U-boats destroyed in the ports increased dramatically as Allied airpower achieved virtual air supremacy.

Dönitz had three plans for the *Ubootwaffe*. First was that those boats capable of diving should proceed to Norway, where a large concentration of combat-ready boats would, he believed, provide a major role in the forthcoming surrender negotiations. Secondly, he issued preparatory orders for *Unternehmung Regenbogen* (Operation Rainbow) under which all those U-boats unable to leave German ports for Norway would be scuttled by their crews. Thirdly, if all else failed he intended to surrender the Navy and then to find some form of redemption by seeking his own death in battle, although quite how he expected to achieve this after a surrender has never been explained.

Dönitz's situation underwent two sudden, unexpected, and dramatic changes, however, when, first, he was appointed commissioner for northern Germany (April 24), giving him total responsibility for the whole region, and, secondly, when he was appointed *Reichspräsident* on Hitler's death on April 30 1945. Dönitz's reign was short-lived and his only real function was to oversee the surrender in the north, which was signed on May 4 1945, becoming effective at 0800 on May 5 1945, at which moment the U-boat war ended.

Footnotes:
1. Kretschmer was the most successful U-boat co mmander of World War II, sinking 44 ships (266,629grt). He spent the remainder of the was as a prisoner, joined the *Bundesmarine* in the 1950s and ended his career as a widely respected NATO commander with the rank of *Flotilleadmiral*.

MONTH	ANNUAL		CUMULATIVE	
	Ships	Tonnage	Ships	Tonnage
1939	147	509,321	147	509,321
1940	573	2,435,586	660	2,944,907
1941	436	2,235,674	1,096	5,180,581
1942	1,043	5,760,485	2,139	10,941,066
1943	423	2,036,674	2,463	12,977,740
1944	73	371,698	2,536	13,349,438
1945	60	256,574	2,596	13,606,012

ALLIED MERCHANT SHIPS SUNK IN THE ATLANTIC AND ARCTIC OCEANS

THE MEN
U-BOAT OFFICERS

As with any group of human beings, U-boat officers were, despite the selection process, a mixed bag. Some were excellent commanders and skilled tacticians, while a few proved to be poor leaders or unfit to command in battle; the vast majority fell somewhere in between.

In the prewar period, all potential naval officers started their training as infantrymen and attended a three-month basic training course at Stralsund. That was followed by three months' training aboard a sail-training ship and then another three months aboard a modern training cruiser. All this time the men were ranked as ordinary sailors, but they then sat an examination and if they passed they were appointed midshipmen and sent to the *Marineschule* (= naval academy) at Mürwick, just outside Flensburg. The course lasted for 10 months, at the end of which the young men sat the *Offiziershauptprüfung* (officers' main examination) and, provided they passed, then went on another and much longer cruise aboard a training cruiser, at the end of which they were commissioned as a *Leutnant zur See* (lieutenant).

Those who opted for the *Ubootwaffe* (submarine service) then had to attend the submarine school at Neustadt-in-Holstein for nine months, followed by torpedo school for five months. Only then, after no less than five years' training, would the young men report for their first tour of duty aboard a U-boat. They then worked their way up through the appoint-

ments of *Zweite Wachoffizier* (= second watchkeeper [2WO]) and *Erste Wachoffizier* (= first watchkeeper [1WO]) until being selected for commanding officer.

This orderly process of producing a steady stream of naval officers was seriously disrupted in the years 1931/32. In the first of those years the intake was small, anyway, but then on February 26 1932 the sail-training ship *Niobe* sank in a storm while on a training cruise with the 1932 Entry aboard. Many of the cadets were drowned and Admiral Raeder appealed to the Merchant Marine to help in this emergency, as a result of which 15 young officers were transferred to the *Reichsmarine*.

During the war it became the practice for midshipmen to join U-boats as part of the crew, where they were given tasks by the commanding officer and also understudied the watchkeepers. If recommended by their commanding officer they would then go for the officers' training course before returning to a U-boat as 2WO.

COMMANDING OFFICERS

Depending upon the type, U-boats had between three and six officers, at the head of which was the Commanding Officer (CO), whose rank was normally either *Oberleutnant zur See* or *Kapitänleutnant*, although a few were *Korvetten-Kapitän* or *Fregattenkapitän* and, in a very few cases (for example, Freiwald of *U-181*) *Kapitän zur See*. The CO occupied a lonely position: he alone knew what the higher command's and his own plans were; he alone saw the attack through the periscope; and he alone made the decisions. The CO wore a white cover on his cap, the only officer on board allowed to do so. No fewer than 73 COs came from the aristocracy: 8 held the title '*graf*' (= count); 8 '*freiherr*' (= baron); and 57 '*von*' (= knight).

The normal case was for officers to work their way up through the chain of experience, ultimately attaining command after a progressive and carefully managed career in U-boats. Under this ideal system it was usual for an officer to be transferred to another boat when he took command, although later in the war it was not unknown for an officer to step into the captain's shoes in the same boat.

Others, especially later in the war when losses were mounting, came to command of a U-boat by more circuitous paths. Two surface ship officers who had been aboard the *Graf Spee* during the Battle of the River Plate escaped from internment and returned to Germany. *Fregattenkapitän* Jürgen Wattenberg had been *Graf Spee*'s gunnery officer and was interned with the rest of the crew in Argentina but escaped in May 1940, went to Chile and then returned to Germany by air. He transferred to U-boats and took command of the new *U-162* (Type IXC) in September 1941, in which he sank 86,000 tons of Allied shipping (rather more than the 50,000 tons sunk by the *Graf Spee*), before being sunk in September 1942. The other was *Kapitänleutnant* Kurt Diggins who had been *Graf Spee Kapitän zur See* Langsdorff's

▽ Eight commanding officers at a conference in early 1940. Among the most famous are Kretschmer (left); Prien (2nd from left) and Lüth (4th from left, back row). Of these 17 men, eight lost their boats in action (four died, four survived to become PoWs); two died when their boats were lost, cause unknown; one (Lüth) survived the war but was shot in an accident days later; and one (Kretschmer) became a rear-admiral in the Federal German Navy.

Flag Lieutenant and had been left in Uruguay when his ship sailed to be scuttled. Diggins eventually escaped from Uruguay and reached Germany via Brazil, where he, too, joined the U-boats. He was a watchkeeper aboard *U-751* (Type VIIC) before getting command of *U-458* (Type VIIC), in which he was sunk in the Mediterranean in 1943. Like Wattenburg, he spent the rest of the war in various prisoner-of-war camps.

Another officer, Johann Fehler, took command of *U-234* (Type XB) in 1944 at the age of 34. He was originally in the merchant navy but enlisted as an officer-cadet in 1936 and by 1939 was commanding a small minesweeper. He then served as gunnery officer aboard the successful raider *Atlantis* (March 1940-November 1941) and on his return he became an instructor at the *Marineschule* (= naval academy) at Mürwik. He then applied for an appointment as a U-boat commander and after the usual course and one cruise 'under instruction' he was appointed to command *U-234*.[1]

At least five commanders came to U-boats from the *Luftwaffe*. *Kapitänleutnant* Manfred Kinzel, for example, was an ex-*Luftwaffe* officer who commanded *U-338* (a Type VIIC), which was sunk with all hands on September 20 1943. Other ex-*Luftwaffe* officers included *Kapitänleutnant* Werner Otto, who commanded *U-285* from May 1943 to April 1944, and Paul Just, commander of *U-546* from June 1943 until it was sunk by US Navy warships on April 24 1945.

It is not surprising that in a large body of men and under the enormous stress of U-boat operations there should be a few problems. Dönitz did not hesitate to get rid of men he considered unsound, although he could also be very forgiving towards men he regarded highly. Some thrived on command – Prien, Lüth, and Kretschmer, for example – but others fared less well. *Kapitänleutnant* Heinicke did not impress Dönitz with his performance in command of *U-53* (Type VIIB) on patrol between October 21 and November 30 1939 and was removed from command; *Kapitänleutnant* Franzke, who took command of *U-3* (Type IIA) in July 1940, was removed in November and reduced to the ranks;[2] while *Kapitäleutnant* Hewicker, former commander of *U-671* (Type VIIC), was dismissed from the officer corps on May 4 1943.

Some paid an even greater price. *Kapitänleutnant* Hirsacker, commanding officer of *U-572*, tried and failed to penetrate the Straits of Gibraltar in 1941, and in November 1942 his boat was the first on the scene of the Allied Torch landings, where he was considered to have shown 'cowardice in the face of the enemy' for which he was charged (the only U-boat CO to face such an indictment) court-martialed, sentenced to death and shot on April 24 1943.

Oberleutnant Kusch of *U-154* (Type IXC) returned from patrol in December 1943 to be denounced by his 1WO, Ulrich Abel, a Nazi party member, for 'lacking in aggression', 'undermining morale' (*Wehrkraft zersetzung*), making remarks against Hitler and the Nazi Party, and for removing Hitler's picture from

△ Wilhelm Dommes (b. 1907, d. 1990) entered the *Kriegsmarine* in 1933, after service in the merchant navy. He served aboard *Nurnberg* (cruiser) followed by *Scharnhorst* (battlecruiser), but transferred to U-boats in April 1940. Following a cruise as 'CO under instruction' he took command of *U-431* (ten, patrols April 1941-December 1942). He then commanded *U-178* (Type IXD₂), leaving Bordeaux in March 1943 and reaching Penang, Malaya, in August. He commanded the German base at Penang and in January 1945 became commander of all U-boats in the Far East. He sank 11 ships (45,646grt).

the boat. In January 1944 Kusch was sentenced by a court-martial to be reduced to the ranks and shot; the sentence was confirmed by Dönitz, and Kusch was shot on May 12 1944.[3]

Not all of those who found the strain too great were treated harshly. Heinrich Bleichrodt, known as 'Ajax' to all U-boat men, was one of the merchant navy officers who joined the Navy in 1933 after the *Niobe* disaster. He transferred to U-boats in 1939 and commanded *U-48* (Type VIIB) (August-December 1940), then *U-67* (Type IXC) (January-May 1941), before taking over *U-109* (Type IXB) in June 1941. He broke down at sea on December 26 1943 and requested an immediate return to base. This was denied by *BdU* but on December 31 Bleichrodt insisted and handed over command to his 1WO, who took *U-109* back to St Nazaire, arriving on January 23 1943. Bleichrodt had served Dönitz well, having commanded three U-boats, carried out nine operational patrols, and sunk one British sloop (HMS *Dundee*) and 28 merchant ships (162,171grt), for which he had been awarded the Knight's Cross with Oak Leaves. Appreciating this record, Dönitz did not dismiss him from the U-boat arm, but transferred him to a training job, where he was promoted in July 1944 and given command of 22 Training Flotilla at Gdynia.[4]

GOING DOWN WITH THE SHIP

The tradition of 'going down with the ship' was followed by a number of COs and there may have been more than records show, although in the chaos accompanying the final moments their actions may not have been fully observed. *Kapitänleutnant* Ralph Kapitsky, for example, commanding *U-615* (Type VIIC), was attacked on August 7 1943 and having ordered abandon ship he first ensured that his crew were all in liferafts and, secondly, checked that the scuttling charges had been set; all his responsibilities completed, he then deliberately went down with his boat. In a similar incident, *Korvetten-Kapitän* Georg von Wilamowitz-Möllendorf, a 50-year-old veteran of World War I, went down with *U-459* (Type XIV) on July 24 1943.

A degree of uncertainty shrouds the death of *Kapitänleutnant* Fritz-Julius Lemp, commanding *U-110* (Type IXB). The boat was forced to the surface by a British ASW group on May 8 1941 and, unable to dive, Lemp ordered 'abandon ship.' He also ordered that the demolition charges be set and blown, but the detonators failed and the British got aboard and captured the boat. Lemp's fate remains unclear, since his body was never recovered. One report claims that on becoming aware that the charges had failed he returned to his boat but was shot by the RN boarding party, while another suggests that, having realized the implications of the capture of his command, he allowed himself to drown.

SUICIDES

There were a number of suicides among U-boat COs. *Kapitänleutnant* Peter Zschech took command of *U-505* (Type IXC) in September 1942 and on his first cruise (October 4-

December 12 1942) sank a merchant ship off Trinidad, but was then attacked by a Hudson which caused much damage, although the boat managed to limp back to France. Following lengthy repairs *U-505* sailed again on July 1 1943, but several faults were discovered and Zschech returned for them to be resolved, sailing again on July 3. *U-505* was attacked twice on July 8, first by aircraft and later by ships, forcing Zschech to return again, reaching Lorient on July 13. He then sailed on August 1, 14 and 21, returning to port within 24 hours on each occasion, due to faults discovered when the boat submerged, and for which some French dockyard workers were later executed. The boat sailed yet again on September 18 1943 but when it was attacked by an Allied aircraft (September 23) Zschech crash-dived and the main ballast pump was so severely overstressed that yet another return to base was necessary. *U-505* sailed again on October 9 and this time got well clear of the Bay of Biscay, but on October 23 it was attacked by surface ships, in the course of which Zschech, presumably finding this the last straw in an apparently endless train of disasters, shot himself in the head, and died instantly.

The suicide of *Kapitänleutnant* Horst Höltring of *U-604* (Type VIIC) was even more melodramatic. *U-604* was attacked on three separate occasions on July 30/31 1943 and was so seriously damaged that Höltring rendezvoused with *U-172* (Emmermann) and *U-185* (Maus) on August 11, where his crew was split between the two, with Höltring going to the latter, following which *U-604* was scuttled. On August 24, however, *U-185* was attacked by two US Navy aircraft and very badly damaged. When water reached the battery, chlorine gas spread through the submarine and Höltring rushed to assist two of his crew in the fore-ends who had been wounded in *U-604* and were unable to move. It proved impossible to carry them out and in response to their pleas he shot them both, following which he turned his pistol on himself.

An unsuccessful suicide was attempted when *U-231* (Type VIIC) was sunk by depth-charges from a British aircraft on January 13 1944. Seven men were killed and the CO, *Kapitänleutnant* Wolfgang Wenzel, gave the order to abandon ship. He then took his pistol, placed the muzzle in his mouth and pulled the trigger but, although the gun went off, the bullet lodged in the back of his neck without killing him and he was one of the 43 saved.

ACCIDENTS

There were also some avoidable accidents, such as the death of *Kapitänleutnant* Rolf Mützelberg, CO of *U-203* (Type VIIC). On September 27 1942 *U-203* was three weeks out of Brest and south of the Azores when Mützelberg surfaced to allow the hands to bathe. He decided to join them, but totaly misjudged his dive off the bridge, hit the saddle-tank head first, broke his neck and died. The 1WO assumed command, buried Mützelberg's body at sea the following morning, and took *U-203* back to base.

▽ *U-852* lies aground on Cape Gardefui after an attack by RAF aircraft from Aden on May 2 1944. The commanding officer, Eck, was the only U-boat officer to be tried as a war criminal and was shot in West Germany by a British firing squad in 1945.

THE YOUNGEST CO

The youngest commanding officer was *Oberleutnant zur See der Reserve* (= senior naval lieutenant of the reserve) Hans-Georg Hess, who took command just a few months after his twenty-first birthday. Born in Berlin (May 6 1923), Hess volunteered for the *Kriegsmarine* in April 1940 and served initially in minesweepers, before transferring to the *Ubootwaffe* in April 1942. He then joined *U-466* (*Kapitänleutnant* Thäter) which carried out five war patrols. Promotion was rapid: *Oberbootsmann* – May 1942; commissioned as *Leutnant zur See* – March 1943 (two months before his 20th birthday); *Oberleutnant* – March 1944. He left *U-466* in May 1944 to attend the COs' course and took command of *U-955* (Type VIIC/41) in September. *U-955* operated in Norwegian waters and carried out five patrols under Hess's command. He carried out unsuccessful attacks on Convoy JW.61 (October 27 1944) and another convoy on December 4, but on December 5 he sank one Soviet ship (6,000grt) and damaged another (7,000grt). On February 9 1945 he made a daring entry into Kirkenes harbour, where he launched a torpedo at a steamer alongside a jetty, but missed. He was awarded the *Ritterkreuz* on February 11 1945, almost certainly the youngest man ever to receive such an award, and was in Trondheim on May 8 1945 at the time of the capitulation.

THE ONLY WAR CRIMINAL

Kapitänleutnant Heinz Eck was commanding officer of *U-852* (Type IXD₂), which was sent on a long voyage to the Indian Ocean, Eck's first voyage in command. He sank the Greek tramp steamer, SS *Peleus* (March 13 1944), but remained in the vicinity and over a period of several hours systematically sought to kill the few survivors in lifeboats and rafts. Eventually he headed away and his boat was sunk on May 2 1944, following which his crew was captured. Unknown to Eck, three of the *Peleus* crewmen had survived and made reports about his conduct, as a result of which Eck, the 2WO, doctor and LI, and one sailor were arraigned before a war crimes tribunal in November 1945. Eck pleaded operational justification in that he was seeking to prevent the survivors from reporting his boat's presence, but he, together with his 2WO and doctor, were found guilty and shot on

November 30 1945. The LI and the seaman were sentenced to prison terms. The LI's defense was based primarily on the fact that he had tried hard to persuade Eck to stop the shootings, while the seaman was following orders. Eck and his two officers were the only operational U-boat officers to be found guilty of a war crime and shot after the war.

DETERMINED TO THE END

Some COs simply never gave up fighting. One such was *Kapitänleutnant* Heinz Sternberg, commanding *U-473* (Type VIIC), which was operating in the North Atlantic when it was attacked by the British 2nd Escort Group. *U-473* was subjected to a continuous attack over an 18-hour period and Sternberg was eventually forced to surface in the early hours of May 6 1944. The U-boat came under gunfire from three sloops and some of the crew leapt overboard, but Sternberg immediately attacked, launching all his remaining torpedoes at his attackers. They missed, but he then tried to ram HMS *Starling* and very nearly succeeded. Undaunted, he then headed for HMS *Wild Goose*, also with intent to ram, but the boat sank underneath him. Thirty men survived to become prisoners, but Sternberg and 24 of his men did not.

THE CREW

The second-in-command was designated the *Erste Wach Offizier* (= first watchkeeping officer [1WO]) and was usually an *Oberleutnant zur See*, whose prime responsibility was to understudy the CO, so that he could take command if his superior became ill or died. His responsibilities included the boat's primary weapons system: the torpedoes, and their control and aiming systems. Normally, the only other deck officer was a very

△ *Kapitänleutnant* (*Ingenieur*) Wessels was engineering officer aboard *U-47* (Prien) and *U-198* (Hartmann). He was one of only 14 engineering officers to be awarded the Knight's Cross. He survived the war and died in 1988.

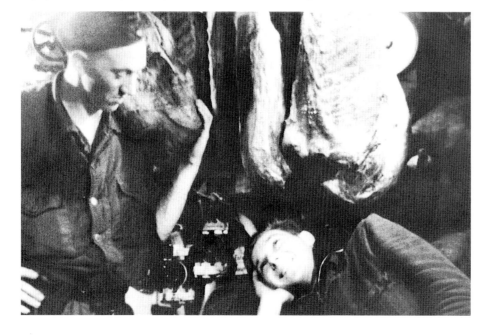

▽ Two U-boat crewmen relax among hanging joints of meat at the start of a long cruise. The loyalty of the U-boat crews never faltered and despite very heavy losses there was rarely a shortage of volunteers to man the new boats.

junior *Leutnant zur See*, designated *Zweiter Wach Offizier* (= second watchkeeping officer [2WO]), who was responsible for the deck and *Flak* weapons, and also oversaw the communicators.

The other commissioned officer on most U-boats was the *Leitender Ingenieur* (= leading engineer [LI]), an experienced officer (sometimes more experienced than the CO), whose action station was in the main control room. His responsibilities included engines, motors, batteries, and the trim, and he also set the demolition charges if the boat had to be scuttled. This meant that he was the last to leave and a number of LIs died as a result, some of them intentionally. For example, *U-801* (Type IXC/40) was severely damaged in an attack by US destroyer-escorts (March 17 44) and was forced to the surface, where the CO was killed as he came on to the bridge. Unfortunately, the 1WO and 2WO then jumped overboard leaving the LI to sort out the crew, which he did and then re-entered the U-boat where he deliberately waited for the end. Junior engineer officers were sent to sea for one voyage under an experienced engineer before being given a boat of their own.

The enlisted men were led by four chief petty officers. The *Obersteuermann* was responsible for navigation and provisioning. The *Oberbootsmann* (boatswain [bosun]) was responsible for the discipline and, generally, dealt with such matters himself, referring only the most serious or intractable problems to the CO. The technical department was headed by the LI who was assisted by the *Obermaschinist*, who was responsible for the diesels and the *Elektro Obermaschinist* who was responsible for the electric motors and battery.

The rest of the crew was made up of *Unteroffiziere* (petty officers) and various types of specialist: *Mechaniker* (mechanics; eg, for torpedoes); *Machinisten* (machine-men [stokers]); *Bootsmänner* (bosuns); *Funkmaat* (radiomen); and the general-duty seamen, *Matrosen*. COs were often able to take at least some of their most trusted crewmen with them when they moved to a new boat.

MEDICAL STAFF

One aspect of life aboard which frequently presented problems was medical care, which came under the general direction of the *Marineärztliches Forschungsinstitut für Ubootmedezin* (= naval medical research institute for U-boat medicine), which was located at Carnac on the French Atlantic coast from January 1942 to August 1944. Larger boats, such as Type XB minelayers and Type XIV tankers, carried a qualified *Stabarzt* (staff doctor), as did most Type IXs sailing to the Indian Ocean. Other boats did not and one of the petty officers was trained to give certain types of treatment. These amateurs did the best they could, but in difficult cases a rendezvous with another U-boat carrying a doctor had to be arranged or the patient transferred to a home-going boat. Infectious complaints such as venereal diseases, crabs, pubic lice and rashes caused particular problems where so many men lived in such close proximity, especially where communal washing, sanitary facilities and hot-bunking were concerned. Many U-boat crews attended a one-week health 'cure' at Carnac as part of their preparations for their next patrol.

ENTERTAINMENT

Despite all the routine work and periodic periods of excitement when they were either attacking targets or themselves being attacked, there were, inevitably, times when the men had little to do. The one official gesture to alleviate this was the provision of a record-player, which could be connected to the ship's loud-speaker system, using the Radione receiver in the *Funkraum* as an amplifier. The Radione could also be used to listen to Axis broadcasts from France and Germany, although some U-boats also used it to listen to the British *'Atlantiksender* '(Atlantic transmitter) and *'Secret Transmitter No 1"* both of which mixed the latest 'pop' music with propaganda designed to lower the crews' morale.

The more enterprising COs devized all sorts of entertain-ment to keep their men's minds occupied. One of the most suc-cessful COs, *Kapitänleutnant* Wolfgang Lüth, made a particular study of the subject, organizing talks; competitions covering activities as diverse as games (chess and skat), poetry or strength; availability of newspapers; musical evenings; and dis-cussions about a wide variety of topics. He made a great point of celebrating birthdays, not only of leaders such as Hitler, but also of every member of the crew. He also ensured that there was an adequate supply of books and records before they sailed, although he vetted both, not only for political content, but also to ensure that they were not prurient, which would encourage 'base thoughts' among a crew far from home. He was not totaly humorless, however, and also organized lying or singing compe-titions, to which every man aboard had to contribute and with the entire crew acting as judges.

CREW OF A NEW BOAT

INITIAL TRIALS

When a new boat was being built, the crew assembled progres-sively at the shipyard, starting with the CO and LI some two months prior to completion. These were followed by the engine-room chief petty officers, then the other officers and petty officers and, finally, just before commissioning, the remaining hands. The first tests were carried out by the builders, using their own technical officers, who examined everything in the boat and carried out an initial trim. The results were passed to *Ubootabnahmekommando* (= U-boat Acceptance Commission [*UAK*]), which then took over, using a team comprising an engineer officer, a constructor officer and a design engineer to conduct local trials to test the engines, steering gear and operation of the hydroplanes. If these were satisfactory, the commanding officer was given six days in which

△ One of a hardy breed of U-boat medical officers, *Marineoberstabsarzt* (senior naval doctor) Pollakowski served aboard *U-1227* (Type IXC-40) from August 1944 to January 1945, when this photograph was taken.

▷ The U-boat arm had a never-ending requirement for trained men, which was met by a large training organization. Here, trainee crewmen solve problems under the watchful eye of an instructor at *2. U-bootsausbildungs-Abteilung* (No. 2 U-boat Training Center) at Plön, July 1940.

to prepare for the formal commissioning ceremony, following which he had a further three days to settle in his crew before sailing either to Kiel, or, if the boat had been built in East Prussia, to Danzig.[5]

ACCEPTANCE TESTS

At Kiel or Danzig the boat was tested by another team, desig-nated a *Ubootabnahmegruppe* (= U-boat acceptance team [*UAG*]),[6] similar in composition to the first, but with the addi-tion of an executive officer (usually a World War I U-boat offi-cer), who was in charge. This team checked everything again and also carried out two further trims, while the commanding offi-cer took the opportunity to acquaint his crew with the operation of their new boat. The *UAG* tested the embarkation and loading of torpedoes, but was not responsible for live testing the launch systems. Altogether, this constituted a comprehensive test of all equipment and systems in the boat and involved thorough checks of its performance; provided all went well, it took two weeks.

TRAINING

Having passed the *UAK* tests the boat and its crew became the responsibility of the *Ausbildungsgruppe für Front Uboote* (= train-ing group for operational U-boats), normally known as *Agrufront*. Once the CO was certain that his crew was familiar with the boat and its systems, the next stage was individual boat exercises against single surface targets, which included making, retaining and reporting a contact, gaining a bearing on the target without

disclosing the U-boat's presence, and simulated torpedo attacks.

The *Torpedoversuchsanstalt* (= torpedo test establishment [*TVA*]) supervized the loading and launching of torpedoes from all tubes, following which the commanding officer carried out a 'shakedown' cruise in the Baltic. The boat then joined the 'Tactical Flotilla' where it carried out attacks against simulated escorted convoys, practising penetrating the screen, launching torpedoes, and deep evasion at silent speeds. On satisfactory completion of this process the boat was allocated to an operational flotilla and sailed on its first active duty patrol.

There was no retraining program to educate operational crews in new equipments and techniques, since, as Admiral Godt dryly informed a post-war British interrogator, the average life expectancy of a U-boat was three cruises and the opportunity for further training simply did not arise.

The whole process, from commissioning to being declared operational and passed to the control of *BdU*, took between five and seven months. So, quite apart from the U-boats permanently committed to the training organization, there were always numerous newly commissioned U-boats undergoing training in the Baltic. Thus, the operational availability of a U-boat dated not from the date of commissioning but from the date it departed on its first operational mission.

ACCIDENTS IN TRAINING

A number of boats were allocated specifically to training, where they took officers, cadets and sailors to sea for individual and collective practice in the skills they had been taught in classrooms. This organization lost a total of nine U-boats and 182 men in five collisions with surface ships, three diving accidents and one sinking alongside. Even more accidental losses were incurred by recently completed U-boats during their work-up process, with 17 boats and 420 men being lost. Of these, 15 were due to collisions – 10 with other U-boats, five with surface vessels – while one was in a diving accident and the other has never been explained. The loss of 26 U-boats and 602 men – not one of them due to enemy action – seems an inordinately high price to pay for training.

THE CREW AT SEA

In combat every man in the crew was on duty, either doing his designated task or standing by to deal with any emergency that might arise. At all other times the crew was divided into watches. The seaman's division worked a three-way system (8 hours on duty, 8 hours of sleep, and 8 hours of miscellaneous duties about the boat), while the engineers worked a two-way system (6 hours in the engineroom, 6 hours sleep) and the communicators worked a split system with their day being divided into three four-hour watches between 0800 and 2000, and two six-hour watches between 2000 and 0800.

When on the surface there was a bridge watch, consisting of an officer and four lookouts. The watchofficer was found from the 1WO and 2WO, who did two four-hour shifts each day, and the *Obersteuermann* and *Oberbootsmann,* each of whom did one four-hour shift per day. The lookouts were found from the seamen who each did one four-hour shift per day and these men were crucial, since the survival of the boat and all in it depended upon their rapid reactions to a threat, particularly from the air. From the bridge they could see about 6 nautical miles (12km) at sea-level on a clear day, but obviously much less in fog, rain, clouds, and at night. One feature which made life more difficult for the lookouts was that U-boat bridges were deliberately low to make them difficult to spot by enemy ships or aircraft, but for the watchkeepers this meant that spray and waves frequently interfered with their effectiveness.

PASSENGERS

U-boats often had to carry passengers, which was almost invariably an unpopular task, partly because they either caused overcrowding or, on some occasions, actually displaced crew members, thus increasing the strain on watchkeeping rosters, but also due to a variety of sailors' superstitions. Such passengers included meteorological specialists, spies, technical specialists examining various aspects of U-boat performance, members of the *B-Dienst,* public relations officers, and photographers, as well as potential commanding officers and leading engineers.

▽ Electricians at work in the electrical control room. Note the narrow space between the banks of instruments and controls in which the men had to work and down which other members of the crew had to pass.

DEATH OF THE U-BOAT MEN

There can be no doubt that the U-boat men dealt out death and suffering to many victims, both in merchant ships and in warships, and that many of those victims died horribly from wounds, burns, exhaustion, drowning, and privation. By the same token, the U-boat men themselves died in large numbers, frequently under extremely unpleasant circumstances. A large number of U-boats sank with all hands, mostly in action, but some simply disappeared – 'cause unknown' – making it possible only to guess what horrors the men experienced in their final hours or minutes.

The crew's lives were very much in the hands of the commanding officer and some of these were just plain careless. *Oberleutnant zur See* Leupold, for example, was outward bound for Penang in *U-1059* in March 1943 when, despite radio warnings that US carrier groups were in the area, he chose to remain stationary on the surface in broad daylight to allow members of the crew to have a swim. His boat was duly surprised and sunk with the loss of 47 lives, including Leupold's.

FIGHT TO THE LAST

When trapped in a corner most U-boats fought to the bitter end. *U-358* (Manke), for example, was under virtually constant attack for 38 hours by four very experienced British ASW escorts – the longest known continuous attack. The action started on February 29 1944 and from then on *U-358* changed depth and course constantly. Despite the harassment, Manke remained defiant. After some 34 hours, by which time conditions inside the U-boat must have been dreadful, two escorts departed to refuel. Possibly sensing this (and, in any case, desperately needing to recharge the batteries) Manke brought *U-358* to periscope depth on the evening of March 1, where he launched a torpedo which sank HMS *Gould,* one of the two remaining attackers. Immediately following that success, however, *U-358* broke surface, was hit by gunfire from HMS *Affleck,* submerged at once, and was then attacked yet again with depth-charges. It sank with all 50 of its crew.

U-616 (Koitschka) was the target of what proved to be the longest hunt against a single U-boat, which took place in the Mediterranean. Koitschka attacked and sank a merchant ship early in the morning of May 14 1944, but *U-616* was then detected by the British escorts, although contact was lost when they had to rejoin their convoy. Eight US destroyers, with RAF aircraft in direct support, had already been called to the scene however. When they arrived *U-616* was found, attacked, and damaged by USS *Hilary P Jones.* Koitschka managed to shake off the hunters until dusk, when he was forced to surface to recharge batteries. *U-616* was quickly detected and attacked by an RAF aircraft, which dropped six depth-charges, causing a leak in a fuel tank which meant that, for the rest of the action, *U-616* left a tell-tale oil slick. Despite this, Koitschka managed to evade the hunting destroyers and aircraft throughout May 15 and for most of 16th,

△ Crewmen relax during a quiet period aboard *U-889* (Type IXC-40). In the Atlantic, crews seldom had much spare time, but on longer voyages, such as those to the Far East, filling in the crew's spare time became a serious concern to the commanding officer.

but late that afternoon he surfaced, was spotted, and crash-dived once again. As soon as darkness had fallen Koitschka was forced back to the surface by conditions inside the boat and one of the US destroyers detected *U-616* by radar, firing star-shell and attacking with its 4in gun. Koitschka crash-dived yet again but could not shake off the searching destroyers which carried out continuous depth-charge attacks throughout the remainder of the night. Just after 0800 Koitschka had no alternative but to surface among the waiting destroyers, where he ordered his men to abandon ship and fired the scuttling charges; there were 47 survivors, including the intrepid captain.

Some COs took the traditional seaman's view that if their U-boat had put up a good fight but was clearly incapable of fighting on then there was no point in further and unnecessary loss of life; they then surrendered. Kretschmer, CO of *U-99*, whose courage, determination, and sense of duty were beyond question, took such a course on March 17 1941 when his boat, which had used up all its torpedoes in the course of some very successful attacks on convoy HX-112, was attacked and fatally damaged by British destroyers. *U-99* descended to a depth of 720ft (220m) before Kretschmer and his LI managed to bring it under control, although they then had no alternative but to surface. All hatches were opened to scuttle the boat and the men had already taken to the water when the LI realized that *U-99* was not sinking and returned aboard to flood the ballast tanks. The boat sank before a British boarding party could reach it, taking the LI and two others with it, while Kretschmer and the remainder of the crew were saved.

Others were, perhaps, not so determined. *U-573* (Heinsohn) was running on the surface off the Spanish coast when it was attacked and disabled by an RAF Hudson (May 1 1942). It was unable to dive and when the Hudson approached for another attack the boat was emitting white smoke and there were 10 men on the bridge with their hands raised in surrender, making no effort to man the nearby AA cannon. The Hudson then had to leave the scene to refuel and Heinsohn took the opportunity to take his boat into the neutral Spanish port of Cartagena, where boat and crew were interned.[7] The British Admiralty was infuriated by this apparent misuse of surrender and ordered that, in future, aircraft were to continue to attack U-boats until a surface vessel arrived to accept a proper surrender.

Very occasionally, attempts to ram led to the hunter and hunted becoming locked together. In such a situation the surface ships were usually unable to depress their main armament sufficiently and the situation degenerated into a fistfight. When USS *Borie*, for example, rammed *U-405* (November 1 1943) the US ship settled on the U-boat's fo'c'sle and one German was killed by a knife thrown by an American sailor.

UNDERWATER EXPLOSIONS

Allied ASW ships often reported that when attacking a deep-running U-boat there was a large underwater explosion, followed by silence. For example, on the morning of January 9 1944 *U-238* (Hepp) was spotted closing on convoy ON.223 and was attacked all morning by two sloops, which were joined by a third at noon. The hunters carried out a series of 'creeping' attacks, in the course of which 262 depth-charges were dropped, together with eight 'Hedgehog' anti-submarine mortar attacks, while the U-boat itself retaliated with two attacks using *Gnat* torpedoes. The last of the hedgehog attacks resulted in a double explosion underwater, following which debris and human detritus rose to the surface. Similarly, *U-338* (Kinzel) was attacked by HMCS *Drumheller* (June 25 1942) and apparently ran deep following which there was a very violent explosion, not caused by depth-charges. *U-880* (Schötzau) was part of the Sea Wolf group en route to the United States in March 1945 when it was attacked by US destroyers, which also culminated in a very powerful underwater explosion.

No explanation for such explosions was known at the time, but in 1947 the Royal Navy conducted a series of trials in which unmanned, surplus submarines were lowered until they collapsed. These showed that rather than, as had been thought, the hull giving way gradually, it actually suffered a sudden, catastrophic implosion, and it seems probable that this was the cause of many of the violent underwater explosions reported by Allied ASW ships.

U-BOAT SURVIVORS

When U-boats were sunk by surface warships there was a reasonable chance that those men who reached the upper deck and abandoned ship would be picked up by the victors, although Allied captains in such a situation were always very wary of becoming a target for another U-boat in the area. When the U-boats were sunk by aircraft, however, as became increasingly the case from 1943 onwards, there was little the aircraft could do for survivors, apart from reporting on them to any nearby ship and, if they were carried, dropping dinghies. However,

there were numerous cases where, following a successful attack, aircraft saw some of the crew either in the water or already in rafts, but none of them ever reached land or was picked up by other ships.

U-625 (Straub), for example, was attacked west of Ireland on February 29 1944 by an RCAF Sunderland flying-boat and was seen by the flying-boat's crew to remain afloat long enough for many of the U-boat crew to take to their dinghies; not one was ever found. Similarly, an RAF Liberator attacked and sank *U-388* (Sues) in the North Atlantic on October 3 1943 and, on seeing survivors struggling in the water, dropped three dinghies, which men were seen to board; none ever reached land. Survivors were also seen from *U-426* (Reich), *U-540* (Kasch) and *U-279* (Finke), but none was ever rescued.

There were, of course, other cases where some survivors were eventually rescued. Only one man survived when *U-512* (Schultze), was sunk by a USAAF B-18 in the Caribbean (October 2 1942). The aircraft dropped him a liferaft in which he spent 10 days before being found by chance by a US destroyer. The CO (*Kapitänleutnant* Müller) and one crewman of *U-662* spent even longer – 17 days – in a liferaft following an aircraft attack off the Brazilian coast on July 21 1943. In another incident, the cruiser USS *Marblehead* (CL-12) found a liferaft containing a single survivor from *U-848* (Rollmann) no less than 30 days after his boat had been sunk southwest of Ascension on November 5 1943, but the unfortunate man was delirious and died a few days later. Some survivors of *U-701* (Degen) were more fortunate when their U-boat was attacked off Cape Hatteras (July 7 1942). Seventeen men remained afloat for 48 hours supported only by their Dräger apparatus until they were spotted by a US Navy blimp (July 9), which dropped a liferaft and summoned help. A USCG seaplane reached them late that afternoon and recovered the remaining seven survivors.

UNDERWATER ESCAPES

There can be no doubt that men often survived for lengthy periods in sunken U-boats and they must have died in distressing circumstances. The escape equipment was primitive by today's standards, but there were occasional escapes from sunken submarines. *U-413* (Sachse) was sunk in the English Channel (August 20 1944). When it bottomed at approximately 90ft (27m) the LI went forward to investigate the damage, where he was blown out of the boat in an air-bubble and reached the surface safely, the only man to do so. *U-512* (W. Schultze) bottomed at 140ft (43m) after an attack (October 3 1942) and was unable to surface. When seawater reached the batteries, chlorine was released and the crew started to collapse, but three managed to escape using Dräger apparatus; one was rescued.

One of the more remarkable escapes was made from *U-1199* (Nollmann), which was lying on the bottom unable to surface after an attack on January 21 1945. A petty officer managed to escape through the conning-tower hatch, using his Dräger

△ A U-boat crewman shouts for help after his boat, *U-175* (Type IXC) has been sunk by USCG *Spencer* (April 17 1943). Allied warships always tried to rescue survivors, but had to be aware of their vulnerability to an attack by another U-boat in the process.

apparatus on the way to the surface. This escape from a depth of 240ft (73m) remains to this day the deepest known operational escape from a submarine.

When *U-533* (Hennig) was attacked and sunk in the Gulf of Oman by an RAF Bisley on October 16 1943, three men remained sufficiently calm to unclip a hatch cover and wait until the pressure inside the sinking boat blew them clear. All reached the surface, although one became unconscious during the ascent and died shortly afterwards, while a second died after about an hour, possibly because none of them had used an escape apparatus. The third man spent some 30 hours in the water before reaching land.

Not all were so fortunate and many crews must have perished one by one inside their boats as they lay trapped on the bottom. *U-526* (Möglich) was on its final approach to Lorient on April 14 1943 when it detonated a British magnetic mine. Twelve men who happened to be on deck survived, nine of them seriously wounded, but the U-boat sank with the remainder trapped inside. The boat lay in the shallows but, although divers established that some men were still alive, the hatch housings had been so twisted by the force of the explosion that they could not be opened and everyone inside died, even though they were within a few feet of the surface.

DROWNED U-BOATMEN

A large number of men drowned while rescue operations were in progress. *U-476* (Niethmann), for example, was sunk some 150nm off the Norwegian coast on May 14 1944 and a large proportion of the crew, possibly even all 52, abandoned ship. *U-276* and *U-990* were despatched to the scene, where they picked up 21 survivors, but 31 were drowned in the heavy seas. In another incident, *U-964* (Hummerjohann) was attacked twice by an RAF Liberator in the early evening of October 16 1943. The U-boat had sufficient time to broadcast a radio request for assistance and most of the crew were seen in the water before it sank at dusk. Knowing other U-boats were in the area, Allied surface escorts were reluctant to undertake a rescue in the dark, but when *U-231* arrived it could find only four men, one of whom died shortly afterwards.

U-BOATMEN KILLED ON DECK

There were some tragic misunderstandings, one of which concerned *U-331* (von Thiesenhausen), which was attacked on the surface on November 7 1942 by three RAF Hudsons and was so seriously damaged that it was unable to dive. The three Hudsons circled above the U-boat for several hours, firing machineguns at any sailor attempting to reach the anti-aircraft guns. After two hours the U-boat displayed a white flag and most of the crew, including several wounded, assembled on the upper casing to await further events. An RN frigate was despatched to take the surrender but before it arrived six Fleet Air Arm aircraft came on the scene and a fighter, either unaware of or deliberately ignoring the U-boat's surrender, carried out a machine-gun

△ When U-boats were sunk by aircraft, survivors' prospects were very bleak. Often aircraft, as here, saw men in the water but no survivors were ever recorded as having reached land. They must have suffered bleak and lonely deaths.

attack, killing and wounding many of the crew, following which an Albacore attacked with a torpedo, sinking the U-boat. Seventeen men were eventually rescued, but 33 were lost.

Such events were not one-sided, however. When *U-664* (Graef) was sunk by US Navy aircraft on August 9 1943 and the commander gave the order to abandon ship, the US Navy did their best to rescue the survivors. Seeing men in the water, circling US aircraft dropped rafts and life vests to them and called up USS *Borie* (DD-215), which arrived seven hours later to rescue them. It was in the process of doing so when *U-262* (Franke) came on the scene and launched five torpedoes at *Borie*, all of which missed. Not surprisingly, the American ship ceased any further attempts at rescue, leaving eight U-boat crew members unaccounted for.

GOOD FORTUNE

For the fortunate few, however, survival sometimes proved to be remarkably straightforward. *U-260* was proceeding submerged when it struck a moored mine off the Irish coast on March 12 1945. It surfaced but eventually had to be abandoned, although by then they were so close to the Irish coast that the entire crew were able to use dinghies to reach the shore, where they were interned.

Footnotes:
1. As a basis for comparison, a contemporary British submarine officer would have to start as Fourth 'Hand' and then work his way up to First Lieutenant, with a compulsory move to another boat to vary his experience. Provided he had received specific recommendations, he then attended the commanding officers' selection course (popularly known as the 'Perisher') and only after that could he be appointed to command. The whole process could take between two and four years, even in wartime.
2. He attained the rank of *gefreiter* (corporal) and was killed aboard VP-boot on April 25 1944.
3. His accuser, Abel, had been killed only two weeks earlier when his boat, U-193, was sunk in the Bay of Biscay (April 28 1944).
4. Unusually, the IWO (Schramm) was confirmed in command of *U-109*. He carried out one successful patrol, but the boat was sunk with all hands on the second.
5. Again, as a comparison, the captain on a new British submarine 'stood-by' his boat about four weeks prior to completion, with the full crew arriving about a week later. Following commissioning, the training period (which was inter-mixed with trials) lasted about 4-5 weeks, after which the boat went on its first operational patrol, usually in a 'quiet' area.
6. There were 10 such teams, seven at Kiel and three at Danzig.
7. The boat was eventually sold to the Spanish Navy, while the crew returned to Germany for reassignment.

DECORATIONS FOR U-BOAT PERSONNEL

Like servicemen in every country, U-boat men derived great satisfaction from the award of medals. The decorations awarded to U-boat personnel can be divided into two categories:

- Those awarded to the German armed forces as a whole.
- Those specific to the U-boat arm.

GENERAL DECORATIONS

DAS EISERNE KREUZ (THE IRON CROSS).

The most frequently awarded and famous German war decoration, the Iron Cross consisted of a number of classes:

- *Eisernes Kreuz 2. Klasse (EK 2)*

The Iron Cross 2nd Class was awarded on a very wide basis, the first award during World War II being to the entire crew of *U-29* on the day after they sank the British aircraft carrier HMS *Courageous* (September 17 1939). The insignia was worn as a ribbon in the button-hole of the jacket.

- *Eisernes Kreuz 1. Klasse (EK 1)*

The next grade up, the Iron Cross 1st Class, was awarded for major achievements on operations. Some commanders received both *EK 2* and *EK 1* together after their first patrol. The metal insignia of the *EK 1* was worn on the left side of jacket.

- *Spange zum Eisernen Kreuz 1914*

This was a World War II award to a man who had already received an Iron Cross during World War I. The bar was worn above the *EK 1* or on the ribbon of the *EK 2*, as appropriate.

- *Das Deutsche Kreuz*

The German Cross, initiated on September 28 1941, took precedence between the Iron Cross 1st Class and the Knight's Cross, there being two classes. *Das Deutsche Kreuz in Silber* was awarded for distinguished service not in the face of the enemy; for example, one was awarded to *Kapitän zur See* von Friedburg, an officer on Dönitz's staff in June 1942. *Das Deutsche Kreuz in Gold* was a higher form of award for operational service and consisted of a golden star enclosing a swastika. A total of 530 were awarded to officers and men in the U-boat service: *Kommandant* (Commander) – 112; *Leitender Ingenieur* (Leading Engineer) – 66; *Wachoffizier* (Watch Officer) – 9; *Obersteuermann* (Petty Officer–Helmsman) – 50; *Obermaschinist* (Petty Officer-Machinist) – 88; *Seemannischer Maat* (Leading Seaman) – 81; *Technischer Maat* (Leading Technician) – 71; *Funkmaat* (Leading Radio Operator) – 27; *Torpedomaat* (Leading Torpedoman) – 16; *Seemann/Heizer* (Seaman/Stoker) – 5; *others* – 5.

DAS RITTERKREUZ DES EISERNEN KREUZES

The Knight's Cross of the Iron Cross was the highest class of the Iron Cross, with 7,318 awarded during the course of the war, of which 144 went to the U-boat service. Recipients were known as *Ritterkreuzträger* (= wearers of the Knight's Cross) and there were four grades of concern to the U-boat crews:

- *Ritterkreuz des Eisernen Kreuzes*

The Knight's Cross of the Iron Cross was the basic level of which recipients in the U-boat arm numbered: *Kommandanten* (Commanders) – 124; *Leitender Ingenieur* (Leading Engineers) – 14; *Mannschafts-dienstgrade* (Petty Officers) – 7.

- *Eichenlaubs zum Ritterkreuz des Eisernen Kreuzes*

The next higher level was Oakleaves to the Knight's Cross of the Iron Cross, with 853 recipients in all services, of which 29 were in the U-boat arm. All the latter were U-boat commanders, except for Dönitz (*BdU*) and Hartmann (*FdU* Mediterranean).

- *Eichenlaubs mit Schwertern zum Ritterkreuz des Eisernen Kreuzes*

Five of the 150 awards of Oakleaves with Swords to the Knight's Cross of the Iron Cross went to U-boat men: Brandi, Kretschmer, Lüth, R Suhren, and Topp.

- *Eichenlaubs mit Schwertern und Brillanten zum Ritterkreuz des Eisernen Kreuzes.*

The very highest combat decoration was the Oakleaves with Swords and Diamonds to the Knight's Cross of the Iron Cross. Twenty-seven were awarded, two of them to U-boat men: Lüth and Brandi.

- *Grosskreuz des Eisernen Kreuzes*

The Grand Cross of the Iron Cross was created specifically for Hermann Göring in July 1940 and, as befitted his rather inflated opinion of himself, he remained the only recipient.

SPANIENKREUZ

The Spanish Cross was instituted on June 6 1939, the day members of the *Legion Condor* returned from Spain and paraded in front of Hitler in Berlin. There were six classes of award – four with swords and two without – and a total of 26,117 of all classes were awarded. Approximately 50 U-boat men wore the Spanish Cross, although only six had earned the award while serving in U-boats in Spanish waters, these receiving the Spanish Cross in Bronze without Swords. The remainder were men who transferred to the U-boat arm after the Spanish Civil War, and who had earned the Spanish Cross while serving in other parts of the *Legion Condor*. For example, *Kapitänleutnant* Gerhard Bigalk earned the Spanish Cross with Swords for 31 sorties in *Luftwaffe* reconnaissance aircraft, while other U-boat men earned their Spanish Cross aboard surface warships such as *Deutschland* and *Admiral Scheer*, or torpedo boats.

KRIEGSVERDIENSTKREUZ

The lower levels of the cross were awarded for achievements of major significance to the war effort, but not in a combat role; for example, training, staff appointments, ship design, and ship construction. The highest level was the *Ritterkreuzes zum*

▽ Crews took great pride in awards made to their commanders and here an artistic *Obersteuermann* (chief petty officer) decorates the bridge to celebrate the tonnage sunk and his captain's award of the Iron Cross with Oak Leaves.

△ Dönitz realized the values of personal contacts with the crews and of presenting awards. Thus, as here, he always tried to greet returning crews in person and his ability to recognize old shipmates and those who had done well was greatly appreciated by the men.

COMMAND AND CONTROL

Like any military organization, the *Ubootwaffe* expanded and contracted, and units and headquarters moved according to the progress of the war. The basic organization was quite simple: the operational U-boats were grouped into flotillas, which were based on either a particular port or on a particular type. A number of flotillas reported to a *Führer der Uboote* (*FdU*) who was responsible for a geographical area; and the FdUs reported to the *Befehlshaber der Uboote* (*BdU*). However, things were never quite that straightforward, principally because Dönitz chose to exercise command through HQ *BdU* direct to the U-boats in the Atlantic, the English Channel and the Far East, a control which he did not relinquish when he became commander-in-chief of the Navy, nor, indeed, when he briefly became *Reichspräsident* on Hitler's death.

From 1936 until August 1939, Dönitz, then *Führer der Uboote* (*FdU*), commanded the ever-growing U-boat force with a relatively small staff. When his title was changed to *Befehlshaber der Uboote* (*BdU*) on September 19 1939, however, he divided his staff into two: *BdU-Operationsabteilung* (*BdU-Op*), the operational department; and the organization department – *BdU-Organisations-abteilung* (*BdU-Org*). The latter was responsible for the overall organization of the *Ubootwaffe*, the selection, training, and promotion of its officers and men, legal matters, and for land-based logistic support; it remained static at Wilhelmshaven until April 1945 when it moved to Mürwick.

BdU-Op (usually simply known as *BdU*) was the operational headquarters and moved to follow Dönitz's requirements and promotions or, in the case of the 1942 move from Kerneval to Paris, as a result of an order by Hitler. Its various wartime locations were:

September – November 1939: Marinestation, Wilhelmshaven.
November 1939 – September 1940: Sengwarden.
September – October 1940: Boulevard Souchet 18, Paris.
October 1940 – March 1942: Kerneval near Lorient, France.
March 1942 – March 1943: Avenue Marechal Maunoury, Paris.
March – December 1943: Hotel am Steinplatz, Berlin.
December 1943 – March 1945: 'Koralle', Bernau.[1]
March – April 1945: Plön, south-east of Kiel.
May 1945: Mürwik, near Flensburg.

The *BdU* staff was headed throughout the war by Dönitz's loyal subordinate *Kapitän-zur-See* (*Konter-admiral* from 1943) Godt, who had first met Dönitz when they both served aboard *Emden* and who transferred to the *Ubootwaffe* in 1935. He commanded *U-23* and *U-25* until January 1938 when he joined *BdU* as *Asto 1* (see below) and in the September 1939 reorganization he became *Chef der Operationsabteilung des BdU* (chief of *BdU* operations branch). Later, when Dönitz became commander-in-

continued on page146

Kriegsverdienstkreuz mit Schwerten (Knight's Cross of the War Service Cross with Swords) and 11 senior officers and civilians received this award for services to the U-boat arm. These included, *Admiral* von Friedeburg, *Korvetten-Kapitän* Salmann, *Montage-Ingenieur* (construction-engineer) Brauweiler (Brown-Boveri, Mannheim), and *Professor* Walter, the inventor and head of the *Walterwerke*.

U-BOAT DECORATIONS

DAS UBOOTSKRIEGSABZEICHEN

The U-boat war badge, instituted on October 13 1939, was usually awarded on completion of a second patrol, although some commanders received the award following a particularly successful first patrol (eg, *Kapitänleutnant* Thomsen [*U-1202*]). The U-boat war badge with Diamonds was instituted in 1941 and was similar in design to the basic *UBootskriegsabzeichen*, but made of silver gilt with nine small diamonds. Approximately 30 were awarded and usually accompanied the award of the Knight's Cross with Oak Leaves. Admiral Dönitz was one of the recipients.

DIE UBOOTSFRONTSPANGE.

The U-boat combat clasp was instituted in 1944 to bring the U-boat service into line with other services, all of which had a similar decoration. There were three grades.

This award, instituted on May 15 1944, was intended to recognize close combat and courageous service. Recommendations were made by the U-boat commander, subject to approval by Admiral Dönitz, and were based upon the number of combat voyages, risks incurred, or personal bravery. The silver grade was introduced on November 24 1944 to recognize even higher degrees of courage or a greater number of missions completed.

GROSSADMIRAL KARL DÖNITZ

Few men have impressed their name and personality on a campaign in the way that Karl Dönitz did upon the U-boat campaign of 1939-1945. Dönitz was born in Berlin on September 16 1891, the youngest son of an engineer. Despite there being no naval tradition in the family, he joined the Imperial Navy in 1910 and was commissioned in 1912. He was assigned to the light cruiser *Breslau*, which on the outbreak of World War I was handed over to Turkey, under whose flag it operated in the Black Sea.

In 1916 Dönitz volunteered for the U-boat service and returned to Germany for the three month conversion course. His first posting was as 2WO aboard *U-39* in the Mediterranean. Its commander, Walter Forstmann, was then Germany's second highest scoring 'ace.' After four patrols in *U-39*, during which 32 ships were sunk, Dönitz was given command of a small minelayer, *UC-25*, in which he conducted two patrols, on completion of which he was awarded the Knight's Cross of the House of Hohenzollern and given command of the larger *UB-68*, one of the latest UB-III class. Shortly after midnight on October 4 1918 he sank a merchant ship and then caught up with the rest of the convoy to claim more victims. Once in position, Dönitz dived but lost control of the boat which plunged downwards, so he ordered an over-correction to prevent the boat being crushed.

◁ *Grossadmiral* Karl Dönitz, the head of the *Ubootwaffe* from 1936 to 1945. Few men have imposed their personalities on their command in quite such a comprehensive fashion.

UB-68 shot upwards, surfacing in the middle of the convoy, where it came under heavy fire from the escorts. With no compressed air remaining, Dönitz had no option but to set demolition charges and abandon ship. Four men, including the LI, were lost, but Dönitz and the remainder of his crew were rescued and taken to England, being released in July 1919.

On returning to Germany, Dönitz joined the much-reduced *Reichsmarine*, where he commanded a torpedo-boat for several years. He then had a short tour (1923-24) with the Torpedo Inspectorate before moving to naval headquarters in Berlin, where he worked for Rear-Admiral Raeder, who was clearly impressed, since from then onwards he actively supported his young subordinate's career. Promoted to *Korvetten-Kapitän* in 1928, Dönitz commanded a half-flotilla of destroyers (1928-1930), following which he was principal staff officer at North Sea High Command (1930-34). This was capped by a prize appointment as commanding officer of the light cruiser *Emden*, in which he undertook a world cruise in 1934-35.

Dönitz was selected to command the newly formed *1. Ubootflotille* in September 1935 and was subsequently appointed *Führer der Uboote* (FdU = leader of the U-boats) on January 1 1936. His old enthusiasm for U-boats quickly returned and he set about devizing new strategies and tactics for what were now his U-boats in the war which he was convinced would come. He organized regular exercises for the U-boats, the largest of which took place in the Bay of Biscay in May 1939, which was clearly aimed at disrupting British overseas trade. He was full of ideas and bombarded his superiors with papers showing his prophesies on the shape of such a war and his calculations on the numbers of U-boats required.

Dönitz was an energetic leader, went to sea frequently, and set high and clearly defined standards of efficiency for his captains and crews. The U-boat force slowly expanded and Dönitz's reputation and influence grew with it. He was appointed *kommodore* [1] in June 1939 but shortly afterwards was promoted to *konter-admiral* (equivalent to rear-admiral), while on October 17 his title was changed to that of *Befehlshaber der Uboote* (commander of the U-boats).

When war broke out Dönitz had already deployed what few U-boats were available to their war positions and thereafter he pursued his conviction that U-boats could strangle British overseas trade, provided he had sufficient of them. Throughout the war he was convinced that the North Atlantic was the one theater that mattered and strenuously resisted requests to transfer U-boats elsewhere, although he was usually forced to give in, especially when the directive came from Hitler.

Raeder resigned in January 1943 after a particularly acrimonious disagreement with Hitler, and Dönitz was appointed in his place, being promoted to *Grossadmiral* and appointed *Befehelshaber der Kriegsmarine* (January 30). From that time on he was drawn into Hitler's inner circle, although the two men did not always agree over naval policy.

DÖNITZ AND HIS CREWS

For the greater part of the war Dönitz made a point of welcoming crews returning to French bases in person, walking down the line of grubby, smelly men paraded in the town square. He encouraged success with praise for the crew as a whole, personal remarks to the men he knew, and the generous award of medals. Captains or crews who had not been successful still got the parade, but it was accompanied by straight-talking on their faults and without the award of quite so many medals. He also regularly addressed conferences and training courses, particularly of commanding officers.

Dönitz ensured that U-boatmen received a special allowance, almost doubling their pay, that there were plenty of decorations, and that there was shore entertainment for them, ranging from bars and brothels in the ports to alpine ski resorts and special leave trains to Germany. He also ensured that important personal news, such as births, promotions and decorations, were passed by radio to the men at sea.

He was known to the sailors as *Onkel Karl* (= uncle Charles), but he could be stern and dismissed people (especially officers) who failed to live up to his exacting standards. He could also be harsh, as, for example, when he confirmed court martial proceedings against two commanding officers, both of whom were subsequently shot.[2] On other occasions he could be remarkably lenient, moving officers who became sick or who made mistakes to shore jobs within the *Ubootwaffe* or elsewhere in the *Kriegsmarine*.

FAMILY

Dönitz enjoyed a happy marriage. His wife, Ingeborg, was the daughter of a German general; they wed on May 27 1916 and had three children: Ursula born in 1917, Klaus (1920), and Peter (1922). The two boys followed in their father's footsteps and joined the Navy, both dying in action: Peter, as 2WO aboard *U-954* (May 19 1943) and Klaus aboard the fast torpedo-boat, *S-141* (May 12/13 1944). Ursula married a very successful U-boat officer, Günther Hessler, in 1937.

DÖNITZ AS REICHSPRÄSIDENT

During his final visit to the Chancellery in Berlin on April 20 1945, Dönitz was appointed by Hitler to be his viceroy for northern Germany, making him responsible for its military defense and civil administration, whilst retaining his command of the Navy. Just 10 days later, Hitler shot himself and in his Will he named Dönitz as his successor as *Reichspräsident*. By then, however, there was no alternative to defeat and on May 4 Dönitz sent General-Admiral Friedburg to meet the British Field Marshal Montgomery. As a result, all German forces in northwest Germany, the Friesian Islands, the Netherlands and Denmark surrendered, and on the afternoon of May 5 Dönitz sent a valedictory radio message to 'My submariners.'

Dönitz was taken into custody by the British on May 23 and

MAJOR EVENTS IN THE LIFE OF GROSSADMIRAL KARL DÖNITZ		
YEAR	**EVENTS**	**PROMOTIONS**
1891	Born (September 16)	
1910		April 1: *Fähnrich zur See* (cadet)
1913	Joined cruiser *Breslau*	September 27: *Leutnant zur See*
1915		March 22: *Oberleutnant zur See*
1916	Joined U-boat course (October)	
1917	Joined *U-39* as 2WO (January)	
1918	*UC-25*, in command (January) *UB-68*, in command (September) *UB-68* sunk. Prisoner-of-war (October 4)	
1919	Released; returns to Germany (July)	
1920	Rejoined the navy	
1921		*Kapitän-Leutnant* (January)
1928	In command of half-Flotilla of destroyers	
1930	Staff officer at North Sea Command	
1934	Cruiser *Emden*, in command	
1935	Commander *1. Ubootflotille* (September 28) *Führer der Uboote* (October 1)	*Kapitan zur See* (October 1)
1939	*Befehlshaber der Uboote* (BdU) (CinC U-boats) (October 17)	*Kommodore* (June) *Kontor-Admiral* (October)
1942		*Admiral* (March)
1943	*Befehlshaber der Kriegsmarine* (CinC Navy) (January 30)	*Grossadmiral* (January 30)
1945	Succeeds Hitler (April 30)	*Reichspräsident*
1946	Sentenced to 10 years imprisonment	
1956	Released from Spandau prison	
1980	Died	

was subsequently charged with war crimes. He was charged on four counts and his trial caused considerable controversy. He received support from some surprising sources, notably Fleet Admiral Chester Nimitz, US Navy, who sent a document to Dönitz's defense lawyer, stating that from the day the United States entered the war, US submariners had been under orders to engage in unrestricted warfare. Dönitz was found guilty of failing to rescind Hitler's 'commando order' which stipulated that all enemy soldiers caught behind German lines were to be killed out of hand. The second was failing to prevent the use of slave labor in shipyards. He was sentenced to 10 years' solitary confinement, which he served in Spandau prison, Berlin. He was released in 1956. He died in 1980, his funeral being attended by many U-boat veterans.

Footnotes:

1. In the arcane world of naval ranks, *kommodore* was a temporary appointment given to a *Kapitän-zur-See* and not a promotion, as such. Thus, at least in theory, the rank of *kommodore* could be relinquished on vacating the appointment to which it applied.

2. *Kapitänleutnant* Hirsacker (*U-572*) was found guilty of 'cowardice in the face of the enemy' in 1943, and *Oberleutnant* Oskar Kusch (*U-154*) of 'lacking in aggression' and 'undermining morale' in 1944.

Directly below *BdU* were *FdUs* in the rank of *Kapitän zur See*, their organization depending partly on geography and partly on mission:

FdU West, located in Paris until September 1944 when he transferred to Bergen, Norway.

FdU Norwegen/Nordmeer (Norway/North Sea), located in Narvik, Norway.

FdU Mitte (Central), established from May to August 1944 to command the anti-invasion U-boat force.

FdU Italien/Mittelmeer (Italy/Mediterranean) in Rome.

Beneath these *FdU* there were flotillas, most of which occupied just one base (eg, *9. Ubootflotille* at Brest).

Dönitz believed strongly in the value of personal briefing and debriefing. Thus, U-boat commanders about to sail from French ports were always briefed on their missions and given the latest intelligence by *BdU* staff. On a U-boat's return to France Dönitz endeavored to greet each crew personally with a small parade, and he then held a debriefing session with the U-boat commander which was attended by the relevant staff officers. The same could not apply to other commands, where the local *FdU* performed the tasks.

CONTROL AT SEA

Dönitz's original concept was for tactical command of 'wolf-packs' to be exercised by the senior officer on the spot and this was tested several times. In August 1939 *Korvetten-Kapitän* Hartmann, who was both commanding officer of *U-37* (Type IXA) and commander of *6. Ubootflotille*, was despatched to Spanish waters to take command of a group, should this be required. It was not and he returned to Germany, only to attempt a similar operation in early October. Hartmann should have had four other boats under command but two were sunk en route to the rendezvous off the Irish coast. The remainder attempted one group operation against convoy HG.3, but it was not particularly successful and the boats then operated independently. Another attempt was made by group *Rösing* in June 1940 but results were meager. The problem was that the officer afloat had few command and control facilities, could see little from his bridge, and could not communicate when submerged; as a result, the trials were discontinued and Dönitz decided to exercise command from *BdU* at Kerneval.

The Imperial Japanese Navy also attempted to exercise command at sea, but went even further than the Germans by using special flagship submarines complete with dedicated accommodation and additional communications for an admiral and his staff. It proved equally unsuccessful; submarines are, by their very nature, lone hunters.

chief of the Navy in March 1943, Godt became C*hef der 2. Abteilung OKM/Skl* (= chief of the second division of the high command of the Navy), which was *BdU-Op* in all but name and where Godt ran the U-boat war on Dönitz's behalf.

BdU headquarters was divided into six branches, each headed by an *Admiralsstabsoffizier* (= admiral's staff officer), known as '*Asto*' for short. The senior branch, responsible for U-boat operations and deployment, was *Asto 1* (*A 1*), which was headed by Godt from January 1938 to October 1939, then, briefly, by two other officers, and finally *Fregattenkapitän* Hessler (Dönitz's son-in-law) from November 1941 to May 1945. Originally established in October 1942 and subordinated to *Asto 1, A 1 op* (*operativ*) was responsible for tracking enemy convoys (hence the alternative title of '*Geleitzugs-Asto*' (= convoy staff officer), which was held from October 1942 to July 1944 by the very experienced *Kapitänleutnant* Adalbert Schnee.

Asto 2 was responsible for home waters (minesweeping, patrols, ports, and port entrances); *Asto 3* for intelligence about Allies (mostly from *B-Dienst*); and *Asto 4* for communications and torpedoes. *Asto 5* had the important task of producing statistics and was run by just two officers: *Kapitänleutnant* Winter from November 1939 to May 1941 and then *Korvetten-Kapitän* Teufer from June 1941 to May 1945. Finally, there were two important specialists: the command engineering officer (*Verbands-Ingeniuer*) and the command medical officer (*Verbands-Sanitätsoffizier*).

△ Günther Prien, commanding *U-47*, during his third operational patrol, November 16 to December 18 1939. Great responsibility rested on the shoulders of U-boat commanders and most, such as Prien, thrived on it.

Footnote:
1. *Koralle* (= coral) was the codename for a purpose-built complex some 18 miles (30km) north of Berlin. It was located in the middle of a pine forest and consisted of a series of timber buildings and just two brick buildings: one for the operations room (*Zentral*), the other the Dönitz family home.

AIR SUPPORT FOR THE U-BOAT WAR

Aircraft should have played a major supporting role in the U-boat campaign, but the story of the U-boat arm and the *Luftwaffe* is a saga of high-level personality clashes, personal pique (especially where *Reichsmarschall* Göring, the head of the *Luftwaffe*, was concerned), inadequate equipment, and missed opportunities. Even the few suitable aircraft that were allotted were frequently taken away for other tasks, usually transport.

Grossadmiral Raeder appears to have had little interest in air support, but soon after taking over as *FdU,* Dönitz tried to ensure that aircraft would be in place for a U-boat campaign in a future war. Unfortunately for him, Göring suspected that the *Kriegsmarine* was plotting to start an independent naval air arm and did everything within his power to thwart it. Thus, when war broke out in 1939, all that was available to the *Kriegsmarine* was the *Seeluftstreitkräfte* (= fleet air-arm), a force of several hundred mostly obsolescent seaplanes, which was under the operational control of the *Kriegsmarine* but organized and administered by the *Luftwaffe*, with the aircrew, many of them originally from the Navy, wearing Air Force uniforms.

Dönitz held the first aircraft/U-boat cooperation exercise in 1938 and believed that he would receive support from the *Luftwaffe* in war, which formed a *Transozeanstaffel* (= trans-oceanic squadron), operating Dornier Do-26 seaplanes for this purpose. This unit was diverted to transport duties during the Norwegian campaign and when the three surviving aircraft finally reached France in August 1940 they proved inadequate and were quickly returned to Germany.

By November 1940 there was a loose form of cooperation with the *Luftwaffe* in both France and Norway, but there were too few aircraft, low availability, and poor reliability. Of greatest significance to Dönitz was that he did not have operational control over the *Luftwaffe* units and naval requests were met entirely at air force commanders' discretion. Further, reconnaissance reports were routed from the squadrons through *Fliegerkorps IV* to *Marine Gruppe West* before reaching Dönitz's headquarters, always a time-consuming process,

On January 2 1941 Dönitz went to Berlin to discuss the situation with General Jodl, Chief of the Operations Staff in the Supreme Command. Although still relatively junior, Dönitz demanded more aircraft and the operational control of the squadrons, expressing himself so forcibly that Jodl persuaded Hitler that *II/KG.40* would be subordinated to *BdU* from January 7.[1] Göring was absent on a hunting trip and when he returned was livid with rage and traveled to France, where he saw Dönitz on February 7 1941 and tried, by a mixture of bullying, bluster, and

▽ *Luftwaffe General-leutnant* Kessler was *Fliegerführer Atlantik* (air commander Atlantic) in 1942–43 and worked hard to cooperate with the U-boats, although Göring allocated him few resources. In May 1945 he was a passenger aboard *U-234* en route to Japan when it surrendered to the US Navy; here, grim-faced but immaculately dressed, he comes ashore at Portsmouth, NH.

wheedling, to persuade the admiral to agree to the cancelation of the *Führerbefehl* (= Hitler order), but Dönitz remained adamant. Göring departed muttering threats, but once back in Berlin he succeeded in persuading Hitler to change his mind, although at the cost of being forced to agree to the establishment of a new post of *Fliegerführer Atlantik* (*FlFü Atlantik* = air commander, Atlantic) who arrived on February 28 1941. Despite this and a few examples of successful aircraft/U-boat cooperation, there were still insufficient aircraft available to meet his needs and many aircrews were inadequately trained for the task, frequently giving wrong locations or bearings of enemy convoys they found.

Unaware of these problems, the British found the Focke-Wulf Fw-200 *Kondor* a substantial addition to the anti-shipping campaign, with Churchill giving it the nickname of 'scourge of the Atlantic.' In the first three months of 1941 *Kondors* sank 171,00grt of enemy shipping but, while the aircraft was adequate for attacks on unarmed merchantmen and general reconnaissance, its effectiveness diminished as Allied anti-aircraft defenses improved, especially once carrier-borne fighters became available.

When *Generalleutnant* Kessler took over as *FlFü Atlantik* in January 1942 he found that his command was not well placed. Dönitz's U-boats were engaged in the Caribbean, far outside the range of his aircraft, while the British had moved the convoy routes well away from the Bay of Biscay, thus denying the *Kondor* aircraft a strike role. Kessler asked for increased resources, including more and better aircraft, radar and improved bomb-sights, but these were denied and within months of taking his post he wrote suggesting that his command be disbanded. In July 1942 Dönitz, with Kessler's agreement, visited General Jeschonneck, chief of staff of the *Luftwaffe*, to request fighter-bombers for both short- and long-range missions, and managed to obtain 24 Junkers Ju-88C-6 for use as heavy fighters above coastal waters. A further request for new four-engined Heinkel He-177s for use in the long-range maritime strike role was also agreed by Jeschonnek but turned down by Hitler, who was scraping together every large aircraft he could lay his hands on to be used as transports on the Eastern Front.

On taking over as commander-in-chief of the Navy from Raeder in January 1943, Dönitz seized the opportunity to ask Hitler yet again for more air cover for his U-boats. Hitler authorized the transfer of three Blohm+Voss Bv-222 flying boats, which were being employed on the Eastern Front, and 10 Junkers Ju-88H very long-range reconnaissance aircraft. Thus, by mid-November 1943 *FlFü Atlantik* had two Bv-222, six Junkers Ju-290 and 10 Junkers Ju-88H, as well as a number of Bv-138s. He also had 19 Focke-Wulf Fw-200, although few were available at any one time and not all were fitted with radar. The *Kondors,* did score some successes, however, of which the most spectacular was the sinking on July 11 1943 of two large troopships, *Duchess of York* (22,021grt) and *California* (16,792grt).

The Bv-222s and land-based Ju-290s took over the long-distance reconnaissance role from the *Kondors,* but there were

never enough aircraft on task. The last strike mission was conducted on February 12 1944 when a number of He-177s and *Kondor*s attacked convoy OS.69, but fighters from the British carrier *Pursuer* shot down 50 percent of the attackers.

In the Bay of Biscay itself *FlFü Atlantik* sought to keep RAF Coastal Command aircraft 'off the backs of the U-boats' but this proved to be a losing battle, especially when the British introduced Beaufighters and later Mosquitoes, which provided more than a match for the German Ju-88s. With *Luftwaffe* fighters out of the way, British ASW aircraft were then able to conduct increasingly effective attacks on U-boats crossing the Bay of Biscay.

NORWAY

In 1940 Norway became the base for *Luftflotte 5*, which was originally sub-divided into *Fliegerführer Nord* (*Ost*), *Fliegerführer Nord* (*West*) and *Fliegerführer Lofote*n (although these were later changed to *Fliegerführer 3, 4* and *5*, respectively) with a separate *Jagdfliegerführer Norwegen* for the fighters. Their main task was to prevent Allied supplies reaching the USSR, which was achieved partly by independent *Luftwaffe* operations, but also by cooperation with surface ships and U-boats. As in France, high-level liaison between the *Kriegsmarine* and the *Luftwaffe* was poor, with the Air Force always ready to break-off to pursue its own agenda.[2]

Initial contact with convoys was made by reconnaissance aircraft operating in the Iceland-Spitzbergen gap, which was originally done by Bv-138Cs operating mainly out of Tromso. In September 1942, however, escort carriers made this too dangerous and radar-equipped *Kondor*s took over. On sighting a convoy the aircraft signaled positions and courses to *Luftwaffe* bases and *1 Uboot Flotille*, which then mounted attacks.

Despite the high-level problems, liaison at lower levels

△ Once out of range of *Luftwaffe* aircraft, U-boats had no air cover, although some carried a Fa-330 observation kite. Pilots, like this one seen practising in a wind tunnel outside Paris in 1942, had little chance of survival.

between U-boats and Bv-138 squadrons was particularly good, resulting in a refueling technique not practised in any other German theater. In this, seaplanes met U-boats at a pre-arranged rendezvous, where the aircraft was supplied with aviation fuel and the crew given meals and rest, thus considerably extending the flying-boats' range. Most rendezvous took place in sheltered bays in Spitzbergen, but in the late summer of 1943 two U-boats set up a forward base for seaplanes on Novaya Zemlya, off the Soviet Siberian coast, which enabled the aircraft to carry out reconnaissances deep into the Kara Sea in search of potential targets.

FAR EAST

During the period 1943-45 the German base at Penang operated

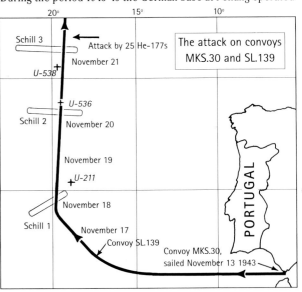

The attack on convoys MKS.30 and SL.139

its own aircraft for local reconnaissance, especially when U-boats were arriving or leaving. Two of these were Arado Ar-196 single-engined floatplanes which had been left behind at the base by German armed merchant cruisers, but there are reports that several Japanese Yokosuka E14Y1 'Glen' collapsible floatplanes were also used, which had been exchanged for Focke-Achgelis 'Bachstelze' drones.

LUFTWAFFE/U-BOAT COOPERATION:

THE ATTACK ON CONVOYS MKS.30 AND SL/139 (SEE MAP)

On November 13 1943 an Allied convoy (MKS.30) left Gibraltar bound for the UK, its departure being reported to the Germans by a Spanish observer. Once at sea MKS.30 steamed due west until it reached 20°W when it joined a second homebound convoy (SL.139) and swung northwards. This presented the Germans with a target consisting of 66 merchant vessels escorted by seven warships. *Luftwaffe* aircraft were despatched to search for this mass of shipping and a sighting report was transmitted by a Ju-290[3] of *FAGr 5* (November 15), confirmed by a Bv-222 of *1(F)SAGr 129* on the 16th.[4] The convoy headed slowly northwestwards at 8 knots, with six more warships reinforcing the escort on the morning of the 18th. Meanwhile, *BdU* ordered the available U-boats to form three reporting lines (*Schill 1, 2* and *3*) which were spaced so that the convoy would cross them (at its estimated speed of advance) on the nights of November 18/19, 19/20 and 20/21, respectively.

Unfortunately, the estimates were wrong, as *U-515* (Henke), which was already on the *Schill 1* line, discovered when it was overrun by the convoy in the early afternoon of November 18. *U-515* took evasive action although, due to the mass of Allied shipping, it was unable to surface and transmit this information to

△ The Blohm+Voss BV-138 flying-boat was flown by the *Luftwaffe* in support of U-boats in the Arctic, Mediterranean, and Atlantic. On several occasions Norway-based U-boats were used to refuel BV-138s, extending their range into the Kara Sea.

△△ A BV-222 *Wiking* confirmed the sighting of convoys MKS.30/SL.139 on November 16 1943.

BdU until about 2300. *BdU* immediately ordered *Schill 1* boats to catch up with the convoy and during this pursuit *U-211* (Hause) was caught on the surface by a Leigh Light Wellington and sunk. The others were too far behind and dispersed. At the same time, *BdU* ordered the *Schill 2* boats to move north so that they would be ahead of the convoy on the night of November 19/20.

During daylight on November 19 the British reinforced the escort with another nine vessels. At dusk the *Schill 2* boats surfaced and were vectored onto the convoy by a Ju-290, in a successful example of air/U-boat cooperation. The convoy escort force and RAF overhead cover was now so strong, however, that they managed to keep the U-boats at bay all through the night.

On the morning of November 20 two Fw-200s of *III/KG 40* tried to re-establish contact with this large group of enemy ships, but one had a faulty radar and the second was shot down by escorting fighters, as was the sole Fw-200 of the evening patrol. During the night the U-boats of *Schill 3* failed to find the convoy, although there were some scattered actions against surface escorts and RAF aircraft, and two of the latter were shot down – one, an RAF Liberator, by *U-648* (Stahl).

On November 21 seven more Allied warships joined the escorting force and, when a patroling German aircraft found the convoy, *Flfü Atlantik* swung into action, despatching no fewer than 25 He-177 heavy bombers, 20 of which found the convoy, some 800 miles (1,280km) from land. Three He-177s were shot down, but 40 Hs-243 glider bombs were launched, although the success rate was very poor: one warship (HMS *Chanticleer*) was damaged.

The whole operation was not at all successful from the German point of view. They had been presented with many merchant and warship targets and had responded by deploying numerous U-boats and aircraft. On the other side, however, the Allied surface escort force was very strong, while UK-based aircraft entered the scene on November 20, adding greatly to the problems of U-boats and *Luftwaffe* alike. The comparison of losses was by no means in the Germans' favor. They lost three U-boats and five aircraft, while the U-boats shot down two Allied aircraft and damaged one warship; the *Luftwaffe* sank one small merchant ship and damaged another. Despite this, the operation did show that cooperation between the *Kriegsmarine* and the *Luftwaffe* could be effective, that aircraft could be of considerable assistance to U-boats in finding convoys, and that He-177s could find and attack targets far from the coast. This first major He-177 operation seemed to augur well for the future, but the *Luftwaffe* then moved the He-177 squadrons to the Mediterranean, and that was that.

Footnotes:
1. II/KG40 indicated the second squadron (*staffel*) of *Kampfgruppe* 40 (40 Bomber Wing).
2. An example was when 21 RAF Lancaster bombers attacked the battleship *Tirpitz* in broad daylight (November 12 1944), which resulted in *Tirpitz* capsizing with the loss of some 900 lives. The incoming bombers were tracked by radar and the nearest *Luftwaffe* fighter base was a mere 50 miles (80km) distant, but not one fighter intercepted the bombers. Commander *Jagdgruppe 5* was court-martialed and found guilty of dereliction of duty.
3. This as the first operation by a Ju-290.
4. In fact, *B-Dienst* intercepted Allied reports of sighting the German aircraft and had decrypts (which included precise locations) at *BdU* before the *Luftwaffe* reports arrived.

U-BOAT REPLENISHMENT AT SEA

The provision of logistic support for U-boats at sea taxed Dönitz and his staff at *BdU* throughout the war, leading to many complicated plans and resulting in numerous losses. For the *BdU* the two main problems were that the U-boats were increasingly used at greater ranges than they had been designed for, which meant that they needed more fuel, while, at least until 1943, the boats were operating in a target-rich environment which frequently meant that the original torpedo supply was quickly used up. The availability of other commodities, such as food, drinking water, and lubricating oil also become critical from time to time, but the crucial factors were fuel and torpedoes.

For the Allies, the U-boats' 'logistic tail' provided them with an opportunity in which they could blunt the U-boats' ability to attack convoys and thus seriously limit their activities.

The Germans did not have overseas bases, nor, with few exceptions, were they able to use neutral ports. On the other hand, the British had an extensive network of dominions and colonies, providing them with a huge network of harbors, where their ships could be replenished and repaired, and where their crews could rest and recuperate. The French enjoyed similar

▽ *U-124* (Type IXB) replenishes from supply ship, *Kormoran* (also known as *Schiff-41*), March 18 1941, north of St Paul's Rock (off the coast of Brazil). Here the crew eases a torpedo through the forward hatch, a task which was by no means easy in port, but fiendishly difficult at sea, even when calm.

facilities in their colonies until their defeat in 1940. But this was not all, because both the British and French were also able to make extensive use of 'neutral' ports in a way that was denied to the Germans by virtually all countries. Finally, when the United States entered the war in 1941, not only did they acquire some bases from the British and Canadians, but they were also able to use the facilities in many 'neutral' ports.

The one stroke of good luck which befell the Germans – and which had not been predicted by the Navy's prewar planners – was that the defeat of France made the Atlantic ports available to the Navy, giving it a number of relatively secure bases, particularly at Brest, Lorient, and Bordeaux. However, when the Type VII boats became committed to operations in North American waters and the Type IXs started to operate in the South Atlantic and Indian Oceans the resupply problems became serious again.

Realizing only too well how acute the logistic problem was to the German U-boats, the Allies did everything in their power to make it even more difficult. In particular, they targeted, first, the surface supply ships and, subsequently, the U-tankers; all became priority targets and were steadily eliminated. A major factor in this achievement was the breaking of the German Navy *Enigma* codes and the related ability to read the radio traffic between the Japanese embassy in Berlin and their government in Tokyo. In this the Allies were helped by one of the major weaknesses of the German resupply system, which was that each rendezvous at sea required numerous radio messages to enable it to be set up, the great majority of which were intercepted by the British, decrypted, and then used to plan counter-action.

U-BOAT DESIGN CHANGES

One measure to reduce the logistics problem was to increase the endurance of the boats, which in the early stages of the campaign was essentially a matter of trial and error. Surprisingly, the real endurance of both the Type VII and the long-range Type IX had never been properly tested before the war. Thus, once operations started each boat's engineering officer conducted practical experiments, in the course of which it was discovered that the maximum surface range could be obtained by using diesel-electric propulsion with the diesels at half-speed, giving a speed through the water of 7-10 knots.

Next came increases in bunker capacity. The Type VII's capacity was increased from 67 tons in the Type VIIA to 159 tons in the Type VIIC/42 and to 199 tons in the Type VIIF, more than doubling endurance from 4,300 to 9,500 nautical miles. This was achieved by finding new spaces inside the boat in which to store fuel and also by putting fuel in the saddle tanks, where it simply floated on top of the water. A similar process with the Type IX saw bunkerage increase from 165 to 441 tons, extending the range from 12,000 to 31,500 nautical miles, a performance never equaled by any other diesel-electric submarine in history, not even the large Japanese I-type boats.

Increasing the number of torpedoes proved to be a more intractable problem, because their large size made it difficult to find places to store them, while the combination of size and weight made it difficult to move them inside the U-boat. Increasingly, as the war continued, additional torpedoes were stored in pressure-tight containers under the upper decking, but this meant that the U-boat had to surface in order to release the torpedoes and then move them below, which was very hard work. More importantly, it was time-consuming and time spent on the surface was fraught with danger as Allied air patrols covered ever greater areas of the oceans.

THE USE OF SPANISH HARBORS

The Naval Operations Staff had realized before the war that facilities would be necessary for replenishment in the southern oceans and made arrangements for both shore and afloat resupply. One of the earliest of these involved positioning two tankers – *Charlotte Schliemann* and *Culebra* – at Las Palmas in the Spanish-owned Canary Islands in September 1939, while another ship, *Thalia*, was in Cadiz. To take advantage of these facilities, however, the U-boats had to enter the harbor after dark, replenish rapidly and then sail before dawn to escape detection by British observers or spies. This clandestine practice was totaly illegal under the Laws of War, but it continued until July 1941, when the British brought pressure to bear on Spain to stop it.

The submarine *U-109* (Bleichrodt), for example, replenished in Cadiz harbor on the night of July 21/22 1941, going alongside *Thalia* at about 0100 and completing replenishment by 0500, when it cast off. During these four hours it had completely topped up its bunkers, and had also taken on three torpedoes and fresh provisions, including fruit and vegetables.

The British were so concerned about the benefits to the U-boats of the facilities in the Canary Islands that they gave serious consideration to an invasion of the islands in 1941. The operation would have involved a large task force, but would have been politically difficult to justify. In the event, intense diplomatic pressure was sufficient to force Spain's leader Franco into withdrawing the German facilities.

SURFACE SUPPLY SHIPS

German supply ships were originally deployed to support surface warships, such as the raiders *Graf Spee* and *Admiral Scheer*. A major effort was made to support the planned operation *Rheinübung* in early 1941, in which the new battleship *Bismarck*, accompanied by the cruiser *Prinz Eugen*, was to have broken out from Germany into the Atlantic where they would have been joined by the battlecruisers *Scharnhorst* and *Gneisenau* from Brest. The four ships would then have roamed the North and Central Atlantic, causing havoc among the British convoys. In the

△ The crew of a Type VIIC loads provisions aboard their boat inside a bunker in Norway. As Dönitz sent his boats ever further afield, logistic support became a major limitation and departing boats were filled to the maximum to enable them to survive for as long as possible.

event, RAF bombing prevented the two battlecruisers sailing from Brest and the *Bismarck* was sunk by the British on May 27 1941. The supply ships which had been positioned to replenish the task force were left at sea, but with their task changed to that of replenishing U-boats. Knowing this from their Ultra intercepts, the British decided to mount a major effort to eliminate them all.

The British operation started on June 3 in the Davis Strait 80 miles (130km) south-west of Greenland, where the supply ship *Belchen* (6,367grt) was in the process of refueling *U-93* (Korth). They were surprised by the British cruisers *Aurora* and *Kenya*, and *Belchen* was sunk, but not before *U-93* had managed to disconnect, submerge and escape; it returned later to rescue the survivors. On the following day, June 4, the supply ship *Gonzenheim* (4,000t), which was in position north of the Azores, was scuttled when directly threatened by the British battleship *Nelson*, while *Gedania* (8,923t), which was en route to relieve *Egerland* (9,798t), was captured June 4 1941 by the ocean boarding vessel Marsdale.[1] The day continued badly for the Germans when the supply tanker *Esso Hamburg* (9,849t) was scuttled itself off the west coast of central Africa after the cruiser *London* appeared over the horizon. *London* struck again the following day when it found another tanker, *Egerland*, just north of St Paul's Rock, whereupon *Egerland*, which was the first ship specifically fitted out to support U-boats, was also scuttled.

The cruiser *Sheffield* was en route to Britain when, on June 12, it met the homeward-bound *Friedrich Breme* (10,397t) WNW of Cape Finisterre and, like most of the others, the crew of the

which had been fitted out for use at the proposed base in Dakar, was escorted into the central Atlantic by two U-boats, only to be intercepted and sunk by gunfire from the cruiser *Kenya* north of the Azores on October 3 1941. *Ship 16*, another of the supply ships, was sunk north of Ascension in late November, followed by *Python*, some 800 miles (1,280km) south of the island of St Helena on December 1 1941.

U-BOAT TO U-BOAT

U-boats frequently replenished each other; for example, when a returning boat with spare fuel or torpedoes would pass them to another boat capable of spending more time on station. Since neither boat was properly fitted for such a task, it usually proved both difficult and exhausting for the men involved. Transferring the torpedoes was a particular problem, since electrical torpedoes required a special type of inflatable dinghy, while compressed-air torpedoes had to be wrapped in 18 lifejackets and floated from one boat to the other. The boats involved were also very vulnerable to a surprise attack, as occurred on July 30 1943 when *U-43* (Schwantke) was refueling *U-403* (Heine) southwest of the Azores when two patroling US carrier aircraft chanced upon them. *U-403* managed to escape, but *U-43* was too slow and was hit by an air-dropped homing torpedo (Fido).

THE TECHNIQUES OF REPLENISHMENT

The methods used by the U-boats were relatively unsophisticated. With surface ships, the supplying ship positioned itself ahead of the U-boat and passed a tow to the U-boat. The supply ship then started to tow the U-boat at a speed of some 3-4 knots and floated down the fuel hose which was recovered and secured to an inlet pipe in the submarine's foredeck. Other stores were lowered into a ship's boat and then taken to the U-boat where the crew struggled on the narrow and slippery upper deck to drag them aboard. Since the deck hatches could not be opened except in the very calmest of seas, everything usually had to be passed up to the bridge and then down through the conning-tower hatch. Such procedures were time-consuming; at best it took most of a day for the operation to be completed, sometimes even longer. It was particularly fraught in bad weather, when the two vessels had no option but to wait where they were for conditions to improve or to proceed in company in an effort to find somewhere more favorable.

The specialized supply U-boat was intended to overcome most of these problems. This idea originated in a letter Dönitz wrote to Supreme Naval Command in September 1939 in which he recommended a variety of U-boat developments, the last of which was for three supply tankers. This led to the Type XIV, which was based generally on the contemporary Type IXD, but with the hull lines altered to enable it to carry 432 tons of fuel oil and 45 tons of provisions, although only four torpedoes were

German tanker quickly scuttled their ship. The U-boat supply ship *Lothringen* was not so quick, however, and was captured by the cruiser *Dunedin* in the central Atlantic on June 15 while en route to its station in the south Atlantic.

The British blitz continued when the blockade-runner *Babitonga* (4,442t), returning to Germany from Brazil, became another victim of the cruiser *London*, being scuttled on June 21. Finally, *Alstertor* (3,039t), a supply ship returning from the Indian Ocean, was forced to scuttle off Cape Finisterre on June 23.

Such an ambitious operation could not hope for total success and a few German ships did manage to elude the hunters. Thus, the patrol ship *Kota Pinang*, the supply ships *Ermland* and *Spichern*, and the blockade runners *Atlanta* (Italian), *Todaro* (Italian), and *Regensburg* (German) all managed to reach French ports.

Having lost so many surface supply ships, the *BdU* staff tried another tactic and sought the agreement of the Vichy French authorities for the use of Dakar to supply U-boats operating in the southern Atlantic. The negotiations were carried out through the Joint Commission which had been set up in Paris after the Armistice and outline agreement was reached within the Commission. However, Hitler refused to agree to certain concessions demanded by the French and the latter then stalled so effectively and for so long that the Germans eventually gave up and Dakar was never used by U-boats.

Despite the earlier losses, one more attempt was made to use surface supply ships. In September 1941 the *Kota Pinang*,

△ In the early part of the war U-boats were able to meet in mid-Atlantic to transfer torpedoes, fuel or passengers, or even just to exchange news. By 1943, however, Allied Ultra intercepts and rapid reactions by aircraft made such meetings extremely hazardous.

carried. Even the Type XIV used substantially the same methods of surface transfer, although the heavy losses led to the idea of refueling underwater and several trials were carried out in the Baltic in 1942-43, using the ex-Dutch boat, *UD-4* (Bernbeck), as the supplying boat. In its final form this system involved the two boats meeting on the surface, where the supplying boat streamed a 315ft (96m) hawser and a telephone cable, which were kept afloat by the air-filled fuel hose. As soon as the receiving boat had made these fast (a time reduced by practice to nine minutes), both boats submerged to about 100ft (35m) with the supplying boat towing the receiving boat at about 4 knots. It took about four hours to transfer 2,800cu ft (80m₃), at the end of which the supplying boat gave a signal over the telephone link and both boats surfaced together. The receiving boat then cast-off the telephone link, fuel line and hawser, and turned away immediately, leaving the supplying boat to recover the lines.

This relatively simple system was, as far as is known, used only once operationally when *U-445* (Fenn) was refueled in the mid-Atlantic by *U-460* (Schnoor) on December 7 1942. The process took some three hours and was completely successful.

Meanwhile, operations were gradually extended southwards and when, in late 1942, *Gruppe Eisbär* (= polar bear) U-boats were sent to Capetown, they were successfully replenished by the first of the Type XIV U-tankers, *U-459* (von Wilamowitz-Möllendorf), some 600 miles (960km) South of St Helena on September 22-26. On the same day that the *Eisbär* boats arrived off the Cape, however, *U-179* (Sobe), one of the first of the new Type IXD₂ long-range boats, also arrived, having steamed direct from Germany without once having to replenish.

Gruppe Monsun's experiences

The refueling difficulties incurred by *Gruppe Monsun*, the first group destined for the Indian Ocean, illustrate just how complicated and dangerous such logistic problems could be. This group consisted of nine Type IXCs and two Type IXD₁s and the intention was for them to replenish from a Type XIV U-tanker in the South Atlantic and then from surface tankers, based on Singapore, when in the southern Indian Ocean.

The first snag occurred with two of the Type IXD₁ operational boats: *U-200* (Schonder) was sunk south-west of Iceland while on the way to join the group, and *U-847* (Kuppisch) was diverted to refuel other U-boats in the Sargasso Sea, where it was sunk by US Navy aircraft. The group's designated Type XIV tanker, *U-462* (Vowe), was then so heavily attacked by Allied aircraft while still in the Bay of Biscay that it was forced to return to port for repairs. *BdU* then hastily cobbled together a new and complicated replenishment plan, which involved diverting another Type XIV, *U-487* (Metz), already at sea in the Atlantic, southwards to a refueling point some 800 miles (1,280km) south of the Azores. Unfortunately, *U-487* had already replenished

△ The forward torpedo room of *U-532*, Type IXC-40, which was involved in the *Gruppe Monsun* voyage, during which replenishment was such a typically hazardous operation.

eight other U-boats since July 6, and thus, while it had sufficient provisions and other stores, it was 150 tons short of the total fuel oil required to give all of the *Monsun* boats the minimum 40 tons that each of them needed to reach Penang. To overcome this problem *U-160* (von Pommer-Esche), another Type IXC, outward-bound for a mission in the central Atlantic, was ordered to rendezvous with *U-487* and to transfer to the tanker all the fuel it could spare, leaving itself the bare minimum needed to return to France.

Setting up such a complicated operation required a great deal of radio traffic, most of which was duly intercepted by the Allies, giving them a head-start. Thus, on July 13 the tanker *U-487* was caught on the surface with many of the crew sunbathing on deck by two US Navy aircraft from the carrier, USS *Core*. Despite a spirited fight in which one F4F fighter was shot down, the U-boat was sunk by depth-charges. The embattled *U-487* failed to send any radio messages that it was under attack, so when the *Monsun* boats reached the replenishment area on July 14 they spent three days searching for it, until *BdU* reluctantly came to the conclusion that it had been lost. In addition, three of the *Monsun* boats failed to arrive and, in the absence of any radio messages from them, they, too, had to be presumed lost.

U-160, which had been tasked to top-up the ill-fated *U-487* was still available, but had insufficient fuel for all the seven surviving *Monsun* boats, so yet another Type IXC, *U-155* (Piening), which was also in the area on another mission, was instructed to join in the refueling operation. Then, just as this new plan swung into operation, *U-160* itself went missing (it had been sunk by aircraft on July 14) and eventually *BdU* was forced to use not only *U-155*, but also one of the *Monsun* boats, *U-516* (Tillessen). Meanwhile, yet another *Monsun* boat, *U-509* (Witte), failed to make the RV and it, too, was added to the growing list of 'presumed lost.'[13]

Because various other replenishment operations elsewhere in the Atlantic had failed, a number of other U-boats returning from operations off the American coast were also running short of fuel. So, as a last resort to help these other boats, a Type IXD₂, *U-847* (Kuppisch), outward-bound to the Far East but proceeding independently of *Gruppe Monsun*, was diverted to assist them. It met the boats some 700 miles (1,120km) south-west of the Azores and refueled them over a period of five days (August 23 – 27). But no sooner had this finished than US Navy aircraft appeared and *U-847* was sunk by depth charges.

Thus, of the 13 U-boats proceeding to the Far East, four operational boats were sunk en route to the first replenishment area, while the U-tanker was so badly damaged that it was compelled to return to base. In the revised replenishment operation, two boats summoned to help were both sunk, while two of the Far East-bound boats had to be diverted to replenish other boats and were then so short of fuel themselves that they had to return to France.

All this was a very steep price to pay and just five Type IXCs were left to proceed on the next leg of their voyage. It also shows, only too clearly, why logistic support was such a serious problem for both U-boat commanders and for *BdU*.

THE LOSS OF THE *CHARLOTTE SCHLIEMANN*

The logistic problems arising from the *Monsun* operation, were by no means over, however. The five surviving boats *(U-168, U-183, U-188, U-532,* and *U-533)* proceeded around the Cape to rendezvous with the surface tanker *Brake*, which had arrived safely from Penang. The meeting took place some 450 miles (720km) due south of the island of Mauritius, an area the Germans were to use on several occasions over the next few months. On this occasion, at least, all went well and the boats were soon on their way to their operational areas.

The British had been aware for some time of the existence of two German replenishment tankers operating in Asian waters. The first of these was the *Charlotte Schliemann* (7,747grt), a twin-screw motor vessel, which had been built in Germany in 1928. It had first come to British notice when based in Las Palmas in the Azores between 1939 and 1941. On leaving the Azores, *Charlotte Schliemann* sailed to the Indian Ocean and remained there for some months during which time the raider *Schiff 28* was refueled three times (April 13-15, May 6-14, June 21-27 1942) as well as being relieved of numerous prisoners. *Charlotte Schliemann* then sailed to Japan to undergo a short but badly needed refit.

In early January 1944 the British Far East Fleet was

▷ The captured *U-532* enters Liverpool on May 10 1945, with a mixture of German and British sailors on the upper deck. It had left Batavia in the Dutch East Indies on January 13 1945 carrying 173 tons of strategic materials for Germany, but surrendered at sea on May 4, the last 'Far East transport' to be accounted for.

informed through Ultra channels that the *Charlotte Schliemann* would replenish an unknown U-boat at 1230 hours on an unknown day in late January 1943 in an unknown position. Further information told them that the tanker had sailed from Singapore on January 4 at a speed of 11 knots and had passed through the Sunda Straits. A task group was immediately assembled consisting of an aircraft carrier, three cruisers, an armed merchant cruiser, two destroyers and a frigate. As the British began their search *Charlotte Schliemann* refueled two U-boats on January 28 some 100 miles (160km) SE of Mauritius: *U-178* (Spahr), which was returning from Penang to France, and *U-510* (Eick) which had just successfully rounded the Cape and was on its way to Penang. The tanker then steamed to a new rendezvous 900 miles (1,440km) east of Mauritius.

The British searched fruitlessly for several weeks, but the ships remained in the area and a new Ultra intercept on February 11 indicated three new replenishment areas at distances of 840 miles (1,345km), 440 miles (705km) and 680 miles (1,090km) from Mauritius. Late that afternoon an RAF Catalina flying-boat spotted the German tanker and signaled its position to the flagship, which tasked the destroyer HMS *Relentless* to administer the *coup de grace*, which it did just after midnight; there were no survivors. *U-532* had seen the RAF Catalina circling the area of the rendezvous and when the tanker could not be found assumed that it had been sunk by aircraft as a result of a chance encounter, which was duly reported to *BdU*.

THE LOSS OF *BRAKE*

The German Navy now had several U-boats in the southern ocean in need of refueling and the other tanker, *Brake*, which was lying in Singapore was instructed to load with fuel, lubricating oil, and provisions, and to sail as soon as possible. Its destination was a position between Madagascar and Australia, where

it was to remain for two months to supply 12 U-boats on their way to and from the Far East. *Brake* reached the area successfully and rendezvoused with three of the *Gruppe Monsun* boats (*U-168*, *U-188* and *U-532*) on the morning of March 11 at a point some 1,000nm SE of Mauritius.

Once again, the British had discovered *Brake*'s plans from Ultra and they assembled another cruiser squadron. The commander was given very precise information that *Brake* had sailed from Singapore at 0001hours on February 26 and was heading at 111/2 knots for Batavia, from where it would proceed into the Indian Ocean for its first rendezvous on March 11.

The British force for this operation comprised: two cruisers; the aircraft carrier HMS *Battler*, with Swordfish aircraft embarked; two destroyers; and RAF Catalina flying boats from Mauritius. When the first three U-boats arrived in the refueling area they carried out a careful reconnaissance and only when they found no trace of air or surface activity did they approach the tanker. *Brake* successfully replenished *U-188* (Lüdden) and *U-532* (Junker) on March 11, but refueling *U-168* (Pich) on the following day was interrupted by bad weather, and hoses were disconnected so that all four vessels could proceed south-westwards to find smoother water.

At 1056hours, however, a watchkeeper in *U-188* spotted an aircraft and all three submarines had no choice but to dive, leaving *Brake* to face the enemy alone. *U-188* surfaced near *Brake* during the action and saw an unidentifiable warship shelling the tanker. But, since the enemy ship was out of range of the U-boat's guns and because *U-188* had run out of torpedoes, it had no choice but to submerge again. The crew then suffered the very unpleasant experience of hearing the noises of the tanker sinking.

As before, the British carrier and cruisers remained out-of-sight over the horizon and the destroyer despatched the tanker with gunfire. Also, as in the case of *Charlotte Schliemann*, the

THE CAREERS OF GERMAN TANKER U-BOATS

U-BOAT TYPE	BOAT: DATES OF OPERATIONAL CAREER AS SUPPLY BOAT	NUMBER OF SUPPLY VOYAGES	TOTAL U-BOATS REFUELLED	FATE	DEAD	SURVIVED
Type XIV	*U-549* November 15 1941– July 24 1943	6	65	Sunk by RAF aircraft (172 and 159 Sqns.) Depth charges	19	?
	U-460 January 30 1942– October 4 1943	6	82	Sunk by USN aircraft (VC.9) USS *Card* North of Azores	62	0
	U-461 January 30 1942– July 30 1943	6	69	Sunk by RAF aircraft (502 Sqn) North of Cape Finisterre	53	0
	U-462 July 23 1942– July 30 1943	4	54	Sunk by RAF aircraft (502 Sqn) Northwest of Cape Ortegal	53	0
	U-463 April 2 1942– May 15 1943	5	73	Sunk by RAF aircraft (58 Sqn) Southwest of Scillies	56	0
	U-464 April 30 1942– August 20 1942	1	0	Scuttled after attack by CSN aircraft (VP.73) Northwest of Rockall	2	52
	U-487 December 21 1942– July 13 1943	2	22	Sunk by CSN aircraft (VC.13) from USS *Core* North Atlantic	31	33
	U-488 May 18 1943– April 26 1944	3	41	Sunk by US DEs *Barber*, *Frost*, *Snowden* Northwest of Cape Verde Islands	64	0
	U-489 July 22 1943– August 4 1943	1	0	Sunk by RAF aircraft (424 Sqn) South of Iceland	1	53
	U-490 March 27 1943–June 12 1944	1	0	DEs *Frost*, *Huse* and *Inch* Northwest of Azores	0	53
TYPE XB	*U-116* July 26 1941– October 6 1942	3	23	Missing October 6 1942	55	0
	U-117 October 1942– August 7 1943	4	26	Sunk by USN aircraft (VC.1) from USS *Card* West of Azores	62	0
	U-118 December 6 1941– June 43 1943	4	24	Sunk by USN aircraft (VC.9) from USS *Bogue* West of Canary Islands	43	16
	U-119 April 2 1942– June 24 1943	2	16	Depth-charged by DEs *Starling* and *Woodpecker* Northwest of Cape Ortegal	57	0
	U-219 October 16 1943– January 1 1944	2	5	Later used as transport. Taken over by Japanese as *I-505* May 8 1945	–	–
	U-220 March 7 19432– October 28 1943	1	0	Sunk by USN aircraft (VC.1)) from carrier *Block Island*	56	–
	U-461 January 30 1942– July 30 1943	6	69	Sunk by RAF aircraft (502 Sqn) North of Cape Finisterre	62	0

weather closed down the air search. When the search was resumed on March 11 an RAF Catalina looking for *U-178*, chanced, instead, upon *UIT-22* and damaged it in a surprise attack. Several more Catalinas were directed to the scene and *UIT-22* was sunk with all hands. *U-178*, whose radio signal had caused all this, searched for *UIT-22* but was eventually forced to assume that it was lost and resumed course for Bordeaux, which it reached on May 25 1944.

THE LAST OF THE SUPPLY U-BOATS

Despite the loss of all the other Type XIV U-tankers it was decided that the situation in the Far East was so critical that it required despatching the last of the class, *U-490* (Gerlach). This boat sailed from Norway on May 16 1944 but once again the Allies knew its precise movements and the U-boat got no further than north-west of the Azores when it was sunk by aircraft from USS *Croatan*, supported by three US destroyers (June 12).

TORPEDO RESUPPLY

Apart from fuel, torpedoes were also a major problem for the Germans in the Far East, especially as the Japanese torpedoes, including the excellent Long Lance, could not be launched from German tubes. As described above, torpedoes could be transferred from one U-boat to another, but the major hope in this sphere was the base at Penang, which had started operations with a small stock of torpedoes obtained from armed merchant cruisers and blockade runners. However, a large additional stock of torpedoes and spares was despatched in the first two of the new Type VIIF torpedo-carriers to become operational. Both captains were warned not to seek any action during the voyage, except in the most favorable circumstances, and to be very wary of air attack, especially in the South Atlantic.

U-1062 (Albrecht) sailed from Norway on January 18 1944 and had an uneventful voyage, except that by the time it reached the southern Indian Ocean, both the tankers it intended to use for replenishment had been sunk. It had no choice but to keep going and was eventually replenished by *U-532* (Junker) on April 10, reaching Penang without further incident on April 19 where it delivered its eagerly awaited stores. The second Type VIIF, *U-1059* (Leupold), sailed from Norway on February 25 1944 but, early on the morning of March 20, while off the Cape Verde Islands – and despite the many warnings about air attack – the captain hove-to on the surface so that his crew could relax and swim, and they were caught by aircraft from USS *Block Island*; there were eight survivors, including the commanding officer.

German crew was left to fend for themselves, although on this occasion the U-boats waited until just after sunset when they surfaced to rescue their compatriots.

As usual, the British were able to monitor the subsequent events, learning the following day that one U-boat would proceed to Bordeaux while the other two were to return to Penang, although the destination of one of these was later changed to Batavia.

THE LOSS OF *UIT-22*

Meanwhile, *UIT-22* (Wunderlich), one of the ex-Italian submarines taken over by the *Kriegsmarine*, was also on its way to Penang, and it, too, was in trouble, having been attacked and damaged by United States aircraft off Ascension. It survived the attack, but lost a lot of diesel fuel and could not reach its destination without replenishment. So, *BdU* ordered *U-178*, one of the U-boats that had successfully replenished from *Charlotte Schliemann*, to rendezvous with *UIT-22* 600 nautical miles southwest of the Cape of Good Hope. There, the homeward bound boat would transfer sufficient fuel for *UIT-22* to reach Singapore, while *U-178* itself would collect a new radar warning device and *Enigma* keys to use when transitting the Bay of Biscay.

The British knew about both boats through Ultra, but were hesitant to attack in case the Germans guessed their secret. However, on March 5, *U-178* transmitted a long signal which enabled the South African Navy to get a good direction-finding 'fix,' which justified an operation being mounted against the two U-boats. British and South African aircraft found and attacked *U-178* on March 8, but it managed to escape, following which bad

△ This daylight repenishment of a U-boat at a dockyard indicates that there was no apparent threat of attack, but it was frequently not so easy to resupply the boats with vital fuel, torpedoes, fresh food and drinking water, especially at sea. Apart from the logistical difficulties of U-boats locating a replenishment vessel (transport U-boat or surface vessel), as the war drew on there was the increasing danger of being spotted and attacked by Allied aircraft or warships.

Footnotes:
1. A great deal of secret material was captured, including cypher machines and coding information.
2. All had been sunk by aircraft: *U-200* (Schonder) – June 24; *U-514* (Auffermann) – July 8; and *U-506* (Würdmann) – July 12.
3. It had been sunk by US Navy aircraft on July 16.

WEATHER REPORTING

The weather in the North Atlantic and Arctic was a source of continuous concern to all three German armed forces throughout the war, accurate forecasting being needed to plan major land operations, air raids, and naval operations. Dönitz in particular needed continuous forecasts to plan his U-boat operations and to inform boats of impending bad weather. However, the problem was that, since weather in the northern hemisphere moves from west to east, German forecasters needed data from the western and central Atlantic, with a particular requirement in the areas of the polar front and the North Atlantic drift. To Dönitz's indignation, his U-boats became heavily involved in both collecting the data on which the forecasts were based, and in transporting weather personnel and equipment to and from their sites.

Two U-boats provided a weather-reporting service from August 1940 to January 1941, but this mid-ocean service was insufficient for the meteorologists' needs and what they really wanted was a base in Greenland. The first attempt to achieve this (Operation Nanok)1 took place in August 1940 when a civilian ship, *Furenak*, tried but failed to reach Greenland and landed its weather observation party on Jan Mayen Island instead. The party was resupplied by an Fw-200 in October and taken off by ship sometime later.

Up to the end of 1940 the German meterological service was responsible for the Arctic program, but in January 1941 full responsibility for command, deployment, resupply, and removal was transferred to the *Kriegsmarine*, who delegated most of these responsibilities to Commander Northern Fleet in Norway. The men, however, were still selected, trained, and equipped by the meteorological service.

U-boats became heavily committed to the program, which involved them in sailing to Greenland, Bear Island, Jan Mayen Island, and Spitzbergen. A U-boat was sufficient to transport small parties, but for the larger parties a trawler was used, although this was often escorted by a U-boat. U-boats were also used to take supplies to the deployed parties. U-boats also deployed automatic weather stations, which were set up on land by an expert, or weather-reporting buoys, both of which transmitted regular reports (usually four times a day). Such automatic stations had a limited life and had to be replaced from time to time, which was, again, done by U-boat.

U-BOATS AS WEATHER STATIONS

Despite his opposition to U-boats being diverted to what he regarded as a secondary tasks, Dönitz was ordered in late August 1940 to provide two U-boats to serve full-time on weath-

▽ A meteorologist checking his instruments aboard a U-boat. Denied access to peacetime weather forecasts, the *Kriegsmarine* was compelled to employ U-boats for weather reporting.

er duties in the central Atlantic, mainly for the benefit of the *Luftwaffe* during the Battle of Britain. As a result, two boats were on weather duties from mid-August 1940 to the end of January 1941, although, due to turn-overs, transits and refits, such a commitment actually tied down six boats.

Although the full-time provision of U-boats as weather ships ceased in January 1941, U-boats were often tasked with observing the weather for short periods, while on other missions. In addition, all U-boats were required to send weather data back to base as a matter of routine, although the Allies' Ultra files are littered with constant reminders from *BdU* to send this information, suggesting that it was often overlooked.

WEATHER SHIPS

The *Kriegsmarine*'s first attempt at weather reporting was most unsuccessful. Six small trawlers were equipped as weather ships to maintain two (sometimes three) on station. The first pair were deployed in January 1941, but the whole operation was being monitored by the British and on February 22 1941 the first of these weather ships, *Krebs* (NN-04), was captured together with some *Enigma* rotors and setting keys, as a result of which the British were able to read *Heimische Gewässr* (the German code for 'Home Waters') for February 13-23 and for periods in March and April. Then, on May 7 1941, the trawler *München* (WBS-6) was also surprised and captured off Jan Mayen Island. Three British cruisers and four destroyers were employed, but this overwhelming force was justified by the intelligence 'take,' which included cryptographic items of priceless value. Two more weather ships were also lost: *August Wriedt* was sunk (May 29) and *Lauenburg* (WBS-2) was captured off Jan Mayen Island (June 28), again with the capture of much cryptographic material.

The *Kriegsmarine* realized that these weather reporting ships were too vulnerable and, with one exception, the Atlantic weather reporting system for the remainder of the war was based on land stations, both automatic and manned, in both of which U-boats played a large part. The sole exception to this was in November 1944 when the weather ship *Wuppertal* was escorted by a U-boat to a position near Jan Mayen Island (Operation *Zugvogel*). *Wuppertal* started transmitting on December 1 1944, but in early January reported that it had been hit by a hurricane. After U-boats and aircraft had searched for it in vain it was declared lost on January 22 1945.

MANNED LAND STATIONS

The most satisfactory stations from the meteorological point-of-view were the land-based stations, which were staffed by between 12 and 20 experts. Deployment and recovery was either by trawler (usually with a U-boat escort) or by U-boat alone. The parties were landed with supplies for about a year, but in emergency they were resupplied by the *Luftwaffe*, which occasionally also recovered the personnel.

GREENLAND

Major efforts were made to maintain at least one party on Greenland, the first, codenamed *Holzauge*, landing on Sabine Island from the trawler *Coburg* in September 1942. It remained there, sending regular weather reports, until March 1943 when it was discovered by a small party of US troops on foot and subsequently bombed. Two Germans were later captured, but the remainder were removed by Fw-200s from Norway.

The next party to go to Greenland was the *Bassgeiger* group,

△ A floating weather-reporting buoy lying ashore. Such buoys were deployed by U-boats and although early types, used in 1943, proved of little value, the 1944 models were much more effective. They were supposed to self-destruct, but often failed to do so.

part of which disembarked from the trawler *Coburg* in late August 1943 and was soon transmitting messages from Shannon Island. The remainder of the men on *Coburg* went ashore later on Shannon Island (codenamed *Roderich*) and started sending weather messages in November 1943. Both groups were resupplied by air on several occasions, one of them by Bv-222 flying-boat. A patrol from the *Bassgeiger* party was ambushed by US troops in May 1944, as a result of which the party was evacuated by air in June.

In August 1944 another party, *Edelweiss*, was sent to Greenland, but its ship was intercepted and sunk by a US Coast Guard cutter and the survivors captured on the island of Little Koldewey. A second mission, *Edelweiss II*, was then mounted, which also landed on Little Koldewey, where it, too, was captured on October 4 1944, together with a great deal of valuable documents.

SPITZBERGEN

Spitzbergen was occupied by a mix of manned and automatic stations. Kisfjord was occupied on December 1 1941 by a party brought by trawler which remained in the area until the following August. Meanwhile, a party of British troops on the island discovered an automatic station in July which they destroyed, but this was replaced by another, delivered by U-boat in September, although it was removed a month later.

In October 1942 a new party, codenamed *Nussbaum*, was delivered by U-boat to Krossfjord, and another U-boat delivered yet more stores in November, following which two air resupply flights were made in May and June 1943. The party was attacked by British troops on June 20 but, although the camp (including many documents) and one man were captured, the remainder of the party were taken off by *U-302* (Sickel).

In October 1943 another group, *Kreuzritter*, was landed by trawler escorted by a U-boat. It was resupplied by air on several occasions and was eventually extracted by *U-737* (Brasack) in June 1944.

The *Haudegen* group arrived in Spitzbergen by trawler, with a U-boat escort, in October 1944 and was still there on May 8 1945 when German forces capitulated (it was recovered by a Norwegian trawler in September). Another party, *Landvik*, went to a different location in Spitzbergen in October 1944 and was also still there in May 1945, but its fate is unknown. Two other small parties, *Taaget* and *Helhus*, were deployed by U-boat and the British heard meteorological reports from both, but their fates are unknown.

FRANZ JOSEF LAND

The first party sent to Franz Josef Land (*Schatzgräber*) arrived in September 1943, having been taken there by a trawler, escorted by a U-boat. It was resupplied several times by air and was then due to be removed by *U-354* (Herbschleb) but this was prevented by ice and they were taken back to Norway by air. Almost alone among these Arctic groups, nine out of the ten in the *Schatzgräber* group became very ill, probably due to poor food and scurvy. A second group intended for Franz Josef Land in mid-1944 was diverted to Greenland, becoming *Edelweiss II*.

HOPE ISLAND

A small party (*Svertisen*) was landed on Hope Island by *U-354* (Herbschleb) in October 1943. It was extracted by the same U-boat in July 1944.

UNMANNED STATIONS

AUTOMATIC LAND STATIONS

The land-based automatic meteorological stations were considered by the British to be most ingenious. Powered by batteries, they transmitted data according to a pre-set schedule, usually four times in every 24 hour period, but the harsh environment meant that battery life was only about two months. The signals were short, usually consisting of two four-letter groups, which were repeated several times, and were transmitted at frequencies around 7MHz.

These automated land stations were given men's first names as codenames (eg, *Hermann*, *Edwin*). A serious program of deploying these automated stations began in 1943, all being emplaced by U-boats. The earliest stations were taken to Bear

△ The weather-buoy, shown opposite, in the water, where it was extremely difficult to spot from any distance. Each buoy contained barometer, thermometer, anemometer, and transmitter, and broadcast readings four times in each 24-hour period.

Island by U-boats, with new ones delivered as the old ones ran down; thus, *Edwin* (December 1942-February 1943) was replaced by *Brausewetter* (March-July 1943), *Robert* (July-August 1943) and finally *Gerhard* (August 1943). Among other examples were automatic stations on Hope Island: *U-636* (Schendel), October 1944; the northern tip of Jan Mayen Island: *U-992* (Falke), November 1944; Alexandra Land: *U-387* (Büchler); the southern tip of Spitzbergen; and Iceland. However, there were some problems, the most important being that signals were sometimes weak and the station's measurements of wind direction and force were usually much more inaccurate than its measurement of temperature and pressure.

WEATHER REPORTING BUOYS

Weather reporting buoys were dropped by U-boats at positions ordered by *BdU*. Each buoy contained a barometer, thermometer, anemometer and a transmitter, and the data was broadcast automatically, again four times during each 24 hour period. The buoys also included a timed self-destruct charge, although since several fell into Allied hands it can be assumed that this did not always work properly. The first tests were conducted in November 1943 when *U-277* (Lubsen) laid some buoys off Hammerfest and then laid some more further offshore, but the experiment was a failure. Later buoys worked more effectively.

COMMUNICATIONS

All these meteorological stations depended upon radio communications to fulfil their purpose, and therein lay their greatest weakness. The manned stations, for example, whether afloat or ashore, encrypted their messages in a special cypher known to the Germans as *Wasserhuhn* (= waterhen) and to the British as 'LMT.' This was received at Thrums, Norway, from where they were passed to Germany, either by landline or by radio. The resulting weather forecasts were then broadcast on the normal weather service (eg, *Norddeich*). Unfortunately for the Germans the British had broken this cypher and were able to work out the positions of the weather stations from them, which led to the attacks on *München* and *Lauenburg*, and which gave up material which resulted in the breaking of naval *Enigma*. Later, the capture of the documents belonging to the *Nussbaum* and *Holzauge* groups resulted in yet further penetration of the *Kriegsmarine* communications and cryptographic systems.

One of the ironies of the German meteorological reports was that, having broken the German codes, the British gained virtually as much value from them as did the Germans — RAF Bomber Command and the 8th US Army Air Force Command being particularly enthusiastic customers.

Footnote:
1. Named after a popular 1930s film about Eskimos: 'Nanook of the North.'

TRANSPORTS TO THE FAR EAST

The story of the U-boat campaign in the western hemisphere is well documented but the campaign in the Far East is less well-known, even though it involved a large number of boats and demanded considerable resources. Overland and air travel between Europe and Japan was possible until Germany invaded the USSR in June 1941, following which the only practicable means was by sea.[1] Such movement involved personnel (diplomats and military specialists), strategic materials, and samples of the latest military equipment. Initially, the requirement was met by surface blockade-runners, and between January 1941 and December 1943 21 ships sailed from Europe for the Far East: six were lost en route, but the other 15 delivered 56,000 tons to their Japanese allies. Traffic in the opposite direction comprised 35 ships, of which 19 were lost, while the 16 arrivals delivered 110,800 tons of cargo: fats – 49,000 tons; rubber – 44,000 tons; ores – 4,800 tons; and mixed cargo – 13,000 tons. Losses grew so alarmingly, however, that in January 1944 Hitler ordered that surface blockade-running was to cease.

Germany needed rubber; metals such as bismuth, selenium and caesium; and medicines, such as quinine and opium. In the reverse direction, the Japanese needed specialized steels, mercury, and optical glass. In addition both sides sought to learn the details of their partner's latest military equipment, including plans, handbooks, and actual hardware. These exchanges were formalized in an agreement which was initialled on November 8 1942, although it was not formally ratified until March 2 1944. The Japanese also sent at least two shipments of gold to their embassy in Berlin.

▽ German and Japanese officers in Penang, where the *Kriegsmarine* used the former British Imperial Airways seaplane base. The tall officer (left, rear) is the German commander, Dommes, while the Japanese officer in the center is Captain Ariizumi, the senior staff officer and also a submariner, who later committed suicide to avoid war crimes charges.

THE *U-180* EXCHANGE

The first link arose from the need to return the Indian nationalist leader Subhas Chandra Blose and an aide to the Far East.[2] *U-180* (Musenberg), one of the two Type IXD1s with six Mercedes-Benz diesels, was selected and, in addition to the two passengers, her cargo included ammunition, secret weapon plans, and some miscellaneous items.[3] *U-180* sailed on February 9 1943 (the date selected by Blose as being astrologically 'propitious') and duly met the Japanese submarine *I-29* on April 23, but they had to move nearer Madagascar in a search for calmer waters. The actual transfer took place between April 25-27, the difficulties of such a mid-ocean exchange being compounded by the transfer of gold ingots to *U-180* and the inability of the two allies to speak each other's languages. Nevertheless, the operation was completed and *U-180* returned to France, loaded with gold, prototype inventions, quinine, three of the latest Japanese torpedoes, and several Japanese officers on their way to Germany to study German methods. According to *U-180*'s log, the Japanese also supplied cockroaches, beetles, and small mites, which conspired to make the voyage homewards in an overcrowded boat somewhat less than enjoyable! *U-180* reached Bordeaux on July 2 1943 after a successful mission, which included not only the mid-ocean exchange, but also sinking a tanker (8,132grt) on the outward voyage and a freighter (5,166grt) on the homeward leg.

U-BOATS FOR JAPAN

At a *Führer* Naval conference (March 5 1943) Dönitz informed Hitler that the Japanese Naval Attaché, Admiral Nomura, had asked for two German submarines. Dönitz was lukewarm about the proposal but Hitler endorsed it and the first to be supplied was *U-511* (Type IXC/40), which had already carried out three war patrols but was in reasonable condition and was immediately available at Bordeaux. It sailed on May 5 1943 with seven Japanese officers aboard and, having sunk two merchant ships (14,370grt) en route, arrived at Kure on August 7, where it was handed over and commissioned as *RO-500*.[4] The second U-boat was the brand-new *U-1224* (Type IXC/40), which was commissioned into the IJN on February 15 1944 as *RO-501*. During the voyage to Japan it was tracked by Ultra and sunk on May 13, 500 miles (800km) west of the Cape Verde islands by a US destroyer.

GERMAN TRANSPORT SUBMARINES

When attrition of surface blockade-runners to and from the Far East reached serious proportions in mid-1942, design work started on the specialized Type XIX U-boat transport. This was quickly abandoned, however, in favor of another design, the Type XX, which, with a submerged displacement of 3,425 tons, was estimated to carry 800 tons of cargo. After repeated delays the project was canceled in May 1944. Another design was then prepared for a variant of the Type XXI, designated Type XXIE. This was intended to carry the same 800 ton cargo load as the Type XX, but this proved impossible, leading to the Type XXIT, which would have carried only 275 tons of cargo. This project, too, was canceled.

Four Type VIIFs were built as specialized torpedo transports: two were sent to the Far East, of which one reached Penang (*U-1062*, April 19 1944). It set out on the return voyage on June 19, an unusually rapid turnaround for that base, with its torpedo storerooms and bilges loaded with cargo, but was forced back to Penang by engine trouble. It sailed again on July 15, but was sunk on September 30 off the Cape Verde islands.

The two Type IXD₁ (*U-180, U-195*) had already carried out one trip each to the Indian Ocean, but their six E-boat diesels had proved unsuitable, so four were removed, as were all six torpedo tubes and the 105mm deck-gun, enabling them to carry 252 tons of cargo. The conversion took place in Bordeaux between October 1943 and April 1944, and both boats sailed for the Far East in August 1944. *U-180* (Riesen) was sunk by a mine in the Bay of Biscay (August 22), but *U-195* (Steinfeldt) reached Jakarta (December 28), having refueled the homeward bound *U-843* on December 20. *U-195* set out on the homeward voyage on January 26 1945, but was forced back by engine trouble on

△ Japanese submarine *I-8* arrives in the French port of Brest on August 4 1943. A number of Japanese submarines made the voyage between Japan and France, carrying men, strategic supplies and, on at least two occasions, gold bullion to replenish the coffers of the Japanese Embassy in Berlin.

March 4, and was still in Jakarta on May 8, when it was taken over by the Japanese. *U-195* and *U-219* delivered some very valuable equipment for the Japanese, among it optical instruments, mercury, and torpedoes, as well as electronic equipment, including the very latest radars. In addition to this, however, they carried a dismantled Fieseler Fi-103 (*V-1* flying bomb), together with its Argus As 109-14 pulse-jet motor.

Two of the large Type XB minelayers were also pressed into service as transports, the first of which, *U-219* (Burghagen), was given only very minor modifications. It sailed from Bordeaux on August 23 1944, reached Jakarta on December 11 and was still there in May 1945, when it was seized by the Japanese.

The penultimate transport to leave for Japan was *U-864* (Wolfram), a Type IXD₂, which sailed from Norway on February 5 1945 and was sunk by a British submarine (HMS *Venturer*) on February 9 in the only recorded engagement in which both submarines were fully submerged throughout. The final Far East transport, *U-234* (Fehler), did not sail for the Far East until April 17 1945 and surrendered to the United States Navy on May 16; its voyage is described in more detail below.

OPERATIONAL U-BOATS AS CARGO CARRIERS

Numerous Type IX operational U-boats made the long voyage to and from the Far East and all were overcrowded with food, supplies, and spares, simply to survive the voyage. Despite this, *BdU* decided in mid-1943 that all operational boats should carry some cargo. Strategic metals were substituted for the usual keel ballast, for example: mercury and lead on the outward voyage, and tin and wolfram ores on the return. In addition, homeward-bound boats were required to carry as much as possible internally, usually rubber, molybdenum, opium, and quinine. Most of the tin was fashioned into ingots and stowed in the keel and was also used to make containers for other cargo, which were then stowed in the bilges, as well as in the bow and stern compartments and in any empty torpedo tubes. The rubber was placed in bales which were stowed in the free-flooding compartments under the upper casing. In addition, any nook or cranny within the boat was used for stowage. Many operational U-boats were fitted-out in this way, but of those that set out on the return voyage to Europe only six actually reached European waters. Even then only two were actually successful in delivering their cargoes.

UNDERWATER BARGES

Another proposal was for U-boats to tow submerged, cargo-carrying dumb barges, either in the Mediterranean or on the Far East route. A prototype 90 ton barge was tested in October 1943, where it was found that towing, depth-keeping, and directional control were not difficult, provided that speed was not less than 4.1 knots; below that, the dynamic force keeping the barge submerged was lost and it surfaced. Above that speed, however, the submarine's battery rapidly lost its charge, dramatically reducing the boat's underwater endurance and greatly increasing the time spent on the surface or at *schnorchel* depth while recharging the batteries. Two further prototypes were constructed – one an improved 90 ton barge, the second a much larger 300 ton lighter – which were also tested successfully in mid-1944. The problems of low-speed control and of underwater endurance remained intractable and the whole project, including orders for 50 of the 90 ton type, was canceled in December 1944.

THE ITALIAN TRANSPORTS – AQUILA AND MERKATOR

Admiral Dönitz considered the large Italian submarines unsatisfactory for operational service in the Atlantic and in early 1943 it was proposed they should be converted for use as Far East transports, although still manned by Italians. Dönitz proposed this at his first *Führer* Naval conference in February 1943 and obtained Hitler's approval.

The Italian *Supramarina* (Admiralty) struck a hard bargain, obtaining no fewer than 10 brand-new Type VIICs in exchange for their 10 Atlantic boats then operating from Bordeaux. Two were lost on their final Atlantic patrols, leaving eight for conversion, under the codename *Aquila*. The Germans also tried to obtain the two *Romolo*-class transport submarines then completing for the Italian Navy, but even though, with the loss of North Africa, the Italians had no further requirement for them, they turned this down in June 1943.

After a six-week conversion the Italian boats were able to

OPERATIONAL U-BOATS CARRYING CARGO BACK TO EUROPE			
SUBMARINE	**DEPARTED**	**ARRIVED**	**COMMENTS**
U-178	Penang November 27 1943	France May 24 1944	Successful
U-188	Penang January 9 1944	France June 19 1944	Successful
U-843	Jakarta December 10 1944	Norway April 9 1945	Sunk while continuing on to Germany
U-861	Jakarta January 14 1945	Norway April 18 1945	Surrendered: Insufficient time to complete voyage
U-510	Jakarta January 11 1945	France April 24 1945	Surrendered; short of fuel
U-532	Jakarta January 13 1945	England May 14 1945	Surrendered following German capitulation

carry 150 tons of cargo (90 tons in external bunkers, 60 tons internally), but they required refueling on both outward and inward voyages. The first three sailed in May 1943, followed by two more in June, of which only three had reached Singapore by August: *Aquila II* (ex-*Giuliani*), *Aquila III* (ex-*Cappellini*) and *Aquila VI* (ex-*Torelli*). As Italy's future membership of the Axis was in doubt, the Japanese delayed the return of the three boats in Singapore, while the Germans acted similarly for the remaining two boats preparing to leave Bordeaux.

When the Italian surrender came, the last boat intended for conversion, *Cagni*, was still at sea and it was surrendered to the British. The three boats in Singapore were taken over by the Japanese, but after some discussion they were handed over to the Germans. The five boats became *UIT-21* (ex-*Finzi*), *UIT-22* (ex-*Bagnolini*), *UIT-23* (ex-*Giuliani*), *UIT-24* (ex-*Cappellini*), and *UIT-25* (ex-*Torelli*), while the cover-name for the operation was changed to *Merkator*.

Of the Bordeaux boats, *UIT-21* proved to be riddled with engine defects and was scuttled in August 1944, while the second, *UIT-22* (Wunderlich), sailed on January 26 1944, but was sunk with all hands on March 9 1944. That left three in Singapore. *UIT-23* (Striegler) sailed for Penang on February 13 1944, but was sunk by a British submarine the following day, when just short of its destination. *UIT-24* (Pahls) set out on the return voyage to Europe (February 8 1944) carrying 115 tons of rubber, 55 tons of tin and 10 tons of miscellaneous goods, including quinine. It was due to replenish from the tanker *Charlotte Schliemann* but after that ship had disappeared (February 11) the task was taken on by the other German tanker, *Brake*. When that vessel was also sunk (March 12) yet another plan was made for *UIT-24* to be replenished from *U-532*, which was in the area, but *UIT-24*'s fuel shortage, coupled with repeated engine trouble, led to a decision for it to return to Penang, which it reached on May 4 1944. Once unloaded, *UIT-24*, accompanied by *UIT-25* (Schrein) sailed to the German base at Kobe, Japan, for repair, where both were given engine overhauls. They were ready by August 1944, but by that stage of the

Type	Cargo Capacity							TOTALS	Notes
	Rubber	Tin	Wolfram	Molybdenum	Tunsten	Quinine etc	Misc.		
IXC/40	10	115		10	9	0.5	0.5	145	
IXD$_1$								252	3
IXD$_2$	80	120		15		1.0	0.1	216	
XB								160	4
XX	400	200	150			50		800	5
XXIT	125	67	67	12			4	275	5
XXIE$_2$	290	170	100	25		83		668	5

The header title row reads: **TRANSPORT U-BOATS; DESIGNATED CARGO-CARRYING CAPACITIES**

Notes:
1. These are planning figures. Actual loads varied according to demands from Berlin and availability.
2. On outward voyage, boats carried ammunition, weapons, documents, mercury, high quality steel, etc.
3. Actual load carried by *U-180* on outbound voyage in 1944.
4. Actual load carried by *U-234* after conversion to special transport, on outbound voyage, April 1945.
5. Types XX and XXIT/E2 were never built.

war there was no possibility of them being replenished en route and their departure was canceled. Following the German surrender in Europe they were taken over by the Japanese.[5]

The original *Aquila* program had resulted in considerable effort being expended on the conversion of the boats, fitting German equipment (such as radars and intercept sets) and in overhauling the unreliable engines. Then, following the Italian surrender, the *Merkator* program required even more effort as German crews had to be found to man them and to be trained on the unfamiliar boats. The outcome of the program was that some goods were delivered to Singapore, but not one ton of the urgently needed supplies was ever brought back to Europe.

THE ENDURING MYSTERY OF *U-234*

The voyage of the Type XB, *U-234* (Fehler) remains a mystery. *U-234* was damaged during construction in a bombing raid, delaying commissioning until March 3 1944, but then, following the usual work-up period in the Baltic, it was converted to a transport for a special mission. The major part of the work, which started on August 30 1944, involved removing the 24 vertical mine tubes from the side tanks to create two large holds; the cargo being loaded into watertight cylinders normally used to carry spare torpedoes. The six vertical mine tubes forward of the bridge were also used for cargo, using special watertight steel cylinders, held in place by the usual mine-release mechanism. Finally, the keel duct was filled with cargo, mainly mercury and optical glass.

Other modifications included the installation of a *schnorchel*, additional radios (including the latest *Kurier* [burst transmitter]), a *Balkon* sonar, and the latest air-search radar. Work was completed on December 22 and following trials final loading took place, part of which was supervised by two

Japanese naval officers. The cargo amounted to 260 tons, of which the most unusual item was 0.55 tons (560kg) of Uranium Oxide (U$_{235}$); there were also 12 passengers.

U-234 sailed from Kiel on March 25 1945, arriving in Horten, Norway, on March 28. The order to sail onward, signed by Dönitz in person, was received on April 14 and *U-234* sailed on April 16, even though Germany was on the verge of defeat. *U-234*'s radios picked up the announcement of Hitler's death on May 3, followed by news of the appointment of Dönitz as his successor. On May 4 they received the order for all U-boats to surrender at 0800 hours the following morning.

The two Japanese officers aboard committed suicide by taking massive overdoses of sleeping tablets and their bodies had just been committed to the deep when *U-234* surrendered to USS *Sutton* (DE-771). *U-234* was escorted into the naval base at Portsmouth, New Hampshire, where the crew were interrogated, while the uranium oxide was removed and taken away. From that day to this the reason the uranium oxide was being sent to Japan and the use to which it was put by the USA have remained closely guarded secrets.

It is quite clear that planning for *U-234*'s mission started in early 1944. *U-234* entered refit to prepare for this voyage in August 1944, but designing the installation and allocating space in the overcrowded shipyards must have started much earlier, in February or March 1944. At first sight, the decision of the two Japanese naval officers to commit suicide seems to follow the traditional Japanese code, but not one of the many other Japanese diplomats and officers in Germany at the time of the German surrender is known to have taken this course. A detailed inspection of the minutes of the CinC Navy's meetings with Hitler do not show anywhere any mention of this U-boat or its mission, which suggests that it was of such secrecy that it could not be recorded.

JAPANESE SUBMARINES TO EUROPE

The seaborne traffic between the two Axis partners was not one way only. Five Japanese submarines set out from the Far East for Europe; three (*I-30*, *I-8*, and *I-29*) reached their destination and returned to Singapore. The other two (*I-34* and *I-52*) were sunk en route to Europe. *I-8* carried the stores and 48 officers and ratings needed to crew *U-1224*, the German U-boat being presented to the IJN (*RO-501*).

Footnotes:
1. Several attempts at flying between Europe and the Far East were made and one or two flights may have been successful. Air travel over such distances did not become a feasible proposition during the war, however.
2. The Japanese raised an anti-British army from Indian soldiers captured during their invasion of Southeast Asia. Bhose, a long-time anti-British agitator, had taken refuge in Germany and was required to return to the Far East to control the so-called Indian National Army.
3. One item was a sample of *Bolde*, a container filled with calcium hydride, which reacted with seawater to produce a cloud of hydrogen bubbles to confuse enemy sonar.
4. *RO-500* was closely examined by the IJN and subjected to a series of trials, but was then used as a training boat, while the Germans were dispersed among the various German bases in the Far East. *RO-500* was surrendered at Maizuru in August 1945.
5. *UIT-24* (ex-*Cappellini*) became *I-503*, and *UIT-25* (ex-*Torelli*) became *I-504*. They were the only two warships to fly the flags of all three Axis navies during the war.

U-BOATS SUNK BY ACCIDENT 1935-1945

The *Ubootwaffe* lost no fewer than 40 U-boats and 926 men due to accidents, as shown in the tables. The great majority of these occurred in the training organization and can be divided into two groups: boats of the training flotillas, and recently commissioned boats working-up prior to joining an operational flotilla. Losses due to accidents while on operations are also shown.

COLLISIONS ON OPERATIONS

Collisions between U-boats were an ever-present danger during the melees in and around convoys, especially during the hours of darkness, although only three major incidents are known to have taken place. The first was on the night of December 8 1942 when *U-254* (Gilardone) was rammed by *U-221* (Trojer) while both were submerged and attacking convoy HX.217. *U-221* suffered little damage and no loss of life, but *U-254* was forced to the surface, where it was attacked by an RAF Liberator and sunk, going down very quickly and leaving just four survivors.

The worst accident disaster to befall the *Ubootwaffe* occurred on May 4 1943 when *U-439* (von Tippelskirch) and *U-659* (Stock) were operating as part of *Gruppe Drossel* off Cape Finisterre. During the morning of May 3 a *Luftwaffe* Fw-200 reported sighting a convoy nearby and the *Drossel* group immediately headed in its direction. The convoy consisted of 15 tank-landing craft (LCTs) with two escorts. At the best of times, flat-bottomed LCTs were particularly difficult targets for U-boats, since torpedoes ran underneath them, but on this occasion the sea was very rough as well, and an attack was postponed. Early next morning, however, the group carried out a surface attack, during which *U-439*, traveling at about 7 knots, was overtaken on its port side by *U-659*. Despite their proximity none of the lookouts on either bridge appears to have spotted the other boat, possibly because they were looking at a British ship which had just been hit by a torpedo and was burning brightly. At that moment, *U-439*'s captain came on the bridge and ordered the course to be altered to port, which almost immediately led to the collision, in which his boat's bows penetrated the starboard side of *U-659* abreast the bridge.

The damaged boat sank within seconds, leaving just a few men from the bridge-watch struggling in the water. Von Tippelskirch immediately ordered *U-439*'s engines full astern, but at that moment a following sea swept over his boat, flooding the diesel exhausts and stopping the engines. The captain ordered the conning tower hatch to be closed, but his boat sank rapidly, although it may have remained just below the surface because two hours later a British trawler reported striking a submerged object. Another British vessel passing through the area was alerted by the smell of diesel fumes and when its look-

outs spotted lifebuoy lights in the water it stopped to pick up the survivors. There were nine survivors from *U-439* and three from *U-659*, a total of 84 being lost in the two boats.

The only other collision between operational U-boats occurred on October 24 1944, when *U-382* (Wilke) collided with *U-673* (Gehrke) off Stavanger, when both were en route from Bergen to Germany. *U-673* sank, but all the crew were rescued.

U-BOATS SUNK WHILE WORKING-UP						
DATE	**U-BOAT**	**TYPE**	**PLACE**	**CAUSE**	**MONTHS IN SERVICE**	**LIVES LOST**
November 11 1941	U-560	VIIC	Baltic	Collision with surface ship. Raised; used for training	8	0
November 11 1941	U-580	VIIC	Baltic	Collision with target vessel *Angelburg* during night exercises	4	12
November 15 1941	U-583	VIIC	Baltic	Collision with *U-153*	3	45
August 6 1942	U-612	VIIC	Baltic	Collision with *U-444*	5	6
September 2 1942	U-222	VIIC	Baltic	Collision with *U-626*	3	42
November 12 1942	U-272	VIIC	Baltic	Collision with German depot ship	1	28
February 24 1943	U-649	VIIC	Baltic	Collision with *U-232*	3	36
August 21 1943	U-670	VIIC	Baltic	Collision with target ship *Bolkoberg*	7	21
September 8 1943	U-983	VIIC	Baltic	Collision with *U-988*	3	5
September 20 1943	U-346	VIIC	Baltic	Diving accident: sabotage was suspected	3	36
November 18 1943	U-718	VIIC	Baltic	Collision with *U-476*	5	43
November 20 1943	U-768	VIIC	Baltic	Collision with *U-745*	1	49
March 17 1944	U-1013	VIIC	Baltic	Collision with *U-286*	0.5	25
May 15 1944	U-1234	VIIC/40	Baltic	Collided with tug; raised and returned to service	1	13
May 19 1944	U-1015	VIIC/41	Baltic	Collision with *U-1014*	2	36
October 10 1944	U-2331	XXIII	Baltic	Lost	1	16
February 18 1945	U-2344	XXIII	Baltic	Collision with *U-2336*	3	7
TOTALS	17					420

TOTAL LOSSES IN U-BOAT ACCIDENTS								
	U-BOATS SUNK				**MEN KILLED**			
	Training	Working up	Operations	TOTALS	Training	Working up	Operations	TOTALS
Collision — surface ship	5	5	5	15	86	74	105	265
Collision — U-boat	0	10	4	14	0	294	125	419
Diving	3	1	1	5	95	36	45	176
Alongside	1	0	1	2	1	0	0	1
Unexplained	0	1	0	1	0	16	0	16
Heavy seas	0	0	1	1	0	0	0	0
Sunk in error	0	0	1	1	0	0	45	45
Grounded	0	0	1	1	0	0	4	4
TOTALS	9	17	14	40	182	420	324	926

SUNK IN HARBOR

Perhaps the most humiliating accidental loss was when *U-43*, a Type IXA commanded at the time by *Kapitänleutnant* Wolfgang Lüth, one of the most efficient of the U-boat captains, sank alongside at Lorient. *U-43* had returned from patrol on December 171940 and after the usual refit was due to sail on its next patrol at dawn on February 4 1941. Final preparations were made the previous day and somehow – whether by accident or design, was never established – a valve was left in the wrong position, as a result of which water slowly seeped into the bilges.

To compound the problem, the majority of the crew had gone ashore for a final night 'on the town,' leaving a few new arrivals to guard the boat. Since the boat sank very slowly and on an even keel, nothing was noticed until it was too late. To cap it all, the watertight doors had not been closed, as laid down in orders, so the boat sank until only the top of the bridge was visible. *U-43* was raised and refitted, and did not leave on the next patrol until May 11 1941. The petty officer of the watch and the sentry were punished, and Lüth was doubtless reprimanded by Dönitz (although it did not affect his subsequent career). Due to carelessness *BdU* was deprived of a valuable boat and crew for three months at a time when Dönitz needed every boat he could lay his hands on.

U-BOATS LOST BY ACCIDENTS WHILE ON OPERATIONS (* = no survivors)					
DATE	**U-BOAT**	**TYPE**	**PLACE**	**CAUSE**	**LIVES LOST**
January 31 1940	*U-15*	IIB	North Sea	Rammed by torpedo boat *Iltis*	0
September 3 1940	*U-57*	IIC	North Sea	Rammed by Norwegian ship at entrance to Kiel Canal	0
December 4 1941	*U-43*	IXA	France	Sank alongside	0
December 6 1941	*U-557*	VIIC	Mediterranean	Rammed by Italian torpedo boat, *Orione*	43*
December 8 1942	*U-254*	VIIC	Atlantic	Rammed by *U-221* during convoy attack	41
May 4 1943	*U-659*	VIIC	Atlantic	Collided with *U-439* during Atlantic operation	44
May 4 1943	*U-439*	VIIC	Atlantic	Collided with *U-659* during Atlantic operation	40
December 21 1943	*U-284*	VIIC	North Atlantic	Severely damaged by heavy seas; scuttled	0
October 21 1944	*U-957*	VIIC	Norway	Collided with merchant ship; damaged beyond repair	0
October 24 1944	*U-673*	VIIC	Norwegian Sea	Collided with *U-382*	0
December 19 1944	*U-737*	VIIC	Norwegian Sea	Collided with minesweeper *MRS-25*	31
February 15 1945	*U-1053*	VIIC	Norwegian Sea	Accident during deep diving test	45*
April 14 1945	*U-235*	VIIC	North Sea	Sunk in error by torpedo boat *T-17*; mistaken identity	45*
Aprl 14, 1945	*U-1206*	VIIC	North Sea	Grounded; navigational error	4
TOTALS	14				324

SCHOOL BOATS SUNK DURING TRAINING (* = no survivors)					
DATE	**U-BOAT**	**TYPE**	**PLACE**	**CAUSE**	**LIVES LOST**
November 20 1936	*U-18*	IIB	Baltic	Colided with escorting ship: *T.156*	8
March 19 1943	*U-5*	IIA	Baltic	Diving accident during exercises	21
August 5 1943	*U-34*	VII	Baltic	Collision with U-boat depot ship *Lech*	4
February 14 1944	*U-738*	VIIC	Baltic	Collision with SS *Erna*	22
February 18 1944	*U-7*	IIB	Baltic	Diving accident	26
March 17 1944	*U-28*	VIIA	Baltic	Sank alongside jetty; cause unknown	1
April 8 1944	*U-2*	VIIC	Baltic	Collided with trawler *Fröse*	16
November 28 1944	*U-80*	VIIC	Baltic	Diving accident	48*
December 17 1944	*U-416*	VIIC	Baltic	Collided with minesweeper *M-203*	36
TOTALS	9				182

◁ A surprising number of U-boats were lost in training; here the crew of *U-957* (Type VIIC) smile at their lucky escape after colliding with the bottom of a surface ship, March 20 1943.

THE END FOR
THE U-BOATS

As the war in Europe drew to its end the remaining U-boats were scattered: some in German ports, some in Norway, a number in the Atlantic, and a few in the Far East. The *Kriegsmarine* issued instructions on April 30 1945 that all warships would be sunk on receipt of the codeword '*Regenbogen*' (= rainbow), the only exceptions being vessels needed for Germany's post-war recovery, such as minesweepers and transports. The surrender terms for all German forces in northern Germany, the Netherlands, and Denmark were laid down by Britain's Field Marshal Montgomery on May 3 and were transmitted to all German forces in those areas on May 4, coming into force at 0800 hours May 5 1945. A general surrender was then imposed by General Eisenhower, which came into effect at 0001 hours on May 9 1945. These surrender terms included instructions that boats in German ports were to surrender to the Allies, those in Norway were to await Allied orders, and that U-boats at sea were to surface and broadcast their positions, whereupon they would receive further instructions.

U-BOATS IN GERMAN PORTS

Many U-boats were scuttled in German waters in two phases. The first of these took place on May 1-4 and was the captains' response to the impending capture of their ports by advancing British and Soviet troops. A total of 136 serviceable, incomplete and damaged U-boats were scuttled in this phase: Bremen – 1; Bremerhaven – 11; Eckenförde – 1; Hamburg – 11; Heikendorf – 1; Kiel Canal – 2; Kiel – 48; Laboe – 1; Nordenham – 1; Travemünde – 32; Vegesack – 1; Warnemünde – 3; Wassersleben -1; and Wilhelmshaven – 22.

The second phase took place on May 4/5 when a large number of U-boat captains, who had been briefed for Operation *Regenbogen*, interpreted the announcement of the capitulation to Field-Marshal Montgomery on May 4 as the signal to scuttle their boats, even though the surrender terms included clear instructions to the contrary. They deliberately ignored the fact that the codeword *Regenbogen* was never issued, their justification being that Dönitz signed the surrender terms under duress, which may have been true, but surrenders are seldom signed under any other circumstances.

Thus, on the night of May 4/5 a further 83 U-boats were scuttled: Aarhus – 1; Cuxhaven – 2; Eckenförde – 1; Flensburg – 1; Flensburger Förde – 9; Geltinger Bay – 44; Holnis – 1; Hörup Haff – 6; Kupfermühlen Bay – 9; Lübeck Bay – 1; Schleimünde – 1; Solitüde – 1; Wassersleben Bay – 2; and Wesermünde – 4. Since the Allies eventually scuttled all but a few of the captured U-boats, this presumably did not run counter to their long-term interests; in any event, no disciplinary action was ever taken.

△ The end of the campaign, and a U-boat flies the black flag, as ordered in the surrender agreements, as it sails towards the US coast on May 10 1945.

U-BOATS AT SEA

At the moment of surrender, 48 U-boats were at sea or in foreign waters: 17 on operational patrols in the Atlantic, six in the Arctic and 14 in the waters around the British Isles. Nine were involved in traffic with Germany's only remaining ally, Japan, with six in the Far East, one outward bound and two homeward bound. The remaining two U-boats were involved in supplying the port of St Nazaire, where a German garrison was holding out against the Allies.

On the evening of May 4, *BdU* issued instructions by radio to these boats instructing them to end any current pursuit immediately, and to cease aggressive action from 0800 hours the following morning. This was followed on May 8 by a signal announcing Germany's total surrender and banning the sending of encrypted messages; all old cypher keys were to be destroyed and any current or future keys surrendered. Allied radio stations then broadcast instructions telling U-boats to surface immediately, switch on navigation lights, and fly a black flag from the periscope. In addition, all torpedoes were to be disarmed, gun ammunition jettisoned and the guns locked facing aft.

The boats were also to report their position by radio and when a few failed to comply a peremptory signal told them that any U-boat failing to do so would be treated as a pirate and its captain tried after capture. On establishing contact, U-boats in

\multicolumn{5}{c}{U-BOATS WHICH SERVED WITH FOREIGN NAVIES (EXCLUDING OPERATION DEADLIGHT)}
COUNTRY	U-BOAT	TYPE	ACQUIRED	FATE
Canada	U-190	IXC/40	Surrendered to RCN, May 16 1945	Commissioned into RCN June 1945. Sunk October 21 1947
France	U-123	IXB	Captured in Lorent, 1945	Named *Blaison*. Served 1947–49. Scrapped 1960
	U-129	IXB	Stricken in Lorient in 1944. Captured by French in 1945	Broken up for spares 1946
	U-471	VIIC	Sunk Toulon 1944. Raised 1945	Named *Mille*. Served 1946–63. Scrapped 1963.
	U-510	IXC	Captured by French in St Nazaire, 1945	Named *Bouan*. Served 1945–59. Scrapped 1960
	U-766	VIIC	Captured at La Pallice, France, 1944	Named *Laubie*. Served 1945–63
	U-2518	XXI	Handed over by British	Named *Roland Worillot*. Served 1946–68
	U-2326	XXIII	Handed over by British (N-35)	Served 1945 until lost in accident in 1946
Germany	U-2365	XXIII	Sunk 1945. Raised 1956	In service 1956 as *S-170 Hai* until lost in 1946
	U-2367	XXIII	Sunk 1945. Raised 1956	In service 1957–69 as *S-171 Hecht*. Scrapped 1969
	U-2540	XXI	Sunk 1945. Raised 1958	Named *Wilhelm Bauer*; in service as trials boat 1960–82. Scrapped
Norway	U-310	VIIC	Abandoned in Trondheim 1945	Scrapped March 1947
	U-315	VIIC	Abandoned in Trondheim 1945	Scrapped March 1947
	U-324	VIIC	Abandoned in Bergen 1945	Scrapped March 1947
	U-926	VIIC	Abandoned in Norway. Allocated to Norway as war booty	Named *Kya*. Served January 1949 to March 1964. Scrapped
	U-975	VIIC	Abandoned in Trondheim 1945	Scrapped
	U-995	VIIC	Abandoned in Norway. Allocated to Norway as war booty	Named *Kaura*. Served 1952 to 1965. Returned to Germany; museum since 1971 at Laboe
	U-1202	VIIC	Abandoned in Norway. Allocated to Norway as war booty	Named *Kynn*. Served 1951 to 1961. Scrapped 1963
	U-1275	VIIC	Abandoned in Bergen 1945	Scrapped in Norway
	U-4706	XXIII	Abandoned in Norway. Allocated to Norway as war booty	Named *Knerter*. Served 1950 to 1953. Scrapped 1954
Spain	U-573	VIIC	Interned in 1944, then purchased from Germany	Designated *G7*, later *S-01*. In service 1945–70. Scrapped
Sweden	U-3503	XXI	Sunk in Swedish waters 1945. Raised in 1946	Examined in detail, then scrapped
USSR	U-250	VIIC	Sunk by Soviet ships July 1944. Salvaged August 1944	Examined in detail, later scrapped
	U-1058	VIIC	Handed over by British (N-21)	Soviet S-82
	U-1064	VIIC	Handed over by British (N-21)	Soviet S-83
	U-1305	VIIC	Handed over by British (N-21)	Soviet S-84
	U-2353	XXIII	Handed over by British (N-31)	Baltic Fleet 1947–63. Scrapped 1963
	U-2529	XXI	Handed over by British (N-28)	Baltic Fleet 1946–55. Scrapped 1958–59
	U-3035	XXI	Handed over by British (N-29)	Baltic Fleet 1946–55. Scrapped 1958–59
	U-3041	XXI	Handed over by British (N-30)	Baltic Fleet 1946–55. Scrapped 1972
	U-3515	XXI	Handed over by British (N-27)	Baltic Fleet 1946–55. Scrapped 1958–59
UK	U-570	VIIC	Captured at sea August 27 1941	Served in RN. HMS *Graph*. Wrecked in 1944
	U-792	Wa-201	Scuttled May 4 1945. Raised by British	Used for trials. Fate unknown

△ Continued over

the eastern Atlantic were told to head for the nearest suitable port; the majority (26) went to British ports, while seven in the western Atlantic went to the nearest North American port: five to the USA and two to Newfoundland. Two tried and failed to return to Germany: one was mined, the other ran aground. Of five in the Bay of Biscay one went to France, two to Gibraltar and two were scuttled by their crews off the Portuguese coast. The captains in the Far East had no choice but to give themselves and their crews up to the Japanese, where they were interned in relative comfort for the remainder of the war. Their boats were impressed into the Imperial Japanese Navy on July 15 1945, although they were little used before the Japanese surrender on September 2 1945, when they were taken over by the Allies. That left *U-530* (Wermuth) and *U-977* (Schäffer), which made two remarkable voyages to Argentina, reaching their goal on July 10 and August 17, respectively.

OPERATION DEADLIGHT – THE PLAN

Despite the scuttlings, the Allies found themselves with a large number of U-boats in their hands and no plan for their disposal. Their first reaction was to move as many as possible to British ports, with Norwegian-based U-boats sailing for the UK on May 30, followed by those from German ports in mid-June.

Country	U-boat	Type	Acquired	Fate
	U-793	Wk-201	Scuttled May 5 1945. Raised by British	Used for trials. Fate unknown
	U-953	VIIC	Surrendered May 9 1945 at Drontheim	N-?. Sscrapped June 1949
	U-1023	VIIC	Surrendered Weymouth May 10 1945	N-83. Used for tests, then sunk January 7 1946
	U-1108	VIIC/41	Surrendered Horten, Norway May 1945	British N-19. Scrapped May 1949
	U-1171	VIIC/41	Surrendered Stavanger May 1945	British N-19. Scrapped April 1949
	U-1407	XVIIB	Scuttled 1945. Raised and taken to UK 1945	British N-25, later named *Meteorite*. Scrapped 1949
	U-2348	XXIII	Surrendered Stavanger May 1945; taken to UK	Broken up April 1949
	U-3017	XXI	Surrendered Horten, Norway May 1945. Taken to UK	British N-41. Scrapped 1949
USA	U-234	XB	Surrendered Portsmouth, NH, USA May 16 1945	Used for trials; sunk off Cape Cod November 1946
	U-505	IX	Captured at sea June 4 1944	Used for trials. Became museum in Chicago 1954
	U-530	IXC/40	Interned in Argentina July 1945. Transferred to USA 1946	Used for trials. Sunk off Cape Cod November 1947
	U-977	VIIC	Interned in Argentina August 1945. Transferred to USA November 1946	Used for trials. Sunk off Cape Cod November 13 1947
	U-1105	VIIC/41	Surrendered in UK at Loch Erriboll May 1945. Transferred to USA 1946	British N-16. Used for trials; sunk November 18 1948
	U-1406	XVIIB	Scuttled May 5 1945. Raised and taken to USA	Used for trials 1946–48. Scrapped 1948
	U-3008	XXI	Surrendered at Wilhelmshaven May 1945. Transferred to USA June 1945	Used for propulsion trials. Scrapped 1954 November 1947
	U-2513	XXI	Surrendered at Horten, Norway May 1945. Transferred to USA 1946	Used for trials. Sunk during trials October 1951

△ *U-2513*, one of many U-boats which surrendered in the Norwegian bases. As a Type XXI it was of great interest and reached the USA in August 1945. It was examined and tested in detail before being expended as a target in October 1951.

▽ Surrender in Germany and U-boat crews break ranks to form around *Korvetten-Kapitän* 'Ajax' Bleichrodt for a final speech before they pass into captivity. These lucky ones had survived; tens of thousands of their shipmates had not.

Some went to Loch Ryan in Scotland, the others to Lisahally in Northern Ireland.

At the Potsdam Conference of Allied leaders it was agreed that up to 30 U-boats would be distributed to the Allies for experiments and research, although in the event, 28 were actually distributed: Canada – 1; France – 6; Norway – 4; UK – 3; USA – 4; USSR – 10. A Tripartite Naval Commission was established and met in Berlin between August 14 and December 6 1945, and among the decisions reached was that '...all unallocated submarines which are afloat shall be sunk in the open sea in a depth of not less than one hundred metres by February 15 1946.'

This decision resulted in *Operation Deadlight*, carried out by the British on behalf of all Allied navies. It was decided to carry out some realistic training, with a number of U-boats allocated as air or submarine targets, but the remainder would be sunk by demolition charges installed by RN specialists. A deep area in the Atlantic some 130 miles (210km) off the coast of Northern Ireland was selected, with three main locations for the sinkings:

Datum position (XX) – 56° 00'N 10° 05'W
Main scuttling position (YY) – 56° 10'N 10° 05'W
Air target position (ZZ) – 55° 50'N 10° 05'W.

LOCH RYAN

U-boats in Loch Ryan were towed to sea by a collection of destroyers, frigates, and a few tugs, and the task proved more difficult than anticipated: warships were not ideal, unmanned submarines were difficult to tow, and the weather was appalling. There were 14 'flights,' each of 6-7 U-boats, between November 25 and December 28 (with short breaks for bad weather and the Christmas holiday) and trouble was experienced from the start. Tows parted en route and as the U-boats were unmanned there was no prospect of restoring them; sometimes the U-boat solved the problem by foundering, otherwise gunfire was used. Even when some did reach the correct spot the elaborate charges could not be detonated, so the majority had to be sunk by gunfire and only a few were sunk by aircraft or submarines, as planned. The last three U-boats were taken to sea on December 28 (Flight 14); two parted their tows en route and were sunk by gunfire, leaving *U-1103* as the last Loch Ryan boat to be sunk, also by gunfire, in the designated scuttling area at 1010 on December 29.

LISAHALLY

The second phase of *Operation Deadlight* was mounted from Lisahally on the River Foyle, 2 miles (3.2km) down-river from the city of Londonderry. The U-boats had to motor down-river to an anchorage off the Irish port of Moville, where they were passed a tow by their designated towing vessel. Each day's sailing was designated a 'lift,' the first of which (five U-boats) sailed on December 29. Not one of the U-boats in Lifts 1-5

BOAT		FATE			
Number	Type	Date	Sunk	Location	Remarks
U-143	IID	December 22	Gunfire	55°58'N 09°35'W	Tow parted
U-145	IID	December 22	Gunfire	55°47'N 09°56'W	Tow parted
U-149	IID	December 21	Gunfire	55°40'N 08°00'W	Tow parted
U-150	IID	December 21	Gunfire	56°04'N 09°35'W	
U-155	IXC	December 21	Gunfire	55°35'N 07°35'W	Tow parted
U-170	IXC/40	November 30	Gunfire	55°44'N 07°53'W	Towing badly
U-218	VIID	December 4	Sank in tow	Inistrahul Light 301° 8.9n miles	30 fathoms
U-245	VIIC	December 7	Foundered	55°25'N 06°19'10"W	Tow parted
U-249	VIIC	December 13	Torpedo	56°10'N 10°05'W	
U-255	VIIC	December 13	Aircraft	55°50'N 10°05'W	
U-281	VIIC	November 30	Foundered	55°32'N 07°38'10"W	
U-291	VIIC	December 21	Gunfire	55°50'N 09°08'W	Tow parted
U-293	VIIC	December 13	Gunfire	55°50'N 10°05'W	
U-293	VIIC	December 17	Gunfire	56°14'N 10°37'W	
U-298	VIIC	November 29	Gunfire	55°35'N 07°54'W	Tug slipped tow
U-299	VIIC	December 4	Foundered	55°38'N 07°54'W	Tow parted
U-312	VIIC	November 29	Foundered	55°35'N 07°54'W	Sank in tow
U-313	VIIC	December 21	Foundered	55°40'N 08°24'W	55 fathoms
U-318	VIIC	December 21	Gunfire	55°47'N 08°30'W	Tow parted
U-328	VIIC	November 30	Aircraft	55°50'N 10°54'W	
U-368	VIIC	December 17	Gunfire	56°14'N 10°37'W	
U-369	VIIC	November 30	Foundered	55°31'N 07°27'W	
U-427	VIIC	December 21	Gunfire	56°04'N 09°35'W	500 fathoms
U-481	VIIC	November 30	Gunfire	56°11'N 10°00'W	Tow parted
U-483	VIIC	December 16	Gunfire	56°10'N 10°05'W	
U-485	VIIC	December 8	Torpedo	56°10'N 10°05'W	
U-532	IXC	December 9	Torpedo	56°08'N 10°07'W	Using CCR pistol
U-539	IXC/40	December 4	Foundered	55°38'N 07°57'W	Sank in tow
U-637	VIIC	December 21	Foundered	55°35'N 07°46'W	38 fathoms
U-680	VIIC	December 28	Gunfire	55°24'N 06°29'W	Tow parted
U-716	VIIC	December 11	Aircraft	55°50'N 10°05'W	
U-720	VIIC	December 21	Gunfire	56°04'N 09°35'W	Over 500 fathoms
U-739	VIIC	December 16	Aircraft	55°50'N 10°05'W	
U-760	VIIC	December 13	Aircraft	55°50'N 10°05'W	
U-773	VIIC	December 8	Torpedo TANTIVY	56°10'N 10°05'W	
U-775	VIIC	December 8	Gunfire	55°40'N 08°25'W	Tow parted
U-776	VIIC	December 3	Foundered	55°08'N 05°30'W	48 fathoms
U-778	VIIC	December 4	Sank in tow	Inistrahull light 308° 11.2n miles	34 fathoms
U-779	VIIC	December 17	Gunfire	55°50'N 10°05'W	
U-806	IXC/40	December 21	Gunfire	55°44'N 08°18'W	Tow slipped
U-826	VIIC	December 1	Gunfire	56°10'N 10°05'W	
U-868	IXC	November 30	Foundered	55°48'N 08°33'W	Sank in steep dive
U-907	VIIC	December 7	Foundered	55°17'N 05°59'W	Dived to bottom
U-928	VIIC	December 16	Aircraft	55°50'N 10°05'W	

To Sea From Lock Ryan, Scotland

△ Continued over.

BOAT			FATE		
Number	**Type**	**Date**	**Sunk**	**Location**	**Remarks**
U-956	VIIC	December 17	Gunfire	55°50′N 10°05′W	
U-968	VIIC	November 28	Foundered	55°24′N 06°22′W	Sank in 80 fathoms
U-978	VIIC	December 11	Torpedo	55°50′N 10°05′W	
U-991	VIIC	December 11	Torpedo	56°10′N 10°05′W	
U-992	VIIC	December 16	Gunfire	56°50′N 10°05′W	
U-994	VIIC	December 5	Foundered	55°50′N 08°30′W	Sank in tow
U-997	VIIC	December 11	Aircraft	55°50′N 10°05′W	
U-1002	VIIC	December 13	Torpedo	56°10′N 10°05′W	
U-1004	VIIC	December 1	Gunfire	56°10′N 10°05′W	
U-1005	VIIC	December 5	Foundered	55°33′N 08°27′W	Sank in tow
U-1009	VIIC	December 16	Gunfire	55°31′N 07°24′W	
U-1019	VIIC	December 7	Gunfire	55°27′N 07°56′W	U-boat sinking
U-1052	VIIC	December 9	Aircraft	55°50′N 10°05′W	
U-1061	VIIC	December 1	Gunfire	56°50′N 10°05′W	
U-1102	VIIC	December 21	Gunfire	56°04′N 09°35′W	Over 500 fathoms
U-1103	VIIC	December 30	Gunfire	56°03′N 10°05′W	
U-1104	VIIC	December 15	Demolition	55°35′N 10°05′W	Sunk early
U-1110	VIIC	December 21	Gunfire	55°45′N 08°19′W	Tow parted
U-1163	VIIC	December 11	Aircraft	55°50′N 10°05′W	
U-1165	VIIC	December 31	Gunfire	55°44′N 08°40′W	Released and sunk
U-1194	VIIC	December 22	Gunfire	55°59′N 09°55′W	Tow parted
U-1198	VIIC	December 17	Gunfire	56°14′N 10°37′W	
U-1203	VIIC	December 8	Aircraft	55°50′N 10°05′W	
U-1230	IXC40	December 17	Gunfire	55°50′N 10°05′W	
U-1233	IXC40	December 29	Gunfire	55°51′N 08°54′W	Tow parted
U-1271	VIIC	December 8	Foundered	55°28′N 07°20′W	
U-1272	VIIC	December 8	Aircraft	55°50′N 10°05′W	
U-1301	VIIC	December 16	Gunfire	56°50′N 10°05′W	
U-1307	VIIC	December 9	Aircraft	55°50′N 10°05′W	
U-2321	XXIII	December 27	Gunfire	56°10′N 10°05′W	
U-2322	XXIII	November 27	Gunfire	56°10′N 10°05′W	
U-2324	XXIII	November 27	Gunfire	56°10′N 10°05′W	
U-2325	XXIII	November 28	Gunfire	56°10′N 10°05′W	
U-2328	XXIII	November 27	Foundered	56°12′N 09°48′W	Tow parted
U-2329	XXIII	November 28	Gunfire	56°10′N 10°05′W	
U-2334	XXIII	November 28	Gunfire	56°10′N 10°05′W	
U-2335	XXIII	November 28	Gunfire	56°10′N 10°05′W	
U-2337	XXIII	November 28	Gunfire	56°10′N 10°05′W	
U-2345	XXIII	November 27	Demolition	56°10′N 10°05′W	
U-2350	XXIII	November 28	Gunfire	56°10′N 10°05′W	
U-2354	XXIII	December 22	Gunfire	56°10′N 10°05′W	
U-2361	XXIII	November 27	Gunfire	56°10′N 10°05′W	
U-2363	XXIII	November 28	Gunfire	56°10′N 10°05′W	

ed the planned operations from Lisahally, but two U-boats (*U-975* and *U-3514*) remained, and were disposed of on February 10.

OPERATION DEADLIGHT IN RETROSPECT

Precisely 50 percent (58 boats) failed to reach the designated scuttling area in what was a rather unsuccessful operation. The warships (mostly small Hunt-class destroyers) proved most unsuitable for towing and, for reasons never established, the towing cables frequently parted, although this was not due to weakness, since when U-boats sank the towing vessel could not proceed until the tow had been slipped.

U-BOATS IN POST-WAR USE

Not all war-end U-boats met their fate in *Operation Deadlight*. Canada retained one of the two boats that had surrendered to the RCN and used it for trials until it was sunk on October 21 1947, which happened (not by chance) to be Trafalgar Day. The British had operated the captured *U-570* as HMS *Graph* in 1942-44, but they still took four Type VIIs, which they used for trials between 1946 and 1948. However, the British were more interested in the Walter propulsion system, which seemed to offer a cheaper alternative to nuclear propulsion. To this end, they raised a scuttled Type XVIIB (ex-*U-1407*) and took it to England together with Dr Walter, the inventor. He returned to Germany in 1948 and the boat was scrapped in 1949, but the work led to two new submarines (HMS *Excalibur* and *Explorer*) using hydrogen peroxide propulsion, although the system proved so dangerous that it was discontinued. The British were also allocated two Type XXIs, of which one (ex-*U-3017*) was tested for several years, while the other (ex-*U-2518*) was transferred to France in 1947. The British also tested a single Type XXIII (ex-*U-2348*). All these British war prizes had been scrapped by 1949.

A few pre-war French submarines had survived the war, but were very dated and the French Navy seized the opportunity offered by the German booty to restart their submarine arm. They already held five U-boats, captured in French ports in 1944-45, four of which were commissioned into the *Marine Nationale*, serving until the early 1960s. Two modern boats were also handed over from Allied stocks held by the British and both were commissioned into the navy: one Type XXI (ex-*U-2518*) was named *Roland Morillot* and served until 1968, while the other, a Type XXIII (ex-*U-2326*), was lost in an accident in 1946.

When the U-boats were taken from their Norwegian bases in May/June 1945, a number were left behind and handed over to the Norwegians. Four were scrapped in 1947, a single Type XXIII survived until 1953, but three Type VIICs were refurbished and gave some 10 years' service.

Eleven U-boats passed into US ownership. *U-505* (captured at sea June 4 1944) was used for trials, before becoming a museum at Chicago in 1954. One Type XB and four Type IXs sur-

reached Point YY (see above) and a single boat in Lift 6, which sailed on January 5 1946, became the first from Lisahally to actually reach the datum point. Lift 7 complet-

OPERATION DEADLIGHT: TO SEA FROM LISAHALLY, NORTHERN IRELAND					
BOAT		**OPERATION DEADLIGHT**			
Number	Type	Date	Fate	Location	Remarks
U-244	VIIC	December 30	Gunfire	55°46′N 08°32′W	Tow parted
U-278	VIIC	December 31	Gunfire	55°44′N 08°21′W	Tow released
U-294	VIIC	December 31	Gunfire	55°44′N 08°40′W	Released and sunk
U-363	VIIC	December 31	Gunfire	55°45′N 08°18′W	Tow released
U-516	IXC	January 3	Foundered	56°06′N 09°00′W	
U-541	IXC/40	January 5	Gunfire	55°38′N 07°35′W	Tow parted
U-764	VIIC	January 3	Gunfire	56°06′N 09°00′W	
U-802	IXC/40	December 31	Foundered	55°30′N 08°25′W	Tow parted
U-825	VIIC	January 3	Gunfire	55°31′N 07°30′W	Tow parted
U-861	IXD₂	December 31	Gunfire	55°25′N 07°15′W	Tug broke down
U-874	IXD₂	December 31	Gunfire	55°47′N 09°27′W	Tow parted
U-875	IXD₂	December 31	Gunfire	55°41′N 08°28′W	Tow parted
U-883	IXD/42	December 31	Gunfire	55°44′N 08°40′W	Released early
U-901	VIIC	January 6	Gunfire	55°50′N 08°30′W	In planned location
U-930	VIIC	December 29	Gunfire	55°22′N 07°35′W	Tow parted
U-975	VIIC	December 10	Squid	55°42′N 09°01′W	Deadlight (2)
U-1010	VIIC	January 7	Gunfire	55°37′N 07°49′W	Tow parted
U-1022	VIIC	December 29	Gunfire	55°40′N 08°15′W	Tow parted
U-1023	VIIC	January 8	Foundered	55°49′N 08°24′W	
U-1109	VIIC	January 6	Torpedo	55°49′N 08°31′W	
U-1165	VIIC	December 31	Gunfire	55°44′N 08°40′W	Released early
U-2336	XXIII	January 3	Gunfire	56°06′N 09°00′W	
U-2341	XXIII	December 31	Gunfire	55°44′N 08°19′W	
U-2351	XXIII	January 3	Gunfire	56°06′N 09°00′W	
U-2356	XXIII	January 6	Gunfire	55°50′N 08°20′W	
U-2502	XXI	January 3	Gunfire	56°06′N 09°00′W	
U-2506	XXI	January 5	Gunfire	55°37′N 07°30′W	Tow parted
U-2511	XXI	January 7	Gunfire	55°33′N 07°38′W	Tow parted
U-3514	XXIII	February 11	Shark	56°00′N 10°05′W	Deadlight (2)

rendered in US waters in May 1945 and all were used for a variety of trials, but had been scuttled or scrapped by 1948. Three boats were transferred to the USA from the Allied pool held in the UK: one Type VIIC/41 (*U-1105*) and two Type XXIs (*U-2513*, *U-3008*). In addition, the two boats which sailed to Argentina (*U-530* and *U-977*) were both taken to the United States in 1946 to be scrapped.

U-573 (Type VIIC) was interned in Spain in 1944 and was subsequently purchased by the Spanish Navy. It was refurbished and commissioned as *G-7* (later *S-01*), remaining in service until 1970.

Sweden had long possessed a small force of Swedish-designed and -built submarines but, as a neutral power, it was denied access to the latest German technology which became available to the Allies in 1945. Fortunately for them, *U-3503* (Type XXI) was scuttled in Swedish territorial waters in the last weeks of the war and this was quietly raised by the Swedes and taken to a dry dock where it was examined in minute detail before being scrapped.

Finally, when it joined NATO in 1955, West Germany wished to restart a U-boat arm and to speed this process it raised three boats which had been sunk in 1945: two Type XXIIIs (ex-*U-2365* and ex-*U-2367*) in 1956 and one Type XXI (ex-*U-2540*) in 1958. All were refurbished and the two Type XXIIIs were commissioned into the *Bundesmarine*, while the Type XXI spent its second career solely involved in various trials.

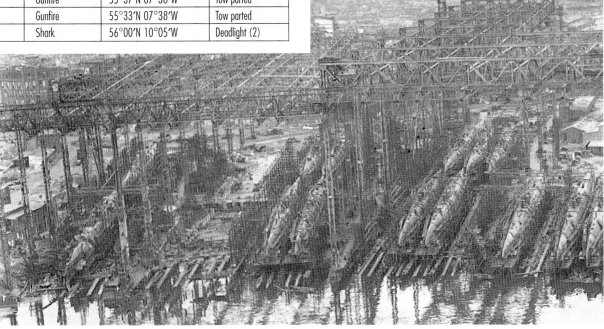

▷ Three minutes after the surrender on May 3 1945 and the U-boat yards in Hamburg lie silent, surrounded by a shattered city which had so often been the target of Allied air attacks. Many hard months lay ahead for the German population, but they would recover.

APPENDIX (see notes on pages 202-203)

						U-Boats Lost at Sea:
U-Boat	**Type**	**Builder**	**Commissioned**	**Fate**	**Date**	**Captain**
U-1	IIA	Deutsche	June 15 1935	Operational loss	April 6 1940	Deecke, J
U-2	IIA	Deutsche	July 25 1935	Training loss	April 8 1944	Schwarzkopf, W
U-5	IIA	Deutsche	August 31 1935	Training loss	March 19 1943	Rahn, H †
U-7	IIB	Germania	July 18 1935	Training loss	February 18 1944	Loeschke, G †
U-12	IIB	Germania	September 30 1935	Sunk	October 8 1939	von der Ropp, D †
U-13	IIB	Deutsche	November 30 1935	Sunk	May 31 1944	Schulte, M
U-15	IIB	Deutsche	March 7 1935	Collision	January 31 1940	Frahm, P †
U-16	IIB	Deutsche	May 16 1935	Sunk	October 24 1939	Weingaertner, H †
U-18	IIB	Germania	January 4 1936	Training loss	November 20 1936	Pauckstadt, K
U-19	IIB	Germania	January 16 1936	Scuttled	September 11 1944	Verpoorten, H
U-20	IIB	Germania	February 1 1936	Scuttled	September 10 1944	Grafen, K
U-22	IIB	Germania	August 20 1936	Operational loss	April 25 1940	Jenisch, KH †
U-23	IIB	Germania	September 24 1936	Scuttled	September 10 1944	Arendt, R
U-24	IIB	Germania	October 10 1936	Scuttled	August 25 1944	Lenzmann, D
U-25	IA	Deschimag	April 6 1936	Sunk	August 3 1940	Beduhn, H †
U-26	IA	Deschimag	May 11 1936	Sunk	July 3 1940	Scheringer, H-G
U-27	VIIA	Deschimag	August 12 1936	Sunk	September 10, 1939	Franz, J
U-28	VIIA	Deschimag	September 12 1936	Training loss	March 17 1944	Sachse, D
U-31	VIIA	Deschimag	December 28 1936	Sunk	March 11 1940	Habekost †
U-32	VIIA	Deschimag	April 5 1937	Sunk	October 30 1940	Jenisch, H
U-33	VIIA	Germania	July 25 1936	Sunk	February 12 1940	von Dresky, HW †
U-34	VIIA	Germania	September 12 1936	Collision	August 5 1943	Fresnki, H
U-35	VIIA	Germania	November 3 1936	Sunk	November 29 19390	Lott, W
U-36	VIIA	Germania	December 16 1936	Sunk	December 4 1939	Frölich, W †
U-39	IXA	Deschimag	December 10 1938	Sunk	September 14 1939	Glattes, G
U-40	IXA	Deschimag	February 11 1939	Sunk	October 13 1939	Barten, W †
U-41	IXA	Deschimag	April 22 1939	Sunk	February 5 1940	Mugler, G-A †
U-42	IXA	Deschimag	Juky 15 1939	Sunk	October 13 1939	Dau, R
U-43	IXA	Deschimag	August 26 1939	Sunk	July 30 1943	Schwantke, H-J †
U-44	IXA	Deschimag	November 4 1939	Sunk	March 20 1940	Mathes, L †
U-45	VIIB	Germania	June 25 1938	Sunk	October 14 1939	Gelhaar, A †
U-47	VIIB	Bremer Vulcan	December 17 1938	Operational loss	March 7 1941	Prien, G †
U-49	VIIB	Germania	August 12 1939	Sunk	April 15 1940	von Goszier, C
U-50	VIIB	Germania	December 12 1939	Operational loss	April 6 1940	Bauer, M-H †
U-51	VIIB	Germania	August 6 1938	Sunk	August 20 1940	Knorr, D †
U-53	VIIB	Germania	June 24 1939	Sunk	February 23 1940	Grosse, H †
U-54	VIIB	Germania	September 23 1939	Operational loss	February 13 1940	Kutschmann, G †
U-55	VIIB	Germania	November 21 1939	Scuttled	January 30 1940	Heidel, W †
U-63	IIC	Deutsche	January 18 1940	Sunk	February 25 1940	Lorentz, G
U-64	IXB	Deschimag	December 16 1939	Sunk	April 13 1940	Schulz, W
U-65	IXB	Deschimag	February 15 1940	Sunk	April 28 1941	Hoppe, J †
U-66	IXC	Deschimag	January 2 1941	Sunk	May 6 1944	Seehausen, G †
U-67	IXC	Deschimag	January 22 1941	Sunk	July 16 1943	Müller-Stockheim, G †
U-68	IXC	Deschimag	February 11 1941	Sunk	April 10 1944	Lauzemis, A †
U-69	VIIC	Germania	November 2 1940	Sunk	February 17 1943	Gräf, U T

1939–1945

Place	Means	Dead	Saved
Off Heligoland	Possible mine	25	0
Off Pilau, Baltic	Collided with trawler *Fröse*, sank. Salvaged. Stricken	17	18
Baltic, off Pillau	Diving accident	20	16
Off Pilau	Diving accident	26	0
Straits of Dover	Mine	27	0
NW of Newcastle	RN ship: *Weston* (S)	0	26
North Sea	German torpedo boat *Iltis*	25	0
Straits of Dover	Grounded during attack	28	0
Lübeck Bay	Collisioin with *T-136*; raised, returned to service	8	12
Black Sea	Konstanza under attack; crew interned in Turkey	0	0
Black Sea	Konstanza under attack; crew interned in Turkey	0	0
Black Sea	Possible mine	27	0
Black Sea	Konstanza under attack; crew interned in Turkey	0	0
Off Konstanza	Beyond repair after air attack	0	0
Off Terschelling	Mine	49	0
SW of Bishop's Rock	RAAF aircraft	7	39
NW of Hebrides	RN ships: *Fortune* (D), *Forester* (D)	0	38
Neustadt, Baltic	Sank alongside	1	0
Jade Bright	RAF aircraft (later raised)	58	0
NW of Ireland	British destroyers *Harvester* (D), *Highlander* (D)	9	33
Firth of Clyde	British minesweeper *Gleaner* (M/S)	23	17
Off Memel	Collided with tender *Lech*	4	39
North Sea	RN ships: *Kingston* (D), *Kashmir* (D), *Icarus* (D)	0	43
North Sea	RN submarine; *Salmon*	40	0
W of Hebrides	RN ships: *Faulkner* (D), *Foxhound* (D), *Firedrake* (D)	0	44
Straits of Dover	Mine	45	3
S of Ireland	RN ships: *Antelope* (D)	49	0
SW of Ireland	RN ships: *Imogen* (D), *Ilex* (D)	26	20
SW of Azores	USN aircraft: VC-29	56	0
N of Shetlands	RN ship: *Fortune* (D)	47	0
SW of Ireland	RN ships: *Icarus* (D), *Inglefield* (D), *Intrepid* (D), *Ivanhoe* (D)	38	0
W of Ireland	Cause unknown during attack on convoy OB.293	45	0
Vaagsfjord, Norway	RN ships: *Fearless* (D), *Brazen* (D)	1	41
NNE of Shetlands	Possible mine	44	0
Biscay	RN submarine: *Cachalot*	43	0
W of Orkneys	RN ship: *Gurkha* (D)	42	0
North Sea	Possible mine	41	0
North Atlantic	Scuttled after damage by RN ships, RAF aircraft	1	41
S of Shetlands	RN ships: *Escort* (D), *Inglefield* (D), *Imogen* (D)	1	23
Norwegian Sea	RN aircraft (*Warspite*)	8	37
North Atlantic	RN ship: *Douglas* (D)	50	0
Central Atlantic	USN ship: *Buckley* (DE)	24	36
Sargasso Sea	USN aircraft: VC-13 (*Core*)	48	3
NW of Madeira	USN aircraft: VC-58 (*Guadacanal*)	56	1
North Atlantic	RN ship: *Viscount* (D)	46	0

U-Boat	Type	Builder	Commissioned	Fate	Date	Captain
U-70	VIIC	Germania	November 23 1940	Sunk	March 7 1943	Matz, J
U-73	VIIB	Bremer Vulcan	September 30 1940	Sunk	December 16 1943	Deckert, H
U-74	VIIB	Bremer Vulcan	Octo ber 31 1940	Sunk	May 2 1942	Friedrich, Km †
U-75	VIIB	Bremer Vulcan	December 19 1940	Sunk	December 28 1943	Ringelmann, H †
U-76	VIIB	Bremer Vulcan	December 3 1940	Sunk	April 5 1941	von Hippel, F
U-77	VIIC	Bremer Vulcan	January 18 1941	Sunk	March 28 1943	Hartmann, O †
U-79	VIIC	Bremer Vulcan	March 13 1941	Scuttled	December 23 1941	Kauffmann, W
U-80	VIIC	Bremer Vulcan	April 8 1941	Training loss	November 28 1944	Keerl, H †
U-82	VIIC	Bremer Vulcan	May 14 1941	Sunk	February 7 1942	Rollmann, S †
U-83	VIIB	Flender	February 8 1941	Sunk	March 4 1943	Wörishoffer, G †
U-84	VIIB	Flender	April 29 1941	Sunk	August 23 1943	Uphoff, H †
U-85	VIIB	Flender	June 7 1941	Sunk	April 14 1942	Greger, E †
U-86	VIIB	Flender	July 8 1941	Sunk	November 23 1943	Schug, W †
U-87	VIIB	Flender	August 19 1941	Sunk	March 4 1943	Berger, J †
U-88	VIIC	Flender	October 15 1941	Sunk	September 12 1942	Bohmann, H †
U-89	VIIC	Flender	November 19 1941	Sunk	May 14 1943	Lohmann, D †
U-90	VIIC	Flender	December 20 1941	Sunk	July 24 1942	Oldörp, H †
U-91	VIIC	Flender	January 28 1942	Sunk	February 25 1944	Hungershausen, H
U-93	VIIC	Germania	July 30 1940	Sunk	January 15 1942	Elfe, H †
U-94	VIIC	Germania	August 10 1940	Sunk	August 28 1942	Ites, O
U-95	VIIC	Germania	August 31 1940	Sunk	November 28 1941	Schreiber, G
U-97	VIIC	Germania	September 28 1940	Sunk	June 16 1943	Trox, H-G †
U-98	VIIC	Germania	October 12 1940	Sunk	November 15 1942	Eichmann, K †
U-99	VIIB	Germania	April 18 1940	Sunk	March 17 1941	Kretschmer, O
U-100	VIIB	Germania	March 16 1940	Sunk	March 17 1941	Schepke, J †
U-102	VIIB	Germania	April 27 1940	Sunk	July 1 1940	von Klot-Heydenfeldt, H †
U-104	IXB †	Deschimag	August 19 1940	Operational loss	November 27 1940	Jürst, H †
U-105	IXB	Deschimag	September 10 1940	Sunk	June 2 1943	Nissen, J †
U-106	IXB	Deschimag	September 24 1940	Sunk	August 2 1943	Damerow, W
U-107	IXB	Deschimag	October 8 1940	Sunk	August 18 1944	Fritz, KH †
U-109	IXB	Deschimag	December 5 1940	Sunk	May 4 1943	Schramm, J †
U-110	IXB	Deschimag	November 21 1940	Captured	May 9 1941	Lemp, F-J †
U-111	IXB	Deschimag	December 19 1940	Sunk	October 4 1941	Kleinschmidt, W †
U-116	XB	Germania	July 26 1941	Operational loss	October 19 1942	Grimme, W †
U-117	XB	Germania	October 25 1941	Sunk	August 7 1943	Neumann, H-W †
U-118	XB	Germania	December 6 1941	Sunk	June 12 1943	Czygan, W †
U-119	IXB	Germania	April 2 1942	Sunk	June 24 1943	von Kameke, H-J †
U-122	IXB	Deschimag	March 30 1940	Oprational loss	June 22 1940	Looff, H-G †
U-124	IXB	Deschimag	June 11 1940	Sunk	April 3 1943	Mohr, J †
U-125	IXB	Deschimag	March 3 1941	Sunk	May 6 1943	Folkers, U †
U-126	IXC	Deschimag	March 22 1941	Sunk	July 3 1943	Kietz, S †
U-127	IXC	Deschimag	April 24 1941	Sunk	December 15 1941	Hansmann, B †
U-128	IXC	Deschimag	May 12 1941	Sunk	May 17 1943	Steinert, H
U-130	IXC	Deschimag	June 11 1941	Sunk	March 13 1943	Keller S †
U-131	IXC	Deschimag	July 1 1941	Sunk	December 17 1941	Baumann, A
U-132	VIIC	Bremer Vulcan	May 29 1941	Operational loss	November 5 1942	Vogelsang, E †
U-133	VIIC	Bremer Vulkan	July 5 1941	Operational loss	March 14 1942	Mohr, E †

Place	Means	Dead	Saved
SE of Iceland	RN ships: *Camelia* (C), *Arbutus* (C)	20	26
NW of Oran	USN ships: *Woolsey* (D), *Trippe* (D), *Edison* (D)	17	35
E of Gibraltar	RN ships: *Wishart* (D), *Wrestler* (D)	46	0
Mediterranean	RN ship: *Kipling* (D)	14	30
S of Iceland	RN ships: *Scarborough* (S), *Wolverine* (D)	1	40
E of Cartagena	RAF aurcraft: Hudson (233 Sqn)	37	9
Off Bardia	RN ships: *Hasty* (D), *Hotspur* (D)	0	43
Danzig Bay	Diving accident	48	0
S of Cape Race	RN ships: *Tamarisk* (C), *Rochester* (S)	45	0
E of Cartagena	RAF aircraft: Hudson (500 Sqn)	50	0
North Atkantic	USN aircraft; VC-13 (*Core*)	46	0
off Cape Hatteras	USN ship: *Roper* (D)	45	0
E of Bermuda	USN aircraft: VC-19 (*Bogue*)	50	0
North Atlantic	RCN ships: *Ste Croix* (C); *Shediac* (C)	49	0
NW of Bear Island	RN ship: *Faulkner* (D)	46	0
N of Azores	RN ships: *Broadway* (D); *Lagan* (F)	48	0
E of Cape Race	RCN ship: *St Croix* (D)	44	0
North Atlantic	RN ships: *Affleck* (DE), *Gore* (DE), *Gould* (DE)	37	16
W of Cape St Vincent	RN ship: *Hesperus* (D)	6	40
Off Haiti	RCN ship: *Oakville* (C)/USN aircraft: VP-92	19	26
E of Gibraltar	RNethN S/M: *O-21*	35	12
Mediterranean	RAAF aircraft: 459 Sqn	27	21
SW of Cape St Vincent	RN ship: *Wrestler* (D)	46	0
SE of Iceland	RN ships: *Walker* (D), *Vanoc* (D)	3	38
SE of Iceland	RN ship: *Vanoc* (D)	38	6
Biscay	RN ship: *Vansittart* (D)	43	0
North Atlantic	Cause/position unknown	49	0
Off Dakar	Fench AF: 141 Sqn	53	0
Off El Ferrol	RAF aircraft: 228 Sqn/RAAF aircraft: 461 Sqn	25	24
Bay of Biscay	RAF aircraft: 201 Sqn	59	0
Biscay	RAF aircraft: 86 Sqn	52	0
E of Cape Farewell	Captured by RN ship *Bulldog* (D); sank in tow	15	32
SW of Teneriffe	RN ship: *Lady Shirley* (T)	8	44
North Atlantic	Cause unknown	55	0
North Atlantic	USN aircraft: VC-41 (*Card*)	62	0
W of Canary Islands	USN aircraft: VC-9 (*Bogue*)	44	15
NW of Cape Ortegal	RAF aircraft: 172 Sqn	55	0
W of Orkneys	RN ships: *Starling* (S), *Woodpecker* (S)	57	0
W of Oporto	RN ships: *Stonecrop* (C), *Black Swan* (S)	53	0
Off Newfoundland	RN ships: *Oribi* (D); *Vidette* (D)	54	0
NW of Cape Ortegal	RAF aircraft: 172 Sqn	55	0
W of Gibraltar	RAN ship: *Nestor* (D)	51	0
S of Pernambuco	USN aircraft: VP-74/USN ships: *Moffet* (D), *Jouett* (D)	7	47
W of Azores	USN ship: *Champlin* (D)	53	0
NE of Madeira	RN ships/aircraft	47	1
SE of Cape Farewell	Possibly sunk in explosion of target tanker	45	0
Off Salamis	Possible German mine	45	0

U-Boat	Type	Builder	Commissioned	Fate	Date	Captain
U-134	VIIC	Bremer Vulkan	July 26 1941	Sunk	August 24 1943	Brosin, H-G †
U-135	VIIC	Bremer Vulkan	August 16 1941	Sunk	July 15 1943	Luther, O
U-136	VIIC	Bremer Vulkan	August 30 1941	Sunk	July 11 1942	Zimmermann, H †
U-138	IID	Deutsche	June 27 1940	Sunk	June 18 1941	Gramitzkty, K
U-144	IID	Deutsche	October 2 1940	Sunk	July 28 1941	von Mettelstaedt, G †
U-147	IID	Deutsche	December 11 1940	Sunk	June 2 1941	Wetjen, E†
U-153	IXC	Deschimag	July 19 1941	Sunk	July 3 1944	Gemeiner, G †
U-154	IXC	Deschimag	August 2 1941	Sunk	July 13 1942	Reichmann, W †
U-156	IXC	Deschimag	September 41941	Sunk	March 8 1943	Hartenstein, W †
U-157	IXC	Deschimag	September 15 1941	Sunk	June 13 1942	Henne, W †
U-158	IXC	Deschimag	September 25 1941	Sunk	June 30 1942	Rostin, E †
U-159	IXC	Deschimag	October 4 1941	Sunk	July 15 1942	Beckmann, H †
U-160	IXC	Deschimag	October 16 1941	Sunk	July 14 1943	von Pommer-Esche, G †
U-161	IXC	Deschimag	Julu 8 1941	Sunk	September 17 1943	Achilles, A †
U-162	IXC	Seebeck	September 9 1941	Sunk	September 30 1942	Wattenburg, J
U-163	IXC	Seebeck	October 21 1941	Sunk	March 13 1943	Engelmann, K-E †
U-164	IXC/40	Seebeck	November 28 1941	Sunk	January 6 1943	Fechner, O †
U-165	IXC	Seebeck	February 3 1942	Operational loss	September 27 1942	Hoffmann, E †
U-166	IXC	Seebeck	February 23 1942	Sunk	August 1 1943	Kuhlmann, H-G †
U-167	IXC/40	Seebeck	July 4 1942	Scuttled	April 6 1943	Sturm, K
U-168	IXC/40	Seebeck	September 10 1942	Sunk	October 6 1944	Pich, H
U-169	IXC/40	Seebeck	November 16 1942	Sunk	March 27 1943	Bauer, H †
U-171	IXC	Deschimag	October 25 1941	Mined	October 9 1942	Pfeffer, G
U-172	IXC	Deschimag	November 5 1941	Sunk	December 13 1943	Hoffmann, H
U-173	IXC	Deschimag	November 15 1941	Sunk	November 16 1942	Schweichel, H †
U-174	IXC	Deschimag	November 26 1941	Sunk	April 27 1943	Grandefeld, W †
U-175	IXC	Deschimag	December 5 1941	Sunk	April 17 1943	Bruns, H †
U-176	IXC	Deschimag	December 5 1941	Sunk	May 15 1943	Dierksen, R †
U-177	IXD2	Deschimag	March 14 1942	Sunk	February 6 1944	Buchholz, H †
U-179	IXD2	Deschimag	March 7 1942	Sunk	October 8 1942	Sobe, E †
U-180	IXD1	Deschimag	May 16 1942	Operational loss	August 22 1944	Riesen, R †
U-182	IXD2	Deschimag	June 30 1942	Sunk	May 16 1943	Clausen, N †
U-183	IXC/40	Deschimag	April 1 1942	Sunk	April 23 1942	Schneewind †
U-184	IXC/40	Deschimag	May 29 1942	Operational loss	November 20 1942	Dangschat, G †
U-185	IXC/40	Deschimag	June 13 1942	Sunk	August 24 1943	Maus, A
U-186	IXC/40	Deschimag	July 10 1942	Sunk	12 May 1943	Hesemann, S †
U-187	IXC/40	Deschimag	July 23 1942	Sunk	February 4 1943	Munnich, R †
U-189	IXC/40	Deschimag	August 15 1942	Sunk	April 23 1943	Kurrer †
U-191	IXC/40	Deschimag	October 20 1942	Sunk	April 23 1943	Fiehn, H †
U-192	IXC/40	Deschimag	November 16 1942	Sunk	May 5 1943	Happe, W †
U-193	IXC/40	Deschimag	December 10 1942	Sunk	April 28 1944	Abel, Dr U †
U-194	IXC/40	Deschimag	January 8 1943	Sunk	June 24 1943	Hesse, H †
U-196	IXD2	Deschimag	September 11 1942	Operational loss	November 30 1944	Striegler, W †
U-197	IXD2	Deschimag	October 10 1942	Sunk	August 20 1943	Bartels, R †
U-198	IXD2	Deschimag	November 3 1942	Sunk	August 12 1944	H von Waldegg, B †
U-199	IXD2	Deschimag	November 28 1942	Sunk	July 31 1944	Krauss, H-W †
U-200	IXD2	Deschimag	December 22 1942	Sunk	June 24 1943	Schonder, H †

Place	Means	Dead	Saved
SW of Cape Finisterre	RAF aircraft: 179 Sqn	48	0
North Atlantic	RN ships/USN aircraft	5	41
W of Madeira	RN ships: *Pelican* (S), *Spey* (F), *Lépard* (D) (Fr)	45	0
W of Cadiz	RN ships (5): 6th Destroyer Group	0	27
Gulf of Finland	Soviet submarine: Shch-307	28	0
NW of Ireland	RN ships: *Wanderer* (D), *Periwinkle* (C)	26	0
Caribbean	USN ship: *Lansdowne* (D)	52	0
W of Madeira	USN ships: *Inch* (DE), *Frost* (DE)	58	0
Off Barbados	USN aircraft: VP-53	53	0
Gulf of Mexico	USCG ship: *Thetis* (Cutter)	52	0
Caribbean	USN aircraft: VP-74	53	0
Caribbean	USN aircraft: VP-32	54	0
Central Atlantic	USN aircraft: VC-13 (Santee)	54	0
Off Bahia, Brazil	USN aircraft: VP-74	52	0
Caribbean	RN ships: *Vimy* (D), *Pathfinder* (D), *Quentin* (D)	2	49
Biscay	RCN ship: *Prescott* (PC)	57	0
Off Brazil coast	USN aircraft: VP-83	54	2
Off Lorient, France	Cause unknown	50	0
Gulf of Mexico	USCG aircraft: 212 Sqn	52	0
Central Atlantic	Scuttled in shallows after attack by aircraft	0	54
Java Sea	RNethN S/M: *Zwaardfisch*	23	28
S of Iceland	RAF aircraft: 206 Sqn	54	0
Off Lorient	Mine	22	30
NW of Cape Verde	USN ships: *Clemson* (D), *Ingram* (D), *Badger* (D)	14	46
Off Casablanca	USN ships: *Woolsey* (D), *Swanson* (D), *Quick* (D)	57	0
S of Newfoundland	USN aircraft: VB-125	53	0
SW of Ireland	USCG ship: *Spencer* (Cutter)	13	41
Off Havana, Cuba	USN aircraft: VS-62/Cuban ship: *SC-13* (PC)	53	0
W of Ascension Island	USN aircraft: VB-107	51	10
Off Cape Town	RN ship: *Active* (D)	61	0
Bay of Biscay	Possibly mined	56	0
NW of Madeira	USN ship: *Mackenzie* (D)	61	0
Java Sea	USN submarine: *Besugo*	55	1
Mid-Atlantic	Cause unknown	50	0
Central Atlantic	USN aircraft: VC-13 (*Core* — *U-604* survivors aboard)	43	36
N of Azores	RN ship: *Hesperus* (D)	53	0
North Atlantic	RN ships: *Vimy* (D), *Beverley* (D)	9	45
E of Cape Farewell	RAF aircraft: 120 Sqn	54	0
SE of Cape Farewell	RN ships: *Hesperus* (D), *Clematis* (C)	55	0
North Atlantic	RN ships: *Loosestrife* (C)	55	0
W of Nantes	RAF aircraft: 612 Sqn	60	0
S of Iceland	USN aircraft: VP-84	54	0
Sunda Strait, Indonesia	Cause unknown	65	0
SW of Madagascar	RAF aircraft: 259 Sqn, 265 Sqn	67	0
Indian Ocean	RN ship: *Findhorn* (F)/RIN ship: *Godavari* (S)	66	0
Off Rio de Janeiro	USN aircraft: VP-74/Brazilian aircraft	50	12
SW of Iceland	RAF aircraft: 120 Sqn	62	0

U-Boat	Type	Builder	Commissioned	Fate	Date	Captain
U-201	VIIC	Germania	January 25 1941	Sunk	February 17 1943	Rosenberg, G †
U-202	VIIC	Germania	March 22 1941	Sunk	June 2 1943	Poser, G
U-203	VIIC	Germania	February 18 1941	Sunk	April 25 1943	Kottmann, H
U-204	VIIC	Germania	March 8 1941	Sunk	October 19 1941	Kell, W †
U-205	VIIC	Germania	May 3 1941	Sunk	February 17 1943	Bürgel, F
U-206	VIIC	Germania	May 17 1941	Operational loss	November 30 1941	Opitz, H †
U-207	VIIC	Germania	June 7 1941	Sunk	September 11 1943	Meyer, F †
U-208	VIIC	Germania	July 5 1941	Sunk	December 7 1941	Schlieper, A †
U-209	VIIC	Germania	October 11 1941	Operational loss	May 4 1943	Brodda, H †
U-210	VIIC	Germania	February 21 1942	Sunk	August 6 1942	Lemcke, R †
U-211	VIIC	Germania	March 7 1942	Sunk	November 18 1943	Hause, K †
U-212	VIIC	Germania	April 25, 1942	Sunk	July 21 1944	Bogler, H †
U-213	VIID	Germania	August 30 1941	Sunk	July 31 1942	von Varendorff, H †
U-214	VIID	Germania	November 1 1941	Sunk	July 26 1944	Conrad, G †
U-215	VIID	Germania	November 22 1941	Sunk	July 3 1942	Hoeckner, F †
U-216	VIID	Germania	December 15 1941	Sunk	October 20 1942	Schultz, K-O †
U-217	VIID	Germania	January 31 1942	Sunk	June 5 1943	Reichenbach-Klinke, K †
U-220	XB	Germania	March 27 1943	Sunk	October 28 1943	Barber, B †
U-221	VIIC	Germania	May 9 1942	Sunk	September 27 1943	Trojer, H †
U-222	VIIC	Germania	May 23 1942	Training loss	September 2 1942	von Jessen, R
U-223	VIIC	Germania	June 6 1942	Sunk	March 30 1944	Gerlach, P †
U-224	VIIC	Germania	June 20 1942	Sunk	January 13 1943	Kosbadt H-C †
U-225	VIIC	Germania	July 11 1942	Sunk	February 15 1942	Leimkühler, W †
U-226	VIIC	Germania	August 1 1942	Sunk	November 6 1943	Gänge, A †
U-227	VIIC	Germania	August 22 1942	Sunk	April 30 1943	Kuntze, J †
U-229	VIIC	Germania	October 3 1942	Sunk	September 22 1943	Schetelig, R†
U-230	VIIC	Germania	October 24 1942	Scuttled	August 21 1944	Eberbach, H-E †
U-231	VIIC	Germania	November 14 1942	Sunk	January 31 1944	Wenzel, W
U-232	VIIC	Germania	November 28 1942	Sunk	July 8 1943	Ziehm, E †
U-233	XB	Germania	September 22 1943	Sunk	July 5 1944	Steen, H †
U-235	VIIC	Germania	December 19 1942	Sunk	April 10 1945	Huisgen †
U-236	VIIC	Germania	January 9 1943	Scuttled	May 5 1945	Mumm, H
U-238	VIIC	Germania	February 20 1943	Sunk	February 9 1944	Hepp, H †
U-240	VIIC	Germania	April 3 1943	Sunk	May 16 1944	Link, G †
U-241	VIIC	Germania	July 24 1943	Sunk	May 18 1944	Werr, A †
U-242	VIIC	Germania	August 14 1943	Operational loss	late April 1945	Riedel, H †
U-243	VIIC	Germania	October 2 1943	Sunk	July 8 1944	Märtens, H †
U-246	VIIC	Germania	January 11 1943	Operational loss	early April 1945	Raabe, E †
U-247	VIIC	Germania	October 23 1943	Sunk	September 1 1944	Matschulat, G†
U-248	VIIC	Germania	November 20 1943	Sunk	January 16 1945	Loos, J-F †
U-250	VIIC	Germania	December 12 1943	Sunk	July 30 1944	Schmidt, W-K
U-251	VIIC	Bremer Vulkan	September 20 1941	Sunk	April 19 1945	Sauerbier, J †
U-252	VIIC	Bremer Vulkan	October 4 1941	Sunk	April 4 1942	Lerchen, K †
U-253	VIIC	Bremer Vulkan	October 21 1941	Operational loss	late September 1942	Friedrichs, A †
U-254	VIIC	Bremer Vulkan	November 8 1941	Collision	December 8 1942	Loewe, O †
U-257	VIIC	Bremer Vulkan	January 14 1942	Sunk	February 24 1944	Rahe, H †
U-258	VIIC	Bremer Vulkan	February 4 1942	Sunk	May 20 1943	Koch, L †

PLACE	MEANS	DEAD	SAVED
Off Newfoundland	RN ship: *Ffame* (D)	50	0
Off Cape Farewell	RN ship: *Starling* (S)	18	29
SE of Cape Farewell	RN ship: *Pathfinder* (D)/RN aircraft: 811 NAS	11	39
W of Gibraltar	RN ships: *Rochester* (S), *Mallow* (C)	46	0
Mediterranean	RN ship: *Paladin* (D)	9	34
Biscay	Cause unknown	46	0
Denmark Straits	RN ships; *Leamington* (D), *Veteran* (D)	41	0
W of Gibraltar	RN ships: *Harvester* (D), *Hesperus* (D)	45	0
North Atlantic	Possibly due to damage by RCAF aircraft: 5 Sqn	46	0
S of Cape Farewell	RCN ship: *Assiniboine* (D)	6	37
NE of Azores	RAF aircraft: 179 Sqn	54	0
English Channel	RN ship: *Curzon* (DE), *Ekins* (DE)	50	0
W of Azores	RN ships: *Erne* (S), *Sandwich* (S), *Rochester* (S)	50	0
English Channel	RN ship: *Cooke* (DE)	46	0
Off Boston, USA	French ship; *Le Tigre* (T)	48	0
North Atlantic	RAF aircraft: 224 Sqn	45	0
Central Atlantic	USN aircraft: VC-9 (*Bogue*)	50	0
Central Atlantic	USN aircraft: VC-1 (*Block Island*)	51	0
S of Ireland	RAF aircraft: 58 Sqn	50	0
Off Pillau, Baltic	Collision with *U-262*	42	4
Mediterranean	RN ships: *Laforey* (D), *Tumult* (D); three DEs	24	27
Mediterranean	RCN ship: *Ville de Quebec* (C)	44	1
North Atlantic	RAF aircraft: 120 Sqn	46	0
E of Newfoundland	RN ships: *Woodcock* (S), *Starling* (S), *Kite* (S)	51	0
NE of Faroe Islands	RAAF aircraft: 455 Sqn	49	0
SE of Cape farewell	RN ship: *Keppel* (D)	50	0
Toulon roads	Ran aground, blown up to avoid capture	0	49
N of Azores	RAF aircraft: 172 Sqn	7	43
W of Oporto	USAAF aircraft: 2/480 Group	46	0
Off Halifax, Nova Scotia	USN ships: *Baker* (DE), *Thomas* (DE)	31	30
Kattegat	Sunk in error by German *T-17*	47	0
Kattegat	Damaged by RAF aircraft; scuttled next day	0	47
SW of Cape Clear	RN ships; *Kite* (S), *Magpie* (S), *Starling* (S)	50	0
NE of Shetland Islands	RAF aircraft: 300 Sqn	50	0
NE of Shetland Islands	RAF aircraft: 210 Sqn	51	0
Irish Sea	Cause unknown	44	0
Bay of Biscay	RAAF aircraft: 10 Sqn/USN aircraft: VP-105	12	38
English Channel	Cause unknown	48	0
English Channel	RCN ships: *St John* (F), *Swansea* (F)	52	0
North Atlantic	USN ships: *Varian, Otter, Hubbard, Hayter* (all DEs)	48	0
Gulf of Finland	Soviet ship: *MO-103* (SC)	46	6
Kattegat	RAF aircraft: 143, 235, 248, 333 Sqns	39	5
S of Ireland	RN ships: *Stork* (S), *Vetch* (C)	44	0
NE of Iceland	Possible mine	46	0
Greenland	Sank after collision with *U-221*; attack by RAF aircraft	41	4
North Atlantic	RCN ship: *Waskesiu* (F)	31	18
North Atantic	RAF aircraft: 120 Sqn	49	0

U-Boat	Type	Builder	Commissioned	Fate	Date	Captain
U-259	VIIC	Bremer Vulkan	February 18 1942	Sunk	November 15 1942	Köpke, K †
U-260	VIIC	Bremer Vulkan	March 14 1942	Sunk	March 14 1945	Becker
U-261	VIIC	Bremer Vulkan	March 28 1942	Sunk	September 15 1942	Lange, H †
U-263	VIIC	Bremer Vulkan	May 6 1942	Operational loss	January 20 1944	Nölke, K †
U-264	VIIC	Bremer Vulkan	May 22 1942	Sunk	February 19 1944	Looks, H
U-265	VIIC	Bremer Vulkan	June 6 1942	Sunk	February 3 1943	Auffhammer, L †
U-266	VIIC	Bremer Vulkan	June 24 1942	Sunk	May 15 1943	von Jessen, R †
U-268	VIIC	Bremer Vulkan	July 29 1942	Sunk	February 19 1943	Heydemann, E †
U-269	VIIC	Bremer Vulkan	August 19 1942	Sunk	June 25 1944	Uhl, G †
U-270	VIIC	Bremer Vulkan	September 5 1942	Sunk	August 12 1944	Schreiber, H †
U-271	VIIC	Bremer Vulkan	January 28 1944	Sunk	January 28 1944	Barleben, K †
U-272	VIIC	Bremer Vulkan	October 7 1942	Training loss	November 12 1942	Hepp, H
U-273	VIIC	Bremer Vulkan	Octdober 21 1942	Sunk	May 19 1943	Rossmann, H †
U-274	VIIC	Bremer Vulkan	November 7 1942	Sunk	October 23 1943	Jordan, G †
U-275	VIIC	Bremer Vulkan	November 25 1942	Sunk	March 10 1945	Wehrkamp, H †
U-277	VIIC	Bremer Vulkan	December 21 1942	Sunk	May 1 1944	Lubsen, R †
U-279	VIIC	Bremer Vulkan	February 3 1943	Sunk	October 4 1943	Finke, O †
U-275	VIIC	Bremer Vulkan	February 13 1943	Sunk	November 16 1943	Hungershausen, W †
U-282	VIIC	Bremer Vulkan	March 13 1943	Sunk	October 29 1943	Müller, R †
U-283	VIIC	Bremer Vulkan	March 31 1943	Sunk	February 11 1944	Ney, G †
U-284	VIIC	Bremer Vulkan	April 14 1943	Scuttled	December 21 1943	Scholz, G
U-285	VIIC	Bremer Vulkan	May 15 1943	Sunk	April 15 1945	Bornhaupt, K †
U-286	VIIC	Bremer Vulkan	June 5 1943	Sunk	April 29 1945	Dietrich, W
U-288	VIIC	Bremer Vulkan	June 26 1943	Sunk	April 3 1944	Meyer, W†
U-289	VIIC	Bremer Vulkan	July 10 1943	Sunk	May 31 1944	Hellwig, A †
U-292	VIIC/41	Bremer Vulkan	August 25 1943	Sunk	May 27 1944	Schmidt, W †
U-296	VIIC/41	Bremer Vulkan	November 3 1943	Sunk	March 22 1945	Rasch, K-H †
U-297	VIIC/41	Bremer Vulkan	November 17 1943	Sunk	December 6 1944	Aldegarmann, W †
U-275	VIIC/41	Bremer Vulkan	December 29 1943	Sunk	February 22 1945	Hein, F †
U-301	VIIC	Flender	May 9 1942	Sunk	January 21 1943	Korner, W-R †
U-302	VIIC	Flender	June 16 1942	Sunk	April 6 1944	Sickel, H †
U-303	VIIC	Flender	July 7 1942	Sunk	May 21 1943	Heine, K-F †
U-304	VIIC	Flender	August 5 1942	Sunk	May 28 1943	Koch, H †
U-305	VIIC	Flender	September 17 1942	Sunk	January 17 1944	Bahr,-R †
U-306	VIIC	Flender	October 21 1942	Sunk	October 31 1943	von Trotha, C †
U-307	VIIC	Flender	November 18 1942	Sunk	April 29 1945	Krüger, E †
U-308	VIIC	Flender	December 23 1942	Sunk	June 4 1943	Mühlenpfort, K †
U-309	VIIC	Flender	January 27 1943	Sunk	February 16 1945	Loeder, H †
U-311	VIIC	Flender	March 23 1943	Sunk	April 22 1944	Zander, J †
U-314	VIIC	Flender	June 10 1943	Sunk	January 30 1944	Basse, G-W †
U-317	VIIC/41	Flender	October 23 1943	Sunk	June 26 1944	Rahlf, P †
U-319	VIIC/41	Flender	December 4 1943	Sunk	July 15 1944	Clemens, J †
U-320	VIIC/41	Flender	December 30 1943	Scuttled	May 8 1945	Emmrich, H †
U-321	VIIC/41	Flender	January 20 1944	Sunk	April 2 1945	Berends, F †
U-322	VIIC/41	Flender	February 5 1944	Sunk	November 25 1944	Wysk, G †
U-325	VIIC/41	Flender	May 6 1944	Sunk	April 30 1945-	Dohrm, E †
U-326	VIIC/41	Flender	June 6 1944	Sunk	April 25 1945	Matthes, P †

Place	Means	Dead	Saved
N of Algiers	RAF aircraft: 500 Sqn	48	0
Off Irish coast	Severely damaged by mine; scuttled; crew interned	0	49
S of Faroe islands	RAF aircraft: 58 Sqn	43	0
Bay of Biscay	Cause unknown	51	0
North Atlantic	RN ships: 2nd Escort Group	0	50
S of Iceland	RAF aircraft: 220 Sqn	48	0
North Atlantic	RAF aircraft: 58 Sqn	47	0
Bay of Biscay	RAF aircraft: 172 Sqn	45	0
English Channel	RN ship: *Bickerton* (DE)	16	33
W of La Rochelle	RAAF aircraft: 461 Sqn. Carrying extra passengers	10	71
West of Limerick	USN aircraft: VB-103	51	0
Baltic	Collision with unidentified ship	28	19
S of Iceland	RAF aircraft: 269 Sqn	46	0
S of Iceland	RAF aircraft: 224 Sqn/RN ship: *Duncan* (D)	48	0
English Channel	British mine	49	0
S of Bear Island	RN aircraft: 842 NAS (*Fencer*)	50	0
S of Iceland	USN aircraft: VP-128	50	0
North Atlantic	RAF aircraft: 86 Sqn	49	0
North Atlantic	RN ships: *Vidette* (D), *Duncan* (DE), *Sunflower* (C)	48	0
S of Faroe Islands	RAF aircraft: 407 Sqn	50	0
North Atlantic	Damaged in heavy seas; men transferred to *U-629*	0	49
SW of Ireland	RN ships: *Grindall* (DE), *Keats* (DE)	46	0
Off Kola Inlet	RN ships: *Loch Shin* (F), *Anguilla* (F)	51	0
Barents Sea	RN aircraft: 819/826 NAS (*Activity/Tracker*)	49	0
Barents Sea	RN ship: *Milne* (D)	51	0
N of Shetlands	RAF aircraft: 59 Sqn	51	0
Irish Sea	RAF aircraft: 120 Sqn	43	0
Pentland Firth	RN ships: *Loch Inch* (F), *Goodall* (DE)	50	0
SE of Cape St Vincent	RN ships: *Pincher* (MS)/USN ship: *Evadne* (MS)	11	42
W of Corsica	RN submarine: *Sahib*	45	1
N of Azores	RN ship: *Swale* (DE)	51	0
S of Toulon	RN submarine: *Sickle*	19	20
SE of Cape Farewell	RAF aircraft: 120 Sqn	46	0
S of Ireland	RN ships: *Wanderer* (D), *Geranium* (C)	51	0
NE of Azores	RN ships: *Whitehall* (D), *Geranium* (C)	51	0
Off Kola Inlet	RN ship: *Loch Insh* (F)	37	14
NE of Faroe Islands	RN submarine: *Translucent*	44	0
Moray Firth	RCN ship: *St John* (F)	47	0
S of Ireland	RCN ships: *Matane* (F), *Swansea* (F)	51	0
SE of Bear Island	RN ships: *Whitehall* (D), *Meteor* (D)	49	0
NE of Shetland Islands	RAF aircraft: 86 Sqn	50	0
Norwegian Sea	RAF aircraft: 206 Sqn	51	0
Norwegian Sea	Damaged by RAF aircraft, then scuttled	0	49
SW of Ireland	RAF aircraft: 304 (Polish) Sqn	41	0
NE of Orkney Islands	RAF aircraft: 330 (Norwegian)Sqn/RN ship: *Ascension* (DE)	52	0
Irish Sea	RN ships: *Hesperus* (D), *Havelock* (D)	44	0
S of Ireland	USN aircraft; VP-103	43	0

U-Boat	Type	Builder	Commissioned	Fate	Date	Captain
U-327	VIIC/41	Flender	July 18 1944	Operational loss	mid-February 1945	Lemcke, H †
U-331	VIIC	Nordsee	March 31 1941	Sunk	November 17 1942	Fhr von Thiesenhausen, H-D
U-332	VIIC	Nordsee	June 7 1941	Sunk	April 29 1943	Hüttemann, E †
U-333	VIIC	Nordsee	August 25 1941	Sunk	July 31 1944	Fiedler, H †
U-334	VIIC	Nordsee	October 9 1941	Sunk	June 14 1943	Ehrich, H †
U-335	VIIC	Nordsee	December 17 1941	Sunk	August 3 1942	Pelkner, H-H †
U-336	VIIC	Nordsee	February 14 1942	Sunk	October 5 1943	Hunger, H †
U-337	VIIC	Nordsee	May 6 1942	Operational loss	January 15 1943	Ruwiedel, K †
U-338	VIIC	Nordsee	June 25 1942	Sunk	September 20 1943	Kinzel, M †
U-340	VIIC	Nordsee	October 16 1942	Sunk	November 2 1943	Klaus, H-J
U-341	VIIC	Nordsee	November 28 1942	Sunk	September 19 1943	Epp, D †
U-342	VIIC	Nordsee	12 January 1943	Sunk	April 17 1944	Hossenfielder, A †
U-343	VIIC	Nordsee	February 18 1943	Sunk	March 10 1944	Rahn, W †
U-344	VIIC	Nordsee	March 26 1943	Sunk	August 22 1944	Pietsch, U †
U-346	VIIC	Nordsee	June 7 1943	Training loss	September 20 1943	Leisten, A †
U-347	VIIC	Nordsee	July 7 1943	Sunk	July 17 1944	de Buhr, J †
U-352	VIIC	Flensburg	August 28 1941	Sunk	May 9 1942	Rathke, H
U-353	VIIC	Flensburg	March 31 1942	Sunk	October 16 1942	Römer, W
U-354	VIIC	Flensburg	April 22 1942	Sunk	August 24 1944	Sthamer, H-J †
U-355	VIIC	Flensburg	October 29 1941	Sunk	April 1 1944	La Baume, G †
U-356	VIIC	Flensburg	December 20 1941	Sunk	December 27 1942	Ruppelt, G †
U-357	VIIC	Flensburg	June 18 1942	Sunk	December 26 1942	Kellner, A †
U-358	VIIC	Flensburg	August 15 1942	Sunk	March 1 1944	Manke, R
U-359	VIIC	Flensburg	October 5 1942	Sunk	July 28 1943	Förster, H†
U-360	VIIC	Flensburg	November 12 1942	Sunk	April 2 1944	Becker, K †
U-361	VIIC	Flensburg	December 18 1942	Sunk	July 17 1944	Seidel, H †
U-362	VIIC	Flensburg	February 4 1943	Sunk	September 5 1944	Franz, L †
U-364	VIIC	Flensburg	May 3 1943	Sunk	January 30 1944	Sass, P-H †
U-365	VIIC	Flensburg	June 8 1943	Sunk	December 13 1944	Todenhagen, D †
U-366	VIIC	Flensburg	July 16 1943	Sunk	March 5 1944	Langenberg, B †
U-367	VIIC	Flensburg	August 27 1943	Operational loss	March 15 1945	Stegemann, H†
U-371	VIIC	Howaldt	March 15 1941	Scuttled	May 4 1944	Fenski, H-O
U-372	VIIC	Howaldt	April 19 1941	Sunk	August 4 1942	Neumann, H-J
U-373	VIIC	Howaldt	May 22 1941	Sunk	June 8 1944	von Lehsten, D †
U-374	VIIC	Howaldt	June 21 1941	Sunk	January 12 1942	von Fischel, U †
U-375	VIIC	Howaldt	July 19 1941	Sunk	July 30 1943	Könenkamp, J †
U-376	VIIC	Howaldt	August 21 1941	Sunk	April 10 1943	Marks, F-K †
U-377	VIIC	Howaldt	October 2 1941	Operational loss	mid-January 1944	Kluth, G †
U-378	VIIC	Howaldt	October 31 1941	Sunk	October 20 1943	Mäder, E †
U-379	VIIC	Howaldt	November 29 1941	Sunk	August 8 1942	Kettner, P-H †
U-381	VIIC	Howaldt	February 25 1942	Sunk	May 19 1943	Graf von Pückler und Limpburg †
U-383	VIIC	Howaldt	June 6 1942	Sunk	August 1 1943	Kremser, H †
U-384	VIIC	Howaldt	July 18, 1942	Sunk	March 20 1943	von Rosenburg-Guszczynski, HA †
U-385	VIIC	Howaldt	August 29 1942	Sunk	August 11 1944	Valentiner, H-G
U-386	VIIC	Howaldt	October 10 1942	Sunk	February 19 1944	Albrecht, F
U-387	VIIC	Howaldt	November 24 1942	Sunk	December 9 1944	Büchler, R †
U-388	VIIC	Howaldt	December 31 1942	Sunk	June 20 1943	Sues, P

PLACE	MEANS	DEAD	SAVED
English Channel	Cause unknown	46	0
NW of Algiers	RN aircraft: *Formidable*/RAF aircraft: 500 Sqn	33	17
Off Cape Finisterre	RAF aircraft: 224 Sqn	45	0
English Channel	RN ships: *Starling* (S), *Loch Killin* (F)	46	0
SW of Iceland	RN ships: *Pelican* (F), *Jed* (F)	47	0
NW of Shetland Islands	RN submarine: *Saracen*	41	1
SW of Iceland	RAF aircraft: 269 Sqn	50	0
SW of Iceland	Cause unknown	47	0
SW of Iceland	RCN ship: *Drumheller* (C)	52	0
Off Gibraltar	Scuttled after damage by RN ship: *Fleetwood* (S)	1	48
SWE of Iceland	RCAF aircraft: 10 Sqn	50	0
S of Iceland	RCAF aircraft: 162 Sqn	51	0
S of Sardinia	RN ship: *Mull* (T)	51	0
Arctic Ocean	RN aircraft: 825NAS (*Vindex*)	50	0
Off Hela, Baltic	Diving accident; details unknown	36	0
W of Narvik	RAF aircraft: 210 Sqn	49	0
Off Cape Hatteras	USCG ship: *Icarus* (cutter)	17	32
Central Atlantic	RN ship: *Fame* (D)	6	39
NW of Bear Island	RN ship: *Mermaid* (F)	51	0
S of Bear Island	RN aircraft: 826NAS (*Tracker*)/RN ship: *Beagle* (D)	52	0
North Atlantic	RCN ships	46	0
NW of Ireland	RN ships: *Hesperus* (D), *Vanessa* (D)	37	6
N of Azores	RN ships; *Gould, Affleck, Gore, Garlies* (all DE)	50	0
S of San Dimingo	USN aircraft: VP-32	47	0
NW of Hammerfest, Norway	RN ship: *Keppel* (D)	51	0
W of Narvik	RAF aircraft: 86 Sqn	52	0
Kara Sea	Soviet ship: *T-116* (MS)	51	0
W of Bordeaux	RAF aircraft: 172 Sqn	49	0
Barents Sea	RN aircraft: 813 NAS (*Compania*)	50	0
N of Hammerfest	RN aircraft: 816 NAS (*Chaser*)	51	0
Off Hela, Baltic	Cause unknown; possibly British mine	43	0
Off Constantine	After damage by US, British and French ships	4	49
East Mediterranean	RN ships; *Sikh* (D), *Croome* (DE), *Tetcott* (DE)	0	47
Bay of Biscay	RAF aircraft: 224 Sqn	4	47
E of Catania, Italy	RN submarine: *Unbeaten*	42	1
NW of Malta	USN ship: *PC-624* (SC)	45	0
Bay of Biscay	RAF aircraft: 172 Sqn	47	0
N of Azores	Cause unknown	52	0
N of Azores	USN aircraft: VC-13 (*Core*)	48	0
SE of Cape Farewell	RN ship: *Dianthus* (C)	40	5
SE of Cape Farewell	RN ships: *Snowflake* (C), *Duncan* (D)	47	0
NW of Cape Ortegal	RAF aircraft: 228 Sqn	54	0
North Atlantic	RAF aircraft: 206 Sqn	47	0
W of La Rochelle	RAAF aircraft: 461 Sqn/RN ships: 2nd Escot Group	1	41
N of Azores	RN ship: *Spey* (S)	33	18
Off Kola Inlet, Russia	RN ship: *Bamborough Castle* (C)	51	0
SE of Greenland	USN aircraft: VP-84	47	0

U-Boat	Type	Builder	Commissioned	Fate	Date	Captain
U-389	VIIC	Howaldt	February 6 1943	Sunk	October 4 1943	Heilmann, S †
U-390	VIIC	Howaldt	March 13 1943	Sunk	July 5 1944	Geissler, H †
U-391	VIIC	Howaldt	April 24 1943	Sunk	December 13, 1943	Dültgen, G †
U-392	VIIC	Howaldt	May 29 1943	Sunk	March 16 1944	Schümann, H †
U-394	VIIC	Howaldt	August 7 1943	Sunk	September 2 1944	Borger, W †
U-398	VIIC	Howaldt	December 18 1943	Operational loss	late April 1945	Cranz, W †
U-399	VIIC	Howaldt	January 22 1944	Sunk	March 26 1945	Buhse, H †
U-400	VIIC	Howaldt	March 18 1944	Sunk	December 17 1944	Creutz, H †
U-401	VIIC	Danzig	April 10 1941	Sunk	August 3 1941	Zimmermann, G †
U-402	VIIC	Danzig	May 21 1941	Sunk	October 13 1943	Freiherr von Forstner. S
U-403	VIIC	Danzig	June 25 1941	Sunk	August 17 1943	Heine, K-F †
U-404	VIIC	Danzig	August 6 1941	Sunk	July 28 1943	Schönberg, A †
U-403	VIIC	Danzig	September 17 1941	Sunk	November 1 1943	Hopman, R-H †
U-406	VIIC	Danzig	October 22 1941	Sunk	February 18 1944	Dieterichs, H †
U-407	VIIC	Danzig	December 18 1941	Sunk	September 19 1944	Kolbus, H
U-408	VIIC	Danzig	November 19 1941	Sunk	November 5 1942	von Hymmen, R †
U-409	VIIC	Danzig	January 21 1942	Sunk	July 12 1943	Massmann, H-F †
U-411	VIIC	Danzig	March 18 1942	Sunk	November 13 1942	Spindlegger, J †
U-412	VIIC	Danzig	April 29 1942	Sunk	October 22 1942	Jahrmärker, W †
U-413	VIIC	Danzig	June 3 1942	Sunk	August 20 1944	Sachse, D †
U-414	VIIC	Danzig	July 1 1942	Sunk	May 25 1943	Huth, W †
U-415	VIIC	Danzig	August 5 1942	Mined	July 14 1944	Werner, H
U-416	VIIC	Danzig	November 4 1942	Mined	March 30 1943	Reich
U-417	VIIC	Danzig	September 26 1942	Sunk	June 11 1943	Schreiner, W †
U-418	VIIC	Danzig	October 21 1942	Sunk	June 1 1943	Lange, G †
U-419	VIIC	Danzig	November 18 1942	Sunk	October 8 1943	Giersberg, D
U-420	VIIC	Danzig	December 16 1942	Sunk	October 26 1943	Reese, HJ †
U-422	VIIC	Danzig	February 10 1943	Sunk	October 4 1943	Poeschel W †
U-423	VIIC	Danzig	March 3 1943	Sunk	June 17 1944	Hackländer, K †
U-424	VIIC	Danzig	April 7 1943	Sunk	February 11 1944	Lüders. G †
U-425	VIIC	Danzig	April 21 1943	Sunk	February 17 1945	Bentzien, H†
U-426	VIIC	Danzig	May 12 1943	Sunk	January 8 1944	Reich, C †
U-431	VIIC	Schichau	April 5 1941	Sunk	October 21 1943	Schöneboom, D †
U-432	VIIC	Schichau	April 26 1941	Sunk	March 11 1943	Eckhard, H †
U-433	VIIC	Schichau	May 24 1941	Sunk	November 16 1941	Ey, H
U-434	VIIC	Schichau	June 21 1941	Sunk	December 18 1941	Heyda, W †
U-435	VIIC	Schichau	August 30 1941	Sunk	July 9 1943	Strelow, S †
U-436	VIIC	Schichau	September 27 1941	Sunk	May 26 1943	Siebicke, G †
U-438	VIIC	Schichau	November 22 1941	Sunk	May 6 1943	Heinsohn, H †
U-439	VIIC	Schichau	December 20 1941	Collisiion	May 4 1943	von Tippelskirch, H †
U-440	VIIC	Schichau	January 24 1942	Sunk	May 31 1943	Schwaff, W †
U-441	VIIC	Schichau	February 21 1942	Operational loss	June 18 1944	Hartmann, K †
U-442	VIIC	Schichau	March 22 1942	Sunk	February 12 1943	Hesse, H-J †
U-443	VIIC	Schichau	April 18 1942	Sunk	February 23 1943	von Puttkamer, K †
U-444	VIIC	Schichau	May 9 1942	Sunk	March 11 1943	Langfeld, A †
U-445	VIIC	Schichau	May 30 1942	Sunk	August 24 1944	Graf von Treuberg, RF †
U-446	VIIC	Schichau	June 20 1942	Mined	September 21 1942	Richard, H †

Place	Means	Dead	Saved
Denmark Straits	RAF aircraft: 120 Sqn	48	0
Seine Bay	RN ships: *Wanderer* (D), *Tavy* (F)	48	1
NW of Cape Ortegal	RAF aircraft: 53 Sqn	51	0
Off Gibraltar	USN aircraft: VP-63/RN ships: 1st Escort Group	52	0
Norwegian Sea	RN ships: *Mermaid* (F), *Peacock* (F), *Keppel* (D), *Whitehall* (D)	50	0
North Sea	Cause unknown	45	0
English Channel	RN ship: *Duckworth* (F)	46	0
S of Cobh, Ireland	RN ship: *Nyasaland* (F)	50	0
SW of Ireland	RN ships: *Wanderer* (D), *St Albans* (D), *Hydrangea* (C)	44	0
NW of Azores	USN aircraft: VC-9 (*Card*)	50	0
Off Dakar	RAF aircraft: 200 Sqn/French aircraft: 697 (FR) Sqn	50	0
NW of Cape Ortegal	USAAF aircraft: 4/479 Group/RAF aircraft: 224 Sqn	50	0
NW of Azores	USN ship: *Borie* (D)	49	0
North Atlantic	RN ship: *Spey* (S)	12	41
Mediterranean	RN/Polish destroyers	6	48
N of Iceland	USN aircraft: VP-84	45	0
NE of Algiers	RN ship: *Inconstant* (D)	12	37
SW of Gibraltar	RAF aircraft: 500 Sqn	46	0
NE of Faroe Islands	RAF aircraft: 179 Sqn	48	9
English Channel	RN ships; *Forester* (D), *Vidette* (D); *Wensleydale* (DE)	45	1
Off Oran	RN ship: *Vetch* (C)	47	0
Brest roads	British, air-laid ocoustic mine	2	47
Baltic	Soviet, submarine-laid mine; raised	n.k.	n.k.
NW of Faroe Islands	RAF aircraft: 206 Sqn	46	0
Bay of Biscay	RAF aircraft: 236 Sqn	48	0
North Atlantic	RAF aircraft: 86 Sqn	48	1
North Atlantic	RCAF aircraft: 10 Sqn	50	0
NW of Azores	USN aircraft: VC-9 (*Card*)	49	0
NW of Faroe Islands	Norwegian aircraft: 333 (Norwegian) Sqn	53	0
N Atlantic	RN ships: *Wild Goose* (S), *Woodpecker* (S)	50	0
Norwegian Sea	RN ships; *Alnwick Castle* (C), *Lark* (S)	53	1
NW of Cape Ortegal	RAAF aircraft: 10 Sqn	50	0
SW of Marseille	RN submarine: *Ultimatum*	52	0
North Atlantic	French ship: *Aconit* (C)	26	20
S of Malaga	RN ship: *Marigold* (C)	6	38
Off Cape St Vincent	British ships: *Blankney* (DE), *Stanley* (D)	3	42
Off Portuguese coast	RAF aircraft: 179 Sqn	48	0
W of Cape Ortegal	RIN ship: *Hyderabad* (C); RN ship: *Test* (F)	47	0
NE of Newfoundland	RN ship: *Pelican* (S)	48	0
W of Cape Ortegal	Colided with *U-659*	40	9
NW of Cape Ortegal	RAF aircraft: 201 Sqn	46	0
Atlantic/English Channel	Cause unknown	58	0
WNW of Cape St Vincent	RAF aircraft: 48 Sqn	48	0
Off Algiers	RN ships: *Bicester* (DE), *Lamerton* (DE), *Wheatland* (DE)	48	0
North Atlantic	RN ship: *Harvester* (D)	41	4
SW of St Nazaire	RN ship: *Louis* (DE)	53	0
Off Danzig	British air-laid mine; raised, stricken	23	26

U-Boat	Type	Builder	Commissioned	Fate	Date	Captain
U-447	VIIC	Schichau	July 11 1942	Sunk	May 7 1943	Bothe, F †
U-448	VIIC	Schichau	August 1 1942	Sunk	April 14 1944	Dauter, H
U-449	VIIC	Schichau	August 22 1942	Sunk	June 24 1943	Otto, H †
U-450	VIIC	Schichau	12 September 1942	Sunk	March 10 1944	Böhme, K
U-451	VIIC	Deutsche	May 3 1941	Sunk	December 21 1941	Hoffmann, E †
U-452	VIIC	Deutsche	May 29 1941	Sunk	August 25 1941	March, J †
U-453	VIIC	Deutsche	June 26 1941	Sunk	May 21 1944	Lührs, D
U-454	VIIC	Deutsche	July 24 1941	Sunk	August 1 1943	Hackländer, B
U-455	VIIC	Deutsche	August 21 1941	Operational loss	April 6 1944	Scheibe, H-M †
U-456	VIIC	Deutsche	September 18 1941	Sunk	May 13 1943	Teichert, M-M †
U-457	VIIC	Deutsche	November 5 1941	Sunk	September 16 1942	Brandenburg, K †
U-458	VIIC	Deutsche	December 12 1941	Sunk	August 22 1943	Diggins, K
U-459	XIV	Deutsche	November 15 1941	Sunk	July 24 1943	von Wiliamowitz-Moellendorf, G †
U-460	XIV	Deutsche	December 24 1941	Sunk	October 4 1943	Schnoor, E †
U-461	XIV	Deutsche	January 30 1942	Sunk	July 30 1943	Stiebler, W
U-462	XIV	Deutsche	March 5 1942	Sunk	July 30 1943	Vowe, B
U-463	XIV	Deutsche	April 2 1942	Sunk	May 161943	Wolfbauer, L †
U-464	XIV	Deutsche	April 30 1942	Sunk	August 21 1942	Harms, O
U-465	VIIC	Deutsche	May 20 1942	Sunk	May 2 1943	Wolf, H †
U-467	VIIC	Deutsche	July 15 1942	Sunk	May 25 1943	Kummer, H †
U-468	VIIC	Deutsche	August 12 1942	Sunk	August 11 1943	Schamong, K
U-469	VIIC	Deutsche	Octob er 7 1942	Sunk	March 25 1943	Claussen, E †
U-470	VIIC	Deutsche	January 7 1943	Sunk	October 16 1943	Grave, G †
U-472	VIIC	Deutsche	May 26 1943	Scuttled	March 4 1944	Freiherr von Forstner, W-F
U-473	VIIC	Deutsche	June 16 1943	Sunk	May 6 1944	Sternberg, H †
U-476	VIIC	Deutsche	July 28 1943	Sunk	May 24 1944	Niethmann, O
U-477	VIIC	Deutsche	August 18 1943	Sunk	June 3 1944	Jenssen, K-J †
U-478	VIIC	Deutsche	September 8 1943	Sunk	June 30 1944	Rademacher, R †
U-479	VIIC	Deutsche	October 27 1943	Operational loss	December 12 1944	Sons, F †
U-480	VIIC	Deutsche	October 6 1943	Sunk	February 24 1945	Förster, H-J †
U-482	VIIC	Deutsche	December 1 1943	Sunk	January 16 1945	Graf von Matschuka, H †
U-484	VIIC	Deutsche	January 19 1944	Sunk	September 9 1944	Schaefer, W-A †
U-486	VIIC	Deutsche	March 22 1944	Sunk	April 12 1945	Meyer, G †
U-487	XIV	Deutsche	December 21 1942	Sunk	July 13 1943	Metz, H †
U-488	XIV	Deutsche	February 1 1943	Sunk	April 26 1944	Studt, B †
U-489	XIV	Deutsche	March 8 1943	Sunk	August 4 1943	Schmandt, A
U-490	VIIC	Deutsche	March 27 1943	Sunk	June 12 1944	Gerlach, W
U-501	IXC	Deutsche	April 30 1941	Sunk	September 10 1941	Forster, H
U-502	IXC	Deutsche	May 31 1941	Sunk	July 5 1942	von Rosenshiel, J †
U-503	IXC	Deutsche	July 10 1941	Sunk	March 15 1942	Gericke, O †
U-504	IXC	Deutsche	July 20 1941	Sunk	July 30 1943	Luis, W †
U-505	IXC	Deutsche	August 26 1941	Captured	June 4 1944	Lange, H
U-506	IXC	Deutsche	September 15 1941	Sunk	July 12 1943	Würdermann, E †
U-507	IXC	Deutsche	October 8 1941	Sunk	January 13 1943	Schacht H †
U-508	IXC	Deutsche	October 30 1941	Sunk	November 12 1943	Staats, G †
U-509	IXC	Deutsche	November 4 1941	Sunk	July 15 1943	Witte, W †
U-512	IXC	Deutsche	December 20 1941	Sunk	October 3 1942	Schultze, W †

Place	Means	Dead	Saved
W of Gibraltar	RAF aircraft: 233 Sqn	48	0
NW of Azores	RN ship: Pelican (S)/RCN ship: *Swansea* (F)	10	42
NW of Cape OrtegAL	RN ships: 2nd Support Group	49	0
Off Italian W coast	RN ships; *Blankney, Blencathra, Brecon, Exmoor* (all DEs)	1	48
Off Tangier	RN aircraft: 812 NAS	44	1
S of Iceland	RAF aircraft: 209 Sqn	42	0
Ionian Sea	RN ships: *Termagent* (D), *Tenacious* (D), *Liddlesdale* (DE)	3	48
NE of Cape Ortegal	RAAF aircraft: 10 Sqn	34	13
W Mediterranean	Cause unknown	51	0
NW of Cape Ortegal	RAF aircraft: 86 Sqn	49	0
Barents Sea	RN ship: *Impulsive* (D)	45	0
SE of Pantellaria	RN ship: *Easton* (D); Greek ship: *Pindos* (D)	8	39
NW of Cape Ortegal	RAF aircraft: 172, 549 Sqns	19	41
NW of Azores	USN aircraft: VC-9 (*Card*)	62	0
NW of Cape Ortegal	Combined attack by RN ships, and RAF/USAAF aircraft	53	15
NW of Cape Ortegal	Combined attack by RN ships, and RAF/USAAF aircraft	3	64
SW of Scilly Islands	RAF aircraft: 58 Sqn	56	0
S of Iceland	USN aircraft: VP-73	2	52
NW of Cape Ortegal	RAAF aircraft: 461 Sqn	48	0
W of Faroe Islands	USN aircraft: VP-84	46	0
E of Dakar	RAF aircraft: 200 Sqn	46	7
W of Faroe Islands	RAF aircraft: 206 Sqn	46	0
SW of Iceland	RAF aircraft: 120, 59 Sqns	46	2
SE of Bear Island	Under attack from RN aircraft/RN ship: *Onslaught* (D)	22	27
North Atlantic	RN ships: 2nd Support Group	24	30
SW of Lofoten	RAF aircraft: 210 Sqn	35	21
W of Drontheim	RCAF aircraft: 162 Sqn	51	0
N of Shetland Islands	RCAF aircraft: 162 Sqn/RAF aircraft: 86 Sqn	52	0
Gulf of Finland	Unknown cause: possibly mined	51	0
SW of Land's End, England	RN ships; *Duckworth* (F), *Rowley* (F)	48	0
Off W coast of Scotland	RN ship: 22nd Escort Group	48	0
S of Hebrides	RN ships: *Portchester Castle* (F), *Helmsdale* (D)	52	0
Norwegian Sea	RN submarine: *Tapir*	48	0
Central Atlantic	USN aircraft; VC-13 (*Core*)	31	33
NW of Cape Verde Islands	USN ships: *Frost, Barber, Snowdon* (all DEs)	65	0
SE of Iceland	RCAF aircraft: 423 Sqn	1	58
NW of Azores	USN ships: *Frost, Huse, Inch* (all DE)/USN aircraft: VC-25 (*Croome*)	1	59
Denmark Strait	RCN ship: Chambly (C), Moosejaw (C)	12	46
W of La Rochelle	RAF aircraft: 172 Sqn	52	0
SE of Newfoundland	USN aircraft: VP-82	51	0
NW of Cape Ortegal	Combined attack by RN ships, and RAF/USAAF aircraft	53	0
W of Cape Blanco	USN ships: Guadalcanal group	1	56
W of Vigo	USAAF aircraft: 1 A/S Sqn, 480 Group	48	6
Off NW coast of Brazil	USN aircraft: VP-83	55	0
N of Cape Ortegal	USN aircraft: VB-103	60	0
NW of Madeira	USN aircraft; VC-29 (*Santee*)	54	0
N of Cayenne	USAAF aircraft: 99 Bomb Sqn	51	1

U-Boat	Type	Builder	Commissioned	Fate	Date	Captain
U-513	IXC	Deutsche	January 10 1942	Sunk	July 19 1943	Guggenberger, F
U-514	IXC	Deutsche	January 24 1942	Sunk	July 8 1943	Auffermann, H-J †
U-515	IXC	Deutsche	February 21 1942	Sunk	April 9 1944	Henke, W
U-517	IXC	Deutsche	March 21 1942	Sunk	November 21 1942	Hartwig, P
U-518	IXC	Deutsche	April 25 1942	Sunk	April 22 1945	Offermann, H †
U-519	IXC	Deutsche	May 7 1942	Operational loss	February 10 1943	Eppen, G †
U-520	IXC	Deutsche	May 19 1942	Sunk	October 30 1942	Schwatrzkopf, V †
U-521	IXC	Deutsche	June 3 1942	Sunk	June 2 1943	Bargsten, K
U-522	IXC	Deutsche	June 11 1942	Sunk	February 23 1943	Schneider, H †
U-523	IXC	Deutsche	June 25 1942	Sunk	August 25 1943	Pietsch, W
U-524	IXC	Deutsche	July 8 1942	Sunk	March 22 1943	Freiherr von Steinecker, W †
U-525	IXC/40	Deutsche	July 30 1942	Sunk	August 11 1943	Drewitz, H-J †
U-526	IXC/40	Deutsche	August 12 1942	Mined	April 14 1943	Möglich, H †
U-527	IXC/40	Deutsche	September 2 1942	Sunk	July 23 1943	Uhlig, H
U-528	IXC/40	Deutsche	September 16 1942	Scuttled	May 11 1943	von Rabenau, G †
U-529	IXC/40	Deutsche	September 30 1942	Operational loss	February 15 1943	Fraatz, G-W †
U-531	IXC/40	Deutsche	October 28 1942	Sunk	May 6 1943	Neckel, H †
U-533	IXC/40	Deutsche	November 25 1942	Sunk	October 16 1943	Hennig, H †
U-534	IXC/40	Deutsche	December 23 1942	Sunk	May 5 1945	Nollau, H
U-535	IXC/40	Deutsche	December 23 1942	Sunk	July 5 1943	Ellmenrich, H †
U-536	IXC/40	Deutsche	January 13 1943	Sunk	November 20 1943	Schauenburg, R
U-537	IXC/40	Deutsche	January 27 1943	Sunk	November 9 1944	Schrewe, P †
U-538	IXC/40	Deutsche	February 10 1943	Sunk	November 21 1943	Gossler, J-E †
U-540	IXC/40	Deutsche	March 10 1943	Sunk	October 17 1943	Kasch, L †
U-542	IXC/40	Deutsche	April 7 1943	Sunk	November 28 1943	Coester, C-B †
U-543	IXC/40	Deutsche	April 21 1943	Sunk	July 2 1944	Hellriegel, H-J †
U-544	IXC/40	Deutsche	May 5 1943	Sunk	January 16 1944	Matke, W †
U-545	IXC/40	Deutsche	May 19 1943	Sunk	February 11 1944	Mannesmann, G
U-546	IXC/40	Deutsche	June 2 1943	Sunk	April 24 1945	Just, P
U-548	IXC/40	Deutsche	June 30 1943	Operational loss	May 19 1945	Krempl, E †
U-549	IXC/40	Deutsche	July 14 1943	Sunk	May 29 1944	Krankenhagen, D †
U-550	IXC/40	Deutsche	July 28 1943	Sunk	April 16 1944	Hänert, K
U-551	VIIC	Blohm+Voss	November 7 1940	Sunk	March 23 1944	Schrott, K †
U-553	VIIC	Blohm+Voss	December 23 1940	Operational loss	January 2 1943	Thurmann K †
U-556	VIIC	Blohm+Voss	February 6 1941	Sunk	June 27 1941	Wohlfarth, H
U-557	VIIC	Blohm+Voss	February 13 1941	Collision	December 16 1941	Paulshen, O †
U-558	VIIC	Blohm+Voss	February 20 1941	Scuttled	July 20 1943	Krech, G
U-559	VIIC	Blohm+Voss	February 27 1941	Sunk	October 30 1942	Heidtmann, H
U-561	VIIC	Blohm+Voss	March 13 1941	Sunk	July 12 1943	Henning, F †
U-562	VIIC	Blohm+Voss	March 20 1941	Sunk	February 19 1943	Hamm, H †
U-563	VIIC	Blohm+Voss	March 27 1941	Sunk	May 31 1943	Borchardt, G †
U-564	VIIC	Blohm+Voss	April 3 1941	Sunk	June 14 1943	Fiedler, H †
U-566	VIIC	Blohm+Voss	April 17 1941	Scuttled	October 24 1943	Hornkohl, H
U-567	VIIC	Blohm+Voss	April 24 1941	Sunk	December 21 1941	Endrass, E †
U-568	VIIC	Blohm+Voss	May 1 1941	Sunk	May 28 1942	Preuss, J
U-569	VIIC	Blohm+Voss	May 8 1941	Sunk	May 22 1943	Johannsen, H
U-570	VIIC	Blohm+Voss	May 15 1941	Captured	August 27 1941	Rahmlow, H-J

PLACE	MEANS	DEAD	SAVED
Off Brazilian coast	USN aircraft: VP-74	46	7
NE of Cape Finisterre	RAF aircraft: 224 Sqn	54	0
S of Azores	USN aircraft/ships: Guadalcanal group	16	44
SW of Ireland	RN aircraft: 817 NAS (*Victorious*)	3	52
NW of Azores	USN ships: *Carter* (DE), *Neal A Scott* (DE)	57	0
SW of Ireland	Cause unknown	50	0
E of Newfoundland	RCAF aircraft: 10 Sqn	53	0
SE of Baltimore	USN ship: *PC-565* (SC)	51	1
S of Azores	RN ship: *Totland* (ex-USCG cutter)	51	0
NE of Azores	RN ships: *Wanderer* (D), *Wallflower* (C)	20	35
S of Madeira	USAAF aircraft: 1/480 Group	51	0
NW of Azores	USN aircraft: VC-1 (*Card*)	54	0
Bay of Biscay	British mine	41	42
S of Azores	USN aircraft: VC-9 (*Bogue*)	40	12
SW of Ireland	Damaged by RN ship: *Fleetwood* (S)/RAF aircraft: 58 Sqn	11	45
North Atlantic	Cause unknown	48	0
NE of Nwfoundland	RN ships: *Snowflake* (C), *Vidette* (D)	54	0
Gulf of Oman	RAF aircraft: 244 Sqn	53	1
Kattegat	RAF aircraft: 86 Sqn	3	48
NW of Cape Finisterre	RAF aircraft: 53Sqn	55	0
NE of Azores	RCN ships: *Calgary* (C), *Snowberry* (C)/RN ship: *Nene* (F)	38	17
E of Soerabaya, Java Sea	USN submarine: *Flounder*	58	0
NE of Azores	RN ships: *Foley* (DE), *Crane* (S)	55	0
E of Cape Farewell	RAF aircraft: 59, 120 Sqns	55	0
N of Madeira	RAF aircraft: 59 Sqn	56	0
SW of Teneriffe	USN aircraft: VC-58 (*Bogue*)	58	0
NW of Azores	USN aircraft: VC-13 (*Guadalcanal*)	57	0
W of Hebrides	RAF aircraft: 407 Sqn	2	48
SE of Cape Farewell	Five USN ships, including *Flaherty* (DE)	24	33
Gulf of Maine	May have been sunk by USN ships, but not confirmed	59	0
W of Canary Islands	USN ships: *Elmore* (DE), *Ahrens* (DE)	59	0
E of New York	USN ships: *Gandy*, *Joyce*, *Peterson* (all DEs)	44	12
Iceland–Faroes Gap	RN ship: *Visenda* (T)	45	0
N Atlantic	Cause unknown	47	0
E of Cape Farewell	RN ships: *Celandine* (C), *Gladiolus* (C), *Nasturtium* (C)	5	41
SW of Crete	Rammed (accidentally?) by Italian torpedo boat: *Orion*	5	41
NW of Cape Ortegal	RAF aircraft: 58 Sqn/USAAF aircraft: 19/479 Group	45	4
NE of Port Said	RN ships: *Pakenham* (D), *Petard* (D)	8	38
Straits of Messina	RN ship: *MTB-81*	42	5
Off Benghazi	RN ships: *Isis* (D), *Hursley* (D)	49	0
SW of Isles of Scilly	RAF aircraft: 228 Sqn/RAAF aircraft: 10 Sqn	53	0
Bay of Biscay	RAF aircraft: 10 OTU	29	18
NW of Cape Ortegal	RAF aircraft: 179 Sqn	0	49
W of Cape Finistere	RN ship: *Deptford* (S)	47	0
Mediterranean	RN ships: *Eridge* (D), *Hero* (D), *Hurworth* (D)	0	47
SE of Cape Farewell	Damaged by USN aircraft: VC-9 (*Bogue*)	0	47
N Atlantic	RAF aircraft: 269, 209 Sqns. Became HMS *Graph*	0	44

U-Boat	Type	Builder	Commissioned	Fate	Date	Captain
U-571	VIIC	Blohm+Voss	May 22 1941	Sunk	January 28 1944	Lussow, G †
U-572	VIIC	Blohm+Voss	May 29 1941	Sunk	August 3 1943	Kummetat, H †
U-573	VIIC	Blohm+Voss	June 5 1941	Sunk	May 1 1942	Heinsohn, H †
U-574	VIIC	Blohm+Voss	June 12 1941	Sunk	December 19 1941	Gengelbach, D †
U-575	VIIC	Blohm+Voss	June 19 1941	Sunk	March 13 1944	Boehmer, W
U-576	VIIC	Blohm+Voss	June 26 1941	Sunk	July 15 1942	Heinicke, H-D †
U-577	VIIC	Blohm+Voss	July 30 1941	Sunk	January 15 1942	Schauenburg, H †
U-578	VIIC	Blohm+Voss	July 10 1941	Sunk	August 10 1942	Rehwinkel, E-A †
U-580	VIIC	Blohm+Voss	July 24 1941	Training loss	November 11 1941	Kuhlmann, H-G
U-581	VIIC	Blohm+Voss	July 31 1941	Sunk	February 2 1942	Pfeifer, W
U-582	VIIC	Blohm+Voss	August 7 1941	Sunk	October 5 1942	Schulte, W †
U-583	VIIC	Blohm+Voss	August 14 1941	Training loss	November 15 1941	Ratsch, H †
U-584	VIIC	Blohm+Voss	August 21 1941	Sunk	October 31 1943	Deecke, J †
U-585	VIIC	Blohm+Voss	August 28 1941	Mined	March 30 1942	Lohse, B †
U-587	VIIC	Blohm+Voss	September 11 1941	Sunk	March 27 1942	Borcherdt, U †
U-588	VIIC	Blohm+Voss	September 18 1941	Sunk	July 31 1942	Vogel, V †
U-589	VIIC	Blohm+Voss	September 25 1941	Sunk	September 14 1942	Horrer, H-J †
U-590	VIIC	Blohm+Voss	October 2 1941	Sunk	July 9 1943	Krüer, W †
U-591	VIIC	Blohm+Voss	October 9 1941	Sunk	July 30 1943	Ziesmer, R †
U-592	VIIC	Blohm+Voss	October 16 1941	Sunk	January 31 1944	Jaschke, H †
U-593	VIIC	Blohm+Voss	October 23 1941	Sunk	December 13 1943	Kelbling, G
U-594	VIIC	Blohm+Voss	October 30 1941	Sunk	June 4 1943	Mumm, F †
U-595	VIIC	Blohm+Voss	November 6 1941	Sunk	November 14 1942	Quaet-Faslam, J
U-597	VIIC	Blohm+Voss	November 20 1941	Sunk	October 12 1942	Bopst, E †
U-598	VIIC	Blohm+Voss	November 27 1941	Sunk	July 23 1943	Holtorf, G †
U-599	VIIC	Blohm+Voss	December 4 1941	Sunk	October 24 1942	Breithaupt, W †
U-600	VIIC	Blohm+Voss	December 11 1941	Sunk	November 25 1943	Zurmühlen, B †
U-601	VIIC	Blohm+Voss	December 18 1941	Sunk	February 25 1944	Hansen, O †
U-602	VIIC	Blohm+Voss	December 29 1941	Operational loss	late April 1943	Schüler, P †
U-603	VIIC	Blohm+Voss	January 2 1942	Sunk	March 1 1944	Bertelsmann, H-J †
U-604	VIIC	Blohm+Voss	January 8 1942	Scuttled	August 11 1943	Höltring, H
U-605	VIIC	Blohm+Voss	January 15 1942	Sunk	November 14 1942	Schütze, H-V †
U-606	VIIC	Blohm+Voss	January 22 1942	Sunk	February 22 1943	Döhler, H †
U-607	VIIC	Blohm+Voss	January 29 1942	Sunk	July 13 1943	Jeschonnek, W
U-608	VIIC	Blohm+Voss	February 5 1942	Sunk	August 10 1944	Reisener, W
U-609	VIIC	Blohm+Voss	February 12 1942	Sunk	February 7 1943	Rudloff, K †
U-610	VIIC	Blohm+Voss	February 19 1942	Sunk	October 8 1943	Frhr von F-E-Allmendingen †
U-611	VIIC	Blohm+Voss	February 26 1942	Sunk	December 8 1942	von Jakobs, N †
U-612	VIIC	Blohm+Voss	March 5 1942	Training loss	August 6 1942	Siegmann, P
U-613	VIIC	Blohm+Voss	March 12 1942	Sunk	July 23 1943	Köppe, H †
U-614	VIIC	Blohm+Voss	March 19 1942	Sunk	July 29 1943	Sträter, W †
U-615	VIIC	Blohm+Voss	March 26 1942	Sunk	August 7 1943	Kapitzky, R †
U-616	VIIC	Blohm+Voss	April 2 1942	Sunk	May 14 1944	Koitschka, S
U-617	VIIC	Blohm+Voss	April 9 1942	Beached	September 12 1943	Brandi, A
U-618	VIIC	Blohm+Voss	April 16 1942	Sunk	August 14 1944	Faust, E †
U-619	VIIC	Blohm+Voss	April 23 1942	Sunk	October 5 1942	Makowski, K
U-620	VIIC	Blohm+Voss	April 30 1942	Sunk	February 13 1943	Stein, H †

PLACE	MEANS	DEAD	SAVED
Off W coast of Ireland	RAAF aircraft: 461 Sqn	52	0
Caribbean	USN aircraft: VP-205	46	0
E of Cartagena	Damaged by RAF aircraft: 233 Sqn. To Spanish Navy as *G-7*	1	43
Off Lisbon	RN ship: *Stork* (S)	28	18
W of Cape Finisterre	USN/RCN ship; RAF/USN aircraft	18	35
Off Cape Hatteras	USN aircraft: VS-9/Rammed by SS *Unicoi* (US)	45	0
NW of Mersa Matruh	RN aircraft: 815 NAS	43	0
W of Land's End	RAF aircraft: 311 (Czech) Sqn	49	0
Baltic, off Memel	Collided with surface ship	12	32
Off Azores	RN ship: *Westcott* (D)	4	39
S of Iceland	USN aircraft: VP-73	46	0
Baltic	Collided with *U-153*	45	0
NW of Azores	USN aircraft: VC-9 (*Card*)	53	0
N of Murmansk	Sunk by German mine	45	0
W of Ushant	RN ships: *Aldenham, Grove, Leamington, Volunteer* (all DE)	42	0
NW of Newfoundland	RCN ships: *Skeena* (D), *Wetaskiwin* (C)	46	0
NW of North Cape	RN ship: *Onslow* (D)	44	0
Off Amazon estuary	USN aircraft: VP-94	45	0
Off coast of Brazil	USN aircraft: VB-127	19	28
W of Cape Clear	RN ships: *Wild Goose* (S), *Starling* (S), *Magpie* (S)	50	0
Mediterranean	After attacks by RN, ship: *Calpe* (DE)/USN ship: *Wainwright* (D)	0	45
S of Cape St Vincent	RAF aircraft: 48 Sqn	50	0
Off Oran	After attack by RAF aircraft: 608 Sqn	0	45
SW of Iceland	RAF aircraft: 120 Sqn	49	0
Off coast of Brazil	USN aircraft: VB-107	43	2
NW of Cape Finisterre	RAF aircraft: 224 Sqn	44	0
NE of Azores	RN ships: *Blackwood* (DE), *Bazely* (D)	54	0
NW of Lofoten Islands	RAF aircraft: 210 Sqn	52	0
Mediterranean	Causes unknown	48	0
N of Azores	USN ship: *Brosntein* (DE)	51	0
S Atlantic	After attacks by USN aircraft: VB-129	0	49
N of Algiers	RAF aircraft: 233 Sqn	46	0
North Atlantic	Polish ship: *Burza* (D); USCG ship: *Campbell* (cutter)	35	12
NW of Cape Ortegal	RAF aircraft: 228 Sqn	46	7
Bay of Biscay	RAF aircraft: 53 Sqn/RN ship: *Wren* (S)	0	51
N Atlantic	French ship: *Lobélla* (C)	46	0
SW of Rockall	RCAF aircraft: 423 Sqn	51	0
N Atlantic	RAF aircraft: 120 Sqn	45	0
Baltic	Collided with *U-144*. Raised, used for training	2	44
S of Azores	USN ship: *George E Badger* (D)	48	0
NW of Cape Ortegal	RAF aircraft: 172 Sqn	49	0
W of Grenada	USN/USAAF aircraft	4	43
E of Cartgena	USN ships (eight DEs)	0	47
Near Melilla, N Africa	After attack by RAF aircraft: 179 Sqn	0	49
Off St Nazaire	RAF aircraft: 53 Sqn	61	0
N Atlantic	RAF aircraft: 269 Sqn	44	0
NW of Lisbon	RAF aircraft: 202 Sqn	46	0

U-Boat	Type	Builder	Commissioned	Fate	Date	Captain
U-621	VIIC	Blohm+Voss	May 7 1941	Sunk	August 18 1944	Stuckmann, H
U-623	VIIC	Blohm+Voss	May 21 1942	Operational loss	February 21 1943	Schröder, H †
U-624	VIIC	Blohm+Voss	May 28 1942	Sunk	February 7 1943	Graf von Soden-Fraunhofen, U †
U-625	VIIC	Blohm+Voss	June 4 1942	Sunk	March 10 1944	Straub †
U-626	VIIC	Blohm+Voss	June 11 1942	Sunk	December 15 1942	Bade, H-B †
U-627	VIIC	Blohm+Voss	June 18 1942	Sunk	October 27 1942	Kindelbacher, R †
U-628	VIIC	Blohm+Voss	June 25 1942	Sunk	July 3 1943	Hasenschar, H †
U-629	VIIC	Blohm+Voss	July 2 1942	Sunk	June 7 1942	Bugs, H-H †
U-630	VIIC	Blohm+Voss	July 9 1942	Sunk	May 3 1943	Winkler, W †
U-631	VIIC	Blohm+Voss	July 16 1942	Sunk	October 17 1943	Krüger, J †
U-632	VIIC	Blohm+Voss	July 23 1942	Sunk	April 6 1943	Karpf, H †
U-633	VIIC	Blohm+Voss	July 30 1942	Sunk	March 10 1943	Müller, B †
U-634	VIIC	Blohm+Voss	August 6 1942	Sunk	August 30 1943	Dahlhaus, E †
U-635	VIIC	Blohm+Voss	August 13 1942	Sunk	April 6 1943	Eckelmann, H †
U-636	VIIC	Blohm+Voss	August 20 1942	Sunk	April 21 1945	Schendel, E †
U-638	VIIC	Blohm+Voss	September 3 1942	Sunk	May 5 1943	Staudinger, O †
U-639	VIIC	Blohm+Voss	September 10 1942	Sunk	August 30 1943	Wichmann, W †
U-640	VIIC	Blohm+Voss	September 17 1942	Sunk	May 14 1943	Nagel, K-H †
U-641	VIIC	Blohm+Voss	September 24 1942	Sunk	January 19 1944	Rendtel, H †
U-643	VIIC	Blohm+Voss	October 8 1942	Sunk	October 8 1943	Speidel, H
U-644	VIIC	Blohm+Voss	October 15 1942	Sunk	April 7 1943	Jensen, K †
U-645	VIIC	Blohm+Voss	October 22 1942	Sunk	December 24 1943	Ferro, O †
U-646	VIIC	Blohm+Voss	October 29 1942	Sunk	May 171943	Wulff, H †
U-647	VIIC	Blohm+Voss	November 5 1942	Operational loss	late July 1943	Hertin, W †
U-648	VIIC	Blohm+Voss	November 5 1942	Sunk	November 23 1943	Stahl, P †
U-649	VIIC	Blohm+Voss	November 19 1942	Training loss	February 23 1943	Tiesler, R
U-650	VIIC	Blohm+Voss	November 26 1942	Operational loss	early January 1945	Zorn, R †
U-651	VIIC	Howaldt	February 12 1941	Sunk	June 29 1941	Lohmeyer, P
U-652	VIIC	Howaldt	April 3 1941	Scuttled	June 2 1942	Fraatz, G-W
U-653	VIIC	Howaldt	May 25 1941	Sunk	March 15 1944	Kandler, H-A †
U-654	VIIC	Howaldt	July 5 1941	Sunk	August 22 1942	Forster, L †
U-655	VIIC	Howaldt	August 11 1941	Sunk	March 24 1942	Dumrese, A †
U-656	VIIC	Howaldt	September 17 1941	Sunk	March 1 1942	Kröning, E †
U-657	VIIC	Howaldt	October 8 1941	Sunk	May 17 1943	Göllnitz, H †
U-658	VIIC	Howaldt	November 5 1941	Sunk	October 30 1942	Senkel, H †
U-659	VIIC	Howaldt	December 9 1941	Collision	May 4 1943	Stock, H †
U-660	VIIC	Howaldt	January 8 1942	Scuttled	November 12 1942	Baur, G
U-661	VIIC	Howaldt	February 12 1942	Sunk	October 15 1942	von Lilienfeld, E †
U-662	VIIC	Howaldt	April 9 1942	Sunk	July 21 1943	Müller, H-E
U-663	VIIC	Howaldt	May 14 1942	Operational loss	May 8 1943	Schmid, H †
U-664	VIIC	Howaldt	June 17 1942	Sunk	August 9 1943	Graef, A
U-665	VIIC	Howaldt	July 22 1942	Sunk	March 22 1943	Haupt, H-J †
U-666	VIIC	Howaldt	August 26 1942	Sunk	February 11 1944	Wilberg, E-A †
U-667	VIIC	Howaldt	October 20 1942	Mined	August 25 1944	Lange, K-H †
U-669	VIIC	Howaldt	December 16 1942	Sunk	September 7 1943	Köhl, K †
U-670	VIIC	Howaldt	January 26 1943	Training loss	August 20 1943	Hyronimus, G
U-671	VIIC	Howaldt	March 3 1943	Sunk	August 5 1944	Hegewald, W †

Place	Means	Dead	Saved
Bay of Biscay	RCN ships: *Ottawa* (D), *Kootenay* (D), *Chaudière* (D)	56	0
N Atlantic	May have been sunk by RAF aircraft: 120 Sqn	46	0
N Atlantic	RAF aircraft: 220 Sqn	45	0
W of Cape Clear	RCAF aircraft: 422 Sqn	54	0
SW of Iceland	USCG ship: *Ingham* (Cutter)	47	0
SW of Iceland	RAF aircraft: 206 Sqn	47	0
NW of Cape Ortegal	RAF aircraft: 224 Sqn	49	0
SW of Ushant	RAF aircraft: 224 Sqn	53	0
NE of Cape Race	RN ship: *Vidette* (D)	47	0
SE of Cape Farewell	RN ship: *Sunflower* (C)	53	0
SW of Iceland	RAF aircraft: 86 Sqn	48	0
SW of Iceland	Rammed by SS *Scorton*	42	0
W of Cape Finisterre	RN ships: *Stork* (S), *Stonecrop* (C)	47	0
SW of Iceland	RAF aircraft: 120 Sqn	47	0
N Atlantic	RN ships: *Bazley* (DE), *Bentinck* (DE), *Drury* (DE)	42	0
N of Cape Race	RN ship: *Sunflower* (C)	44	0
Arctic	Soviet submarine: *S-101*	44	0
S of Cape Farewell	USN aircraft: VP-84	49	0
SW of Cape Clear	RN ship: *Violet* (C)	50	0
S of Iceland	RAF aircraft: 86, 120 Sqns	25	23
SE of Jan Mayen Island	RN submarine: *Tuna*	45	0
NE of Azores	USN ship: *Schenk* (D)	55	0
N of Faroe Islands	RAF aircraft: 269 Sqn	46	0
N Atlantic	Cause unknown	48	0
NE of Azores	RN ships: *Bazeley*, *Blackwood*, *Drury* (all DEs)	50	0
Baltic	Collided with *U-232*	36	11
N Atlantic	Was heading for Irish Sea. Cause unknown	47	0
S of Iceland	RN ships: *Malcolm* (D), *Scimitar* (D), *Arabis* (C), *Violet* (C), *Speedy*	0	44
Off Sollum	After attack by RAF aircraft: 202 Sqn/RN aircraft: 815 NAS	0	45
N Atlantic	RN ships: *Starling* (S), *Wild Goose* (S)	51	0
Off Colon, Panama Canal	USAAF aircraft: 45 Sqn	44	0
SE of Bear Island	RN ship: *Sharpshooter* (MS)	45	0
S of Cape Race	USN aircraft: VP-82	45	0
SW of Iceland	RN ship: *Swale* (DE)	51	0
NE of Newfoundland	RCAF aircraft: 145 Sqn	48	0
W of Cape Ortegal	Collided with *U-439*	44	3
N of Oran	After attacks by RN ships: *Lotus* (C), *Starwort* (C)	2	44
N Atlantic	RN ship: *Viscount* (D)	44	0
Off coast of Brazil	USN aircraft: VP-94	46	2
Bay of Biscay	Possibly due to attack by RAAF aircraft: 10 Sqn	49	0
NW of Azores	USN aircraft: from *Card*	8	44
W of St Nazaire	RAF aircraft: 10 OTU	46	0
N Atlantic	RN aircraft: 842 NAS (*Fencer*)	51	0
Off La Pallice	British air-laid mine	45	0
N Atlantic	RCAF aircraft: 407 Sqn	53	0
Danzig Bay	Collision with target ship, *Bolkoburg*	21	22
English Channel	RN ships: *Stayner* (DE), *Wensleydale* (DE)	47	6

U-Boat	Type	Builder	Commissioned	Fate	Date	Captain
U-672	VIIC	Howaldt	April 6 1943	Scuttled	July 18 1944	Lawaetz, U
U-673	VIIC	Howaldt	May 18 1943	Accident	October 24 1944	Gerke, E-A
U-674	VIIC	Howaldt	June 15 1943	Sunk	May 2 1944	Muhs, H †
U-675	VIIC	Howaldt	July 14 1943	Sunk	May 24 1944	Sammier, K-H T
U-676	VIIC	Howaldt	August 6 1943	Mined	February 18 1945	Sass, W †
U-678	VIIC	Howaldt	October 25 1943	Sunk	July 6 1944	Hyronimus, G †
U-679	VIIC	Howaldt	November 29 1943	Sunk	January 10 1945	Aust, E †
U-681	VIIC	Howaldt	February 3 1944	Scuttled	March 10 1945	Gebauer, W
U-683	VIIC	Howaldt	May 30 1944	Sunk	March 12 1945	Keller, G
U-701	VIIC	Stülcken	July 16 1941	Sunk	July 2 1942	Degen, H
U-702	VIIC	Stülcken	September 3 1941	Operational loss	ealry April 1942	von Rabenau, W-R †
U-703	VIIC	Stülcken	October 16 1941	Operational loss	late September 1942	Brünner, J †
U-705	VIIC	Stülcken	December 30 1941	Sunk	September 3 1942	Horn, K-H
U-706	VIIC	Stülcken	March 16 1942	Sunk	August 3 1942	von Zitzewitz, A †
U-707	VIIC	Stülcken	July 1 1942	Sunk	November 9 1943	Gretschel, G †
U-709	VIIC	Stülcken	August 12 1942	Sunk	March 1 1944	Ites, R †
U-710	VIIC	Stülcken	September 2 1942	Sunk	April 24 1943	von Carlowitz, D †
U-713	VIIC	Stülcken	December 29 1942	Sunk	February 24 1944	Gosejakob, H †
U-714	VIIC	Stülcken	February 10 1943	Sunk	March 14 1945	Schwebke, H-J †
U-715	VIIC	Stülcken	March 17 1943	Sunk	June 13 1944	Röttger, H †
U-718	VIIC	Stülcken	June 25 1943	Training loss	November 18 1943	Wieduwilt, H
U-719	VIIC	Stülcken	July 27 1943	Sunk	June 26 1944	Steffens, K-D †
U-722	VIIC	Stülcken	December 15 1943	Sunk	March 27 1945	Reimers, H †
U-731	VIIC	Schichau	October 3 1942	Sunk	May 15 1944	Graf von Keller, A †
U-732	VIIC	Schichau	October 24 1942	Scuttled	November 1 1943	Carlsen, K-P
U-734	VIIC	Schichau	December 2 1942	Sunk	February 9 1944	Blauert, H-J †
U-736	VIIC	Schichau	January 16 1943	Sunk	August 6 1944	Reff, R
U-737	VIIC	Schichau	January 30 1943	Collision	December 19 1944	Gréus, F-A
U-738	VIIC	Schichau	February 20 1943	Training loss	February 14 1944	Hoffmann, E-M †
U-740	VIIC	Schichau	March 27 1943	Sunk	June 9 1944	Stark, G †
U-741	VIIC	Schichau	April 10 1943	Sunk	August 15 1944	Palmgren, G †
U-742	VIIC	Schichau	May 1 1943	Sunk	July 18 1944	Schwaßmann, H †
U-743	VIIC	Schichau	May 15 1943	Operational loss	September 9 1944	Kandzior, H †
U-744	VIIC	Schichau	June 5 1943	Sunk	March 6 1944	Blischke, H †
U-745	VIIC	Schichau	June 19 1943	Operational loss	February 4 1945	von Trotha, W
U-751	VIIC	KMW	January 31 1941	Sunk	July 17 1942	Bigalk, G †
U-752	VIIC	KMW	May 24 1941	Sunk	May 23 1943	Schroeter, K-E †
U-753	VIIC	KMW	June 18 1941	Sunk	May 13 1943	von Manstein, AM †
U-754	VIIC	KMW	August 28 1941	Sunk	July 31 1942	Oestermann, J †
U-755	VIIC	KMW	November 3 1941	Sunk	May 28 1943	Göing, W †
U-756	VIIC	KMW	December 30 1941	Sunk	September 1 1942	Harney, K †
U-757	VIIC	KMW	February 28 1942	Sunk	January 8 1944	Deetz, F †
U-759	VIIC	KMW	August 15 1942	Sunk	July 26 1943	Friedrich, R †
U-760	VIIC	KMW	Octboer 15 1942	Interned	September 8 1943	Blum, O-U
U-761	VIIC	KMW	December 3 1942	Sunk	February 24 1944	Geider, H
U-762	VIIC	KMW	January 30 1943	Sunk	February 8 1944	Pietschmann, W †
U-765	VIIC	KMW	June 19 1943	Sunk	May 6 1944	Wendt, W

PLACE	MEANS	DEAD	SAVED
English Channel	Abandoned after attack by RN ship: Balfour (DE)	0	52
Stavanger, Norway	Rammed by *U-882*, sank. Later raised and stricken	0	47
NE of Jan Mayen Island	RN aircraft: 842 NAS (*Fencer*)	49	0
Norwegian Sea	RAF aircraft: 4 OTU	51	0
Gulf of Finland	Hit Soviet mine	57	0
English Channel	RCN ships: *Ottawa* (D), *Kootenay* (D)/RN ship: *Statice* (C)	52	0
Gulf of Finland	Soviet submarine; *MO-124*	53	0
English Channel	Hit rocks, attacked by USN aircraft: VPB-103, abandoned	11	40
English Channel	RN ships: *Wild Goose* (S), *Loch Ruthven* (F)	49	0
Off Cape Hatteras	USAAF aircraft: 396 Bomber Sqn	40	7
North Sea	Cause unknown	45	0
N Atlantic	Cause unknown	56	0
W of Ushant	RAF aircraft: 7 Sqn	45	0
NW of Cape Ortegal	USAAF aircraft: 479 AS Group/RCAF aircraft: 415 Sqn	42	4
NE of Azores	RAF aircraft: 220 Sqn	50	0
N of Azores	USN ships: *Bronstein*, *Thomas*, *Bostwick* (all DEs)	54	0
SE of Iceland	RAF aircraft: 206 Sqn	49	0
NW of Lofoten Islands	RN ship: *Keppel* (D)	50	0
North Sea	South African ship: *Natal*	51	0
NE of Faroe Islands	RCAF aircraft: 162 Sqn	35	14
Off Bjornholm, Baltic	Collided with *U-476*	43	7
NW of Bloody Foreland	RN ships: *Bulldog* (D)	52	0
Off Hebrides	RN ships: *Byron*, *Fitzroy*, *Redmill* (all DEs)	44	0
N of Tangier	RN ship: *Kilmarnock* (S), *Blackfly* (T)	53	0
W of Gibraltar	RN ships: *Imperialist* (T), *Douglas* (D)	31	19
Atlantic	RN ships: *Wild Goose* (S), *Starling* (S)	50	0
Bay of Biscay	RN ship: *Loch Killin* (F)	28	19
Vestfjord, Norway	Collided with German *MRS-25* (MS)	31	20
Off Gotenhafen	Collision with SS *Erna*. Raised, stricken	24	24
SW of Isles of Scilly	RAF aircraft: 120 Sqn	51	0
English Channel	RN ship: *Orchis*	0	48
W of Lofoten Islands	RAF aircraft: 210 Sqn	52	0
N Atlantic	Disappeared; cause unknown	50	0
Atlantic	RCN ships: C2 Escort Group	12	40
Gulf of Finland	Cause unknown	48	0
NW of Cape Ortegal	RAF aircraft: 502 Sqn, 61 Sqn	47	0
Off Irish coast	RN aircraft: 819 NAS, 892 NAS (*Archer*)	29	17
Bay of Biscay	RAF aircraft: 423 Sqn/RN ship: *Logan* (F)/RCN ship: *Drumhell*	47	0
S of Nova Scotia	RCAF aircraft: 113 Sqn	43	0
Mediterranean	RAF aircraft: 608 Sqn	40	9
North Atlantic	RCN ship: Morden (C)	43	0
Off Irish coast	RN ships: *Bayntun* (DE), *Camrose* (C)	49	0
SE of Jamaica	USN aircraft: VP-32	47	0
Vigo, Spain	After attack by RAF aircraft: 179 Sqn. To UK later	0	52
Strait of Gibraltar	USN aircraft/RN ships	9	48
W of Cape Clear	RN ships: *Wild Goose* (S), *Woodpecker* (S)	51	0
N Atlantic	RN aircraft: 825 NAS (*Vindex*); RN ships of 5 Support Group	51	0

U-Boat	Type	Builder	Commissioned	Fate	Date	Captain
U-767	VIIC	KMW	September 11 1943	Sunk	June 18 1944	Dankleff, W
U-768	VIIC	KMW	October 14 1943	Training loss	November 20 1943	Buttjer †
U-771	VIIC	KMW	November 18 1943	Sunk	November 11 1944	Block, H †
U-772	VIIC	KMW	December 23 1943	Sunk	December 30 1944	Rademacher, E †
U-774	VIIC	KMW	February 17 1944	Sunk	April 8 1945	Sausmikat, W †
U-801	IXC/40	Seebeck	March 24 1943	Scuttled	June 18 1944	Dankleff, W
U-803	IXC/40	Seebeck	September 7 1943	Mined	April 24 1944	Schimpf, K
U-804	IXC/40	Seebeck	December 4 1943	Sunk	April 9 1945	Meyer, H †
U-821	VIIC	Oderwerke	October 11 1943	Sunk	June 10 1944	Knackfuß, U †
U-841	IXC/40	AG Weser	February 6 1943	Scuttled	Octboer 7 1943	Bender, W †
U-842	IXC/40	AG Weser	March 1 1943	Sunk	November 6 1943	Heller, W †
U-843	IXC/40	AG Weser	March 24 1943	Sunk	April 9 1945	Herwartz, O †
U-844	IXC/40	AG Weser	April 7 1943	Sunk	October 16 1943	Möller, G †
U-845	IXC/40	AG Weser	May 1 1943	Sunk	March 10 1944	Weber, W †
U-846	IXC/40	AG Weser	May 29 1943	Sunk	May 4 1944	Hashagen, B †
U-847	IXD2	AG Weser	January 23 1943	Sunk	August 27 1943	Kuppisch, H †
U-848	IXD2	AG Weser	February 20 1943	Sunk	November 5 1943	Rollmann, W †
U-849	IXD2	AG Weser	March 11 1943	Sunk	November 25 1943	Schultze, H-O †
U-850	IXD2	AG Weser	April 17 1943	Sunk	December 20 1943	Ewerth, K †
U-851	IXD2	AG Weser	May 21 1943	Operational loss	early April 1944	Weingaertner, H †
U-852	IXD2	AG Weser	June 15 1943	Grounded	May 2 1944	Eck, H-W
U-853	IXC/40	AG Weser	June 25 1943	Sunk	May 6 1945	Frömsdorf, H †
U-854	IXC/40	AG Weser	July 19 1943	Mined	February 4 1944	Weiher †
U-855	IXC/40	AG Weser	August 2 1943	Operational loss	mid-September 1944	Ohisen, P †
U-856	IXC/40	AG Weser	August 19 1943	Sunk	April 7 1944	Wittenberg, F
U-857	IXC/40	AG Weser	September 16 1943	Sunk	April 7 1945	Premauer, R †
U-859	IXD2	AG Weser	July 8 1943	Sunk	September 23 1944	Jebsen, J †
U-860	IXD2	AG Weser	August 12 1943	Sunk	June 15 1944	Büchel, P
U-863	IXD2	AG Weser	November 3 1943	Sunk	September 29 1944	von der Esch, D
U-864	IXD2	AG Weser	December 8 1943	Sunk	February 9 1945	Wolfram, R-R
U-865	IXC/40	AG Weser	Otober 25 1943	Operational loss	mid-September 1944	Stellmacher, D †
U-866	IXC/40	AG Weser	November 17 1943	Sunk	March 16 1945	Rogowsky, P †
U-867	IXC/40	AG Weser	December 12 1943	Sunk	September 19 1944	von Mühlendahl, A †
U-869	IXC/40	AG Weser	January 26 1944	Sunk	February 28 1945	Neuerburg, H †
U-871	IXD2	AG Weser	January 15 1944	Sunk	September 26 1944	Ganzer, E †
U-876	IXD2	AG Weser	May 24 1944	Scuttled	May 4 1945	Bahn, R
U-877	IXC/40	AG Weser	March 24 1944	Sunk	December 27 1944	Findeisen, E †
U-878	IXC/40	AG Weser	April 14 1944	Sunk	April 10 1945	Rodig, J †
U-879	IXC/40	AG Weser	April 19 1944	Sunk	April 30 1945	Manchen, E †
U-880	IXC/40	AG Weser	May 11 1944	Sunk	April 16 1945	Schötzau, G †
U-881	IXC/40	AG Weser	May 27 1944	Sunk	May 6 1945	Dr Frischke, K-H †
U-905	VIIC	Stülcken	March 8 1944	Sunk	March 20 1945	Schwarting, B
U-921	VIIC	Neptun	May 30 1943	Sunk	September 30 1944	Werner, A †
U-923	VIIC	Neptun	October 4 1943	Training loss	February 9 1945	Frömmer, H †
U-925	VIIC	Neptun	December 30 1943	Operational loss	mid-September 1944	Knoke, H †
U-927	VIIC	Neptun	June 27 1944	Sunk	February 24 1945	Ebert, J †
U-951	VIIC	Blohm+Voss	December 3 1942	Sunk	July 7 1943	Pressel, K

PLACE	MEANS	DEAD	SAVED
SW of Guernsey	RN ships: 14th Escort Group	48	1
Baltic, Pillau-Gotenhafen	Rammed by *U-745*	49	0
W of Tromso, Arctic	RN submarine: *Venturer*	51	0
English Channel	RCAF aircraft: 407 Sqn	48	0
Off Cape Clear	RN ships: *Bentinck* (DE), *Calder* (DE)	44	0
Off Cape Verde Islands	USN aircraft: VC-6 (*Block Island*)/USN ships: *Bronstein, Corry*	10	48
Baltic	British, air-laid mine	13	35
Kattegat	RAF aircraft: 143 Sqn, 235 Sqn	56	0
N of Ushant	RAF aircraft: 248 Sqn	50	1
E of Cape farewell	After damage by RN ship: *Byard* (DE)	26	27
N Atlantic	RN ships: *Wild Goose* (S), *Starling* (S)	56	0
Kattegat	RAF aircraft: Banff Strike Wing	44	0
SW of Iceland	RAF aircraft: 86 Sqn, 59 Sqn	53	0
Atlantic	RCN/RN ships: *St Laurent* (D), *Owen Sound* (F), *Forester* (D)	10	45
N of Cape Ortegal	RCAF aircraft: 407 Sqn	57	0
Sargasso Sea	USN aircraft: VC-1 (*Card*)	63	0
SW of Ascension Island	USN aircraft: VP-107/USAAF aircraft: 1st Composite Sqn	64	1
W of Congo estuary	USN aircraft: VP-107	66	0
W of Madeira	USN aircraft: VC-19 (*Bogue*)	66	0
Atlantic	Cause unknown	70	0
Somaliland coast	Ran ashore following damage from RAF aircraft: 8 Sqn	7	58
Off US Coast	US ship: *Atherton* (DE)	56	0
Baltic, N of Swinemünde	Allied air-delivered mine	50	7
N Atlantic	Cause unknown	56	0
N Atlantic	USN ships: *Champlin* (D), *Huse* (DE)	27	28
Off Cape Cod	US ship: *Gustavson* (DE)	59	0
Off Penang, Malaya	RN submarine: *Trenchant*	46	19
S of Helena	USN aircraft: VC-9 (*Solomons*)	44	19
Off Ascension Island	USN aircraft: VB-107	68	0
Norwegian Sea	RN submarine: *Venturer*	73	0
N Atlantic	Cause unknown	59	0
Off US Coast	USCG ships: TG 22.14	55	0
Norwegian Sea	RAF aircraft: 224 Sqn	60	0
Off US coast	US ship: *Fowler* (DE)/French ship: *L'Indescret*	57	0
NW of Azores	RAF aircraft: 220 Sqn	69	0
Off Aschau, Baltic	Attacked by RAF aircraft, then scuttled	0	60
NW of Azores	RCN ships: *St Thomas* (C)	0	55
Bay of Biscay	RN ships: *Vanquisher* (D), *Tintagel Castle* (C)	51	0
Off US coast	USN ships: TG 01.10	52	0
N Atlantic	USN ships: *Stanton* (DE), *Frost* (DE)	49	0
Off US coast	USN ship: *Farquart* (DE)	52	0
Off Cape Wrath	RAF aircraft: 86 Sqn	45	0
W of Bear Island	RN aircraft: 813 NAS (*Campania*)	51	0
Baltic	Mine	48	0
Atlantic	Cause unknown	51	0
English Channel	RAF aircraft: 179 Sqn	47	0
Central Atlantic	USAAF aircraft: 1/480 Group	46	0

U-Boat	Type	Builder	Commissioned	Fate	Date	Captain
U-954	VIIC	Blohm+Voss	December 23 1942	Sunk	May 19 1943	Loewe, O †
U-955	VIIC	Blohm+Voss	December 31 1942	Sunk	June 7 1944	Baden, H-H †
U-959	VIIC	Blohm+Voss	January 21 1943	Sunk	May 2 1944	Weitz, F †
U-960	VIIC	Blohm+Voss	January 28 1943	Sunk	May 19 1944	Heinrich, G
U-961	VIIC	Blohm+Voss	February 4 1943	Sunk	March 29 1944	Fischer, K †
U-962	VIIC	Blohm+Voss	February 11 1943	Sunk	April 8 1944	Liesberg, E †
U-964	VIIC	Blohm+Voss	February 18 1943	Sunk	October 16 1943	Hummerjohann, E †
U-965	VIIC	Blohm+Voss	February 25 1943	Sunk	March 27 1945	Unverzagt, G †
U-966	VIIC	Blohm+Voss	March 4 1943	Scuttled	November 10 1943	Wolf, E
U-970	VIIC	Blohm+Voss	March 25 1943	Sunk	June 8 1944	Ketels, H-H
U-971	VIIC	Blohm+Voss	April 1 1943	Scuttled	June 24 1944	Zeplien, W
U-972	VIIC	Blohm+Voss	April 8 1943	Operational loss	mid-January 1944	König, K-D †
U-973	VIIC	Blohm+Voss	April 15 1943	Sunk	March 6 1944	Paepenmöller, K †
U-974	VIIC	Blohm+Voss	April 22 1943	Sunk	April 19 1944	Wolff, H †
U-976	VIIC	Blohm+Voss	May 5 1943	Sunk	March 25 1944	Tiesler, R
U-980	VIIC	Blohm+Voss	May 27 1943	Sunk	June 11 1944	Dahms, H †
U-981	VIIC	Blohm+Voss	June 3 1943	Sunk	August 12 1944	Keller, G
U-983	VIIC	Blohm+Voss	June 16 1943	Training loss	September 8 1943	Reimers, H
U-984	VIIC	Blohm+Voss	June 17 1943	Sunk	August 20 1944	Sieder, H †
U-986	VIIC	Blohm+Voss	July 1 1943	Sunk	April 17 1944	Kaiser, KE †
U-987	VIIC	Blohm+Voss	July 8 1943	Sunk	June 15 1944	Schreyer, H †
U-988	VIIC	Blohm+Voss	July 15 1943	Sunk	June 29 1944	Dobberstein, E †
U-989	VIIC	Blohm+Voss	July 22 1943	Sunk	February 14 1945	von Roithberg, HR †
U-990	VIIC	Blohm+Voss	July 28 1943	Sunk	May 25 1944	Nordheimer, H
U-1001	VIIC/41	Blohm+Voss	November 8 1943	Sunk	April 8 1945	Blaudow, E-U †
U-1003	VIIC/41	Blohm+Voss	December 9 1943	Scuttled	March 23 1945	Strübing, W †
U-1006	VIIC/41	Blohm+Voss	January 11 1944	Sunk	October 16 1944	Voigt, H
U-1013	VIIC/41	Blohm+Voss	March 2 1944	Training loss	March 17 1944	Linck, G
U-1014	VIIC/41	Blohm+Voss	March 14 1944	Sunk	February 4 1945	Glaser, W †
U-1015	VIIC/41	Blohm+Voss	March 23 1944	Training loss	May 19 1944	Boos, H-H
U-1017	VIIC/41	Blohm+Voss	April 13 1944	Sunk	April 28 1945	Riecken, W †
U-1018	VIIC/41	Blohm+Voss	April 25 1944	Sunk	February 27 1945	Burmeister, W †
U-1020	VIIC/41	Blohm+Voss	May 17 1944	Operational loss	early January 1945	Eberlein, O †
U-1021	VIIC/41	Blohm+Voss	May 25 1944	Operational loss	mid-March 1945	Holpert, W
U-1024	VIIC/41	Blohm+Voss	June 28 1944	Sunk	April 13 1945	Gutteck, H-J
U-1051	VIIC	Germania	March 4 1944	Sunk	January 26 1945	von Holleben, H †
U-1053	VIIC	Germania	February 12 1944	Operational loss	February 15 1945	Lange, H
U-1054	VIIC	Germania	March 25 1944	Accident	September 16 1944	Riekberg
U-1055	VIIC	Germania	April 8 1944	Operational loss	April 8 1944	Meyer, R †
U-1059	VIIF	Germania	May 1 1943	Sunk	March 19 1944	Leupold, G
U-1060	VIIF	Germania	May 15 1943	Sunk	October 27 1944	Brammer, H †
U-1062	VIIF	Germania	June 19 1943	Sunk	September 30 1944	Albrecht, K †
U-1063	VIIC/41	Germania	July 8 1944	Sunk	April 16 1945	Stephan, K-H †
U-1065	VIIC/41	Germania	September 23 1944	Sunk	April 9 1945	Panitz, J †
U-1106	VIIC	Nordsee	July 5 1944	Sunk	March 29 1945	Bartke, E †
U-1107	VIIC	Nordsee	August 8 1944	Sunk	April 30 1945	Parduhn, F †
U-1166	VIIC/41	Danzig	December 8 1943	Accident	July 28 1944	Ballert, S

Place	Means	Dead	Saved
N Atlantic	RN ships: *Jed* (F), *Sennen* (S)	47	0
Bay of Biscay	RAF aircraft: 201 Sqn	50	0
NE of Iceland	RN aircraft: 842 NAS (*Fencer*)	53	0
NW of Algiers	USN ships, RAF aircraft	31	22
N of Faroe Islands	RN ships: 2nd Escort Group	49	0
NE of Azores	RN ships: *Crane* (S), *Cygnet* (S)	50	0
Atlantic	RAF aircraft: 86 Sqn	47	3
Off Cape Wrath	RN ship: *Conn* (F)	53	0
NW of Cape Ortegal	Blown-up in Spanish waters after repeated air attacks	8	42
Bay of Biscay	RAF aircraft: 228Sqn	38	14
NW of Ushant	RAF aircraft: 311 (Czech) Sqn/RN ships	2	51
Atlantic	Cause unknown	50	0
Arctic	RN aircraft: 816 NAS (Chaser)	51	0
Off Stavanger, Norway	Norwegian submarine: *Ula*	42	7
Bay of Biscay	RAF aircraft: 618 Sqn	4	45
North Sea	RCAF aircraft: 162 Sqn	51	0
Off La Rochelle	Mined then attacked by RAF aircraft: 502 Sqn	12	40
N of Leba, Baltic	Collided with *U-988*	5	42
W of Brest	RCN ships: *Ottawa* (D), *Chaudiere* (D), *Kootenay* (D)	45	0
N Atlantic	USN ships: *Swift* (MS), *PC-619* (SC)	50	0
W of Lofoten Islands	RN submarine: *Satyr*	52	0
English Channel	RN ships: *Essington, Domett, Duckworth, Cooke* (all DEs)	50	0
N of Shetlands	RN ships: 10th Escort Group	48	0
NW of Trondheim, Norway	RAF aircraft: 59 Sqn	19	31
Near Fastnet	RN ships: *Byron* (DE), *Fitzroy* (DE)	46	0
Atlantic	Damaged after collision with RCN ship and later attacks	20	29
Atlantic	RCN ship: *Annan* (F)	6	44
Baltic	Collided with *U-286*	25	24
Off Irish coast	RN ships: 23 Escort Group	48	0
Baltic	Collided with *U-1014*	36	14
Atlantic	RAF aircraft: 120 Sqn	33	0
English Channel	RN ship: *Loch Fada* (F)	51	2
Off coast of Scotland	Cause unknown	49	0
English Channel	Cause unknown	43	0
Irish Sea	RN ships: 8th Escort Group	9	37
Irish Sea	RN ships: *Bentinck, Aylmer, Calder* (all DEs)	47	0
Norwegian Sea	Cause unknown, but was on deep-diving trials	54	0
Off Hela, Baltic	Rammed by ferry, *Peter Wessel*. Heavy damage; stricken	0	54
Bay of Biscay	Cause unknown	49	0
SW of Cape Verde Islands	USN aircraft: VC-6 (*Block Island*)	47	8
Norwegian coast	Damaged by RN aircraft, ran aground, finished by RAF	16	43
Central Atlantic	USN ship: *Fessenden* (DE)	55	0
Irish Sea	RN ship: *Loch Killin* (F)	29	17
Kattegat	RAF aircraft: Banff Strike Wing	45	0
Atlantic	RAF aircraft: 224 Sqn	46	0
Atlantic	USN aircraft: VP-63	37	0
Eckernförde	Internal explosion during torpedo trials, while submerged	0	46

U-Boat	Type	Builder	Commissioned	Fate	Date	Captain
U-1169	VIIC/41	Danzig	February 9 1944	Operational loss	mid-March 1945	Goldbeck, H †
U-1172	VIIC/41	Danzig	April 20 1944	Sunk	January 27 1945	Kuhlmann, J
U-1191	VIIC	Schichau	September 9 1943	Sunk	June 18 1944	Grau, P †
U-1195	VIIC	Schichau	November 4 1943	Sunk	April 6 1945	Cordes, E †
U-1199	VIIC	Schichau	December 23 1945	Sunk	January 21 1945	Nollmann, R †
U-1200	VIIC	Schichau	January 5 1944	Sunk	November 11 1944	Mangels, H †
U-1206	VIIC	Schichau	March 16 1944	Scuttled	April 14 1945	Schlitt, K-A
U-1208	VIIC	Schichau	April 6 1944	Sunk	February 27 1945	Hagene, G †
U-1209	VIIC	Schichau	April 13 1944	Scuttled	December 18 1944	Hülsenbeck, E †
U-1222	IXC/40	Deutsche	September 1 1943	Sunk	July 11 1944	Bielfeld, H †
U-1225	IXC/40	Deutsche	November 10 1943	Sunk	June 24 1944	Sauerberg, E †
U-1226	IXC/40	Deutsche	November 24 1943	Operational loss	mid-October 1944	Claussen, A-W †
U-1229	IXC/40	Deutsche	January 13 1944	Sunk	August 20 1944	Zinke, A †
U-1234	IXC/40	Deutsche	April 19 1944	Training loss	May 14 1944	Thurmann, H
U-1235	IXC/40	Deutsche	May 17 1944	Sunk	April 15 1945	Barsch, F †
U-1273	VIIC/41	Bremer Vulkan	February 16 1944	Mined	February 17 1945	Knollmann, H
U-1274	VIIC/41	Bremer Vulkan	March 1 1944	Sunk	April 16 1945	Fitting, H-H †
U-1276	VIIC/41	Bremer Vulkan	April 6 1944	Sunk	February 20 1945	Wendt, K-H †
U-1278	VIIC/41	Bremer Vulkan	May 31 1944	Sunk	February 17 1945	Müller-Bethka, E †
U-1279	VIIC/41	Bremer Vulkan	July 5 1944	Sunk	February 3 1945	Falke, H †
U-1302	VIIC/41	Flensburg	May 25 1944	Sunk	March 7 1945	Herwartz, W †
U-2323	XXIII	Deutsche	July 18 1944	Mined	July 26 1944	Angermann, W
U-2331	XXIII	Deutsche	September 12 1944	Training loss	October 10 1944	Pahl, HW
U-2338	XXIII	Deutsche	October 9 1944	Sunk	May 5 1945	Kaiser, H-D †
U-2342	XXIII	Deutsche	November 1 1944	Mined	December 26 1944	Schad von Mittelbiberach, B †
U-2344	XXIII	Deutsche	November 10 1944	Collision	February 18 1945	Ellerlage, H
U-2503	XXI	Blohm + Voss	August 1 1944	Scuttled	May 4 1945	Wächter, K-J †
U-2508	XXI	Blohm + Voss	September 26 1944	Training loss	November 14 1944	Christiansen, U
U-2521	XXI	Blohm + Voss	October 31 1944	Sunk	May 4 1945	Methner, J †
U-2540	XXI	Blohm + Voss	February 24 1945	Scuttled	May 4 1945	Schultze, R
U-3932	XXI	Deschimag	February 12 1945	Sunk	May 3 1945	Slevogt, H
U-3523	XXI	Schichau	January 29 1945	Sunk	May 6 1945	Müller, W †
UIT-22	Italian	Tosi	October 11 1943	Sunk	March 11 1944	Wunderlich, W †
UIT-23	Italian	Tosi	December 6 1943	Sunk	February 15 1944	Schäfer, H
U-1169	VIIC/41	Danzig	February 9 1944	Operational loss	mid-March 1945	Goldbeck, H †
U-1172	VIIC/41	Danzig	April 20 1944	Sunk	January 27 1945	Kuhlmann, J
U-1191	VIIC	Schichau	September 9 1943	Sunk	June 18 1944	Grau, P †
U-1195	VIIC	Schichau	November 4 1943	Sunk	April 6 1945	Cordes, E †
U-1199	VIIC	Schichau	December 23 1945	Sunk	January 21 1945	Nollmann, R †
U-1200	VIIC	Schichau	January 5 1944	Sunk	November 11 1944	Mangels, H †
U-1206	VIIC	Schichau	March 16 1944	Scuttled	April 14 1945	Schlitt, K-A
U-1208	VIIC	Schichau	April 6 1944	Sunk	February 27 1945	Hagene, G †
U-1209	VIIC	Schichau	April 13 1944	Scuttled	December 18 1944	Hülsenbeck, E †
U-1222	IXC/40	Deutsche	September 1 1943	Sunk	July 11 1944	Bielfeld, H †
U-1225	IXC/40	Deutsche	November 10 1943	Sunk	June 24 1944	Sauerberg, E †
U-1226	IXC/40	Deutsche	November 24 1943	Operational loss	mid-October 1944	Claussen, A-W †
U-1229	IXC/40	Deutsche	January 13 1944	Sunk	August 20 1944	Zinke, A †

PLACE	MEANS	DEAD	SAVED
S of Ireland	Cause unknown	50	0
Irish Sea	RN ships: *Bligh* (DE), *Keats* (DE), *Tyler* (DE)	52	0
English Channel	RAF aircraft: 304 (Polish) Sqn	50	0
English Channel	RN ship: *Watchman* (D)	31	18
English Channel	RN ships: *Icarus* (D), *Mignonette* (C)	47	0
Atlantic	RN ships: 30th/40th Escort Groups	52	0
Off coast of Scotland	Took in water while submerged, surfaced, scuttled	3	45
English Channel	RN ships: 2nd Escort Group	49	0
English Channel	Seriously damaged on hitting underwater rock	10	41
Bay of Biscay	RAF aircraft: Sunderland (201 Sqn)	56	0
NW of Bergen	RCAF aircraft: 162 Sqn	56	0
Atlantic	Cause unknown	56	0
SE of Newfoundland	USN aircraft: VC-42 (*Bogue*)	18	?
Baltic	Collided with tug. Raised, in service, scuttled May 5 1945	13	32
Atlantic	USN ship: *Stanton* (DE)	57	0
Oslofjord	Struck mine	57	8
North Sea	RN ship: *Viceroy* (D)	44	0
Irish Sea	RN ship: *Amethyst* (S)	49	0
North Atlantic	RN ships; *Bayntum* (DE), *Loch Eck* (F)	48	0
North Atlantic	RN ships: *Bayntum* (DE), *Braithwaite* (DE), *Loch Eck* (F)	48	0
Irish Sea	RCN ships: *La Hulloise* (F), *Strathadam* (F), *Thetford Mines* (F)	48	0
Kiel Bay	Allied air-delivered mine. First Type XXIII to be lost	2	12
Baltic	Raised but not returned to service	15	4
Off Danish coast	RAF aircraft: 236 Sqn, 254 Sqn	11	2
Baltic	Mined	8	4
Baltic	Collided with *U-2366*	6	0
Danish coast	Badly damaged by RAF aircraft: North Coates Wing. Grounded	14	n.k.
Baltic	Refloated; in service, scuttled, Kiel, May 3 1945	1	0
Baltic	RAF aircraft: 184 Sqn	41	n.k.
Baltic	RAF aircraft: 2nd TAF	n.k.	n.k.
Baltic	RAF aircraft: 184 Sqn	28	n.k.
Baltic	RAF aircraft: 86 Sqn	57	0
Off Cape Town	RAF aircraft: 262 Sqn	43	0
Off Penang	RN submarine: *Tally Ho*	31	14
S of Ireland	Cause unknown	50	0
Irish Sea	RN ships: *Bligh* (DE), *Keats* (DE), *Tyler* (DE)	52	0
English Channel	RAF aircraft: 304 (Polish) Sqn	50	0
English Channel	RN ship: *Watchman* (D)	31	18
English Channel	RN ships: *Icarus* (D), *Mignonette* (C)	47	0
Atlantic	RN ships: 30th/40th Escort Groups	52	0
Off coast of Scotland	Took in water while submerged, surfaced, scuttled	3	45
English Channel	RN ships: 2nd Escort Group	49	0
English Channel	Seriously damaged on hitting underwater rock	10	41
Bay of Biscay	RAF aircraft: Sunderland (201 Sqn)	56	0
NW of Bergen	RCAF aircraft: 162 Sqn	56	0
Atlantic	Cause unknown	56	0
SE of Newfoundland	USN aircraft: VC-42 (*Bogue*)	18	?

U-Boat	Type	Builder	Commissioned	Fate	Date	Captain
U-1234	IXC/40	Deutsche	April 19 1944	Training loss	May 14 1944	Thurmann, H
U-1235	IXC/40	Deutsche	May 17 1944	Sunk	April 15 1945	Barsch, F †
U-1273	VIIC/41	Bremer Vulkan	February 16 1944	Mined	February 17 1945	Knollmann, H
U-1274	VIIC/41	Bremer Vulkan	March 1 1944	Sunk	April 16 1945	Fitting, H-H †
U-1276	VIIC/41	Bremer Vulkan	April 6 1944	Sunk	February 20 1945	Wendt, K-H †
U-1278	VIIC/41	Bremer Vulkan	May 31 1944	Sunk	February 17 1945	Müller-Bethka, E †
U-1279	VIIC/41	Bremer Vulkan	July 5 1944	Sunk	February 3 1945	Falke, H †
U-1302	VIIC/41	Flensburg	May 25 1944	Sunk	March 7 1945	Herwartz, W †
U-2323	XXIII	Deutsche	July 18 1944	Mined	July 26 1944	Angermann, W
U-2331	XXIII	Deutsche	September 12 1944	Training loss	October 10 1944	Pahl, HW
U-2338	XXIII	Deutsche	October 9 1944	Sunk	May 5 1945	Kaiser, H-D †
U-2342	XXIII	Deutsche	November 1 1944	Mined	December 26 1944	Schad von Mittelbiberach, B †
U-2344	XXIII	Deutsche	November 10 1944	Collision	February 18 1945	Ellerlage, H
U-2503	XXI	Blohm+Voss	August 1 1944	Scuttled	May 4 1945	Wächter, K-J †
U-2508	XXI	Blohm+Voss	September 26 1944	Training loss	November 14 1944	Christiansen, U
U-2521	XXI	Blohm+Voss	October 31 1944	Sunk	May 4 1945	Methner, J †
U-2540	XXI	Blohm+Voss	February 24 1945	Scuttled	May 4 1945	Schultze, R
U-3932	XXI	Deschimag	February 12 1945	Sunk	May 3 1945	Slevogt, H
U-3523	XXI	Schichau	January 29 1945	Sunk	May 6 1945	Müller, W †
UIT-22	Italian	Tosi	October 11 1943	Sunk	March 11 1944	Wunderlich, W †
UIT-23	Italian	Tosi	December 6 1943	Sunk	February 15 1944	Schäfer, H

This appendix details all known U-boats lost at sea for any reason. It does not include U-boats sunk or scuttled in harbor, or those which survived the war, but it does include *U-416* which was sunk, raised, returned to service and then sunk a second time.

Builder
Builders' names have been abbreviated; abbreviations and full titles are:
Blohm+Voss: Blohm & Voss, Hamburg.
Bremer Vulkan: AG Bremer Vulkan, Vegesack.
Danzig: Danziger Werft, Danzig.
Deschimag: Deschimag AG, Weser, Bremen.
Deutsche: Deutsche Werft (with yards at Finkenwerder, Gotenhafen, Kiel, Reiherstieg).
Flender: Lubecker Flender Werke, Lubeck.
Flensburg: Flensburger Schiffbau Gesellschaft, Flensburg.
Germania: Friedrich Krupp AG, Germaniawerft.
Howaldt: Howaldtswerke, Hamburg.
KMW: Kriegsmarine-Werft, Wilhelmshaven.
Nordsee: Nordseewerke Emden AG, Emden.
Oderwerke: Stettiner Oderwerke, Stettin.
Neptun: AG Neptun, Rostock.
Schichau: F Schichau GmbH Werk, Danzig and Elbing.
Seebeck: Deschimag Werk, Wesermunde.
Stulcken. HC Stulcken Sohn, Hamburg.
Tosi: Tosi, Taranto, Italy.

Commissioned
The commissioning date is more meaningful than the date laid down or launched, not least because Allied air action frequently caused delays in completion. Note, however, that after commissioning there was frequently a 5-7 month delay while final trials and crew training were carried out before the boat became operational.

Fate
Operational losses: these include U-boats which disappeared at sea for no known reason. By definition, there were no survivors. Note also that it is seldom possible to give a precise date for such losses.
Training losses: U-boats lost while in the training organization, either 'school boats' (ie, those permanently allocated to training tasks) or new boats working-up prior to being declared operational.
Scuttled: this covers only those boats which were sunk at sea because they had been so badly damaged by Allied action or the elements that they could not return to base.

Captain
The name of the captain at the time of the loss. The symbol † after a name denotes that the captain was lost in the action or incident.

Means
a) Aircraft:
i) Service: RAF = Royal Air Force (British); RAAF = Royal Australian Air Force;

Place	Means	Dead	Saved
Baltic	Collided with tug. Raised, in service, scuttled May 5 1945	13	32
Atlantic	USN ship: *Stanton* (DE)	57	0
Oslofjord	Struck mine	57	8
North Sea	RN ship: *Viceroy* (D)	44	0
Irish Sea	RN ship: *Amethyst* (S)	49	0
North Atlantic	RN ships; *Bayntum* (DE), *Loch Eck* (F)	48	0
North Atlantic	RN ships: *Bayntum* (DE), *Braithwaite* (DE), *Loch Eck* (F)	48	0
Irish Sea	RCN ships: *La Hulloise* (F), *Strathadam* (F), *Thetford Mines* (F)	48	0
Kiel Bay	Allied air-delivered mine. First Type XXIII to be lost	2	12
Baltic	Raised but not returned to service	15	4
Off Danish coast	RAF aircraft: 236 Sqn, 254 Sqn	11	2
Baltic	Mined	8	4
Baltic	Collided with *U-2366*	6	0
Danish coast	Badly damaged by RAF aircraft: North Coates Wing. Grounded	14	n.k.
Baltic	Refloated; in service, scuttled, Kiel, May 3 1945	1	0
Baltic	RAF aircraft: 184 Sqn	41	n.k.
Baltic	RAF aircraft: 2nd TAF	n.k.	n.k.
Baltic	RAF aircraft: 184 Sqn	28	n.k.
Baltic	RAF aircraft: 86 Sqn	57	0
Off Cape Town	RAF aircraft: 262 Sqn	43	0
Off Penang	RN submarine: *Tally Ho*	31	14

RCAF = Royal Canadian Air Force; USAAF = United States Army Air Force;
USN = United States Navy.

ii) Ship-board aircraft: The name of the parent ship/carrier is given in brackets.
iii) Squadrons: Sqn = squadron; OTU = operational training unit;
NAS = naval air squadron.

b) Ships:
i) RAN = Royal Australian Navy; RCN = Royal Canadian Navy; RN = Royal Navy
(British); RIN = Royal Indian Navy; RNethN = Royal Netherlands Navy;
USCG = United States Coast Guard; USN = United States Navy.
ii) C = corvette; D = destroyer; DE = destroyer escort; F = Frigate;
MS = minsweeeper; S = sloop; SC = submarine-chaser; T = trawler.

INDEX

Figures in **bold type** indicate references in captions to photographs and diagrams

PICTURE CREDITS